The Struggle for Self-Det

The Struggle for Self-Determination

•

History of
the Menominee Indians
since 1854

DAVID R. M. BECK

University of Nebraska Press

Lincoln and London

Portions of chapters 10–12 have been previously published in the following sources: "Historical Overview,"
in "Designing the Economic Future of the Menominee
Peoples," a report written by Benjamin J. Broome with
LaDonna Harris for Americans for Indian Opportunity, April 1991. "Return to *Namä'o Uskíwämit*: The
Importance of Sturgeon in Menominee Indian History," *Wisconsin Magazine of History* 79, no. 1 (autumn
1995): 32–48. Reprinted with permission of the Wisconsin Historical Society. (Also reprinted in *Menominee Tribal News*, 12 April 1996, 16–19.) "An Urban Platform for Advocating Justice: Protecting the
Menominee Forest," in *American Indians and the Urban
Experience*, ed. Susan Lobo and Kurt Peters, 155–62
(Walnut Creek CA: AltaMira Press, 2001).

Set in Adobe Minion by Bob Reitz. Book designed by
Richard Eckersley. Printed by Thomson-Shore, Inc.

Library of Congress Cataloging-in-Publication Data
Beck, David, 1956–
The struggle for self-determination: history of the
Menominee Indians since 1854 / David R. M. Beck.
p.   cm. Includes bibliographical references and index.
ISBN-13: 978-0-8032-1347-0 (hardcover: alk. paper)
ISBN-10: 0-8032-1347-6 (hardcover: alkaline paper)
ISBN-13: 978-0-8032-2241-0 (paper: alk. paper)
1. Menominee Indians – History. 2. Menominee
Indians – Treaties. 3. Menominee Indians – Govern-
ment relations. 4. Self-determination, National.
5. United States – Politics and government. 6. Meno-
minee Indian Reservation (Wis.) – History. I. Title
E99.M44B435 2005 977.4004'97313–dc22 2005003444

I dedicate this book
to those who work
to strengthen tribal
self-determination.

CONTENTS

ILLUSTRATIONS

Shaping a Tribally Defined Existence

This work is the culmination of a project that developed from a suggestion Sol Tax made in the spring of 1988.[1] After he wrote the preface to my annotated bibliography of the Chicago American Indian community, he casually asked what project I would work on next. When I hesitated, Dr. Tax told me that what was really needed was a study of all the indigenous people across the world who survived the European expansion and colonization. He envisioned a large-scale and broad-scale analysis of these groups, including who they are and how and why they survived.

Dr. Tax proposed a multi-life work, but his vision encouraged me to study the issue as it relates to a single tribal nation. Menominee leaders Ada Deer, Carol Dodge, and Michael Chapman encouraged me to use the Menominee as a case study of survival.[2] I worked closely with the Menominee Historic Preservation Department in framing the questions of the study and in researching the portion of the study conducted on the Menominee reservation.

The resulting work is a modest contribution to Dr. Tax's world vision. Reducing his proposal to a single North American indigenous nation, my guiding question came to be this: How did the Menominee survive the flood of European- and Euro-American-induced incursions into their land, lives, and culture? This question called for both documentation and analysis of the near overwhelming forces that this nation confronted in its battle to survive. It also raised a series of new questions. In what ways have the Menominee constructed the circumstances that define their world? To what extent have tribal actions been simply responsive to outside forces? To what extent have their actions been within the context of their longstanding cultural traditions? Or should their actions be understood as a combination of both? In what ways have the Menominee been able to shape their future on their own terms? In a historical sense, the future is often already part of the past. That means historians can analyze how those futures that have become the past have been shaped and reshaped over time. For the Menominee that shaping has required a combination of survival of the old ways; creation of new cultural, political, and economic institutions; and re-creation of weakened institutions since earliest contact with Europeans.

Studying survival means rethinking the standard telling of Menominee history. Throughout time Menominee tribal leaders from all walks of life have understood their world in a distinct manner and have worked to ensure the continuation of their way of life. Physical survival has often been a primary focus for individual tribal members, but cultural survival has always been the concern of Menominee leaders. Indeed, for the Menominee, survival has been just the first step in an ongoing process of self-definition. Cultural survival encompasses social, political, and economic aspects of tribal life that preserve core cultural values and use those to shape and reshape both community life and interactions with outsiders. From the years of earliest contact in the 1630s through the establishment of the reservation in the 1850s, the Menominee, despite ever-increasing pressures, fought successfully to maintain their own distinct vision of their present and future and to move—fitfully at some times, full bore at other times—along the crooked path to that tribally defined future.

In more general terms, the craft of writing historical tribal studies is undergoing changes as Indian community perspectives are beginning to be incorporated into their stories. Whereas in the past tribal histories have largely reflected questions more relevant to the larger society—focusing, for example, on federal policy—some of the recent works are beginning to focus on questions arising from within tribal communities. [3] The historian Greg Dening has noted that history written from either the political right or left does a disservice to indigenous peoples. From the right, "real history" assumes the primacy of the dominant society's values, placing the Native community in a position of inferiority until it rises to the level of the colonizer. "The political left," on the other hand, "tends to believe that 'real history' is knowing the enemy in imperialism and capitalism." This approach objectifies Native people, consigning them either to mere reactive participants or to museums. [4]

Flawed by analytical shortcomings, both approaches fail to explain Native communities' survival into the present and the ways that they have shaped their changing worlds in the hopes of securing survival into the future. The actors in the story told here are those who survived and those who both impacted and impeded survival. The voices of all these actors need to be heard in this tribal history. Such an approach requires that the motivations of both the Menominees and non-Menominees who have participated in the history be told.

Because tribal histories are mutual stories between others, it becomes necessary to give voice to the Menominee in the telling of their history. Of course, outside scholars, in the process of "giving voice," can themselves become part of imperialist construction. It is not enough to simply add Native voice to the text. It must be part of the analysis. Otherwise, such an approach is akin to Dave Barry's satirical, oft-added comment that "women and minorities were making many contributions" in his lampoon of American history textbooks, *Dave Barry Slept Here*.[5] Native people's perspectives must guide the text as well.

Giving voice, then, means more than providing Menominee reactions to their historical situation. It also involves viewing these historical forces from within the context of Menominee culture. This task requires wiping clear the lens through which we view history, to avoid what Renato Rosaldo has termed "imperialist nostalgia, the curious phenomenon of people's longing for what they themselves have destroyed."[6]

Since tribal and nontribal history share a mutual story line, the cultural context of the Native voice is as important as the cultural context of the Euro-American voice in telling tribal history. Without both, the Native voice becomes either relegated to "imperialist nostalgia" or complicit in imperial mythmaking. As Linda Tuhiwai Smith points out, "the term 'research' is inextricably linked to European imperialism and colonialism." What is needed, she observes, is both a "*re*writing and *re*righting" of indigenous history. For the past to become relevant to indigenous communities, it must be conceptualized outside of Western imperial and colonial definitions.[7]

To accomplish this objective, we sometimes need to utilize the colonizer's story to find the Indian voice. Epeli Hau'ofa, in writing about Pacific Island history, however, warns that the use of Euro-American imperial events as the markers to define indigenous histories is helpful only to a degree. These markers also serve as "a hindrance . . . that marginalizes our peoples by relegating them to roles of spectators and objects for transformation," he writes.[8] The same may be said of Native American histories. The careful historian must expand both the sources used to explicate history and the frameworks in which those sources are analyzed.

Past Menominee histories have generally been told within typical Western frameworks of Euro-American policies. Writing in the 1970s, the historian Patricia Ourada, in *The Menominee Indians*, used colonial and federal policies as her guideposts in telling the Menominee story. The anthropologist Feelix Keesing, who authored a valuable 1930s ethnography, *The Menomini Indians*, wrote later in a text on applied anthropology that he worked on behalf of colonizing governments—conducting research on indigenous peoples in order to aid those governments in controlling them.[9]

Figure 1. Periods in Menominee history: A visual timeline

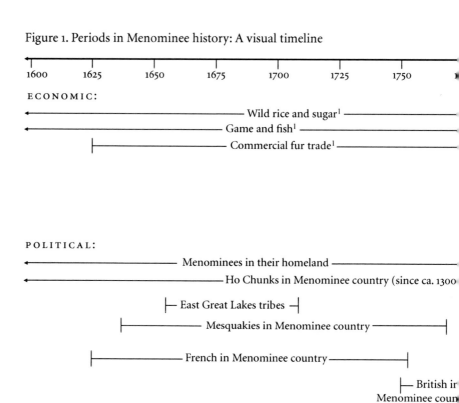

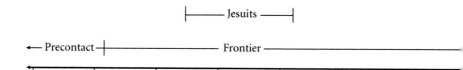

1. The Menominee did not stop using these at the dates indicated, but they became relatively
   unimportant to the tribal economy at those times.

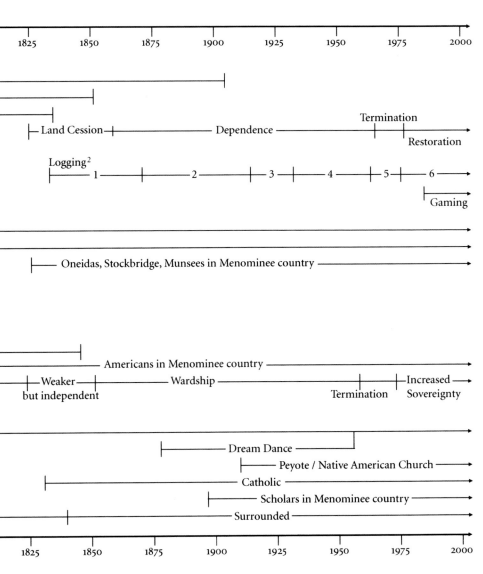

2. The six periods in Menominee logging are (1) 1830s–1871: whites log Menominee timber, legally and illegally; (2) 1871–1908: Menominees and whites log Menominee timber, legally and illegally; (3) 1905–27: gross federal mismanagement of Menominee timber, despite LaFollette Act; (4) 1927–61: selective cutting under various jurisdictions and leaders; (5) 1961–73: termination, outside managemant tries "modernization"; and (6) 1973–present: restoration, tribally run Menominee Tribal Enterprises, Inc., oversees resource.

These approaches tell part of, or different views of, the larger story, but other historical and cultural markers exert greater influence during different historical eras in the Menominee past. This work focuses on the Menominee struggle for survival and self-determination within the larger American context. Here, it is useful to consider the Menominee world as evolving from one of complete autonomy in precontact times to one of substantial dependence and loss of autonomy that occurred after the arrival of the Americans. This loss of control led to a century of underdevelopment and colonial subordination that was not reversed until the end of the twentieth century.

The first part of the Menominee story of survival, from independence to colonial subjugation, was told in *Siege and Survival* and focused on the years 1634–1856, from Jean Nicolet's arrival in Menominee country until the tribe signed its last treaty with the United States. That volume examined the ever-increasing flow of outside forces that challenged Menominee home rule and the strategies the tribe employed to retain a piece of its homeland and a modicum of control over its future.

This volume focuses on the years since 1854, when the Menominee signed the treaty that ensured their future on a piece of their own homeland in Wisconsin. There they repelled attempt after attempt to dispossess them of their remaining land base despite the efforts of outside forces to take it from them. Generation after generation of Menominee leaders beat back individuals and institutions—educational, religious, entrepreneurial, and governmental—that sought to wrest control over their rich forest resources and their land from them. The struggle for home rule often pitted tribal leaders against federal agents; federal agents against entrepreneurs; and tribal leaders, federal agents, and missionaries in various alliances against each other as all tried to shape Menominee life to fit within the northeast Wisconsin world for their own purposes. Local conditions, national agendas of both the federal government and religious institutions, as well as an increasingly broadening regional market for their timber all left their marks on the Menominee world.

The Menominee struggle took various forms but came to focus primarily on the forest and the land base, on the one hand, and on tribal culture, on the other. Tribal members worked to use their resources to support themselves while the United States worked to reshape tribal cultural values. This led to divergent views of the tribal economy. For more than three-quarters of a century U.S. officials hoped to turn the Menominee into agriculturalists while the tribe increasingly worked to manage its forest to provide a living for tribal members.

The Menominee's first success in these efforts came in 1871, a watershed year in which they fought off efforts to remove them from their land base

Map 1. Wisconsin

and instead began harvesting timber themselves on a commercial basis for the first time. Their next landmark success occurred in 1908 with the passage of the LaFollette Act, which required management of the reservation forest in perpetuity. Unfortunately, by this time the U.S. agents had gained near complete control over Menominee actions on their reservation and the tribe could do little but react to federal initiatives. In fact, it was all the tribe could do to fight off various potentially lethal threats to their future that seemed to hurtle upon them on the heels of one another over the course of the first century of reservation life. These threats included allotment, land sales, forest and mill mismanagement, religious repression, and the near strangling of tribal leadership.

Then in 1954 the Menominee struggle was seemingly lost when the process of termination, following the path of federal policy, brought the greatest modern disaster to the tribe. Ironically, however, this action led to a reversal of the process of loss. The tribe began to chart its own route, to break its own path, at this point. Menominee efforts in the past to maintain their identity and resources laid the foundation for the tribal members to achieve restoration in 1973. With this achievement they brought the tribe back from the brink of destruction yet again and began to build a future more completely defined by the Menominee than at any time since the early nineteenth century. The tragic and often depressing narrative thus has a cautiously hopeful ending at the dawn of the twenty-first century.

These stories of the past 150 years of attacks on Menominee land and resources, and on tribal political, economic, and social structures, are almost overwhelming when studied in detail. Yet the detail is important to understand the heroic and daunting nature of the Menominee story of survival and their struggle for self-determination. For this reason the narrative shifts focus between the Menominee and other actors who have played key roles in shaping tribal life, so that the reader may better understand the various forces impacting the development of Menominee self-determination since the establishment of the reservation.

ACKNOWLEDGMENTS

Numerous people helped me in this project with their generosity, hospitality, criticism, advice, input, and encouragement. I would like to especially thank Patricia Albers, Frank Alegria, Rebecca Alegria, Steve Askenette, Bob and Ellie Beatty, Katy Beck, George and Lucy Bennett, Shirley Burton, Bruce Calder, Cawtackasic (Honorable Louis Hawpetoss), Art and Lucille Chapman, Michael Chapman, Mae Chevalier, Brother Keith Clark, Richmond L. Clow, Ron Corn Jr., Bette Crouse, Mary Danowski, Ada Deer, Tom DeLeon, Verna DeLeon, Bob Dignan, Carol Dodge, Sid Dodge, Tara Dowd, Robert V. Dumont Jr., Phyllis Duran, Charles and Nancy Eddis, Ken "Bum Bum" Fish, Scott Forsyth, Neil Froemming, Roy Froemming, Fran Gamwell, JoAnne Gauthier, Connie Goetz, David J. Grignon (Nahwahquaw), Gloria Hamilton, Alice and Jerry Hammett, LaDonna Harris, Bob and Karen Herz, Peggy Hoge, Grace Sims Holt, Brian C. Hosmer, Terri Johnson, Basil Johnston, Rita Keshena, Sally Kitson, Brian Kuehl, Louis B. Kuppenheimer, Rosalyn LaPier, Roxanne LaRock, Nancy O. Lurie, Harvey Markowitz, David Reed Miller, Glen Miller, Marion Miller, Mavis Neconish, Roger L. Nichols, Jay Oleson, Richard Oshkeshequoam, David Oshkosh Sr., Marshall Pecore, Nicholas C. Peroff, Otto Pikaza, David C. Ranney, Patrick Rick, A. LaVonne Brown Ruoff, Sara Satterthwaite, Leo Schelbert, Kathryn Shanley, Honorable Sarah Skubitz, Faith Smith, Robert J. Smith, Donny Spotted Elk, Terry Straus, Jack Sutters, Michelle Sullivan, Gary and Mary Jo Swanson, Sol Tax, Mark Thiel, Scot and Cathy Thomas, Dewey Thunder, Dustin Tourtillott, Bernard Vigue, Angeline Wall, Cheryl Warrington, Allen Washinawatok, Gwen Washinawatok, Karen Washinawatok, Hilary "Sparky" Waukau, Geoffrey M. White, Kristen Wilhelm, Natalia Wilson, and the students I had the pleasure of working with at NAES College. Joerg Metzner deserves special recognition for the maps he created for this document.

Organizations that provided important help were Americans for Indian Opportunity, the Denver Art Museum, the Field Museum of Natural History, the Harold B. Lee Library at Brigham Young University, the Marquette University Archives, the Milwaukee Public Museum, the National Anthropological Archives at the Smithsonian Institution, the National Archives and Records Administration in Washington DC and Chicago, the Newberry Library, Northwestern University Government Publications, the State Historical Society of Wisconsin, the University of Montana Native American Studies

Department, and the University of Montana Mansfield Library Inter-Library Loan desk. Two summer research grants from the University Grant Program of the University of Montana provided assistance in the completion of this project. A 2003 NEH Summer Institute, entitled "Re-Imagining Indigenous Cultures: The Pacific Islands," sponsored by the East-West Center and the University of Hawai'i, provided valuable insights as well.

I would especially like to thank the Menominee Conservation Commission, the Menominee Historic Preservation Department, the Menominee Public Relations Office, the Menominee Treaty Rights and Mining Impacts Office, the Menominee Tribal Archives, the Menominee Tribal Chairman's Office, the Menominee Tribal/County Library, Menominee Tribal Enterprises, the Menominee Tribal Legislature, and NAES College for their help with this project.

Menominee Survival
into the 1850s

God thought proper to have the Indians in this country, and you white men were put on the other side of the ocean. It is you white people who have got our land away from us. We supposed you white people would help us along. You have been buying and selling the lands, and after all you pay about a shilling an acre, and how much you get! All these lands were ours. The little money sent here by government is carried away by mice; you white people are rich and have cities. All the young men are afraid, and we are afraid, to take the money from those not yet born. Those young people would think hard of the chiefs.—Shununiu, 8 September 1855

For thousands of years Menominee Indians lived in what is now north central and eastern Wisconsin and the south central portion of Michigan's Upper Peninsula. They divided the territory into regions controlled by bands consisting of several dozen to more than a hundred members. Social organization also included a clan system that defined people's relationships to each other and their responsibilities to the band and the tribe. The bands traveled extensively through the area, using rivers and lakes as their highways, trading and forging alliances with the nations that would become their neighbors, the Ojibwe (Chippewa), the Santee (Sioux), and the Ho Chunk (Winnebago). They harvested wild rice and fished in those same waterways, planted crops near their shorelines, and hunted and gathered in the lushly wooded forests surrounding them. These activities were directed by the seasons and through the beneficent intervention of their cultural heroes, who resided in the supernatural realm. The different bands traveled separately on foot or by canoe but shared the same language, customs, culture, and world-view, coming together in larger groups only at specified times of the year for particular ceremonial events. They adapted well to a constantly changing environment that provided all their needs—in abundance much of the year and in scarcity through the harsh wintry months.

The Menominee developed a rich, complex society that protected itself with a highly codified, though unwritten, system of justice and social control.

Custom was well defined and sanctified by its connection to the tribe's origins. Each clan and each individual played a specific role in maintaining community welfare. These roles were reinforced by unbreakable tradition that was passed down orally and by participation in community life. Men hunted and gathered and, on those rare occasions when called for, fought in war. Women raised the toddlers, prepared the fish and game brought home by men, gathered berries, and took charge of the home—which meant not only maintaining it but moving it with the changing seasons. Elders educated the youth, who joined the adult roles after ceremonial welcoming to manhood or womanhood at puberty.

The two major clan divisions, the Bear and the Thunderer or Eagle, oversaw domestic and foreign relations, respectively. Leaders made decisions in consultation with the entire community of adults, male and female, in a more true form of political democracy than the one eventually developed on this continent by Europeans and Euro-Americans. Leaders were most successful when they took the community in the directions it wanted to go. Bear clan leaders guided the tribe's bands during peacetime, but Thunder clan leaders decided when to form alliances, share resources, or fight enemies. Individual bands, rather than the nation as a whole, generally made these decisions. Thunder clan members, though, were responsible for enforcing the law. This task fell largely to the *naēnawēhtaw* (warriors) or the providers and defenders. *Naēnawēhtaw* in the fullest sense of the term meant far more than fighting in battle—it meant taking care of the land, as well as those least able to fend for themselves, whether children, elders, the infirm, or women with children. This included, therefore, protecting people from internal and external threats in whatever form they arose. It also required that those who were unable to provide for themselves would receive provisions.

In reality this was a community-wide responsibility. One of the Menominee's core cultural values is reciprocity, or the sharing of resources.[1] Individuals who hunted or fished together shared in the bounty of their success, with the one who killed the game or fish giving the choicest portions to the other. The fall rice harvest was a community-wide event, as was the spring sturgeon catch. One elder today compares the sturgeon catch of old with modern commodities—surplus staples provided to those unable fully to fend for themselves and their families.[2]

Sharing the resources with those in need occasionally applied not only within the community or tribe but also to neighboring tribes. If a band of Ojibwes, Ho Chunks, or Santee Sioux had difficulty finding a winter camp or enough game, their leaders would negotiate use of Menominee land for a specified period of time, and vice versa. The Menominee knew this practice as *apēkon ahkīhih*, which translates literally as "sit down upon." They negotiated use of resources separately. If use of resources was not negotiated, the Menominee retained the rights to them and acted under that assumption. This practice served to establish generally peaceful relationships between neighbors.

Violations of these rules of behavior by taking someone else's resources, within the tribe or between nations, was a serious offense, perhaps more serious than murder. Adjudication of murder cases often required that the offender provide gifts to the family of the victim, although in the most serious cases the offender's life would be taken. Theft of resources could lead to war. A brief civil war once broke out between two Menominee bands, for example, when the downstream band stopped the spring run of sturgeon from advancing upriver. This is the only documented case of major precontact intratribal strife.

Menominees traded many resources as well. They traded such things as wild rice, beaver pelts, and sturgeon for buffalo skins to western Indians who lived in areas lacking abundant water. They were also part of a vast trading network that stretched across much of the North American continent. The life ways that the Menominee developed over long centuries remained relatively undisturbed until the seventeenth century.

By the time the French explorer Jean Nicolet arrived in Menominee and Ho Chunk country in the 1630s, the trade for European-made goods, which the Odawa controlled in the Upper Great Lakes, had already affected Menominee material culture. By the latter half of the seventeenth century, French traders and Jesuit missionaries became a constant, if small, presence in Menominee country. They brought with them ravaging diseases as well as trade goods and entered into relationships with Menominee women that created an increasingly mixed-blood population, forever changing the Menominee world.

A demographic upheaval in Menominee country ensued. During the middle of the seventeenth century the Mesquakie moved into Menominee lands. Then, the dwindling fur trade in the east forced the Iroquois to expand their boundaries in search of commerce to ensure stability. Part of this expansion was to the west. Within a couple of decades nearly a dozen eastern tribes, most of whom would stay for perhaps a generation, fled west into Menominee country, remaining until the early 1700s. This time of invasion and upheaval caused the Menominee and the Ho Chunk, though culturally very different, to strengthen their alliances. Likely these two tribes also cemented their bonds with the Ojibwe, their neighbors to the north and west.

Based on the long-established practice of *apēkon ahkīhih*, the Menominee permitted many of these newcomers to sit down upon their land, to live in Menominee country as guests. Most notably, the Mesquakie and the French took advantage of this policy. When they violated Menominee rules or abused the Menominee generosity as hosts, however, these guests paid the price quickly. A French commandant at the fort at La Baye who misused the tribe forced the Menominee to attack the post and kill eleven Frenchmen, even while the Menominee were the best French allies in the region. Similarly, the Menominee joined the French in a war against the Mesquakie in the first quarter of the eighteenth century when the latter blockaded a river route that was supposed to be accessible to everyone and began to charge tolls, violating a longstanding rule that kept the waterways open to all.

When the British displaced the French as the European colonial agents in the Upper Great Lakes, the previous patterns of the fur trade and interaction remained. The Jesuits had been gone for more than half a century, so it was traders, soldiers, and diplomats, sometimes embodied in the same person, with whom the tribe interacted. The Menominee leader Sekatsokemau invited the British to sit down upon Menominee land in the same way the tribe had previously invited the French and Mesquakie to do so. British soldiers did not stay long in Menominee country, but the British traders did. In fact, the British permitted individual Frenchmen to remain in the *pays d'en haut*, or upper country, and many stayed, maintaining their old positions in the fur trade but now reporting to a different crown and trading with a different Montreal company. Some of the traders married Menominee women, and some learned the Menominee language and customs, becoming allies with different bands of the tribe in negotiations with Euro-Americans.

Some bands dealt regularly with the European traders, while others did not. Throughout this time, despite devastating diseases, the Menominee band system remained intact. By the late 1700s this system slowly expanded as the population began to grow. Menominee bands summered along Green Bay, Lake Winnebago, and the Wolf and Fox Rivers, and they wintered as far southeast as present-day Kenosha; southwest to the Quad Cities area of the Illinois-Iowa border; upstream along the Mississippi River through Prairie du Chien, Wisconsin, and St. Anthony's Falls, Minnesota; and north to Mille Lacs, the southern border of Minnesota's north woods. Menominee bands in the northeast ranged as far as Michilimackinac (now Mackinac).

This residency pattern did not change when the Americans claimed the old Northwest Territory in the wake of their Revolutionary War victory. It held until well after the British finally agreed to leave the area after the War of 1812.

However, when the Americans took over Green Bay in 1815, they established Fort Howard. Shortly thereafter they began an all-out assault on the Menominee political, economic, social, and spiritual realms that left the tribal nation weakened and reeling.

American lumber barons coveted and denuded Menominee forests, and farmers poured into the lands after the loggers left. In this time of Menominee loss, the United States forced a series of treaties on the tribe in which the Americans' ultimate goal was to remove the Menominee from their ancient homeland. Meanwhile Catholics, including Dominicans, Redemptorists, and Franciscans, returned for the first time since the Jesuit efforts of the early 1700s. They worked alternately together and in competition with government agents. Most of the agents assigned to Menominee country were ignorant, incompetent, or corrupt and managed to make life miserable for individual tribal members. Most also pursued the federal policy of converting Menominees into farmers, Christians, and "citizens," attempting to change the Indians' very lifestyle.

Beginning in the 1830s, each treaty the tribe signed shrunk the Menominee estate. The low point occurred in 1848, when the tribe sold all its remaining Wisconsin lands for a tract on the Crow Wing River in central Minnesota. Tribal leaders inserted a stipulation, however, that a tribal delegation would first visit the Crow Wing land, thus reserving for the Menominee the right of disapproval of the move. When the Menominee asserted that right, a difficult process of negotiation followed. Ultimately, with the support of the young state of Wisconsin, the tribe secured the boundaries of its current reservation in two treaties signed in 1854 and 1856. Despite the right-of-refusal clause in the 1848 treaty, and the fact that the Menominee were able to remain in Wisconsin in 1854, U.S. commissioners negotiated a number of the tribe's treaties with the United States in bad faith using bribery, threats—including of forced military removal—and trickery to gain their ends.

Nonetheless, the Menominee faced the challenge, and they retained certain key rights in those treaties. Most tribal members began the painful move to the area surrounding Keshena Falls, although some from the Illinois border to Michigan's Upper Peninsula remained in their old homesites. The Menominee had met their first modern threat to survival and, despite heart-wrenching losses, had survived. In doing so they established a permanent base on a much-reduced portion of their homeland in which their modern communities could take root. Indeed, they would need strong roots to withstand the future flood of threats emanating from federal and state attempts to control their nation over the next 150 years.

By the time the reservation was established the Menominee had virtually no economic base or power. The United States prepared to strip tribal leaders of their political status as well. The United States attempted to do this by manipulating people's social lives, undermining the Menominee nation's social structure and its spiritual base, and controlling the tribe's economy. As in previous eras of Menominee history, the attacks were sometimes large-scale but often piecemeal, creating a debilitating sense of loss of control for tribal members.

Menominee attempts both to counteract these attacks and to shape the direction of their future as a tribal nation were rooted in the tribe's history and social structure. The tribe had long been both divided and unified. Catholic bands lived more closely to the white population and interacted with them on a more regular basis. Those bands that still followed the traditional Mitāēwin religion lived farther away. Bands sometimes disagreed on specific actions to be taken in the face of Euro-American threats, maintaining autonomy in decision making. Yet the bands continued to come together at significant ceremonial times. Neither did Catholic Menominees give up all of their traditional social or religious practices.

In times of grave national crisis, the tribe as a whole made decisions together, often setting aside differences until they had resolved or diminished the crisis. Tribal leaders insisted on waiting for the input of all tribal members before making decisions. This combination of consensus and democracy foiled outsider plans to divide and conquer. The Menominee were also adept at forging alliances with would-be enemies or antagonists. This is evident from their early alliances with the Ho Chunk, their relationships with traders, and their interaction with contacts who lobbied the Wisconsin legislature to regain a piece of the homeland. The factionalism, the unity, and the carefully crafted alliances were to play key roles in shaping the Menominee future.

The new reservation community, despite the carryover of the band structure, was not entirely the same as the old Menominee nation. Not all tribal members moved onto the newly formed reservation. Some remained behind—in the area of Menominee, Michigan, and Marinette, Wisconsin, in the north or Milwaukee County in the south, for example—because of their ties to the land. Others remained behind because they were married to nontribal members who decided not to move. The 1848 treaty bought some, known as forty-niners, out of the tribe. Still others stayed behind with the promise of avoiding military removal to Minnesota.

Those who made the move formed the new Menominee polity, though many of those who remained behind maintained family ties and connections to the tribe as a whole. Despite factional distinctions, members of the new reservation community shared much in common. They had a deeply held reverence for their lands and resources, which they vindicated to some extent when they regained a piece of their homeland. They continued to view the land and waterways of the forest as the basis of their nourishment, in both physical and spiritual terms. The concentration of so many tribal members on so small a land base led to starvation, malnutrition, and want. According to the official count, 2,002 Menominees lived in close proximity after the 1852 move. Many would continue to hunt, fish, and gather in their old homelands until forced to remain on the reservation as the surrounding white population grew. This view of the landscape as a foundation of their society would play a determining role in their history over the next 150 years.

In political terms, tribal leaders consistently acted with the best-perceived interests of the tribe at the forefront, even if the definition of those interests varied among leaders. They viewed their primary responsibility to be to the whole community, even above their own interests. This meant caring for relatives and for those too weak to care for themselves. This would set them at odds with the American perception of individual success time and again—even in cases where they seemed to be following the American model. They wanted for the sake of their children and grandchildren to fulfill the American dream of finding a good living, but they added a Menominee twist: they wanted this for the extended family, band, and tribe, not merely for themselves. Always the community came first. The Menominee recognized that the world around them was changing. And they wanted to change with it. As Roy Oshkosh would say, "We like our modern comforts now."[3] They simply wanted to be able to provide them in a manner they deemed tribally appropriate.

The United States, on the other hand, desired individual Menominees to succeed on their own. Indian Service and other federal officials therefore worked hard to separate the individual from the tribe and the tribe from its resource base. They equated progress with individual effort divorced from the community. Simply put, the two cultures defined success in radically different ways. So while both sides seemed to have the same goals—Menominee success in a modern American culture—their definitions of success differed so drastically that they were constantly at loggerheads with each other. In other words, two different processes were now in conflict. Both had the same purpose, but the definitions of that purpose were almost diametrically opposed.

Ironically, tribal leaders and federal officials often thought the same methods might lead to success, and so at times the Menominee embraced federal initiatives, while at other times they proposed their own initiatives that in the end they would have to fight off. Tribal goals generally centered around maintenance of the tribal way of life and the establishment of a high quality of life for tribal members. They hoped to accomplish this within an evolving economic and political system that was largely driven by their forest resources. Over the years, federal goals were generally to find ways to abandon their trust responsibility and to encourage individual Menominees to enter into a vaguely elaborated, idealized, and unrealistic representation of the larger society.

And so the Menominee struggled in the coming years to make a success in terms they themselves defined. They had to do so as an impoverished nation that was increasingly surrounded by a dominant society that defined success in very different terms. The Menominee would often adopt American means and would even appear to be moving toward American ends. But ultimately, success would only come to them if they could work with their own strengths and overcome their own weaknesses to make a path of their own choosing. Their struggle to meet the future on their own terms, to develop a political voice, and to maintain a semblance of self-determination and cause it to grow over time is the subject of this book.

The Struggle for Self-Determination

ABBREVIATIONS

AAIA	Association for American Indian Affairs
ABN	Alexian Brothers Novitiate
AIO	Americans for Indian Opportunity
AIM	American Indian Movement
AMA	American Missionary Association
BIA	Bureau of Indian Affairs
BIC	Board of Indian Commissioners
CCC	Concerned Citizens Committee
CETA	Comprehensive Employment and Training Act
CHR	community health representative
CMN	College of the Menominee Nation
CNC	Coordinating and Negotiating Committee
DNR	Department of Natural Resources
DOE	Department of Energy
DPI	Department of Public Instruction
DRUMS	Determination of Rights and Unity for Menominee Shareholders
FPC	Federal Power Commission
HEW	Department of Health, Education, and Welfare
IRA	Indian Reorganization Act
MEI	Menominee Enterprises, Inc.
MISC	Menominee Indian Study Committee
MRC	Menominee Restoration Committee
MTE	Menominee Tribal Enterprises
NAES	Native American Educational Services
NAGPRA	Native American Graves Protection and Repatriation Act
NARF	Native American Rights Fund
NCAI	National Congress of American Indians
OEO	Office of Economic Opportunity
OIA	Office of Indian Affairs
PL-280	Public Law 83–280
WPL	Wisconsin Power and Light Company

CHAPTER ONE

The Early Reservation Years

The treaty of 1854 reestablished a legal territorial base for a Menominee home-land in Wisconsin. Tribal members began to settle permanently in communi-ties there based on their historic band affiliation. The numerous bands re-mained territorially separate even after 1854, when each band selected its own site on the reservation, some as many as twenty miles distant from others. In the early reservation years both the Menominee and the federal government would struggle to determine the ways in which the Menominee could survive on this much diminished fraction of their original homeland. Tribal values and ideas would sometimes seem to mesh with American goals and other times to conflict with them as the tribe worked to establish a new way of living in its newly defined home base. As time went on, however, Menominee and federal efforts drifted further apart.

Tribal members attempted to adapt to their new life in a variety of ways. They followed the advice of federal officials until they realized how ineffective it was. They expressed interest in farming and in the American education sys-tem. Many also focused their adaptations on the spiritual realm, and Catholi-cism became an increasingly important part of life for many Menominees. However, self-serving officials in both the government and the church often subverted their efforts to adapt. The reality of life in a land with too few resources struck the Menominee hard. Many of those non-Indians serving among them, both federal agents and missionaries, often failed to take note of this.

THE NEW RESERVATION

In settling the reservation, Catholic bands led by Carron, LaMotte, Kinepoway, and Oshkenaniew moved primarily east of the Wolf River. Tribal members and federal officials often simply called these bands "Christian." The bands that continued to follow the Mitāēwin religion remained separate, based on the Bear (Oshkosh, Souligny, and Mahchakeniew or Chickeney) and Thun-

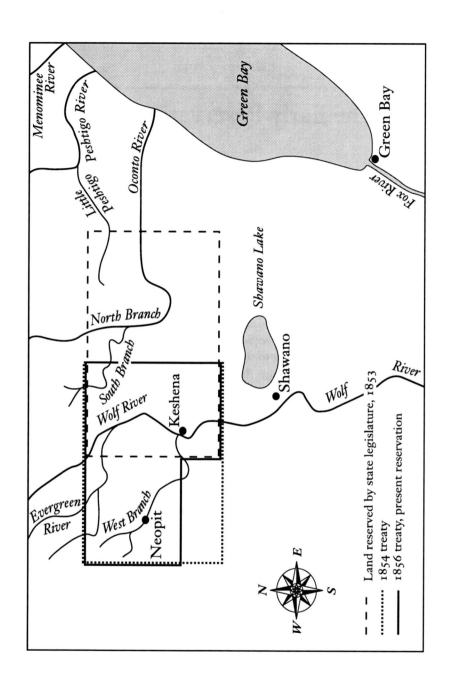

Map 2. Menominee reservation

derer (Wayka, Keso, and Niaqtawapomi) divisions. Bands from along Green Bay arrived later. The Oconto River band, a Catholic band, established South Branch on the Little Oconto River in the northeast corner of the reservation, while the Peshtigo and Menominee River bands established themselves near Keshena Falls. Bands and individual Menominees continued to live off the reservation as well.[1]

This arrangement created an overcrowding that would severely stress a limited resource base. Some two thousand Menominees now lived on approximately a quarter of a million acres. The size of the tribe reflects a 20 percent drop in population from the first land cessions some two decades earlier. Both starvation-induced disease and, more significantly, the number of tribal members who remained in other areas of old Menominee country account for this decline. But alongside this 20 percent decrease in population was an approximately 98 percent decrease in land base, which had diminished from between eight and twelve million acres to twelve townships.[2]

The Wolf River flowed from north to south through the newly established reservation, providing the major water source. Hundreds of miles of rivers and streams, as well as more than one hundred small lakes, also dotted the reservation. The Little Oconto River flowed through the far northeast corner of the reservation. The main body of the Oconto, which flowed through lands to the east and directly into Green Bay, had been reserved for loggers. In fact, federal officials shifted the boundaries originally proposed for the reservation westward and decreased its size by 20 percent especially to serve the loggers' interests. The eastern lands within the original boundaries contained much valuable pine and a river route to run the logs into the waters of Green Bay and directly to market. Because of its accessibility to markets through Lake Michigan, this eastern land was considered more valuable for timber than the land to the west of it. Although the Wolf River flowed through the western land, it did not flow directly to Green Bay. The Menominee had also ceded the most valuable of their agricultural lands in the region, which lay to the south and farther east along the Fox River valley.[3]

The soil on the actual reservation land was a mix of "loam and silt loam soils" in the northwest and "sandy loam and sandy soils" in the southeast and south, all of it "interlaced with peat swamps."[4] This made for good timberland and provided soil for the limited agriculture that southern Menominee bands had long practiced, growing corn and squashes. It was not particularly suitable for the wheat farming brought to Wisconsin by the early Americans settlers.[5] Trees grew in thick, mature stands, depending on soil type. The wide variety of timber included white, red, and jack pine; aspens; and hardwoods such as

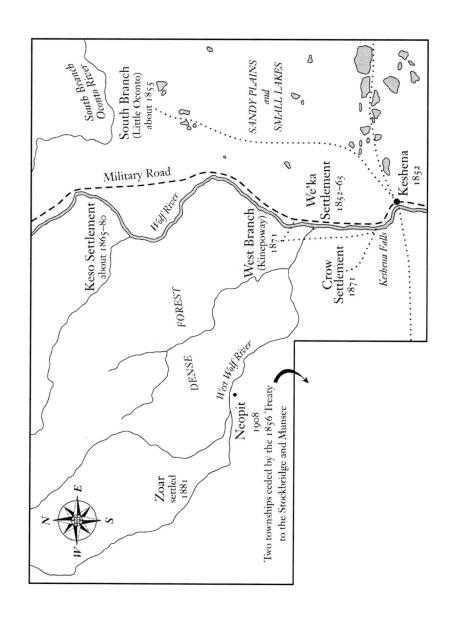

Map 3. Felix Keesing's Menominee reservation settlements

sugar maple, yellow birch, beech, oak, and white ash. Cedar and hemlock grew abundantly in the swamps.[6]

Keshena Falls, the most significant site on the new reservation, had for ages attracted sturgeon and the Menominee who caught the fish in great numbers there. Keshena, the leader of the Menominee River band, was the namesake for both the falls and the village established just southeast of there. The pay grounds were established nearby as well. The village of Keshena became the site of the federal headquarters on the reservation in 1855 when the United States constructed its first agency buildings there.[7]

An 1856 treaty again diminished the size of the Menominee homeland, this time by two townships (17 percent). The Stockbridge and Munsee Indians, whom the United States had previously moved onto Menominee land in the Lake Winnebago–Fox River area, had lost their lands there, and the United States decided to settle them farther west. Superintendent Francis Huebschmann, referred to by a Stockbridge observer as "an unmitigated scoundrel" and a "conscienceless man," lied, bribed, and coerced the Stockbridge and Munsee, a bitterly divided tribe, into signing a treaty accepting land "near the southern boundary of the Menominee reservation." Huebschmann promised the Stockbridge and Munsee a piece of good agricultural land south of Shawano Lake. Instead of taking this land from white settlers, loggers, or speculators, the United States took it from the Menominee, this time at a rate of sixty cents per acre. Six days after the Stockbridge-Munsee treaty, Huebschmann negotiated a treaty with the Menominee to gain the lands for the eastern tribes. Not until after this occurred did Huebschmann inform the Stockbridge and Munsee that they would be moving northwest of the promised site onto Menominee land, which they knew to be of vastly inferior agricultural quality. They agreed to move there unhappily only because they had nowhere else to go.[8]

The primary aim for the Menominee in the 1854 and 1856 treaties was to secure and maintain a portion of the homeland, which they achieved. Secondarily, they needed the federal government to provide them with sustenance, since over a period of less than forty years they had sold to the United States almost their entire birthright under pressure from white expansion. They intended to meet their primary goal at almost any cost, even to the point of letting federal officials deny them portions of their secondary goal. Under tribal custom, they viewed an agreement to be a basis for future negotiations if it did not meet tribal standards. The Menominee viewed these treaties as fatally flawed.

The Americans, through Superintendent Huebschmann, hoped to use the treaties to force the Menominee to restructure their society and economy and to become strictly farmers. Under the American definition, farming would be a full-time occupation, not a supplement to hunting, fishing, and gathering traditional foods. Traditional Menominee farming had occurred in the southern portions of tribal territory, which had now been sold. The primary crops of corn and squashes were well adapted to that region and had supplemented other food sources. American-defined farming meant changing to a diet of dairy products, wheat, and potatoes. American farming had been part of U.S. policy toward the Menominee since the signing of the 1831–32 treaties, which had established a short-lived agricultural colony among the tribe.[9] America was an agrarian nation, and this transition to American-style agriculture seemed the most promising method of incorporating Indians into it.

As a matter of survival, the Menominee indicated a willingness to accept U.S.-imposed changes. After all, this would help them achieve their secondary goal. So when Menominee leaders spoke in support of adapting to American ways to avoid starvation, Agent Benjamin Hunkins believed he was finally making headway in "civilizing" the tribe. A series of 1856 council meetings provides an illustration of how far apart Menominee and American goals were, however, even when they seemed to coincide. The Menominee desired to adapt to reservation life in order to prosper as the white Americans did. Hunkins called for an end to alcohol abuse, and the tribe supported his efforts to control alcohol dispensation and use on the reservation, equating this with becoming "civilized." Tribal leaders also urged tribal members to take up farming and to send their children to school.[10]

At the 12 May council meeting the tribal leader Oshkosh spoke at length to the tribe in Menominee. Unfortunately, what he said was not translated into the record. Then he told the agent that his advice about avoiding strong drink was good. Oshkosh himself had had occasional problems due to drinking. "I am an old man now and cannot expect to derive much benefit from our contemplated change but I wish to pursue a course which will be the best for our children who will follow us," he said. "I have seen those who have adopted the Customs of the whiteman are advancing rapidly towards civilization." He added that he intended to adopt white customs and to send the children to school.

Shoneon spoke next, also thanking the agent for his words of advice and agreeing that the tribe should take up farming. He told the agent and the tribe that he had been to Washington. "I have seen how mighty the whiteman is and this is because they till the earth," he said. "[W]e wish to have clothes like the white men." For these reasons he spoke in favor of cultivation.[11]

Other leaders also spoke against alcohol and in favor of farming and education. Wash-sha-sho promised to join the church if his brother would. Shawanopenass said, "I wish to have clothes like the white man in order to adopt their manners," and he opposed the use of alcohol. Wayka, himself a Thunder clan leader, said, "Those who wished to join the church may do so." Carron said the Menominee wanted to be like whites, adding, "We want some money expended in improvements. We prefer large fields rather than to have it expended in keeping troops among us." LaMotte approved of the plans, and Keshena added that he hoped the Menominee leaders meant what they said and would follow through. [12] The Menominee clearly hoped to create farms that would support their people.

Agent Hunkins reported that the Menominee wished to assist him in eradicating alcohol from the reservation. He also said the tribe requested a system of laws to show their appreciation for the government's efforts to educate them and to bring them agriculture. The laws would forbid alcohol distribution and use as well as require that the Menominee not permit opposition to federal government policy. Since the tribe had spent several decades already opposing federal government policy, the latter clause must have been Agent Hunkins's idea. [13]

Hunkins wanted to change the tribal power structure and leadership roles at the same time. He wrote to Huebschmann, "The danger to Menominee interests is in the chiefs, and the safety with the young men and some regulations that would put the power more in the hands of the young men." [14] But the tribe would not allow Hunkins to take control.

In a meeting in early July, the tribe again discussed the issue of the extent to which the Menominee should adopt American ways, especially agriculture and education. Numerous young men spoke, saying that, if Washington wanted the Menominee to take up white men's ways, Washington ought to protect money due to the tribe from treaty provisions. The young men stated that this money should be for their children and should not be paid to claimants, who consisted largely of traders. This was the same argument that Menominee leaders such as Oshkosh had made time and again in council meetings. [15]

Shawanopenass, a band leader, supported the young men's statement, adding that they provided a good check against tribal leaders. "[W]hen the Indians get into trouble they have to rely on the young men," he said. Wayka also thanked the young men. Besides these two, Oshkosh, Carron, Keshena, LaMotte, and other Menominee leaders signed approval of a document supporting Hunkins's Americanization policy. [16]

Although the agent presented the tribal discussion relating to acceptance of this document as a power struggle between the young men and the tribe's leaders, and to some extent he was correct, the council proceedings show that Menominee decision making was continuing much as it always had. Tribal members' respect for their leaders had long been based on the leaders' ability to make decisions in consultation with the whole tribe or with the whole band, not autocratically. They generally treated their elders deferentially, and the elders sought to include younger tribal members in decision making, which was consensus based. This way one group or the other could not dominate.

The Menominee tried desperately to adapt to their new environment while Hunkins and Huebschmann tried just as hard to change Menominee life ways fundamentally. Tribal-federal relations became mired in conflicting expectations.

CONFLICTING EXPECTATIONS

Unfortunately, Menominee land made poor farm land, and want and privation continued. Federal officials seemed concerned with form while the tribe desired substance. As long as the agent's plan promised positive results—the end of starvation—the Menominee were willing to support it. However, when the promise faded, the Menominee worked for new solutions, while the federal government continued to try to force the tribe into its ill-conceived definition of civilization. In 1856 Agent Hunkins reported, "One hundred [Menominees], who one year ago lived by the chase, and wore their blankets, now dress like the whites, and are clearing and cultivating land and building houses."[17]

But only two years later the agency government farmer, Friederich Haas, provided a more realistic description of farming on the new reservation. Black rust had destroyed all of the wheat, which had looked so good earlier. Indeed, rust, pests, and soil depletion had become a problem for wheat farmers in Wisconsin generally. A frost on 24 August destroyed a large quantity of corn and potatoes and "all the vegetables," so that "it will make the Menomonee Indians destitute of all means of subsistence, and if they should get no assistance from government they will either starve, or fall back to wild life and follow the chase." Unfortunately for the Menominee, their soil was poor and the growing season short, so crops often failed and tribal members lived in a state of near starvation year after year, sometimes surviving on little more than maple sugar.[18]

Both the agent and the tribe expressed a desire that the Menominee become more like their white neighbors. To the agent this meant being formally educated and being agricultural people who shunned alcohol. To the tribe it meant being able to provide homes in which their children would live without want. The Menominee were willing to try agriculture and education if they would end the harsh life forced upon them by being constricted on a small reservation. For the tribe this was a means, but for the federal government it was an end. When the efforts failed, Menominee leaders insisted on trying to find other solutions, while federal officials insisted on continuing to try to make failed policy work.

In 1859 and 1860 Agent Augustus D. Bonesteel recommended allotting Menominee lands for distribution to individual Menominees. Commissioner of Indian Affairs George Manypenny frequently inserted an allotment clause in the 1850s Manypenny treaties. While the United States was making its first treaties with many tribes west of the Mississippi at mid-century, it was organizing agricultural programs for those in the east, primarily where removal efforts had failed. This was a time of massive growth and westward expansion in which the United States sought to define the place of Indians in American society as being on reservations while American individuals increasingly sought to gain control of tribal lands. These tribal lands suddenly no longer seemed infinite, especially on the shrinking frontiers of places like Nebraska, Wisconsin, and Minnesota in the Old West. An agricultural-based yeoman farmer Indian policy would serve to keep mobile tribes on a diminished portion of their homeland if they could not be removed from it altogether. It would also potentially open up more Indian land for sale and distribution to an expanding American population.

In Wisconsin this policy affected different tribes in different ways. The 1856 treaty by which the neighboring Stockbridge and Munsee had secured their two townships of Menominee land included the common allotment clause. The Menominee avoided allotment treaty clauses since the 1854 treaty established a reservation and did not cede land and the 1856 Menominee treaty was negotiated primarily to benefit the Stockbridge and Munsee, who themselves needed a reservation homeland.[19]

At any rate, Bonesteel believed the Menominee reservation should be surveyed in forty- to eighty-acre plots and allotted, with the government to purchase the remainder of the land and to divide the revenues "for the benefit of those [Menominees] who are industrious."[20] This made little sense to tribal members, who were forced to hunt and fish as the only way to provide sustenance for themselves and their families. Bonesteel, seemingly oblivious to the Menominee plight, failed to discuss the situation in his annual reports, noting to the contrary that the tribe had given up the chase (hunting).[21]

Bonesteel was one more in a long string of Green Bay agents who perpetuated an already well-established tradition of fraud, incompetence, and corruption. These agents served not only the Menominee but also the Oneida and the Stockbridge and Munsee. During the eight-year period preceding Bonesteel, six agents (including Hunkins) had served the Green Bay agency—three had been dismissed or left under a cloud, and two more served brief terms.[22]

In 1860 Wisconsin attorney general James Howe, apparently hired by the Menominee, brought charges against Bonesteel for embezzling money from an emergency fund that was to provide food for the Menominee during the winter of 1858–59, a year in which tribal members suffered in near starvation. The case is illustrative of the severe conditions on the new reservation, the federal role in exacerbating rather than ameliorating those conditions, and Menominee attempts to feed their families in the face of federal incompetence.

At the same time that Bonesteel reported optimistically that tribal members were giving up the chase, the schoolteacher Orlin Andrews reported that "hunger, and almost starvation, have forced many of them to retreat to their hunting grounds." The farmer Friederich Haas added, "The Indians had to spend a great part of the time in fishing and hunting to keep themselves and families from starvation," a condition he had foretold in a previous report. The following fall the priest, the Swiss father Anthony Maria Gachet, reported that by early September "two consecutive frosts have come to destroy everything. Famine is at our door. Our Indians will be obliged to disperse into the forests" to find food. He himself was obliged to cook rat-gnawed tallow candles to feed himself that fall.[23]

To make matters worse, while the Menominee suffered, they believed their agent was stealing their money. The Indian Department sent a special agent, Kintzing Pritchette, to investigate Bonesteel.[24] Pritchette fully exonerated Bonesteel of any wrongdoing, which prompted Howe to write an angry report to the commissioner of Indian affairs, resubmitting the charges. Howe charged that Pritchette was wholly unsuited for the investigation, since he was intoxicated most of the time and was also prejudiced against the Indians. Pritchette either dismissed Indian testimony as unfounded or refused to hear it. The case hinged on two problems: (1) the amount of money actually requested by the tribe (from its own Treasury Department funds) versus the amount requested by Agent Bonesteel and (2) the prices Bonesteel paid for the provisions.

Menominee leaders insisted that they had requested three thousand dollars' worth of goods; Bonesteel said they requested five thousand dollars' worth. The Menominee knew that if they requested too much it would be squandered. Howe proved that the prices Bonesteel claimed to have paid were higher than any charged by reputable merchants in the area, but Bonesteel refused to say from whom he purchased the goods. "It is of no consequence," Howe concluded, "whether Bonesteel put money into his own pocket or into a friend's. The wrong to the Indians is the same, and the dreadful responsibility for the starvation of this people, testified to by so many of the Indians, rests upon his guilty head."[25]

Pritchette defended Bonesteel: "The conduct of Agent Bonesteel toward these people has been paternal in the extreme.... But in the vocabulary of the Indians there is no word expressive of thanks; and if the word gratitude ever existed in the language of the Menominee, it is now expunged or obsolete," a gratuitous implication that the Menominee were unable to recognize kindness or help. Although the extent of Bonesteel's help to the tribe is highly questionable, Pritchette's declaration is absurd considering the important role of generosity in the tribe's history and culture. In Menominee terms, generous behavior is an obligation, as is acceptance of it, and the idea of thanking someone verbally for it is not necessarily appropriate. Nonetheless, words for these things exist in the Menominee language. The Menominee word for "thank you" is *wawannon*; gratitude is expressed as *mami yamamāēw*, meaning "he gives thanks to him." Pritchette did not understand the Menominee cultural context of these ideas, nor did he care to.[26]

Howe concurred that many charges made by the tribe did not stand up under evidence. Several of the accusations "would never have been heard of" if Bonesteel or the government employees had explained their actions to the Indians instead of ruling and acting without explanation.[27] The weight of paternalistic action by the agent quashed any Menominee hopes for self-determination.

Keshena's testimony shows that part of the fault lay with the government-appointed interpreter, William Powell. Keshena said "that on Mr. Bonesteel assuming the agency, the tribe objected to the appointment of Mr. Powell, because he did not interpret correctly; that the reason that this is said is because the agent always does different from what they request when Mr. Powell interprets." Bonesteel's arrogant attitude was part of the cause for this disjuncture. But, on the other hand, if the interpreter did not tell Bonesteel what the tribe wanted him to translate, Bonesteel would have no way of knowing. "Powell admits," Howe wrote in one case, "that he refused to interpret to Bonesteel the Indians' complaint . . . because 'he knew himself it was not true.'" Powell testified that Bonesteel had hired him over the protest of Oshkosh and the other Menominee leaders, who had wanted Joseph Gauthier retained as interpreter.[28]

Commissioner of Indian Affairs A. B. Greenwood reported to the secretary of the interior on this affair that "In the opinion of the department, the report of the special agent exculpated that office[r] from all the charges which had been preferred against him." He also believed that "The Menomonees, during the past year, have manifested a spirit of insubordination to the requirements of their local agent."[29]

In reality the Menominee worked relentlessly to reverse the effects of Pritchette's crude prejudices and Bonesteel's harmful paternalism. They knew how much money was due them from treaty stipulations, and they knew how they wanted to spend it. Their families' health depended on it. Indeed, in addition to governing in traditional ways, tribal leaders learned the American system as it affected the tribe. Due to the high turnover of agents, the Menominee usually knew this system better than the American officials. In one case, for example, the Menominee had asked their superintendent about the five thousand dollars due the tribe for industrial improvements under paragraph 9, article 4, of the 1848 treaty. As a result, the superintendent requested the department to send these funds.[30]

Carron testified in the Bonesteel case that his children had nothing to eat but maple sugar, without which they would have perished.[31] The blame for this went in part to Agent Bonesteel. LaMotte testified "that when Mr. Hunkins and Mr. Muscowitz were agents for them they used to go with them when they came out of their sugar camps to the traders and tell the traders they must give them ten cents a pound for their sugar; that now it is quite different; that their traders do not keep flour, and that they are compelled to go to Shawano and sell their sugar at five cents a pound rather than starve."[32]

The licensed traders at this time were George Cown and a Mr. Cavert. Cown—a subordinate bankrolled by Ewing, Chute and Company of Fort Wayne, Indiana—was involved in illicit dealings with the tribe since before removal. Shununiu, the seventy-year-old head military leader of the Menominee, testified that, although Bonesteel told them to come to him if the traders ever took any of their money, "he had never made any complaint to Mr. Bonesteel, because he did not believe he would listen to him."[33]

Others testified that the traders had cheated them in various ways. Three successive agents in the 1860s were likewise accused of cheating the tribe and benefiting from their position: Moses M. Davis, Morgan L. Martin, and Lieutenant John A. Manley.[34] It is little wonder that the tribe did not trust its agents.

Meanwhile the United States continued to insist on pursuing an agricultural economic policy. Agent Davis commented in 1862 that Menominee farmland was poor. Nevertheless, Commissioner of Indian Affairs William P. Dole continued to recommend allotting Menominee lands. In fact, Dole recommended that all the tribes under the Green Bay agency—the Menominee, Oneida, Stockbridge, and Munsee—be placed on the same reservation and given allotments. [35] The next year Davis announced that the Menominee had made real progress in establishing farms but still lacked good farmland. Dole responded by calling for the abandonment of the Menominee reservation. In 1864 both Dole and Davis reported that the Menominee had made "progress" but that their crops had failed. [36] The combination of forced farming and widespread dishonesty or incompetence of the agents laid the framework for the early reservation years, as a corrupt government policy stumbled along.

At the same time, Menominee leaders also showed lasting patterns of self-determination. They had a clear understanding of their rights, especially those derived from or retained in the treaties, and they demanded with varying degrees of success that the federal government fulfill its obligations. They protested corrupt agents and deleterious policies in a variety of ways.

This effort had been easier when an intermediate level of federal authority existed. In 1857 the Green Bay agency gained independence from the northern superintendency, after which the Green Bay agent reported directly to the commissioner of Indian affairs. Tribal trips to Washington to air their complaints cost more and took greater effort, but the Menominee insisted on having their grievances heard. Such was the case in 1865, when Ahconemay Oshkosh, LaMotte, Oshkenaniew, and others sent a petition to the Department of the Interior requesting that they remove Agent Davis from his position. They charged that Davis did not listen to the chiefs of the bands, that he had a pet trader who charged them exorbitant rates, that they received little for what they sold to this trader, and that Davis paid the trader out of their annuities before he paid them. They also alleged that the blacksmith and farmer failed to do their jobs. They commented that they realized the agent must look after the government's interests, but they wanted him to look after their interests also. Davis responded that, with the exception of Ahconemay, the leaders did not know what they had signed. [37] Davis left office shortly thereafter.

When petitions failed, tribal leaders traveled directly to Washington, when possible. These delegations went sometimes with the blessings of the federal government and sometimes against express orders. Often the Menominee lobbyists bypassed the Indian Department entirely, going directly to Congress. Most of those who traveled to Washington were from the old leading families, whose authority the federal government increasingly failed to recognize. These delegations went sometimes with the approval of the tribe and sometimes over the protest of portions of it. The tribe was split into two political factions. This split, based partly on the Catholic-Mitāēwin religious division, had in prereservation years also reflected a geographic division and remained a factor in early reservation life. The two factions disagreed on numerous issues regarding reservation life, including whether government money should be spent on sending tribal delegations to Washington.

Decision making and factionalism were complicated by transitions in leadership as well. After Oshkosh's death the Catholics had pushed for the assignment of his second son, probably Koshka'noqne, a Catholic, as the tribe's primary leader. Ahconemay, Oshkosh's eldest son, who still followed the Mitāēwin but whom Father Gachet said he later baptized into the Catholic faith, had been selected instead.[38] In times of Menominee national crisis, however, these factions overcame their differences and unanimously supported what seemed to be in the tribe's best interest. Someone like Ahconemay, nominally Catholic but still a member of the Mitāēwin, could serve as an effective bridge between the different Menominee religious communities when the tribe's future was at stake.

Since the tribal council could only formally meet in the presence of the agent, he had a large say in what topics the council considered. Nevertheless, he could not control the tribal leaders. When they wanted to bring an issue before the tribal council, they did so. Under Superintendent Huebschmann's rule the United States became increasingly annoyed with the tribe's leadership and tried to eradicate it by creating a "democracy" in which all Menominee men had a voice in decision making. Of course, the Menominee had been operating under a democratic system of decision making for centuries, but it was based on consensus, deference to the elderly, and broad community input rather than on a one-man–one-vote, majority-rule system. The United States found the Menominee to be irritatingly adept at holding onto longstanding cultural methods in the political realm.

THE CATHOLIC CHURCH

During the early years of reservation life in the 1850s and 1860s, federal agents were not the only ones trying to change Menominee culture fundamentally. Catholic Church officials viewed it as their primary aim as well, albeit in the spiritual realm. First Franciscan and then Capuchin missionaries worked to convert tribal members to the Catholic faith and did so with some success. An increasing number of Menominees thought of themselves as Catholic, though generally not of a specific sect, throughout these decades. In some cases the priests worked with Catholic Menominees to spread the faith, but in other cases the priests acted in venal ways. Even under these circumstances Catholicism became the dominant religion on the reservation.

A variety of priests served the reservation mission during the early reservation years, but only irregularly. Although Father Bonduel reported that twelve hundred to fifteen hundred Menominees followed Catholicism, his successor, Father Otto Skolla, still held services in a bark chapel.[39] Indeed, several years after Bonduel left, Father Gachet finally admitted that the official numbers were bloated, and he wondered why this was so. He had observed that many Menominees were Catholic in name only, never even attending church. Upon investigation he learned that at the time of the 1848 treaty negotiations and a threatened removal to Minnesota, a rumor made the rounds that only Catholic Menominees would be allowed to remain in Wisconsin. This led to many hasty and half-hearted conversions of Menominees who he called "Christians whom one counts but whom one does not rely upon." Nonetheless, an increasing number of Menominees identified themselves as Catholic, whether they had nominally or completely converted. In 1859 Gachet estimated that one thousand Menominees followed the Mitāēwin and that the other thousand were Catholic to some degree or other.[40]

Like most priests who served among the tribe, Gachet knew little if anything of the Menominee or even of Indians in general before he came. Most if not all of these priests hailed from Europe. Father Gachet, who served in Keshena from 1859 to 1862, apparently never saw an Indian before moving to Menominee country. Upon passing canoes full of Indian families on the river the day before he arrived in Shawano, Gachet commented from his position on the steamboat: "I had often represented to myself in reading accounts of voyages, the long and straight pirogues of the savages, their visages copper colored, the scenes of Indian life, and now I saw all before me. I had under my own eyes one of the scenes of Indian life of the New World. How often have I sighed for the hour in which it would be given me to preach Jesus Christ to the gentiles, and gliding there so near to me upon the water were the canoes of savages whom I have been called to win for Jesus Christ."[41]

Gachet, in his zeal, began conducting services immediately upon his arrival at Keshena, despite his inability to speak Menominee. He used Rosalie Dousman and the Menominee children as interpreters for services and catechisms. A devout Catholic, Rosalie Dousman was by now in her sixties and had long taught among the Menominee. Apparently, with Mrs. Dousman present to provide both continuity and translation, the steady stream of priests could effectively serve among the tribe, despite the almost constant turnover. When

Gachet taught the catechism to the children, the children did the translating. He had among his pupils three bilingual children: one who spoke German and Menominee; one who spoke French and Menominee; and Keshena's daughter Okemakew, who spoke English and Menominee. All three helped him with his translations.[42]

Father Gachet tried to convince non-Catholic Menominees to convert using argumentative persuasion. Other priests followed his lead, while still others used coercion. Some were kind-hearted, while others were not. The latter caused problems for both the Catholic Menominee and the non-Indian Catholics working and serving on the reservation. The turnover rate of priests was high. Between 1857 and 1875 at least fifteen different priests, some from the Capuchin order but most of them secular priests, served among the Menominee. Some lived among the tribe, but others did not. A Reverend Mignault, who served in 1863, is probably the priest referred to in Agent Moses M. Davis's 1864 report to the commissioner of Indian affairs as "not only dissipated but licentious."[43]

Mignault's successor, the French priest A. M. Mazeaud, who served in 1864 and 1865, proved even more destructive. First, in 1864, he began a battle for schoolchildren between the church and the federal government that resurfaced off and on for the next three-quarters of a century. The teachers at the government school, who were Catholics themselves (Rosalie Dousman and her daughters Kate and Jane), reported in 1864 that student attendance at the government-sponsored school had dropped because the new priest spoke against the school. Rosalie Dousman, who oversaw sixty-six students, reported that she brought up the matter at the behest of Chief Carron, "who insisted it was my duty, as teacher of the Monomonee children, to inform you." Kate Dousman wrote that the priest's "unfavorable remarks" caused the regular attendance of fifty pupils to drop and also caused the students to "sadly neglect their studies. . . . This I deeply regret," she continued, "as we naturally expected words of encouragement from that source, instead of an adverse influence against education." Though she invited Mazeaud to visit the school, he never did. Agent Davis ordered the priest to leave the reservation, but he refused.[44]

The following year Mazeaud continued to disrupt reservation affairs. In addition to continuing to rail against the school, the priest disrupted farming by holding church services on weekdays. Catholic farmers attended these services every day during harvest month.[45] The Catholic Menominees were more likely to be farmers than were the non-Christian Menominees, both because the bands that had practiced farming during the treaty and pretreaty years were among the first converts and because those who converted early were the first to take up farming. Agent Davis called upon Bishop John Martin Henni in January 1865, asking him to replace Mazeaud, who had driven many Catholics away from the church.

Mazeaud cared little for the Menominee. Instead, he seemed concerned with power and money, but whether it was for himself or the church is not clear. Davis reported to Commissioner of Indian Affairs D. N. Cooley that Mazeaud obtained large shares of the bounties due deceased Menominee soldiers from saying mass over their souls after death. Cooley explained how Mazeaud accomplished this, writing in his annual report that Mazeaud was "charged by the agent with obtaining or endeavoring to obtain from the relatives of deceased Indian soldiers, of whom there have been many among the Menomonees, a large share of their arrears of pay and bounty, to pay for masses for the souls of the deceased." Some 120 Menominee warriors went to fight with regiments in the Civil War, and "about one-third were killed." The priest also, according to Davis, "stripp[ed] individuals of their money for saying mass over those off fighting the war."[46]

When smallpox broke out on the reservation in late May 1865, Mazeaud again used the deceased as pawns in his struggles, this time for control of the Catholic Menominees. He held public funerals over the dead with as many as 75–100 individuals attending, which caused the disease to spread further. He also reportedly twice exhumed the body of a woman who had died of smallpox. Approximately 150 Menominees (more than 8 percent of the tribe's population) contracted the disease that year, and at least 50 (2.7 percent of tribal members and more than 5 percent of the Catholics) died. Davis asked the priest to come to the government office in Keshena, where he asked him to discontinue these public funeral services. Mazeaud refused. Davis reported that "he said that he would not obey any such order, that I had no right to give such an order, that he did not care if the soldiers of the President were there, that he would only obey the orders he should receive from the bishop."[47]

Indeed, Davis worked hard to control the spread of the disease. When the outbreak occurred, he brought a Shawano physician to the reservation, who inoculated approximately eight hundred Menominees with serum provided by the agent. The non-Catholics had taken to the woods and avoided the disease entirely, as far as Agent Davis could tell. The physician reported Mazeaud to a magistrate in Shawano, a town several miles south of the reservation boundary. Local authorities arrested the priest and took him there, but Davis allowed him to return to Keshena to get his belongings before the trial. During that time the priest slipped away from the sheriff and placed the body of another smallpox victim in the church doorway, holding services over it as he had done previously. He eventually paid off court costs and left Indian country.[48]

Bishop Henni said he had already had complaints about the priest but wanted to visit him before making a decision. He also had trouble finding a good replacement. Davis apologized in his report to the commissioner of Indian affairs for meddling in church affairs: "I should have complied with the request of the Bishop and permitted this Priest to remain, but for the appearance of the small pox and his conduct in connection therewith." The office of the commissioner of Indian affairs claimed to take the separation of church and state very seriously and did so on a surface level. For example, in his report to the secretary of the interior, the commissioner said he took charge of the financial matters regarding the bounty payments "[a]t the hazard of being charged with interfering with matters of religion."[49]

Unfortunately, no documentation can be found regarding Menominee responses to Mazeaud's handling of the smallpox breakout. A church historian apparently collected oral history from tribal members regarding Mazeaud's work on the reservation but withheld it because Mazeaud disputed its accuracy. The historian reported that he was awaiting from Mazeaud "a personally written account of his activity at Keshena, since the reports given about him by Indians and marked down were incorrect."[50]

Though it provided financial assistance to the church, the government left the church alone to pursue its work among the tribe, except in cases of absolute calamity. In this way it supported the church financially but kept an appearance of retaining separation of church and state. At the same time, the individual priest, in his role as intermediary between the Catholic people and their Lord, wielded tremendous power over his flock. A venal priest could use this power for monetary gain or even in petty political battles with the federal government and could threaten not only his parishioners' economic or financial situations but their very lives.

In an attempt to mend the growing local dissatisfaction with the church, Bishop Henni asked the Province of St. Joseph of the Capuchin order in Mt. Calvary, Wisconsin, to provide mission help. The Capuchins were of a branch long split from the Franciscans, so they could maintain the extreme vow of poverty of the early Franciscan order. Father Cajetan Krauthahn together with Brother Lucius Fuchs arrived during maple sugar season in 1866 and moved into the ramshackle rectory, making it livable with the help of Mrs. Dousman and numerous Menominee Catholics who interrupted their sugar camps to make the missionaries welcome. Father Cajetan remained for a year and a half, but his health suffered partway through his tenure; he and other Capuchins served the mission until 1869, when it "was handed back to Bishop Henni."[51]

The presence of the Dousmans somewhat balanced the irregularity and the sometimes bad-faith service of the priests. By the 1860s they had become a well-established family in reservation life, at least for those Catholics living at Keshena and near Keshena Falls. Together with tribal Catholic families they kept the religion alive in the community. Franciscan officials, oddly enough, later charged that Rosalie Dousman's friendship with Menominees and her facility with the Menominee, French, and English languages worked against the success of visiting and short-term priests and that she turned the tribe against them.[52]

Menominee Catholics remained remarkably devoted to their faith, despite the constant upheaval, as they had done after the departure of the Jesuits in the eighteenth century. Some tribal members who were adapting to the changing world believed their old religious institutions to be outdated—lacking in the spiritual power necessary to see them into the future. The rituals of the Catholic Church were similar enough to their traditional rituals to make sense to them. By the 1860s the church had already been strengthening its hold in the tribal community for about a third of a century.

By 1871 U.S.–Menominee relations typified the federal-Indian relationship of the nineteenth century. An alien society that viewed land as a commodity, ownership as contractual, and work as a means for an individual to accrue profit gradually surrounded the Menominee. The new order glorified individual strength and success rather than family- and tribe-based strength and success. The Menominee faced starvation and high death and illness rates, which resulted from the drastic change in economic conditions that accompanied the removal of the tribe and the restriction of its numerous bands into a small, agriculturally insufficient, seemingly economically forlorn land base. Representatives of the all-powerful society that increasingly surrounded the Menominee assured them that the key to economic stability lay in "civilization," which these representatives defined as based in agriculture, formal education, and religion. They pushed this to the extreme. For example, Morgan L. Martin, who took over the agency in 1866, reported that farming was bound to fail for the Menominee but that the tribe had valuable pine lands. Nonetheless, he encouraged Menominees to become farmers. In one case, he reportedly offered two Menominees help with provisions if they would abandon their tribal ways and turn to farming.[53]

In 1869 Martin echoed previous policy proposals and recommended concentrating the Menominee on "two or three townships of the best farming lands" and selling the remainder to create a "school and improvement fund." This would provide the added advantage of dismantling tribal leadership. "The distinction of *chiefs* and herding into *bands* should be destroyed," he said. [54] The Indian Department continued to insist myopically that the Menominee become farmers. The Menominee, recognizing the power of white America, were willing to believe that agriculture was the key to their well-being and gave it a try. They wanted to be part of the American world. Indeed, they knew they had little choice and tried desperately to make the transition to reservation life.

The toll of their move onto the reservation was high for the Menominee. They lost a great deal of control over their governance and their economics. Individuals lived on the edge of starvation. They began to shift their political energies to mere survival, both physically and culturally, to a larger degree than perhaps ever before. The system pushed tribal leaders toward a reactive stance, yet somehow they maintained a proactive focus. During these harsh times the Menominee population fell by more than 30 percent. From a population of 2,002 counted at the time of removal in 1852, the numbers fell to 1,336 by 1870. [55] This drop was a result of both people dying from diseases that struck those weakened by malnutrition and people leaving the reservation to support their families. Whatever the reason, it signified a deep need for change.

During these years of starvation and despair, Menominees clung to hope, constantly reenvisioning their future. When one option failed, they pursued another. Their survival, both as individuals and as a people, depended upon this resolve. They left the reservation to gather wild rice in the fall, at nearby Shawano Lake and up and down the Wolf River. They fished at Keshena Falls and traveled to the Oconto River and other places in the spring to harvest sturgeon, sometimes bringing them back by the wagonload. They gathered cranberries and other food from the woods, hunted game, tapped maple trees for sugar, and fished the lakes and waterways, both on and off the reservation. They even continued farming, poor though the reservation land was for agriculture. As the woodland surrounding them was slowly deforested and put to farmland, however, they began to recognize the economic value of the timber on their own lands, which timber sharks and speculators increasingly plundered and coveted. This timber would prove to be the key to their future.

CHAPTER TWO

The Pivotal Divide of 1871

The modern divergence between Menominee solutions and federal solutions to Menominee problems began, at least symbolically, in 1871. These solutions centered around the forest resource, of which the Menominee steadfastly refused to let outsiders gain control, despite attempts by some powerful interests to do so. Three events in 1871 stand out above all others: the efforts by the U.S. Congress to open six townships of Menominee land (60 percent) for sale; the attempts by Congressman Philetus Sawyer of Wisconsin to pass a law opening the pines on the Menominee lands for sale to white loggers; and the Menominee's decision instead to harvest their own timber. The commercial timber harvest opened the doors—heavy, at times almost unyielding, doors—to the industry that would sustain the tribe into the twenty-first century.

THE BATTLE FOR MENOMINEE TIMBER

The Menominee had recognized the commercial and utilitarian value of their timber since the early treaty years, long before the establishment of the reservation. As farming continually failed, the Green Bay agents also increasingly recognized the value of Menominee pine timber in their reports. They did not view it as a substitute for farming, however. At least initially, they envisioned the timber primarily as useful for reservation projects. In 1855, at the start of the reservation era, the United States set up a sawmill and immediately began to distribute lumber to Menominees for houses. This mill could process some twelve thousand feet of pine per day and was used to supply lumber for government and farm buildings as well. By 1862 more log and frame houses than wigwams served as dwellings for Menominees.[1]

Loggers had their own hopes for the tribal forest. They cautiously eyed Menominee pine as a potential source of profit. The Menominee had waged a battle for several decades to end continual depredations of their timber by small-scale thieving entrepreneurs who viewed tribal lands as a free source of lumber for the lucrative Great Lakes and Mississippi River markets.[2] Depredations of tribal timber continued even into the reservation era. In 1854 "Sub-agent John Suydam . . . reported that three to five million feet of timber had been cut in the winter," and he "urged immediate investigation of the trespass." In 1857 Superintendent Francis Huebschmann had warned that "the timber stealers" were still after Menominee pine. At the council in which Agent Frederick Moscowitt first met the tribe, Menominee leaders complained of timber depredations. Moscowitt believed that the guilty party resided in Keshena, which would make the perpetrator either a government employee or a trader.[3] In October 1865 Agent Davis wrote to the commissioner of Indian affairs that he had recently discovered a trespass of approximately six hundred thousand feet of pine on the Menominee reservation.[4]

Small-scale loggers simply hired individual Menominees or went on the reservation themselves to steal timber. Agent John A. Manley had some of them arrested, and his successor, Lieutenant W. R. Bourne, helped prosecute them. They ended up paying the tribe for the logs they took, but the price was so low that they trespassed again the next year, hoping to be "penalized" with the same prices.[5] Mysterious fires plagued the reservation in the late 1860s, turning good forest land into burned over timber that these small outfits could harvest.[6]

At the same time, Davis advertised to sell dead and down pine timber from a burned over area of the reservation to non-Indians, but no logging companies bid because it was not worth their while unless they could also cut the standing pine. The burned over area contained twenty to thirty million feet of pine timber, but logging companies simply went elsewhere.[7] Wisconsinites believed their timber resources to be virtually unlimited. In 1870 a commissioner in the General Land Office predicted that Wisconsin timber would last another century.[8] Lumber barons wouldn't be bothered harvesting it in small lots. Menominee timber was apparently worth stealing but not worth purchasing.

Small-scale operators, on the other hand, profited from purchasing small lots, and by the late 1860s they did not need to steal the timber anymore. Often the agents encouraged them to purchase it from the Menominees who were clearing their fields to farm. The combination of federal agricultural policy and the lack of resources for tribal members made a nice source of business for such loggers, as tribal members tried desperately to find ways to earn a little income from their woods. But policy could change when a new agent took charge of the reservation.

Two local non-Indian contractors reported, for example, that on 1 January 1870 around ten Menominees who claimed to be starving wanted to sell a stand of good pine to the contractors to cut, haul, and sell. They said they had authority to enter into such a contract, so the contractors supplied the Menominees with flour, pork, other provisions, and blankets to "enable them to cut haul and deliver said pine timber since nothing else except a small amount of money perhaps near or about one hundred dollars among all." Agent Manley put a stop to the transaction. His successor, Agent Bourne, reported that these two small-time loggers had been making a living from reservation timber for some time. "Bagley and Crawford are purchasing logs from members of the Menomonee Tribe who are engaged in clearing up farms in the Oconto River. This has been done for several years under the advice of former Agents."[9] Policy was shifting to put an end to this profiteering.

By the late 1860s at least one large-scale operator, looking to the future, finally began to take notice of Menominee timber. During that decade Philetus Sawyer, the city of Oshkosh's most powerful lumber baron, had purchased all the pine along the Wolf River and its tributaries above the Menominee reservation and some below it, when it was considered of little value because of its inaccessibility. He then founded the Keshena Improvement Company, which obtained the sole rights to improve the Wolf River by building dams and blasting away obstructions so that logs could be more easily run. For a brief period this caused a boom such that in 1867 an estimated two thousand loggers worked in the Wolf River network. When loggers depleted the rest of the area, Sawyer wanted to exploit the pine on the Menominee reservation.[10]

Loggers such as Sawyer began to look hopefully to the Indian Bureau. By the 1870s logging was big business across much of the Wisconsin woodlands. Whereas most log crews in the 1850s numbered fifteen men or less, by the late 1860s logging camps consisted of fifty to one hundred men.[11] By 1873 loggers had cut approximately 20 billion of an original 129.4 billion feet of Wisconsin's white pine, harvesting some 15 percent of the state's pine timber.[12] Neighbors of the Menominee viewed the tribe's forest with increasing envy and pushed federal officials to open it for logging.

After Sawyer's election to Congress, he tried to rewrite the law to provide him an opportunity to exploit Menominee pine. He introduced two bills into Congress in 1869–70 and again in 1870–71. One bill proposed to sell the lands on the Menominee reservation at public auction, and the other proposed to sell their timber.[13] At the same time, the Indian Department advertised the pine on Menominee land as up for bid in 160-acre lots, except for the two unsurveyed townships that would be sold in their entirety.[14]

Secretary of the Interior Jacob D. Cox wrote to the acting commissioner of Indian affairs in August 1870, just before the advertisement appeared, "I am convinced that such a sale is the only thing which will protect at once, the interest of the Indians, and of the Government." He did not see any other way to stop the "systematic stealing of the [Menominee's] timber."[15] The Democrats charged Sawyer with collusion, but he denied any connection with the Indian Department's proposed sale, and the Department of the Interior abruptly withdrew the offer.[16]

The Menominee saw a different solution—tribal control. On 30 July 1870 eleven chiefs—representing both Christian and non-Christian bands, including Ahconemay, Waukechon, Kinepoway, Niaqtawāpomi, and Neopit—sent a petition to Washington. In it they requested permission to send three delegates with an interpreter and their agent to meet with Commissioner of Indian Affairs Ely S. Parker regarding two issues. Regarding the first issue, the chiefs declared, "We are not satisfied with the Treaty of 1854, the first payment of which we received under protest and only as a part payment, nor do we understand our rights under the provisions of said Treaty." Second, they wanted help from Washington in protecting their timber from outside forces. They had not made such a visit in ten years, they said.[17] The tribe had hoped that an Indian commissioner—Parker was Seneca—would be sympathetic to their needs, but their hopes were dashed.[18] The trip was apparently not authorized or made.

At the same time, hunger remained a problem for the Menominee. If they could sell timber, they could feed their families. "And we would further state that we know that there is much pine timber on our Reservation injured by fire, and going to waste and that we are suffering even for the want of something to eat, and desire that this timber may be sold to relieve our necessities," a petition to Washington in early 1870 stated.[19]

Annuity payments due the tribe for the sale of its land in treaties could also ease hunger by supplying cash for provisions. By 1870 the United States made these annuity payments semiannually. At the end of July Agent Bourne requested the second payment in advance of the fall hunt, working with all speed possible to alleviate the "extreme suffering" among the Menominee. He said that the late nature of the second payment regularly caused problems for the tribe. The tribe had been attempting to resolve this particular problem for some four decades. Writing again in October with the request, he said, "Many of the young men wait for that [payment], until the best of the hunting season is over." Again in November he made the request: "The Menomonee Indians are losing the most valuable portion of their hunting season. Their principal supports sitting around idle: waiting for their Annuity. This tribe is already badly dissatisfied with the management of their affairs, and the delay now makes them worse." He said they were again preparing to select a delegation to travel to Washington to "lay their troubles before the Department." Considering their reluctance to hunt for fear of missing out on the annuity payment, the delay of their annual payments, the failure of American-style agriculture, and, perhaps most frustrating, the knowledge that their most valuable resource, their forest, was in the control of people who let others profit from it while they starved, it is little wonder that Bourne wrote in disgust, "I know they have no respect for an Agent, now."[20]

Farming was proving eminently unsuccessful for the Menominee. As late as 1871, maple sugar, which brought in $15,000–16,000 that year, was the Menominee's best source of income. In a letter to the commissioner of Indian affairs that year, Agent William T. Richardson suggested that the government should support the tribe with provisions for its annual sugar harvest, because it was the Menominee's most profitable business. Furs, which they sold for $2,500 that year (they had brought in $8,000 in furs in 1867), also remained an important basis of tribal members' income. The farm crops they raised in 1871 valued $5,062. They also gathered wild rice worth $150 and cut 505 tons of hay worth $5,050 to feed their stock, which consisted of 125 cattle, 150 horses, and 97 swine. The value of food raised for these 372 animals probably totaled more than the value of the crops raised for the 1,348 Menominee people, but only because of the abundance of the hay, which grew wild in the wetlands.[21] The Menominee's dissatisfaction with farming intensified as the tribe began to realize the economic value of its timberlands.

Philetus Sawyer recognized that value too and continued to press for a law authorizing the sale of Menominee land, finally achieving success. In February 1871 Congress authorized the sale of six of the tribe's ten remaining townships of land. The law required Menominee approval, however.[22] The tribe emphatically and unanimously disapproved the land sale, although the tribal leadership remained sharply divided into two factions, with six band leaders on one side and five on the other. Due to dissatisfaction with the government's management of the tribe's timber and the actions of federal agents, two Menominee delegates traveled to Washington against departmental orders. Six of the band leaders supported them, voting to pay their way from tribal money, while the five others refused. The five in opposition represented about two-thirds of the tribe's members, because their bands were larger. Both sides petitioned the commissioner of Indian affairs over the issue, and he finally paid the delegates' expenses, over the opposition of the agent, because a majority of the tribe's band leaders wished it done.[23]

Yet this disagreement in no way affected the tribe's ability to act in unison.

On 27 March the tribe met in a council that, according to Agent Richardson, "was *fully attended* and *very united* in action." Richardson, the first agent appointed by direction of the American Missionary Association (AMA) under President Ulysses S. Grant's peace policy—another federal failure to separate church and state in Indian country—informed Commissioner of Indian Affairs Parker that the tribe had no desire to sell its lands. "The Indians seem to have a strong attachment to their present home," he wrote, "and they look [upon] any move to deprive them of their *lands* with a jealous eye."[24]

Neopit later said of the meeting, "The Menominees then and there fully and unanimously disapproved, and in the strongest terms portested against the provission of said act, because it provides for the sale of all our pine and agricultural lands, leaving to us for homes and farms four townships of barren sand plains." He then made an emotional plea: "[W]e will not consent to the sale of any more land. We want it for our children and grand children. The Menominees sold to their white brethern all the lands from Milwaukee north to Green Bay and west to the Wisconsin river, containing at present many beautiful cities and villages for about five cents an acre, and we accepted our present reservation when it was considered of no value by our white friends. And all we ask is to be permitted to keep it for a home."[25]

In a statement signed by ten band leaders, overall tribal leadership stated that the law had been fully explained to them. "[W]e do hereby declare ourselves wholly opposed to the provisions of the above named 'Act' inasmuch as we are unwilling to relinquish any portion of the lands ceded to our Tribe, by the Treaty of 1854, except the two townships already ceded to the United States in 1856, for the use of the Stockbridge and Munsee Indians."[26]

At the same time, ironically, Congress had also passed a similar land sale bill regarding those Stockbridge and Munsee lands. The longstanding division between factions of the Stockbridge and Munsee led to its passage. In contrast to the Menominee, the Stockbridge and Munsee were bitterly divided— between a "Citizen Party," which wanted to give up tribal ways and "become citizens of the United States," and an "Indian Party," whose members "desire to retain their tribal character and continue under the care and guardianship of the United States." The money realized from the sale was to be paid out per capita to the former group and held in common by the latter. Separate enrollment rosters were made for each group as well. Congress also reinstated a third group, who had already been bought out of the tribes and become U.S. citizens, and they shared in the wealth.[27]

THE MENOMINEE SOLUTION

In contrast to the government's proposal to sell Menominee lands, the Menominee proposed their own solution to the timber trespass problem. Rather than selling the tribe's land or selling its timber to white loggers, they would harvest the timber themselves. The tribe held a council in May 1871, in which it drafted a petition to Commissioner of Indian Affairs Parker, signed by all eleven band leaders, or "chiefs," as the U.S. government referred to them, and all eleven subleaders, or "second chiefs," within each band. Agent Richardson wrote enthusiastically that the petition seemed to have unanimous approval, since more than two hundred Menominees attended the council.[28] He believed the Menominee would get twice as much for their timber if they harvested it themselves. He also thought the work would "serve very much to encourage and develop the habit of working for their support."[29]

The tribe stated its position concisely.

We are unwilling to part with any portion of our lands, secured to our Tribe, by the Treaty of 1854.

(1) We desire to keep these lands as a permanent home for ourselves and our children.

(2) We wish to secure for our own benefit all the proceeds possible from our lands, and the timber thereon.

(3) We believe this can be done to the best advantage by cutting said timber ourselves.

They therefore requested permission to cut and sell their pine, but did so with four restrictions: that it be managed by Agent Richardson, for whom the AMA vouched credibility; that Menominees do as much of the work as possible; that logs be sold at public sale on the riverbanks; and that the proceeds be invested to be spent on education and agriculture at the demand of the tribe's leaders, with approval of the commissioner of Indian affairs.[30] This latter restriction met with the approval of Richardson and the Indian Department. Richardson pointed out that the proceeds of the funds could be used to help the tribe in its agricultural endeavors.[31]

This historic action by the Menominee, with the help of their agent, forever changed the ways in which the battle for their timber was fought. Though they had been selling timber since 1870 with permission of Agent Manley,[32] trespassers remained a problem. But from this point on, the Menominee battled for the right to exploit the timber themselves.

On 31 July 1871 Secretary of the Interior Columbus Delano authorized the Menominee to cut and sell dead and down timber. That winter, under the direction of Agent Richardson, the tribe sold approximately two million feet of pine for $23,731 and banked $10,000 in the U.S. Treasury while paying out more than $3,000 in wages to Menominee workers.[33] The Menominee requested in council that each member of the tribe be permitted to bring in logs to Richardson at the riverbanks, but the Indian Department disapproved this request because it would lead to wasteful slashing, which would leave too many branches and scraps in the woods. According to a report from a member of the Board of Indian Commissioners (BIC), the Menominee trusted Richardson enough to accept his method of cutting.[34]

This same commissioner recommended selling just the pine on the six townships of Menominee land, not the land itself, and investing the money, which he estimated would produce forty dollars in annual interest per capita.[35] Under the tribe's plan, tribal members would conduct the logging operations themselves and would thus benefit not only from the sale of the timber but from the work involved as well. The tribe consistently desired maximum inclusion of its members in the work and profit of logging, while the government officials desired maximum efficiency.

The tribe's annual cutting brought immediate economic benefits. Individuals cutting and hauling the logs earned money for their labor, while profits went into an account in the U.S. Treasury to be released later for purposes deemed beneficial by the agent, usually for purchases of agricultural or domestic equipment and supplies. In addition, 10 percent of profits went into a "stumpage fund" that supported needy Menominees, including the sick and elderly. A fairly systematic approach to logging developed, but the work was done on a year-to-year basis, with annual permission required every year. This left the process exposed to governmental whim, and several times before the passage of an 1890 law that formalized Menominee logging on a more permanent basis the United States refused permission.

Indeed, in 1873 the U.S. Supreme Court handed down a decision that devastated tribal logging operations in *United States v. Cook*. The case, based on logging that occurred on the nearby Oneida reservation, hinged on whether the United States or the tribes owned the timber on reservation lands. The Court's ruling favored the United States and stipulated that tribes could not conduct commercial logging on trust land. Indians could log only for the purpose of establishing farms; even dead and down timber was ruled out of bounds for commercial purposes.[36] Over the next fifteen years, Menominee logging would be either permitted or halted, depending on the extent to which either tribal members or the agent could convincingly argue that they were conducting the logging in order to establish farms.

From 1872 to January 1876 the commissioner of Indian affairs granted the tribe permission to cut.[37] Some of the Menominee money that was put into the treasury from this work served a double-duty function for the government. A table of statistics accompanying the 1874 *Report of the Commissioner of Indian Affairs* shows $8,214.27 from the sale of pine since 1 November 1873 being "covered into the Treasury under the head of 'Fulfilling treaty with Menomonees—proceeds of land.'" The money was then remitted to the agent, Thomas N. Chase, "for the benefit of the tribe."[38] At this time the Menominee still received annual payments from the government for the lands the tribe had ceded in 1848. Incredibly, the government was paying the Menominee with their own money for the purchase of Menominee land! The Menominee were cutting and selling their timber to pay the government's debt to the tribe for the purchase of millions of acres of the tribe's land in northeastern Wisconsin, land that ironically had benefited non-Indian logging interests before becoming rich farmland for settlers. This was the beginning of what the federal government came to refer to as Menominee economic self-sufficiency.

In 1874 Joseph C. Bridgeman took over as agent. According to Bridgeman, in the winter of 1874–75 approximately one hundred Menominees in four separate camps hauled five million feet of logs. The tribe officially numbered 1,522 that year. The lumberers lived in the camps, where both Menominees and white men cut timber. One camp located twelve miles northeast of Keshena employed eighteen Indians and ten whites, for example.[39] This mixture of Indians and non-Indians carrying out the work of cutting Menominee timber established a long-lasting pattern.

The 1873 financial panic that caused "severe hard times all over the country" also affected the Menominee. Logs cut in 1873 and 1874 were not sold until 1875 under Bridgeman. They had apparently been left on the riverbanks in the hopes of bringing higher prices, which never materialized. The market in 1875, unfortunately, was even more depressed, according to Bridgeman, making the loss greater.[40]

Though Bridgeman supervised timber cutting on a larger scale in 1875–76, in January 1876 the commissioner of Indian affairs suspended Menominee logging. He did so due to illegal cutting activity, including the harvesting of Menominee timber by non-Indians, the cutting of live timber by non-Indians and Menominees, and the firing or burning of areas of the woods to kill timber by both groups so that it could be cut as dead or down timber, which the regulations permitted. Later in the year the commissioner reauthorized tribal logging at the tribe's request but stopped it again in the spring of 1877 until 1881.[41]

Despite the Menominee's fitful steps toward self-sufficiency, the agents for the most part continued to treat the Menominee condescendingly as uncivilized children. This happened time and again when the tribe tried to take the initiative in planning its future. It also happened with events that took place on the reservation, which the agents generally believed they had to control. The Menominee expressed dissatisfaction whenever this occurred. American actions caused the Menominee to distrust their agents. Agent Bourne summed it up well when he said the Menominee "have little confidence in Agents: they look upon all [federal] employees as so many leeches, who live off the money belonging to the tribe."[42]

Political conditions had changed little during this period, and the Menominee understood them well. For example, Neopit, Mahchakeniew, and Niaqtawápomi, along with two other leaders, Moses Ohopasha and Mitchell Oshkenaniew, wrote to Commissioner of Indian Affairs Hiram Price regarding the failure of their agent to make payments to them from their logging fund as he had promised. They said he did not even appear among them on the payment day. "This plainly shows the way he looks at us, he looks upon us as mere brutes and does not care a particle for this people. He would rather see us doomed to death."[43]

Even some Americans who lived away from the reservation recognized that most federal agents gave the Menominee no reason to trust them. Judge Samuel Ryan of Appleton, for example, wrote an angry letter to Secretary of the Interior Samuel J. Kirkwood in 1881 regarding the mistreatment of the Menominee. As a fifty-year Wisconsin resident who had grown up in the vicinity of the Menominee Indians, he demanded "in behalf of those Indians, an honest and careful investigation before permitting the power of the government to be further used to inflict interference with their personal liberties." He pointed out to the secretary that Menominees had fought with U.S. troops against Black Hawk in 1832 and against the Confederacy in the Civil War. "They are really, as a tribe, qualified for citizenship," he insisted, "and yet each succeeding agent seems determined to treat them as barbarians." He added that the latest excuse was that some tribal members were considered "heathens" or "pagans," but he questioned whether more Menominees than whites did not believe in Trinitarianism.[44] Ryan's plea, of course, went unheeded.

The tribe's leaders fought strong battles to gain control of Menominee timber, even while their stature and role diminished under the weight of American colonialist wardship. Federal agents had hoped a turn toward agriculture would also diminish the role of traditional tribal leaders. They continued to meddle in the selection of tribal leaders, as they had since Oshkosh's appointment as head chief in 1827. Ahconemay, son of Oshkosh, had been head chief since 1859. But in 1871, while drunk, he stabbed and killed a man. He was convicted of murder, and the United States replaced him with his brother Neopit, who became the new head chief. Even when Ahconemay returned to the reservation after serving his sentence, he never regained his leadership role. Then in 1872 Richardson suspended Neopit as head chief for striking and seriously injuring Carron with a club. Neopit agreed with the punishment, admitting he was wrong, and even thanked Richardson for his actions.[45] This incident made it clear that the United States no longer considered the selection of tribal leaders as a decision for Menominees to make. It was evidence that the United States increasingly tried to control nearly all aspects of Menominee life.

CHAPTER THREE

Government and Religion

At the same time as the United States attempted to establish hegemony over the Menominee political leadership and economic resources, the heavy hand of the federal government also pressed increasingly into both the religious and educational realms of the Menominee world. The Catholics had a substantial following among the Menominee, but Protestant agents opposed their influence, establishing an additional layer of conflict on the reservation. This conflict between church and government stemmed from President Grant's peace policy, established in 1869 to clean up corruption in the Indian Office and to treat Indians as dependents rather than as enemies. The policy had two foundations or "structural elements." One was the creation of the BIC, a civilian group that would oversee the Office of Indian Affairs (OIA) and act as a watchdog. The other was the creation of a system in which church missionary groups, rather than the federal government, would appoint the local Indian agents. Both of these elements were Protestant controlled.[1]

In 1870 the federal government regularly began to provide education funding for Indian reservations, even when no treaty stipulations required it to do so.[2] This funding might go to government- or mission-operated schools. The conflicts that erupted on the Menominee reservation between the tribe and U.S. officials over education and other issues in the next decade had a religious component to them. A majority of Menominees were Catholic, and most of the rest followed the Mitāēwin religion. Federal officials were Protestant and opposed both. This factor further complicated tribal efforts at self-determination.

PROTESTANT-CATHOLIC CONFLICT

In 1870 the Congregationalist AMA appointed William T. Richardson as the first Green Bay agent under the new peace policy. The AMA conducted mission work among freed slaves but "had no American Indian program." The AMA had not requested the Indian assignments it received. The Menominee were predominantly Catholic, but the other Green Bay agency tribes, the Oneida and the Stockbridge-Munsee, had long been largely Protestant.[3] The Menominee did not welcome this appointment under the peace policy. Catholic-Protestant conflict, dormant since the 1830s, broke out on the reservation almost immediately. Richardson reportedly fired the longtime friend and ally of Catholic Menominees, schoolteacher Rosalie Dousman, because she was Catholic.[4]

Richardson reported three school buildings among the government buildings in Keshena: one a day school, one a sewing school, and one a school in which the teacher lived in half of the building. A church existed in Keshena, but no priest lived on the reservation. After a visit from Reverend Edward P. Smith of the AMA in New York, Richardson urged the government to build a manual labor boarding school on the reservation. It would include a dormitory to house thirty students and a teacher housing wing. The proposed school would serve thirty daytime scholars as well. This school would solve two problems: the lack of space for more pupils and the need to teach students whose families had moved away from Keshena onto better farming land.

This type of school, Richardson believed, would be an ideal place to teach manual labor and agricultural skills to Menominee children. He pointed out to the commissioner of Indian affairs that education had as yet produced few results for the Menominee and that a boarding and manual labor school would succeed five times as well.[5] Richardson apparently dropped the subject in future correspondence, and it was several years before the United States accomplished this plan on the Menominee reservation.

By this time a nationwide clamor had arisen among government officials throughout the bureaucracy for boarding schools. In 1873 Edward P. Smith, who had left the AMA and become the commissioner of Indian affairs, wrote, "Upon no other subject or branch of the Indian service is there such entire agreement of opinion . . . as upon the necessity of labor schools for Indians." The government would use these manual labor schools to teach Indian children agricultural and domestic skills, since "barbarism can be cured only by education." Day schools, the commissioner wrote, had proven inadequate in teaching children English, in dressing them in clothing "suitabl[e] . . . to the school-room," and in regularizing their working hours, the key indicators, apparently, of civilization. "The boarding school, on the contrary, takes the youth under constant care, has him always at hand, and surrounds him by an English-speaking community, and above all, gives him instruction in the first lessons of civilization, which can be found in a well-ordered home."[6]

In 1875 Agent Joseph C. Bridgeman reported to Commissioner Smith, "The

[Menominee] Indians in council have repeatedly expressed a desire that a boarding or manual-labor school might be established among them, and in the opinion of the agent no expenditure of funds could produce more permanent good with this people." He does not say how many Menominees in council requested this nor under what circumstances. Tribal leaders were increasingly concerned that their children needed tools to deal with the future in a reservation community surrounded by white culture and dominated by American laws. In discussing the successful day school in Keshena, which served a mere eighteen students, Bridgeman wistfully mentioned, "[C]ould these same teachers have the scholars under their charge in a boarding-school where the home influence could not counteract their efforts, good scholars, good men and women, would be their reward."[7]

After a U.S. inspector visited the reservation in the summer of 1876 and recommended a manual labor boarding school in Keshena, the government founded such a school. The government closed the day schools in Keshena and Little Oconto (also known as South Branch), while the day school at Kinepoway (also called West Branch) remained open. The farmer, W. W. Wheeler, took charge of the boarding school, with his wife serving as matron. This met with the immediate opposition of Father Amandus Masschelein, the priest who served the Menominee church from 1878 to 1880. He spoke against the government boarding school as Father Mazeaud had spoken against the government day school a decade earlier. Setting a pattern that would reoccur intermittently during the next several decades, the priest expelled any church members who sent their children to the government's school. Because of this, only two children attended the boarding school. Agent Bridgeman then informed Father Masschelein "that so long as he confined his labors to his legitimate church duties and did not interfere with the Government school he might remain upon the reserve, but if he continued to persecute and to excommunicate from his church parents who sent their children to the school, he would not be allowed to labor among the people." Thereafter 102 students signed up for the school, with an average attendance of 76. The tribe approved spending six thousand dollars to construct a new building. The agent did not mention how many students boarded at the school nor how many attended it as a day school.[8] Thus began a new era in Menominee schooling, which lasted well into the twentieth century. An increasing number of Menominee children attended boarding schools, but most did so on the reservation in Keshena rather than at off-reservation schools.

Meanwhile, Protestant-Catholic conflict continued to rage on the reservation, as well as in the surrounding non-Indian world. Agent Bridgeman, the third AMA appointee, was also the third consecutive anti-Catholic agent (Thomas Chase had followed Richardson). These men ignored even a pretense of the separation of church and state that had concerned their pre–peace policy predecessors, inviting Menominees to meetings in the government's council house at which agents and Protestant preachers from Shawano made speeches. The agents and ministers tried to convert both Catholic Menominees and those whom the government considered "pagan"—that is, those members of the non-Catholic bands who continued to belong to the traditional Mitāēwin religion.[9] Despite Protestant efforts in the 1870s and 1880s to convert them, however, most Menominees followed either the Mitāēwin or Catholicism.

Father Masschelein, notwithstanding opposition from the agent, remained on the reservation until Green Bay bishop Francis Xavier Krautbauer assigned the Sacred Heart Franciscans from St. Louis to the mission in 1880. The Franciscans, once a "vast organization," had been greatly reduced in number by the 1800s. They began to rebuild in large part through their work in the United States. The Franciscan Province of the Sacred Heart, established by German Franciscans, conducted "missionary, apostolic, educational, scientific, parochial and social" work from its Midwestern base. The missionary work extended across the United States and the world; in the Midwest they worked among the Ojibwes in northern Wisconsin; the Ottawas at Harbor Springs, Michigan; and the Menominee.[10] The Franciscans found the living quarters in Keshena barely livable—the roof leaked such that during rainstorms "they had to spread an umbrella over the stove to keep it dry." In the end Father Masschelein had grown too old for physical labor and had let the place fall apart around him.[11]

By the time the Franciscans took charge, three Catholic communities existed on the reservation: Keshena, Little Oconto, and Kinepoway. The newly assigned Franciscans built sturdy buildings in all of these communities and finally established an ongoing physical presence in this largely Catholic reservation. The fathers assigned to the reservation apparently stayed in both Keshena and Shawano but traveled throughout the reservation, often remaining overnight. Indeed, the Franciscans used the Keshena site as a base for their work in surrounding reservations and in the white community throughout this region of Wisconsin.[12]

Father Marianus Glahu wrote a colorful description of his first assignment to Kinepoway in 1881. As previous missionaries had done, he wrote an idyllic description of his experience, from his ride through pristine scenery to his first encounters with Indians, who, to his delight, "had more zeal for the good of the mission than I myself." The Menominees offered to translate for him in church, "as it had been the custom in former days." He did not permit them to do this, but since some knew English, he knew they would all be told what he had said. "I assure you," he wrote to the father provincial, "such attentive listeners and such disposed hearts to receive the word of God you will not find . . . I suppose not in any of your Catholic congregations." The listeners paid quiet attention to him throughout the service, apparently not normal behavior in churches where he had previously served. This was simply good manners to the Menominee, many of whom were devout Catholics.

Glahu concluded that all his Menominee parishioners, "old and young, are children at heart; innocent and well disposed (childlike). I always speak to them as children, and treat them thus." He added that if only schools existed with the opportunity to "instruct them more frequently, we would have such good Christians."[13] Despite the father's paternalistic view, the Catholic Menominees in this remote reservation village, who were consistently frustrated by the irregularity of visits by priests, eagerly welcomed Glahu.

At the same time, in 1881 the Sisters of St. Joseph of Carondelet were assigned to the religious education on the reservation. They apparently boarded in Shawano at first but then moved to Keshena within a couple of years, as the peace policy fizzled out by 1882. They and some of the fathers traveled back and forth on a stage coach until a larger facility could be built in Keshena. Father Blasius Krake (Father Blaze) complained in 1883 to his superior that this was "very disagreeable . . . since the passengers, some of them, are bigoted and mean. . . . You can hardly imagine what difficulties we have to reach the mission. Nothing is more unpleasant than to go by stage." The roads, he added, were in poor condition, which made walking "impossible." He wanted to rent a buggy, but apparently the mission could not afford this expense. A Catholic businessman in Shawano ran a livery and lent the Franciscans a horse under a request of anonymity.[14] This was an important step that also added to the stability of the official Catholic presence among the Menominee. With Franciscans now permanently serving the community's church needs, the Catholic population grew to as much as two-thirds or more of all tribal members.[15]

THE 1881 DREAM DANCE

Just as the Catholic Menominees were finally gaining a steady presence of priests and sisters to serve their spiritual needs, the federal agent confronted those Menominees belonging to the Mitāēwin with an intense assault on their practices. The occasion was the introduction in about 1880 of a new ceremonial practice, the Dream Dance, an occurrence that both non-Catholic and Catholic members of the tribe enthusiastically adopted. Though politics often divided the Catholic and traditional bands, their conflicts oddly enough did not carry over to the philosophical realm. While their beliefs differed, neither side proselytized the other, and many continued to share various cultural practices. The agent reacted to the introduction of the Dream Dance in fear, calling in the U.S. Army, although no threat of violence existed. Menominees whose grandparents were there when the army came still remember this event.[16]

In the summer of 1881, Ojibwe and Potawatomi religious leaders brought their sacred drum and celebrated the Dream Dance, or Peace Dance as the Menominee called it, with the Menominee on their reservation.[17] According to Green Bay agent Ebenezer Stephens, the dance taught the Indians that some day "a great drum will tap in heaven, and at that time all the whites and Catholic Indians will be paralized, when all they have got to do is to walk forth and tap them on the head—and take possession of the land."[18]

According to Menominees, the Peace Dance represented either a new religion or a new addition to the older Mitāēwin religion—an addition that symbolized Indian unity. A little over a decade later, some practitioners told the ethnologist Walter James Hoffman that they believed the dance to be a purer form of religion. They told him that the Mitāēwin was becoming impure and that this new religion would resolve that problem.[19] The Dream Dance, like the Mitāēwin, offered the participants access to power through the supernatural. However, it was more easily accessible and open to a broader cross-section of community members.[20]

Federal officials called this dance a "Sioux dance," as did ethnologists, since they traced its origins to the vision of a Sioux woman. In her dream she had been instructed precisely in the ceremony, including songs and rituals. Followers generally performed a large dance in early summer, with other large gatherings occurring occasionally, usually during the warmer months.[21]

At this time approximately one-third of the tribal members still practiced the Mitāēwin, which centered around longstanding Menominee understandings of their world and their relationships to it. Dance and song were among the important ritual aspects of the religion, which helped Menominee spiritual leaders intercede with supernatural powers to guide members along the path of right actions. According to the anthropologist Louise Spindler, "The declared intent of the ritual is to prolong life and insure the good health of its members." The traditional Menominee religion recognized animacy or life in all aspects of their world, and the deities had instructed their spiritual leaders in the proper ways to honor both the cultural heroes themselves and that life way. Whether practitioners believed the Dream Dance to be a new religion or a ceremony to adopt into the old religion, they certainly believed that, as Mahchakeniew articulated, "[t]hat ground" on which the dance occurred "is holy while we are there with the Great Spirit."[22]

Significantly, as with other Indian tribal religions, Menominee spirituality did not necessarily exclude Christian Menominees from participating in their religion in the ways that Christians often attempted to exclude traditional religious practitioners from their religion. In addition, tribal spiritual leaders often sought methods to augment their spiritual powers. In the seventeenth century, for example, they sought teachings from the Jesuits, not in an attempt to replace their religion with Catholicism but in the hopes of bringing some of the Jesuit power into Menominee religious life.[23]

Therefore, when the Dream Dancers spread the word of their religion throughout Menominee country in 1880, the Menominee eagerly sought to incorporate aspects of that religion into their own. Disagreement on exactly how to do this eventually caused a religious split within the tribe. In the initial stages of this religious shift, however, despite opposition of some Catholic tribal members, Catholic and traditional Menominees participated together in ceremonies.

Agent Stephens initially evinced sympathy toward the new religion but later vigorously opposed the practice of the Dream Dance ceremonies. Mahchakeniew responded to negative white perceptions of the dance when questioned by Reverend Clay McCauley: "If I thought that our dance was a step backward, I would have nothing to do with it; neither would Niopet. . . . We are dressed in the old dress of our fathers, and we sing and dance; but I have been in the theater in Washington and have seen the white men do about the same things, with no one to blame them. . . . We do not take the young men from their work. We dance the dance only six times in the year."[24]

Mahchakeniew then described the specific aspects of the dance, emphasizing that the ceremony was a social-kinship healing ritual. They give each other gifts, he said, to emphasize "that we are brothers, and that brothers must help brothers." (Federal anti-Indian religious policy by this time frowned upon gift giving.) Then Mahchakeniew discussed Menominee patriotism, reminding his listener of the Menominee role in the American Civil War. "You saw the flag above us. That is to show that we are friends of the Great Father. You saw some men dancing and acting as though they were firing off guns, hunting, and running hard. They show that some of us helped the Great Father in the big war and are ready to help him again."[25]

Finally, Mahchakeniew lamented the American perceptions of the Menominee. "If our friend [Agent Stephens] could only have understood our speeches he would know that we are trying to do well. We do not take the young men from their work. We try to help them to work better. If I had a flag of my own I should want to have painted on it a picture of a plow and over that my totem, the eagle. This flag I should like to see always waving over our dance. I want all my children to go to school to learn just what white men know. . . . We are doing the best we can. I am sorry that there are some here who wish to do us harm and would make trouble for us if they could."[26]

As with many new religious movements to which American Indians turned, the Dream Dance had socioeconomic as well as philosophical origins in the tribe. The continuing failure of agriculture, the loss of logging, and the steady movement of non-Indians into surrounding lands put increasing pressure on the Menominee, who were never far from starvation in these years. The historian Brian Hosmer observed that "the Dream Dance represented less an adjustment to a new 'culture' than an effort to come to grips with a social and economic order that, while certainly promising, also failed to deliver material security."[27] Dream Dance followers sought ritual power to alleviate their plight. Despite hard times, Stephens threatened to withhold annuity payments from those participating in the dance, but to no avail. Some Menominees simply refused the money; others signed an oath not to dance but started dancing again in August.[28]

On 25 August 1881 Stephens wired the commissioner of Indian affairs that Potawatomis and Ojibwes had joined the Menominee dancers and that many Menominees were now "neglecting their crops" to follow the dance. He commented that the police were "inadequate" to break up the dancing.[29] The Indian police force, established for the Green Bay agency in 1879, fluctuated between ten and twelve Indian policemen in its first few years of existence. Their main task was to help the agent track down illegal liquor traffic and remove trespassers. The Indian police at the Green Bay agency—which oversaw Menominees, Oneidas, and Stockbridge-Munsees—included members of all those tribes. Menominees known to be active members of the force at the time included Captain Joseph Gauthier, Sergeant Michael Kah-pah-o-sha, and perhaps five others.[30]

The commissioner of Indian affairs apparently wired Stephens to authorize him to raise a special police force; as a result, Stephens deputized seventy-seven other Menominees from the various communities and, with them and the ten regular police, attempted to arrest the leading dancers. But once they were on the grounds, most of the police refused to arrest anyone. Stephens said that the "War whoop" raised by the Potawatomi and Menominee dancers terrified the police into not acting. More likely, the police believed the dance was not worth creating conflict over. In all probability they were being asked to arrest friends and relatives. Stephens quickly released those who were arrested, out of fear that their friends would try to help them escape.[31]

With the ceremony in full swing and his police force incapable of stopping it, Stephens convinced the Department of the Interior to call in the army. The War Department dispatched troops from Fort Snelling, Minnesota—the first time since the War of 1812 in which American troops were used against the tribe. Seven Menominee band leaders wired the commissioner of Indian affairs not to send troops. "[W]e are all peaceful, no troops are needed, we will obey all orders from the Commissioner," they wrote.[32] But their efforts were of no avail.

When the troops came at Stephens's request, they discovered no disturbances. In stark contrast to what would occur when the Seventh Cavalry tracked down Lakota Ghost Dancers at Wounded Knee less than a decade later, the troops "shook hands" with the Indians and, after a lengthy stay, departed. Stephens said the troops had a calming influence on the Indians. Most of the Potawatomis and Ojibwes, as well as some Menominee dancers, had left the reservation the night before the troops arrived. The Menominees who stayed on the reservation went to participate in the fall hunt and to gather cranberries, ginseng, and other provisions for winter. Stephens held a council in which Christian members of the tribe denounced the dance, and most promised to give it up. One announced, however, that he would continue dancing until the tribe's lands were allotted in severalty.[33]

Both Major D. W. Benham, the commanding officer sent from Fort Snelling, and Agent Stephens believed that meddling whites from Shawano and other communities near the reservation who wanted to stir up the tribe against the government had encouraged or even caused the dance. Stephens wrote to the commissioner of Indian affairs, "I think if the Indians are not interfered with by unprincipled whites and halfbreeds they will soon submit to orders of the Hon. Commissioner of Indian Affairs." But, he said, Shawano residents had already interfered with them. Benham suggested that these interferers were hoping to get hold of Menominee land and timber this way. He wrote his superior, "I believe the Indians were encouraged to continue the 'dreamers' dance and disobey the orders of their agent for no other purpose than that they would be driven to commit some overt act which would lead to their removal and a forfeiture of their lands."[34]

As usual, the government's officials refused to credit the Menominee with the ability to think or act on their own, instead blaming whites who had negative influences over the tribe for Menominee actions. Conniving whites may well have hoped to take advantage of this uncertain situation. But the Dream Dance was an Indian-run ceremony, and it divided traditional Menominees into two camps: those who incorporated it into their already existing Mitāēwin religion and those who took these new ceremonies and rituals to create something new. The former viewed the Peace Dance as another ceremony to add to a preexisting religious structure. They founded the new community of Zoar in the western part of the reservation.[35] While the division of these groups is denominationally significant, the dance and the ceremonies that were part of it were strictly Indian, and Menominees embraced them because, religiously, they fit into Menominee belief systems.

The Indian Department ignored Menominee guarantees of peacefulness regarding the dance, in part because the agent was concerned for his own safety. The agent also believed that the interruption of farming was a great cause for alarm, and he was upset that Catholic Menominees had joined the dance. His belief that those who followed the dance were enemies or potential enemies of the United States created a division between the tribe and the government. He suspected that three Menominee band leaders—Neopit, Mahchakeniew, and Niaqtawāpomi—were "among the disturbers. And that their loyalty [to the agent] is pretended for the purposes of holding their tribal position and posting the [Dream] Society concerning the action of the Govt. regarding them." The establishment of Zoar created a new community that would remain physically and spiritually isolated from the Catholic communities and the government agency that dominated much of reservation life.[36]

CHURCH AND STATE

Meanwhile, as the United States attacked Menominee traditional religious practice, the government-church, or Protestant-Catholic, conflict continued unabated. This battle pitted a new Protestant agent against a Catholic priest who was fluent in the Menominee language. In their bitter fight with each other they put their own interests above tribal interests. Christian Menominees, who were Catholic, were caught in the middle as the agent and the priest used them as pawns in a battle of egos.

The anti-Catholicism of the surrounding area spilled over to the reservation. In 1883 the "Spiritist" agent D. P. Andrews refused to hire Catholic teachers and failed to reappoint the mixed-blood teachers in the Kinepoway and Little Oconto schools, the latter having apparently reopened.[37] Meanwhile,

Father Zephyrin Englehardt was in the process of building St. Joseph's, which would become a Catholic boarding school.[38]

The building of a Catholic school occurred when a government inspector told church officials, probably in the summer of 1882, that the church could build a school at its own expense. Father Zephyrin observed that all the children might withdraw from the government school, to which the inspector reportedly responded that the government had a lot of money and did not particularly care. Later the Franciscans learned they could apply for federal money to support the students, so they built the school. They also built housing, which would enable the Sisters of St. Joseph to move from Shawano to Keshena. These actions angered Agent Andrews, who threatened "that he would try his utmost to breakup our school."[39]

When Andrews announced that he would open the government school for the start of the new school year on 3 September 1883, Father Zephyrin reacted quickly. "I explained everything on Sunday in Church, that the church law does not allow our children to attend the Protestant school, that I found it necessary to begin our school on Aug. 27, and that I would teach." The father went a step further: he announced in church "that those who would send their children to the Protestant school would not be admitted to the holy communion."[40] This action lacked the approval of the priest's superior, who wrote that, because Father Zephyrin had failed to seek his permission before acting, "God's blessing can not be expected" for the school.[41]

Agent Andrews charged that the father and his followers "commenced threatening the parents of our children" who were attending the government school "and made the children believe that if they attended our school they would surely go to hell." He also charged that the priest had "tampered with" the Catholic policemen, "either directly or indirectly." This caused the commissioner of Indian affairs to write to the Catholic Indian commissioner, "There can be no justification . . . and it will not be tolerated" for the priest "to attempt to break down our school and build up its own by appealing to the superstitious fears of ignorant children" by using "threatenings of Eternal punishment."[42]

Father Zephyrin denied that he threatened eternal damnation. "If I had referred to hell, it would have been in order, but I did not," he wrote. He did, however, insist to the parents that "as Catholics they could not send their children to Protestant or non-Catholic teachers; that their children must learn their Religion, and that therefore they had to send their children to places where this was possible; that they could do as they pleased, but as a matter of course then if their children grew up ignorant of God and their Religion, this would make it impossible for the priest to let them go to Confession or Communion." No doubt many Catholic parents agreed.

Then Father Zephyrin launched a counterattack through the mails. He charged that Agent Andrews had failed to support his temperance society and had done nothing to stop the sale of alcohol on the reservation. He also belittled the agent's previous work experiences and offered the opinion that Andrews should be relieved of responsibility over the government school, "as he is incompetent to run even a small law-office, which years ago he gave up for a book-keeper's place in little Shawano, much less such a work [as a school]." Father Zephyrin also observed that the Catholic school had attracted thirty children immediately upon opening, while the government's school attendance never exceeded "a baker's dozen . . . notwithstanding that there are about 75 *pagan* children in the Reserve over whom I surely had no influence."[43]

In essence, Agent Andrews and Father Zephyrin entered into a recruiting battle for the same schoolchildren. The priest was also charged with tampering with the Catholic members of the police force, whose role was to make sure the children got to school. He denied this. When they asked him for advice, he said, he told them to render unto Caesar that which is Caesar's and unto God that which is God's. Father Zephyrin suggested that Agent Andrews could solve the problem of low enrollment by concentrating his efforts on recruiting "pagan" children, since he could not hope to serve all the children on the reservation anyway. Approximately two-thirds of the tribe was Catholic.[44] However, the Catholic schoolchildren lived in closer proximity to both schools. Many of the non-Christian Menominee families lived remote from Keshena.

Father Zephyrin also made charges that affected Menominees more seriously. He said, "What the agent accuses me of he has been doing himself," that is, threatening children and their parents in order to promote his school. "A rumor was out all over the Reserve that those parents who sent their children to the Sisters school should not be permitted to cut logs in the pineries." He did "not know who spread the rumor, but it had some effect." Some parents sent their boys to the government school, and others withheld their children from school altogether. When the father threatened to write the commissioner of Indian affairs, the rumors stopped, which indicates they may have emanated from official sources. By 1885 the Catholic school reportedly served 125 children.[45]

Other rumors abounded, including one begun by members of Andrews's church in Shawano, in which they stated that the sisters would soon be expelled from the reservation. Father Zephyrin charged that Andrews refused rations to poor women whose children attended the Catholic school. In several cases the father provided flour to widows who had none, whom he said Agent Andrews had refused because their grandchildren attended the Catholic school.[46]

The feud between Andrews and the Catholic school continued. Commissioner of Indian Affairs John D. C. Atkins called for the government to quit funding religious schools, although he supported privately funded missionary efforts on reservations. He also supported opening government day schools even if mission schools existed. According to one historian, "His actions helped to reduce greatly the influence of religion and religious groups on the reservations, an influence that was the basis of the Grant Peace Policy."[47] Despite these efforts, Atkins reprimanded Agent Andrews, in May 1885, for harassing the Catholic schools.[48]

Both the government agent and the Catholic priest pursued their goals with little regard for how their actions affected the well-being of the Menominee parents or children. Neither side could come to a jurisdictional settlement in relation to Menominee children and schooling, so instead they resorted to threats. Menominees were asked to choose, in essence, between feeding their families or saving their souls in this battle to draw students to the respective boarding schools. Since few non-Catholic children attended the schools, the issue disproportionately affected Catholic families. Menominees had said time and again that they wanted their children educated in American schools. But instead of putting education first, the government and religious leaders used the Menominee children to fight their own battles with each other. Many tribal members took sides through their actions, with the Catholic school drawing the lion's share of the students.

Shortly thereafter the tensions eased, when the U.S. government appointed Thomas Jennings, the Catholic livery man from Shawano, as the tribe's new agent in place of Andrews. Menominees had been petitioning for Jennings's appointment since Grover Cleveland's 1884 election to the presidency.[49] They believed a Catholic agent would be more sympathetic to their spiritual needs and would diminish conflict on the reservation.

The Cleveland administration was accused of being too supportive of Catholic missions. Indeed, the Catholic Church thrived on the reservation under Agent Jennings, who held his position throughout Cleveland's first presidency. Jennings's successor even accused him of purchasing land improvements from Menominees and turning them over to the church and of giving to the church farmland that the agency farmer had tilled.[50] But though tensions decreased between the government and the church, the church leadership itself was not entirely stable.

Before Andrews left he accused Father Zephyrin of adultery, apparently because of his habit of sitting on the porch of the sisters' house, well into the evening, "telling jokes and doing foolish things" and in this way carrying on "l'affair d'amour with Sister Augustine." The church reassigned Father Zephyrin and assigned Fathers Oderic Derenthal and Blasius Krake to the Menominee reservation. Several priests believed Father Zephyrin to be a troublemaker. But his dismissal was unpopular with both the sisters and Catholic Menominees; when he left, the tribe lost the only priest (at the time) who spoke the Menominee language.[51]

During these decades both Catholic Menominees and members of the Mitāē-win fought the government to maintain control over their religious practices. The United States bullheadedly attempted to thwart both groups. The same tribal leaders who had fought for logging rights fought for religious rights. The assimilation effort by the United States required pursuit of these two policy initiatives: an economic initiative, carried out through the agricultural program, and an educational initiative, carried out through either government or mission schools. Menominee self-determination also required control of both of these initiatives. The battle was only beginning.

CHAPTER FOUR

Twenty Million Feet a Year

In 1871, when the Menominee began the long and difficult task of taking control of their forest resource—barely snatching it from the greedy hands of local logging interests—the federal government permitted the tribe to do so on the condition that the proceeds of log sales support agricultural endeavors. With the 1873 *Cook* decision as a foundation, this stipulation remained the key to the government's permission to allow the Menominee to log tribal forests, until the passage of an 1890 law that systematized logging on the reservation.[1] Throughout this time, federal officials in Washington continued to insist that the Americanization of the Menominee would require the development of agriculture. Local Indian agents, who also viewed farming as the long-term solution to Menominee economic woes, increasingly viewed the tribal forest as a source of economic stability, but within a context that would eventually lead to an agriculture-based economy on the reservation.

Menominee intentions remained to protect their homeland and to secure survival on their own terms. At times they worked with local agents, at other times in opposition to them. In any case, the United States continually thwarted them, whether on the local or the national level. The Menominee readily recognized the value of their timber resource and constantly worked to find ways to exploit it for the tribal good. This meant a steady tribal shift in focus from agriculture toward logging, as the forest began to provide an increasingly steady source of jobs and income.

As the tribal economy changed in the late nineteenth century, the structure of tribal leadership also began to change in dramatic ways. Old leaders' roles were redefined, and a new group of leadership began to emerge. The main goal of tribal leaders, however, continued to be to pursue economic development and solutions to problems in tribally defined ways.

Focusing on agriculture, federal agents in both Washington and the local agency in Green Bay continued to press for allotment of tribal lands in severalty, both before and after the Dawes or General Allotment Act passed through Congress. In 1880 Agent Ebenezer Stephens reported with enthusiasm that the tribe made a loud cry for timber sales and allotment.[2] The timber and agricultural policies had become linked, since tribal members could log only to prepare agricultural lands, and logging had been halted in 1877. In 1881, "in response to their petitions," the Department of the Interior reauthorized the Menominee to cut and sell timber, and they harvested about five million feet. That year Stephens reported that the tribe requested allotment at every council.[3] They probably did so in desperate hopes of gaining permission to log. Neopit, who was the principal chief and leader of the Bear clan, had himself supported allotment in conjunction with the sale of timber during the 1870s. In February 1882 he said, "We want to sell our pine timber for a fair price, and we will give the purchasers four or five years to take it away, and then we want our lands allotted to us."[4] Neopit saw this as the best available means for the Menominee to remain on their own lands and to utilize their resources. But later he shifted his support to commercial logging.

Neopit managed to fulfill his leadership role in the tribe by maintaining support of, and speaking for, most tribal members. He was able to do so by acting in what he perceived to be the tribe's best interests, despite serious social and political divisions that continued to grow based on community geography, religion, and participation in both logging and the American education system. For example, in 1882, when an act of Congress permitted the Menominee to log dead and down timber, Neopit maneuvered a vote in tribal council that established a "poor fund" to be drawn from logging sales.[5] This tax, modeled after the 1871 stumpage fund, later became the basis for the important 10 percent stumpage fund that supported elderly, disabled, and widowed tribal members. In sanctioning this, Neopit assured tribal members that the tribal leadership would continue to carry out one of its key historic cultural responsibilities: supporting indigent tribal members.

An increasingly powerful group of key tribal loggers bitterly opposed the tax, however. Its successful passage illuminates the continued significance of the traditional leadership system and the continued strength of traditional leaders. "What was developing," according to the historian Brian Hosmer, "was an evolving Menominee politics, with the influence of loggers checked, at least for now, by respect for family, band, and clan."[6]

The Menominee gained permission to cut dead and down timber through much of the rest of the 1880s, but interruptions and difficulties continued to plague them. Lumbermen and mill owners in Oshkosh colluded to deflate prices paid for Menominee timber. Menominee loggers were charged with illegal cutting. And in 1883 the agent kept Menominee timber, already cut and banked, off the market at the request of tribal loggers. This proved disastrous because the logs deteriorated and lost value the next year. Unfortunately, Menominee loggers had already accumulated debt in the logging process. An inspector sent by the Indian Bureau in 1884 concluded that local white logging interests had indeed misused the Menominee. Agent D. P. Andrews, appointed in 1883, opposed logging altogether because he believed it distracted tribal members from agricultural pursuits. He feared that the timber on the reservation would last a half century, which in his mind would greatly delay Menominee advancement toward civilization.[7]

In contrast, Thomas Jennings, the Catholic agent who served from 1885 to 1890, supported both logging and allotment, as Agent Stephens had done earlier in the decade. In the winter of 1885–86 the Indian Department once again halted Menominee logging, due to charges of cutting live timber. Jennings then asked the Indian Bureau for permission to resume cutting, which it granted late the next year (1886–87). It did so only when the tribe and the agent promised that Menominees would not cut green wood and would not set fire to the woods to kill trees, as they had done in the past. The commissioner of Indian affairs reported that year that the Menominee had cut no green wood except as necessary to cultivate land. The tribe sold twenty-one thousand dollars of timber that season.[8]

In 1887 a new sawmill exclusively serving tribal needs, with a cutting capacity of twenty-five thousand feet a day, went into operation on the reservation. This mill, like previous mills on the reservation, was not commercial. It created saw wood for homes, farms, agency buildings, and other reservation projects. In August of that year Agent Jennings enthusiastically reported, "The mill is an indispensable adjunct to the civilization of this tribe of Indians."[9]

Meanwhile, the passage of the Dawes Act, also in 1887, provided the stimulus that Agent Jennings hoped he could use to implement allotment among the Menominee. The act represented the culmination of efforts by federal officials and sympathetic reformers, with the support of land speculators. It had the dual purpose of conforming Indians to white American culture by destroying the tribal basis of life and of dispossessing them of their remaining land. The act would do this by removing Indian land from tribal ownership, doling out parcels to individuals, and giving title of the remaining lands to the federal government to sell. Those who accepted allotments would become citizens. The BIC argued, "The great significance of the general allotment act, known as the Dawes Bill, . . . lies in the fact that this law is a mighty pulverizing engine for breaking up the tribal mass. It has nothing to say to the tribe. It acts directly upon the family and the individual. . . . By making every Indian who comes under its provisions a citizen of the United States it seeks to put a new allegiance and loyalty to our Government in place of the old allegiance to the Indian tribe."[10] Tribally held lands across the United States shrunk by two-thirds during the years when this law was in effect, from 1887 to 1934, and Indian cultures were vigorously assaulted.[11] The Menominee, with astute vision and leadership as well as good luck, avoided this fate.

The Indian Department had long vacillated over the value of the Menominee reservation as farmland. In 1887 Commissioner of Indian Affairs J. D. C. Atkins wrote, "These Indians are to a great extent dependent on [logging] for a living, as their lands are not well suited for farming, nor are they good farmers." Agent Jennings, however, reported that "the larger portion" of the Menominee reservation "is fertile and susceptible of producing large crops of hay, wheat, rye, corn, oats, potatoes, and other grains and vegetables raised in this latitude."[12]

In October 1887, just months after the passage of the Dawes Act, the tribe voted in council to accept allotment. Agent Jennings believed "that the Indians could all be allotted lands without taking any of the solid bodies of pine." The forest could then "be disposed of for their benefit." Jennings stated that "At a Council of the Menominee Indians it was the unanimous feeling that it was for their best interest to have their lands allotted to them in severalty." He added that three hundred Indians attended the council and that he heard no objections to allotment. One hundred and twenty-nine signed the statement agreeing to accept it. In conclusion, Jennings said, "all but a few are in favor of the lands being allotted."[13]

The agent said both that tribal support was unanimous and that some tribal members opposed allotment. He ignored a more important matter, however. It has long been Menominee practice for those who do not support an issue simply to ignore the council meeting at which they discuss it. This means that an overwhelming portion of those who attend the meeting are supporters of the issue.[14] The federal government consistently failed to recognize this cultural practice. But a deeper problem than the meaning of the term *unanimous* was the meaning of the word *allotment*.

The Menominee view of allotment differed greatly from the legal and governmental view, and Jennings, the government's agent, probably misrepre-

sented the governmental view and the legal ramifications of the tribe's decision. In the same letter quoted previously, Jennings said, "All [of the Menominees present at the council meeting] seem to feel that it would be better for
them to know what land was their own and to become citizens." These are
likely the terms in which he explained allotment to the tribal members present.
Jennings would have made the explanation through the interpreter Joseph
Gauthier, since a large portion of the tribe's adults spoke only the Menominee
language.[15] This explanation of allotment, however, ignored perhaps the most
important aspect of it: the loss of tribal control over land and other resources
and the privatization of those resources. The Menominee never meant to
forsake these tribal rights and fought forcibly to retain them.

Jennings pointed out also that tribal members were neglecting their crops
while awaiting the new land assignments they expected to receive under allotment. Jennings believed "that a large majority of the Menominees are suffi-
ciently advanced in civilization to be benefitted by having their lands allotted
to them." He also firmly believed that agriculture could succeed as the foundation of a new tribal economic system. Tribal members themselves wanted
to cultivate farmlands but saw that work as supplemental to logging, which
they viewed as the foundation of the tribal economy.[16]

Jennings, unlike his predecessor, Agent Andrews, believed that logging
would play an important role in the Menominee shift to an agricultural economic base. Even after passage of the Dawes Act, he successfully urged the
Indian Department to permit the Menominee to log. In the winter of 1887–88
after again promising to cut green timber only to clear farmland, the tribe sold
a record eighty-six thousand dollars' worth of logs. The 10 percent stumpage
fund supported the tribe's hospital and its sick and elderly citizens.[17]

The next fall, on 15 October 1888, the tribe held a General Council at which
139 members, including Neopit, Mahchakeniew, and Niaqtawāpomi, signed a
statement. In it they requested "that we shall have our Reservation allotted to
us under the Dawes severalty Bill. Giving us allotments of agricultural lands,
and also an equal share in the Timber of the Timber lands."[18] They clearly
viewed allotment not as part of a process of giving up their forest resource but
rather as part of a process of utilizing that resource to meet tribal needs.

Agent Jennings ignored the issue of tribal rights, however. He gave no indication that he thought it was an issue in this matter. The real issue, he benevo-
lently and paternalistically believed, was helping to improve the tribe. Jennings
believed the government had made little effort to turn Menominees into farmers in the past.[19] Despite decades of evidence to the contrary, he optimistically
opined that "[e]ven the sandy land" would "yield good crops" with "propper

cultivation." He added that the swamps, once deforested, would quickly dry up to provide more good farmland. These he believed to be the only obstacles holding back the advancement of the tribe toward white-conceived definitions of civilization: "[A]s soon as they are settled on land that they know is their own . . . they will take a decided start forward toward a higher civilization."[20]

The reservation had not yet been fully surveyed, however, and perhaps for this reason the United States did not put allotment into effect. Tribal and federal motives clearly differed markedly in this policy. Menominees continued to push for allotment, but apparently only on Menominee terms. When two members of the BIC visited the Menominee reservation, Neopit and Mahchak-eniew spoke (through Gauthier) in favor of both allotment and retention of the timber resource. "They want their lands allotted and patented," reported the visitors, but they also "propose to hold on to their pine timber, and log it themselves from time to time, for they now realize its value, and will make good use of the proceeds."[21] The Menominee clearly did not view acceptance of assigned plots of farmland as inimical to tribal retention and exploitation of their timber resource. Wisconsin's powerful timber lobby helped the tribe in this case by not pushing for allotment, perhaps seeing instead "an advantage in keeping the reservation timberlands intact."[22]

THE 1890 ACT AND TRIBAL LEADERSHIP

The Menominee pine was the best pine left to feed the hungry market in Oshkosh. Throughout the 1880s the lumber baron Philetus Sawyer attempted to get his hands on the Menominee timber. In 1880 he won a seat in the U.S. Senate and during his first year there introduced a bill to auction Menominee timber on the stump in eighty-acre lots. That bill would have permitted the Indians to earn money cutting the wood, but the purchasers would also make a substantial profit. He reintroduced the bill time and again, pushing it through the Senate only to have it fail to pass the House, where Robert "Fighting Bob" LaFollette of Wisconsin would help defeat it.[23]

By 1887 the Oconto representative to Congress, Myron McCord, a friend of the local white lumber industry, was working on the House side to pass a bill to sell Menominee timber. Both the Menominee and Jennings strongly opposed these bills. This opposition led McCord to attack Jennings on both a personal and professional basis. In 1888 Neopit and Mahchakeniew led a delegation to Washington to oppose the Sawyer and McCord bills. They believed that the tribe would best benefit economically if the Menominee could exploit their own timber.

In addition, tribal leaders believed that the presence of coarse white loggers in the Menominee woods weakened the tribe morally. A petition from Menominee veterans of the Civil War supported this contention, charging that white loggers on the reservation seduced Menominee women and, when they were unable to do that, raped them.[24]

When the Menominee sought permission to log in the winter of 1888, the attorney general, in the words of Indian Service forester J. P. Kinney, claimed that "no legal authority for such cutting existed." The *Cook* decision prevented even the cutting of dead and down timber, he ruled. Any cut timber belonged to the United States, not the tribe, he claimed. The attorney general went on to inform the secretary of the interior that Indians did not own reservations but rather simply occupied the land as tenants. "'Therefore the dead-and-fallen timber that is not needed or used for improvements, agricultural purposes, or fuel by the Indians is the property of the United States.'" Only Congress could dispose of it, as it saw fit. This opinion was not reversed until fifty years later.[25]

In February 1889, however, Congress passed a law for all Indian tribes that "gingerly avoided comprehensive legislation," called the Dead and Down Act. It allowed down timber to be cut on a reservation "provided it did not appear that the timber had been injured for the purpose of securing its sale."[26] In this authorization of logging on Indian reservations, Congress "recogniz[ed] an Indian possessory right but [left] its extent still uncertain."[27]

That winter individual Menominees received money for logging only after signing their names next to a statement that read, "We the undersigned Menominee Indians, do hereby acknowledge to have received of Thos. Jennings . . . the sums set opposite our names respectively, being in full for our pay for Logs cut by us from the dead and down timber and from our farms for the purpose of clearing the land for agricultural purposes . . . during the winter of 1888–89."[28] The green timber harvested that winter to clear land for farming brought $138,000. The OIA feared that the Menominee did not plan to build farms on that land and dispatched a special agent to investigate. He reported with surprise that tribal members had made much progress toward this end. The office, therefore, granted permission again in the fall of 1889 for continued cutting.[29]

During this period the logging industry throughout northern Wisconsin expanded rapidly and put increased pressure on the remaining Menominee forest. In the last quarter of the nineteenth century, loggers felled some sixty-six billion feet of Wisconsin pine, more than half the state's total original amount. By 1890 the industry directly employed some twenty thousand people, and about fifty-five thousand Wisconsinites earned a living from the state's timber that year.[30]

For approximately two decades, loggers had cut most Wisconsin pine near riverbanks and streams. But the quick expansion of the railroad in the 1870s brought value to previously remote pine lands. Railroads and spur lines brought lumberjacks and supplies into the woods and brought logs directly to mills. This access to remote pine lands reinvigorated and revolutionized the industry in Wisconsin. Now lumberers could also bring previously unusable hard woods to the mills. By the 1890s more timber was hauled out of Wisconsin by railroads than was transported by river routes. Lumber barons and mill owners quickly recognized the importance of railroads to their livelihoods and supported them fervently, purchasing stock, selling timber to the railroads inexpensively, and supporting subsidies in the state legislature. Railroads themselves eventually became the most important customers of the lumber men, purchasing large quantities of railroad ties.[31]

Railroads did not penetrate the Menominee reservation at this time, however. Menominee loggers continued to haul their timber to riverbanks throughout the winter, where they were scaled (measured), marked, and sold. Then they were floated either down the Wolf River all the way to Oshkosh or down the Oconto River toward Green Bay, along with all the other logs banked along those rivers and their tributaries above and below the reservation.[32]

As Wisconsin's forests began to disappear more rapidly than the white lumbermen had expected, they intensified their attacks on the Menominee forest. They charged that tribal members refused to pay their debts and burned the woods "to increase the amount of dead and down timber."[33] The lumbermen claimed that they should be permitted to log Menominee timber because the Indians received no benefit from the logging and only squandered the money they received. Agent Jennings emphatically denied the lumbermen's claims. "The utter falsity of this charge is best illustrated by the following statement of facts," he wrote to the commissioner of Indian affairs in 1889, and he listed as a conservative estimate $51,495 of timber money the tribe had spent on agricultural and domestic improvements. In addition to this the Menominee had spent $7,500 constructing new homes and stables or replacing old ones. The $51,495 included $22,800 for horses; $1,400 for sewing machines; and money spent for oxen, cattle, wagons, sleds, plows, harnesses, fruit trees, furniture, and stoves. He stressed that the Menominee supported timber work because it allowed them to improve and expand their farms. Jennings believed the work inculcated industriousness in the tribal members; if the United States sold the Menominee's timber and paid the receipts in annuities, tribal members "would lose interest in agricultural pursuits and become lazy and shiftless, retrograding instead of advancing in civilization."[34]

Meanwhile, as part of its assimilation policies, the United States attempted to weaken the tribe's governing structure but softened the blow by retaining tribal leaders in positions of authority. In 1889 the federal government abolished the positions of traditional chiefs, replacing them with the newly created Court of Indian Offenses. The United States initially appointed Neopit, Niaqtawāpomi, and Mahchakeniew, all traditional leaders, as the three judges of the court. The federal government recognized the wisdom of initially appointing band leaders to this newly created judiciary. When these elders passed on, however, the agents would begin to appoint judges educated in boarding schools. This would eventually break the hereditary nature of tribal leadership.

In 1890 Neopit, Niaqtawāpomi, and Mahchakeniew traveled to Washington to relinquish their inherited titles. Their positions in the court were weak and dealt only with "minor offenses," according to Jennings. They adjudicated domestic cases involving alcohol possession, intoxication, seduction, failure to provide for family, stock trespass, and assault while intoxicated. The court succeeded in taking pressure off the agent, and the Indians were more likely to accept justice from their own leaders.[35] The first agents to work with the court pronounced the judges very helpful in furthering government policies and extending the agent's influence.[36] However, the needs it addressed were more federal than Menominee. The federal government froze the tribe out of significant decision making regarding its economic future, relegating the tribal leadership's official jurisdiction to domestic criminal affairs and tribal membership enrollment.

Taking matters into their own hands, in 1889 a tribal group that the historian Brian Hosmer refers to as "emerging political and entrepreneurial 'activists'" retained St. Louis attorney Colonel Fred T. Ledergerber to lobby Congress to defeat the sale of Menominee timber.[37] Reminiscent of a similar action, when the Menominee had hired attorney Richard Thompson to convince Congress to permit them the opportunity to retain a piece of their homeland after the 1848 treaty, a group of tribal leaders turned to an "outside insider"—a nontribal member with special access to Congress—to help them hold onto their precious resources.[38]

An inspector sent from Washington to investigate the Menominee timber situation charged that Jennings had failed to help the tribe. He attempted to replace Jennings with Charles Kelsey, a man who most tribal members believed to be affiliated with the Oshkosh lumber interests that were scheming to get the tribe's timber. The Menominee opposed this change. In a showdown that almost broke out in violence, Neopit took Jennings "prisoner" and ordered him not to turn over agency property to Kelsey. This attempt ultimately failed; Kelsey was the choice of the new administration of President Benjamin Harrison.[39]

In this climate, in 1890 Congress rejected the outright sale of Menominee timber. Sawyer still wanted to be a part of Menominee logging, but he accepted a compromise law that allowed the Menominee to log up to twenty million combined feet of green and dead and down timber annually. Local lumber companies would purchase this timber by bid. The tribe, which was granted the right of approval, met in council and decided to accept the law, after "being informed that on no other terms could they log at all."[40] The first vote was 124–89 in favor of the law, with approximately three hundred Menominees present and numerous abstaining. But after further discussion they then accepted it "nearly unanimously."[41] The closing words of the law itself stated, "[I]f the provisions of this act shall not be accepted [by the tribe] as aforesaid no further cutting of timber shall be permitted upon said reservation until otherwise provided."[42] In such circumstances the tribe's right of approval meant but little, since disapproval would bring the Menominee economic disaster. The United States maintained an iron grip of control on the political front of Menominee affairs. The 1890 act provided some hope on the economic front.

LOGGING UNDER THE 1890 ACT

The 1890 law allowed the tribe to harvest green timber for the first time on a regular basis without specifying that the cutting be done to clear land for farms. Federal officials still hoped the Menominee would become farmers, but now they thought the best way to encourage farming would be to strip the forest clean of timber, after which tribal members would have little choice but to farm. Agent Charles S. Kelsey wrote to the commissioner of Indian affairs on 28 October 1891, "[O]ur aim is to stimulate and encourage habits of industry and thrift, keeping before them the idea that they are soon to have land in severalty and become citizens; and that the logging is to help them to become better farmers."[43]

The law authorized the Menominee to bank logs on the rivers and streams on the reservation and either to scale, advertise, and sell them by bid or to run them down the river if they could obtain a fair price on the riverbanks. The law authorized the Indian agent to employ Menominees to do the work "at all times when in his opinion practicable and for the benefit of the Indians in doing such work." Thus, Congress relied on the agent's judgment in employing

Menominees but encouraged him to do so. The law also authorized appointment of a logging superintendent and assistant superintendent to oversee the work.

In addition, the law permitted a seventy-five-thousand-dollar advancement to pay the expenses of "cutting, banking, scaling, running, advertising, and sale" as well as the expense of the salaries of the logging superintendent and assistant superintendent. It also stipulated the deposit of 20 percent of the net proceeds into the U.S. Treasury for Menominee credit, with 5 percent annual interest from this fund distributed to tribal members on a per capita basis.[44] This provision was crucial: as with the old fur trade and logging industries throughout the region, credit fueled the Menominee logging system. Although the tribe or its fiduciary, the United States, owned the timber, logging debts were considered the responsibility of individuals, not the tribe.[45]

The way the Menominee system developed was that every qualified Menominee person on the reservation had the opportunity to take part in the logging. The first contracts issued the first year were too large and had to be adjusted downward, because all Menominees who wished to log could do so, although the total tribal limit remained twenty million feet. The first year's proceeds for the twenty million feet totaled $204,809.38. After deduction of expenses of $75,000, $129,809.38 remained. This put almost $26,000 into the stumpage fund.[46]

The system developed so that it ran fairly smoothly based on a system of shares.[47] About 450 enrolled Menominees, mostly adult males over twenty-one years of age but also some families, were listed on the official logging roll. Each was issued a logging certificate for both green and dead and down timber, together worth slightly less than forty-five thousand feet of timber. Certificate holders could enter into logging agreements with the government or, under restrictions, could buy certificates from or sell them to other Indians. In 1895, for instance, these certificate shares amounted to approximately forty-one thousand feet each and sold for about fifteen dollars apiece. People too old or too ill to work, or people without logging equipment, sold their shares. The purchasers could build up for themselves a full winter's work in logging. The purchasers might also subcontract the work for some of the shares they owned. The rules permitted purchase of up to one million feet of timber, but no rules restricted subcontracting, so an individual could legally take even more.

According to one observer, the bargaining for shares was speculative and competitive. "An Indian can sell his share for what it will fetch him and frequently is advanced money by several parties most or all of whom lose when he makes the formal transfer at the Agency." The Menominee economy was off and running. One of the biggest purchasers, Joe Gokie (the Menominee rendering of the name Joseph Gauthier), also ran a store on the reservation from which log camps purchased "tools, food, tents and other necessities." He extended credit to individuals who later traded him their logging certificates. In that way, he succeeded better than most at getting hold of shares promised him.[48]

The contractors and subcontractors cut the trees in the winter and then brought logs to the riverbanks for sale. The streams usually needed "improvement" before logs could be floated down them when the snow melt occurred in spring. Obstructions had to be cleared from the streams, and dams had to be built to provide the necessary depth of water. By 1903 at least thirteen such dams existed on the reservation.[49] Some contractors did this work individually, while others hired crews and built large logging camps to do the work. In 1895 the laborers received twenty to thirty dollars per month. A local federal superintendent of logging oversaw the operations. In 1907 the eighty-three contracts let out represented sixteen large camps that were "putting in a few hundred thousand [feet of timber] each," scattered over the reservation. The superintending logger, William Farr, spent five and a half days each week traveling between the camps and inspecting the work.[50]

The larger operations required larger capital outlay, including money to pay and provision laborers and to purchase stock and equipment. Loggers did all their work in the wintertime, cutting trees and hauling them in horse-drawn sleighs across snow-packed trails and ice-covered bogs and swamps to the riverbanks. For those who ran outfits, this meant paying for labor, horses, and the expenses of building and maintaining a camp throughout the winter; yet the first money did not come in until spring, when the snow melted and the rivers carried the logs to the mills. The $75,000 set aside by the 1890 law apparently failed to cover these costs, because the Indians running the larger camps invariably needed white partners to help supply the camps. Agent Thomas Savage pointed this out in his 1895 report to the commissioner of Indian affairs: "An Indian can not log as cheaply as a white man for the reason that the most of them have to obtain credit to purchase shares, teams, sleds, supplies, etc., and in consequence have to pay a larger price than they would if they had the cash."[51] In November 1894 Savage had unsuccessfully requested that the United States raise the credit limit to $110,000. By 1900 Menominee logger debts to traders totaled more than $73,000.[52]

Joe Gokie, for example, formed a profitable partnership with August Anderson of Shawano, an unscrupulous man who schemed a variety of ways to make money from the Menominee. Gokie reportedly served as a figurehead for Anderson's operations "and received one thousand dollars from Anderson for his part in the transaction."[53] General Superintendent of Logging Joseph R. Farr reported to the commissioner of Indian affairs:

> For several years it has been generally believed and rumored on and off the Reservation that Mr. Anderson was the real logger at this camp and gave Mr. Gauthier [Gokie] a certain consideration for getting the contracts. This camp is known far and near as the "Anderson Camp," and he spends a considerable portion of his time there and has frequently given orders in direct contradiction of those of the Superintendent of Logging . . . [who] has frequently protested to Mr. Freeman and myself and urged that he be kept off the reservation or at least out of this logging camp.

Farr added that Anderson was "also under indictments in the West for defrauding the Government."[54]

The OIA investigated the Anderson-Gokie partnership in 1907. The investigator reported that, if this partnership existed, he could not prove it. But he also reported that Agency Superintendent Shepard Freeman and local logging superintendent William Farr had ordered Anderson off the reservation and specifically not to visit Gokie's camps but that Anderson had ignored the orders. His son Charles was Gokie's bookkeeper. Gokie, according to his own statement, had borrowed money from Anderson at no interest, while he was forced to pay 7 percent interest in loans from the First National Bank in Shawano. In exchange, Gokie hired teams, sleighs, chains, and his camp outfit from Anderson, and when he was short of men to work in his camps, Anderson hired them for him.[55]

Just as Gokie loaned supplies from his store, he needed to borrow on credit to supply and work his own camps. With apparently no money from the government to use for this purpose, he had little choice but to deal with someone like Anderson, who made his livelihood preying on Indians unfamiliar with white men's ways. A favorite trick of Anderson's was to serve as log broker, purchasing timber from Indians and selling it to mills. He would pay Indians part of the money he owed them and would then have them sign their "X" mark to a receipt—which said it was paid in full. Those who refused to sign would receive no money at all unless they took the issue to the agent. Indians believed the agent was in collusion with Anderson on this scheme, so many Indians simply took whatever money Anderson would give them. They were beholden to him anyway for the credit he extended them for equipment. Tribal members like Gokie, however, who was more familiar than others with white men's ways, found the relationship mutually beneficial. Anderson probably did not fleece him as badly as he did others.[56] Most were less fortunate; the system lay wide open for abuse.

Recognizing this potential for abuse, the Indian Office prohibited white men from gaining Indian logging contracts. A disputed loophole to this restriction, however, allowed non-Menominee men, white or Indian, to participate in the logging if they were married to tribal members. Menominee women did not otherwise have access to contracts.[57] The Indian Bureau also promised the Menominee that the government would not license white store owners to trade on the reservation, but in the early 1890s Agent Kelsey granted a license to Congressman McCord's son-in-law. He also angered the tribe by appointing McCord's friends and relatives to various positions that Menominees believed tribal members should hold.[58]

TRIBAL ECONOMICS AND LEADERSHIP

The economic system that developed after the 1890 logging law went into effect, though imperfect and open to corruption, nonetheless brought employment and money for subsistence to individual Menominees. It also built up the tribe's fund in the U.S. Treasury, which by 1905 amounted to more than $2,000,000. It did so at a cost, however. Between 1890 and 1907 about 294 million board feet of timber, mostly white and Norway pine, were marketed from the reservation. The logging operations, as is typical of first cuts, "skinned off the cream of the timber on the reservation." Nonetheless, for logging conducted under the 1890 act, an income of $3,901,390.76, with costs of $1,358,894.53, left more than $2,500,000, some of which paid laborers and the bulk of which went into the tribe's U.S. Treasury account.[59] This money, which made the Menominee one of the wealthiest tribes in the United States, formed the basis of federal proposals for tribal incorporation in the 1920s and termination in the 1950s.[60]

Long after the passage of a 1908 law that restructured logging yet again on the reservation, Menominees remembered that, though the 1890 system "handicapped" individual Indians in several ways, it provided a decent living and work for many.[61] This period represents the beginning of a Menominee conception of the lumber industry as an employment tool to benefit Menominee individuals. The Menominee definition of their resource implied that the purpose of exploiting the forest was to support tribal members. They placed an economic value on the forest that was not in conflict with its cultural value. They intended for that economic value to benefit all tribal members.

This era also brought a shift toward the development of what the historian Brian Hosmer calls "entrepreneurs"—individuals who both profited from logging and gained new leadership power in reservation politics. An increasing number of Menominee children who began their education at boarding schools on the reservation were spending a few years at national boarding schools such as Carlisle and Haskell before returning to the reservation. This was especially true of children from leading families. Some of them became part of this new leadership.[62]

After passage of the 1890 law, the tribe immediately demanded a leading role in tribal decision making. By 1892 the Menominee had already drafted the tribe's first constitution, which would have established an elected Business Committee to oversee logging.[63] Mitchell Oshkenaniew and Peter LaMotte are credited with developing this document, which never became law.[64]

The new logging money was enough to cause Menominees from the Marinette-Menominee area who had never joined the tribe on the reservation to petition for membership or at least for access to the pine money. The Menominee Court of Indian Offenses had already responded to these requests in the way Menominees had traditionally dealt with tribal membership, dating long before reservation days: they said that any Menominees from that area who moved to the reservation would be considered part of the tribe and would have the same rights as other Menominees.[65] Here the traditional leaders adjudicated enrollment issues, one of the few areas of decision making the United States was willing to have the tribes control at the end of the nineteenth century. This foreshadowed much of the work of later tribal councils, to the satisfaction of the United States.

The new entrepreneurial leadership consisting primarily of nontraditional leaders began to increasingly oppose the old traditional leadership. Mitchell Oshkenaniew and Peter LaMotte wrote to Secretary of the Interior John W. Noble in May 1892, "The members of the tribe . . . desire to be relieved of the rule of two or three ignorant and superstitious old men, who now maintain themselves in temporary authority as tribal judges, through the agent's influence." Though their roles were limited, and though they increasingly represented the type of Menominees the federal government wanted in tribal leadership roles—that is, those with formal and boarding school education—the new leaders increasingly came into conflict with federal officials. In the 1890s this conflict was over logging, agriculture, and treaties. Some tribal leaders sided with the agent in his push for allotment, while others protested his actions. The latter said in one petition, "[W]e are aware that our Agent . . . is doing all he can to mislead a portion of the ignorant members of our tribe, by misrepresentation."

At this time several tribal leaders, continuing a longtime Menominee tradition, bypassed the local agent and went to Washington to advocate for legislation amending the 1890 logging act and to press old claims. Some of these claims dated to the settlement of the 1848 treaty, some related to claims from resources lost when the 1856 treaty chopped two townships from the reservation for the Stockbridge and Munsee, and some related to land the state claimed. The local agency strongly opposed the Menominee right to bypass its authority, although the Department of the Interior supported the visits by eventually paying the delegates' expenses. [66] Despite valiant efforts, tribal leaders were thwarted time and again in their attempts to make any decisions or changes beyond enrollment and minor domestic criminal issues.

It is interesting to note that, even with the development of a new type of leadership and the lack of power of tribal leaders, the old values continued to permeate Menominee economic life. Part of the logging money was set aside for those unable to care for themselves, and the system remained one in which all tribal members benefited to some extent through shares, never devolving to the American model of "winner takes all."[67]

At the same time, both Indians and whites profited illegally in the business. Poachers could easily change log marks before and after scaling. Log marks were used like cattle brands to identify ownership of logs and to avoid mix-ups with other loggers' timber on the riverbanks, during the float or run to the mill, and at the mill. Loggers pounded the marks into the logs with a tool similar to a hammer but one that had a log mark on the head of it. Changing the marks was a common practice for those who stole logs. [68]

Another logging problem arose because the Wolf River flowed directly through the reservation. Loggers upstream sometimes landed their logs along the river on the reservation, at which time Menominees in cahoots with or in the pay of one of these people could illegally add logs to the pile and sell them downstream as belonging to the party logging above the reservation. [69] Individual tribal entrepreneurs also profited by assigning themselves and family members the better contracts.

Though the abuses were significant, they cannot mask the fact that for most Menominees logging provided a living. For the first time since the creation of the reservation, many Menominees were again able to support themselves to a significant extent by using their natural resources. They did so in ways in which all tribal members, not simply some individuals or a corporate entity, could benefit. Though tribal leadership continually faced pressures from American officials who increasingly reduced their responsibilities, these leaders—including both traditional leaders and the newly emerging leadership class—were able to play significant roles in shaping the Menominee future. Their insistence on developing tribally defined solutions together with their foresight in establishing effective alliances to advocate on their behalf helped bring this about.

CHAPTER FIVE

The 1905 Blowdown
and Its Aftermath

During the years after the passage of the 1890 logging bill, Menominees proved themselves to be successful and skilled lumbermen. They developed an annual pattern of contracting, logging, and selling the timber that brought some stability to the tribe and began to build capital in their federal treasury account. They also tried to use their newly gained economic foundation to leverage some political control over reservation governance. They wrote a new constitution in 1904 through which they created a Business Committee precisely to gain that control over their own economic affairs and over the annual logging of the twenty million feet of timber permitted under the 1890 law.

The Menominee wrote the constitution as an instrument to create a method for the tribe to "better secure the blessings of civilization to ourselves and our posterity." This implied a denunciation of the old system of tribal government and a declaration of the need for tribal governance to enter the modern era. The preamble stated that "the government of the Menominee tribe of Indians is not organized according to civilized principles, but is an old form of government which has existed from the earliest ages, in which the ruling power has been under the control of hereditary chiefs, and handed down from generation to generation from time immemorial to the present time." But now that the tribe was "far enough advanced in civilization" to make the old form of government obsolete, it reputedly needed a new form.[1]

Agency Superintendent Shepard Freeman worked closely with the Business Committee. The tribe could not approve the constitution without a General Council meeting, over which Freeman presided.[2] He probably wholeheartedly approved the plan of "modernization," if he did not have a hand in writing it. Just as the Menominee had accepted farming under Superintendent Huebschmann in the 1850s as a method to gain control of their economy and thus of their future, they apparently embraced a corporate oversight of the forest as the new method touted by the federal government to achieve "civilization."

A new class of tribal leaders, which included membership from both old leading families and the newly developing entrepreneurial class (which some-times overlapped), hoped to use this constitution to take a leading role in guiding the tribe's destiny. This seemed a real possibility now that the tribe had a stable economy for the first time in half a century. But the next half decade would prove the elusive nature of these tribal hopes. Conflicts between tribal members would be dwarfed by a struggle between the tribe and the federal government for control of the Menominee forest, and in these few short years the United States would triumph, effectively shutting the Menominee out of any significant decision making regarding their resource. This would occur just as major changes again redefined management of the tribal forest.

THE 1905 BLOWDOWN

The 1904 constitution created the Business Committee, defined the techni-calities of its selection and meeting procedures, and spelled out some of its powers. The constitution provided for a chairman and a fifteen-member com-mittee, who were initially appointed, pending elections to be held in 1906. The tribe approved the constitution in council on 18 October 1904. The fif-teen committee members listed were Mose Tucker, Mitchell Oshkenaniew, Joseph Okatchecum, Steve Askenet, Peter Lookaround, Reginald Oshkosh, Louis Keshena, Moses Corn, John Perote, Paul Keneboway, Paul Baxter, Alex Peters, Weiskesit, Wehshequanatt, and Henry Wolf.[3] They came into conflict with tribal members almost immediately. A natural disaster that was to shape the destiny of the tribe through the twentieth century exacerbated this conflict.

In the summer of 1905 a cyclone took down a wide swath of forest. On 17 July, during an extreme hot spell, Captain John V. Satterlee reported the following event in his police diary:

> this Day was Severe Hot & caused a Severe Eletrick Storm in afternoon almost a Tornado Created by Heavey Winds at Kanapoways *Sett.* a little West of it to the North Passed a *Strip* Blowing Down a lot of Green Timber Large Trees as well as Dead ones & a few old log & frame Houses Blowed Down to Pieces Blocked up all Passable Roads Accompanied by *Heavey Hail* & a Damage Slightly to Crops Blowing it Down Hay & Grain *oats* no loss of Life but it Scart our Indians thinking almost a Heavey *Tornado.* Main West Branch Road is Blocked of fallen trees it may not be cleared or cut out.[4]

Thirty-five to forty million feet of timber blew down in this storm. The Menominee Business Committee, the federal logging superintendent, and the federal agent all scrambled to gain control of the disposal of it. Much of

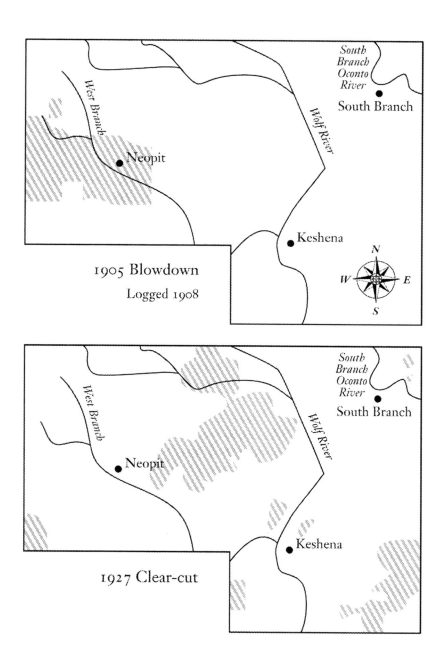

Map 4. 1905 blowdown and 1927 clear-cut

the destroyed timber consisted of hardwood and hemlock, neither of which had been logged on the reservation before because they sink in water. To some degree the exploitation of the blown-down timber was mismanaged. To contemporary observers the mismanagement seemed greater than it actually was.

The Menominee Business Committee wanted to control the contracts for this timber. But federal and state officials believed that the Business Committee had more than it could handle with the twenty million feet of pine cut and sold annually under the 1890 legislation. "I question," wrote Joseph R. Farr, general superintendent of logging for Indian country in Wisconsin, "if in this case it will be good policy to rely on the [I]ndians to do the logging. It costs enough to get hardwood logged by white men of experience and fully equipped for the work." He explained, "[I]t will cost more to pay the Indians for logging this timber than the logs will bring."[5]

The Business Committee strongly opposed the sale of timber on the stump to white loggers, fearing this would provide them with the opportunity they had long been seeking—to open the gates to outside exploitation of all Menominee timber. This had happened to Ojibwe timberlands north and west of Menominee country, and Mitchell Oshkenaniew and others fought hard to be sure it would not occur in their homeland.[6]

On 28 June 1906 Congress passed a law enabling the sale and cutting of the blown-down timber, empowering the Menominee to set up three sawmills in the area and to hire contractors to do the work. According to the historian Brian Hosmer, the Business Committee "defeated a proposal requiring that all contracts be awarded to the highest bidder on the grounds that better-financed off-reservation lumber companies could underbid Menominees and thereby undermine the central goal of providing tribal employment."[7] This dispute between the government and the tribe continued the battle over definitions of the purpose of the Menominee forest, in which the United States emphasized profit and the Menominee focused on providing economic opportunities to a broad base of tribal members, even if at a lower initial economic gain.

Without railroad logging the reservation was not yet equipped to exploit hardwood at all, let alone on this scale. The logging of the blown-down timber finally introduced the railroad to Menominee logging "and greatly enlarged the areas cut over." After this, in fact, and until truck logging became the preferred method of transportation, railroad spurs that were run into rich timberlands determined which areas of the reservation the tribe would cut.[8]

Meanwhile, the various American governmental leaders jumped into the jurisdictional fray. William Farr, the local logging superintendent who reported to his brother Joseph, also in theory worked cooperatively with Superintendent Freeman of the local agency. But in reality, from 1905 to 1908 the Farr brothers and Freeman were involved in disputes against each other.[9] Two other actors became involved, complicating jurisdictional matters further: state forester Edward Merriam Griffith, whose interest was based on Wisconsin's claim to one-sixteenth sections of land in each township, and the Menominee Business Committee.

The arguments over how to effectively log the blown-down timber lasted at least until after 1909, by which point the timber that had not been salvaged had lost its value after rotting in the forest. The fallout from these jurisdictional battles included the firing of at least one federal employee, John Goodfellow, a timber cruiser sent in by the state but paid from Green Bay agency funds; the destruction of the Business Committee; the unearthing of corruption on the part of Superintendent Freeman, including his collusion with non-Indian contractors who tried to get Menominee timber; and passage of the 1908 LaFollette Act, which finally recognized that the Menominee future lay in the utilization of its timber resource.[10]

The 1905 blowdown was partially mismanaged and wasteful because of wrangling over who was in charge and because the timber was not treated as a renewable resource. Federal officials followed practices commonly used by loggers, in which they used up the resource in one area and then moved on to another. The Menominee could not do this to their forest. In the blowdown area, besides the thirty-five million feet of timber that was blown down, up to two hundred million more feet of green timber remained standing. Griffith and the Farrs urged that all this timber be cut at once by bid to contractors, the most cost-effective method for lumberers.[11] "It is the universal custom of lumbermen in handling their own timber," Joseph Farr wrote to Commissioner of Indian Affairs Francis E. Leupp, "if the percentage blown down is great enough to require action, to cut the lands clean." He added, "[We] cannot improve on the methods of handling timber which prevail among lumbermen who have followed the business all their lives and have millions of dollars invested."[12] This solution would avoid the problem of waste, but it would also diminish the tribal resource.

The Menominee Business Committee opposed this plan, because bidding out all this timber for the best prices would give the work to white loggers. The Menominee wanted more than the value of the timber; they desired also the work and its control. The Business Committee indeed had this power on the basis of the 1906 law. Commissioner of Indian Affairs Leupp wrote to Agency Superintendent Freeman that "the power lies clearly with the Committee, and not with the Superintendent of the Green Bay Agency."[13]

Joseph Farr simply attacked the Menominee loggers as incompetent. In 1906 he wrote, "This is the most difficult logging operation on any Indian reservation in the Northwest, for the Indian is not as capable as the white man to carry out a logging job; and besides their experience is decidedly limited in comparison to that of white men. The timber belongs to the Indians, and they assume that they have the right to cut it as they see fit; and it takes all kinds of commanding and coaxing, on the part of the Logging Superintendent, to get them to properly cut the timber and clean up their lands." In 1907 he added, "The handling of this blown down hardwood and mixed timber is, as we have maintained, a proposition that can only be carried out by white men."[14] Unfortunately, the Menominee did not have the limitless resources to which the white lumber barons erroneously believed *they* had access and upon which these barons based their logging methods. The Menominee wished to log the blowdown to gain not only the money from the timber itself but the employment and money from the labor required to get it to market.

Although the blowdown operation was partially bungled, and although the practice of preserving forests while logging them was yet unpopular in the United States, the Menominee actually won the battles both to maintain control of their timber and to preserve their forest while logging it over the long run.[15] At Menominee urging, Congress decided to build a mill on the reservation to cut the timber. Though some of this timber eventually rotted, the idea of a commercial mill on the reservation was an important decision for the tribe's future.

Meanwhile, the Business Committee found itself in the curious position of being attacked from outside the tribe, by the superintendent of logging, as well as from inside the tribe. A federal official, probably General Superintendent Joseph Farr, charged that Agency Superintendent Freeman was cooperating with the Business Committee in illegal dealings.[16] Though the committee's purpose was to safeguard tribal interests, a select handful of members came to control most of the committee's decision making. When the Business Committee gained charge of the blowdown contracting, committee members and their families often received the most lucrative contracts. Of the thirty-eight contracts let by the Business Committee in 1907–8, for example, seven went to the chairman, Mose Tucker, and his relatives.[17]

The awarding of contracts to Menominees was in itself a victory for the tribe, however. The 1906 law not only allowed the Business Committee to let contracts, but it gave the committee charge of the logging operation. It authorized the secretary of the interior "to permit the Business Committee . . . to cause [the blown-down pine] to be cut into logs and hauled to suitable places for sawing and cause [it] to be scaled."[18] The contracts could go to either Menominee or white loggers. This gave the tribe the leverage it needed to overrule Joseph Farr's attempts to sell the blown-down timber to the highest bidders and to instead keep the contracts in Menominee hands.[19]

The Menominee conceived tribal interests as having tribal control of this operation. Indian Department officials later charged that the timber rotted in the woods not because the government mismanaged the operation but because the Menominee Business Committee sabotaged the legislation with unworkable or impractical provisions.[20] The Menominee, in contrast, laid the blame for mismanagement on the federal government, which was always slow to act. Nonetheless, the tribe successfully logged more than thirty-one million feet of the blown-down timber, which represented some 80 percent of the total.[21] Charges that the timber was rotting in the woods probably sped up the congressional process that led to the passage of the 1906 law. The perception on both sides was one of failure, while in reality a significant portion of the timber was brought to market.

The Business Committee created major problems though. Members of the tribe opposed what they saw as the committee's corruption. According to Joseph Farr, the tribe voted in a General Council to abolish the committee in June 1907, but to no avail. When the opposition group planned another meeting, their leader was made drunk. "The meeting never took place. The leader failed to appear. He was found the next day, all cut to pieces."[22] In the spring of 1908, after a Senate investigation, the tribe rescinded the 1904 constitution.[23] On 26 June 1908 the tribal council voted 59–22 to abolish the Business Committee as well.

At that same meeting in June, the tribe decided to discuss charges against the U.S. Forest Service and probably against Agency Superintendent Shepard Freeman. At this point, Freeman left the meeting, apparently in disgust.[24] The meeting, however, continued. Antoine Stick, a Menominee, reported on all the issues discussed by the tribe at that meeting in a letter to the secretary of the interior. He said the tribe refused to recognize any agreements made by the Business Committee because it was corrupt. He also said that the council believed the U.S. Forest Service to be a detriment to the tribe and that Agency Superintendent Freeman, who did not act in the tribe's interest, should step down.[25]

In July the acting commissioner of Indian affairs, C. F. Larrabee, requested a special investigating agent who was already in Keshena to look into these charges. The investigator reported that some of the charges were without foundation but that the bureau should investigate those against the Forest Service.[26]

The Indian Department thoroughly investigated the charges. In August the department apparently sent Robert G. Valentine, the future commissioner of Indian affairs, to Wisconsin to take testimony. Freeman, Edward A. Braniff (the head forester from the Forest Service), Joseph Farr, and several agency employees all testified in hearings that showed Freeman to be either dishonest or incompetent, or, more likely, a combination of both.[27] Braniff presented some of the key testimony in the Freeman hearings, charging that Freeman's system for paying workers in Keshena caused hardships, since most of the work was done in the western part of the reservation near Neopit. Braniff also claimed that Freeman refused to offer him any help in fighting forest fires that burned two sections of land.[28] Recognizing his own lack of forestry experience, Freeman resigned his position.[29] Part of the credit for his resignation must go to the Menominee General Council, which continued its meeting after Freeman left it and sent its report to the secretary of the interior.

According to their new agency superintendent, Edgar A. Allen, the Menominee abolished the Business Committee "because the tribe had become thoroughly disgusted with its methods and believed the most effective way of dealing with it was to put an end to its existence." He added, "A Business Committee made up of honest men who would cooperate with the Agent would be a very useful body."[30] He meant men who would see things his way, not the tribe's way. No doubt Allen was correct, however, about the tribe's disgust with the Business Committee.

FALLOUT FROM THE BLOWDOWN

Local white businessmen jumped in to take advantage of the tribe during this time of upheaval. The attorney Wallace P. Cook, for example, did so in collusion with August Anderson.[31] Cook apparently had his greatest success in a series of claims cases by tribal loggers against the tribe itself and the United States based on their contracts to log the timber blown down in 1905. The complainants had all logged timber under contracts executed based on the 1906 act, but the agency as fiduciary for the tribe had withheld portions of the proceeds to the contractors, citing various violations. When the U.S. Court of Claims finally decided the case, it awarded twenty-nine individuals or partnerships some fifty thousand dollars. More than seventeen thousand dollars of that sum—over one-third—went to the two partnerships that included Cook. Then Cook gathered powers of attorney from as many Menominees as he could to go to Washington to collect the money.

When Cook returned, he refused to pay the Indians, claiming attorney fees and supply bills. For example, on two contracts totaling $699.47, Cook said he paid out $407.05 in bills, quite likely some to Anderson and some to himself, and kept $272.08 to cover attorney fees and expenses. If Indians came to him or complained, he gave them a small amount of money as a "gratuity."

Agency Superintendent Allen wrote, "Mr. Cook has the reputation on the reservation of being a man who would take any possible advantage of the Indians if, by so doing, he could add to his own profits." One Menominee whom Cook had cheated out of thousands of dollars wrote to the commissioner of Indian affairs requesting to retract the power of attorney he had granted Cook, though accepting the fact that he had lost his claim money. Cook apparently got most if not all of the fifty thousand dollars to split between himself and his cronies.[32] These problems of exploitation resulted from a lack of Menominee control over the resource.

Such problems also derived from the credit system on which the entire logging industry depended, because most of the work had to be done before the logs went to market. Individual contractors had to purchase rights to the timber and do the cutting, trimming, and hauling before the logs provided any income. The most expensive time of year, the winter, brought the least income. This dependence on a natural cycle during the years before the railroad, when the amount of snowfall could make or break a lumberman—for example, a large snowfall allowed sleighs to haul logs to the riverbanks and swelled the waterways enough to float logs to market in the spring—proved as much a threat to success as did the occasional disasters such as fires or hard times.[33] Even after railroads, credit by necessity fueled the logging business. Had the federal government judiciously used the money set aside to supply tribal loggers—or, if that were not enough, had they set more aside and acted as creditor instead of allowing people like August Anderson and Wallace Cook to take that role— the Menominee might have been better served. The devastating cycle of the credit system might have been broken.

Such financial problems, together with the failure (in the view of tribal members and U.S. officials) of the Business Committee to provide effective tribal control of logging and the muddled response of the federal government to the 1905 blowdown, spurred the tribe and the U.S. Congress to propose sweeping changes. These changes, formalized in a 1908 law sponsored by Senator Robert LaFollette, defined the twentieth-century tribal economy. They also established the twentieth-century battleground between the United States and the Menominee regarding determination of the tribe's future.

The 1908 LaFollette Act finally gave the tribe the leverage it needed to gain control of its timber resource, at least theoretically. The act was revolutionary not only in Indian forest management but also in overall federal forest management. It was the first federal law providing for sustained-yield timber production and management anywhere.[34] LaFollette, a nationally known Progressive, maneuvered the law through Congress during the heyday of the Progressive era. It was also the dawn of environmental protection in the United States. President Theodore Roosevelt, based on his own experiences in the West, where he had seen the rapid destruction of the bison herds, and on his love of rugged wilderness, had created the national park system to save and protect special American resources. Ironically, this often meant dispossessing American Indians of their lands. During his administration, Congress also created the U.S. Forest Service and "placed the new bureau under the U.S. Department of Agriculture." Roosevelt's staunch ally Gifford Pinchot headed this agency.[35] This early governmental conservation movement coincided with the passage of the 1908 LaFollette Act.

The 1908 law authorized the use of up to three sawmills on the reservation for commercial purposes. It clearly reflected a shift from agriculture to lumbering as the federally defined basis of the Menominee economy. It required that the federal government manage the Menominee forest on a sustained-yield basis and provide employment and training of Menominees in both the logging and milling operations, so that the tribe would eventually run both. The law unfortunately dictated no set methods to accomplish these two goals.

The supporters of LaFollette's bill, in congressional debates and reports preceding its enactment, knew they were shaping the tribe's future. The object of the bill, U.S. Representative Elmer A. Morse of Wisconsin argued, as with all Indian legislation, was "to educate the Indian toward citizenship."[36] Indeed, citizenship had been a primary purpose of the Allotment Act and remained a preeminent federal goal. According to LaFollette, education was now the key to citizenship. The 1890 law had provided money for the tribe, but no education. "The Indian received some financial benefit," LaFollette said, "but the system does nothing to educate him in the practical work of manufacturing the timber nor in the preservation and perpetuation of the forest."[37]

LaFollette recognized that Menominees had proven to be capable woodsmen. "The forest is the natural home of these men," he observed. "The care, the preservation, of these forests should be the Indian's interest and his work." Although white Americans had destroyed the forests elsewhere, LaFollette added, the Menominee should be taught to preserve theirs. The tribe should use its forest as an industry to be self-supporting, but "the harvest of the crop of forest products should be made in such a way that the forest will perpetuate itself." In addition, the federal government should train Menominees to take over the management of the resources. Should the tribe ever be allotted, he added, this would give the Indians practical experience to avoid being exploited the way the Oklahoma Indians were being treated under the allotment system. "In this way," he concluded, "they will become self-reliant, learn to know the value of their heritage, and master the best methods for its preservation."[38]

In accordance with LaFollette's plans, the act states that all jobs "in so far as practical shall at all times" go to Indians. Secretary of the Interior James R. Garfield added that limitation as a precautionary measure because he feared that, if not enough Indians were available in specific instances, operations might be unnecessarily slowed.[39] The bill clearly meant for the United States to train the Indians to run their own business, to educate the tribe for leadership and management of the resource and the mill. Although the original bill was to apply to all Indian reservations in Wisconsin, it was later narrowed to cover only the Menominee. Unfortunately, it said nothing specifically about training Menominees to manage the mill. It did, however, clearly reflect LaFollette's intent: "The Secretary of Interior in so far as practicable shall at all times employ none but Indians upon said reservation in forest protection, logging, driving, sawing, and manufacturing into lumber for the market [the] timber, and no contract for logging, driving, sawing timber, or conducting any lumber operations upon said reservations shall hereafter be let, sublet, or assigned to white men."[40]

The wording in the bill is actually less clear than the intent of the bill as reported in the *Congressional Record*. The bill called for the "protection" and "preservation" of the forest, but it also included a contingency for selling the mill when all work was completed.[41] This wording appears contradictory, in light of developments that actually took place. The bill envisioned temporary mills set up in logging areas, not the massive mill that was eventually built in the town of Neopit.[42] As LaFollette eloquently argued, the purpose of the law was to preserve the forest for the tribe's future use, contrary to the way white lumbermen did their business. In addition, the requirement to employ Menominee workers "in so far as practical" gave the agents too much leeway, even before an amendment to the law specifically permitted the hiring of whites.

As a result, despite the intent of federal lawmakers, the law proved vague enough that agency and mill officials consistently froze Menominees out of most aspects of the business above menial labor. Representative Morse, in response to a question, stated that this bill did not authorize the government to enter into the lumber business; rather, it "proposes that the Government shall allow the Indians to go into that business."[43] Nevertheless, federal officials on the reservation would act as if they, not the tribe, had entered into the logging business. They would use control over the logging industry as a wedge to try to control nearly all aspects of tribal life over the next two decades.

IMPLEMENTING THE LAFOLLETTE ACT

The LaFollette Act gave the U.S. Forest Service charge of supervising Menominee logging operations.[44] In theory, the tribe's leaders were to benefit from Forest Service expertise.[45] In practice, the federal mismanagement of the Menominee forest that had scarred the cleanup of the 1905 blowdown continued unabated. The Forest Service assigned Edward A. Braniff as assistant forester just before the passage of the LaFollette Act. He changed his title to "forester in charge" sometime in early 1909. "I realize the truth of your remark that we have in this Indian work a big and difficult task," he wrote to Edward Merriam Griffith, the state forester, upon assuming his duties. "I hope we will make no bad mistakes."[46] He immediately took charge of the forest and the planning of the mill.

The LaFollette Act authorized the building of mills in logging areas, but Braniff, who was "young, inexperienced and extravagant," instead oversaw the erection of a huge mill at a site originally known as Norway Dam. This mill had a capacity to cut twice the amount of allowable timber. That is, it could cut forty million feet of timber annually—five to seven times as much as the previous noncommercial mills.[47] The decision to create one permanent, high-volume mill would have broad-ranging and long-term impacts on Menominee life throughout the twentieth century.

Among those impacts was the establishment of a new town on the West Branch of the Wolf River, Neopit. Although the West Branch was used to float logs to the mill, a railroad depot was built in Neopit in 1908, the year of the town's founding. Logging rail lines were run out into the woods to bring timber to the mill. The Wisconsin and Northern Railroad passed through the reservation, stopping at Neopit, and apparently hauled finished lumber away from the reservation.[48]

Braniff set right to work on the forest. He began by micromanaging Menominee use of the timber resource to, in hindsight, ridiculous degrees. Braniff believed he needed to gain complete control of the reservation to avoid making "bad mistakes." While he worked out of Neopit, his assistant, James A. Allen, also employed by the Forest Service, worked out of Keshena. They conducted their business by mail. Much of their correspondence involves Menominee applications for permits to gather or cut wood for personal use, made to Allen, who passed them on to Braniff for decisions.

In June 1909, for instance, Braniff wrote to Allen regarding several of these permits. He allowed one man to cut three hundred cedar posts "under the usual conditions." This meant that the posts were for personal use and that the user would clean the dead branches and scraps from the forest. He permitted another man to cut three green pine trees from his field. Yet another could cut eight green tamaracks "for sills for his house." One woman, however, could not cut any tamarack poles until she cleaned up her waste from last year. One man, upon application, was permitted to gather flood wood for use as fuel.[49] In all of these cases, the wood was for personal, not commercial, use.

Braniff wanted control of not only every tree but every stick of wood on the reservation. Indeed, Braniff tried to control all the resources on the reservation, including hunting and fishing. He believed that, unless he controlled these too, he would be unable to control the forest.[50] As is clear from his battles with Indian Office employees, Braniff sought overall control of reservation governance, though his job merely charged him with the task of changing the way the Menominee logged their forest.

Even before the passage of the LaFollette Act on 10 March 1908, a cooperative arrangement between the Forest Service and the Indian Service had gone into effect, dividing federal jurisdiction over the Menominee reservation. It was part of a nationwide cooperative effort that lasted approximately for a year and a half.[51] Yet the arrangement never proved to be very cooperative and was also inefficient. For the first two years after passage of the LaFollette Act, the federal government on the reservation consumed itself in jurisdictional battles between Forest Service employees and the agency superintendent. Braniff reported to the Forest Service, and the agency superintendent reported to the commissioner of Indian affairs. Higher officials in both the Department of Agriculture and the Department of the Interior made final decisions and then reported them back downward, sometimes from the cabinet level all the way to the reservation, through the respective bureaucracies. High-level friction between departments further complicated this system. In 1909, when William Howard Taft became president, he appointed Richard A. Ballinger as secretary of the interior. Ballinger opposed the conservation-minded head of forestry, Gifford Pinchot—a favorite of the previous president, Teddy Roosevelt—whom Ballinger eventually fired. All this made for ineffective troubleshooting and decision making on the Menominee reservation.[52]

During this problematic time, Menominee logging underwent significant changes. The new law canceled contracts made for banking timber that first winter. With the contracts canceled, even logs previously cut or contracted to outsiders would now be milled on the reservation.[53] Suddenly, outsiders could not profit by milling Menominee logs. Rather than being based on individual contracting, the Menominee system of logging would now be an integrated system. Menominees would work in the forest in logging camps built to accommodate railroad routes to the town of Neopit. Menominee men either lived in bunkhouses or, if they brought families, built their own cabins in the vicinity of the camp. Every time such laborers moved to new camps they built new cabins, much as their ancestors had moved their homes to utilize the tribe's resources.[54]

Despite Braniff's authoritarian ways, the forest was well managed under his brief tenure.[55] Nonetheless, the Menominee disliked him from the beginning. He made decisions that were business-smart but that hurt the tribe. For instance, he saved money by hiring teams of horses from off the reservation to haul logs, but this put Menominee drivers out of work. His actions caused more Menominees to quit, and others did not seek work under him. A federal supervisor of Indian employment reported that Braniff's personality caused a 25–40 percent reduction in Indian employment, but he laid the blame on Braniff's misfortunate difficult personality rather than malevolent intent.[56] This supervisor recommended that a personnel manager be hired independent of both the forester and the agency superintendent. Since Braniff opposed this idea, it never happened.[57]

Braniff soon came into conflict with successive agency superintendents Edgar A. Allen and Thomas Wilson over housing. Allen wrote to the commissioner of Indian affairs in February 1909,

> The Forestry Department has made for its officers very comfortable homes and it occurs to me that next Spring the work in this direction should be extended by erecting for Menominee families, members of which are employed at Neopit, suitable quarters for housekeeping. This could be done without great expense and would be a great saving of material over having each Indian interested erecting his own house. It would possess the additional advantage of giving the Forestry Department control so that when the employment of an Indian ceased the room occupied by his family would be available for another.[58]

Wilson, who was Allen's successor, wrote to the commissioner of Indian affairs in August 1909 that he and Braniff were having difficulties over the assignment of land lots and housing in Neopit.[59] Meanwhile, the Menominee protested that all the good housing in Neopit went to white government employees and not to Menominees.[60] The supervisor of Indian employment reported that lavish spending on houses for white employees, even before the mill opened, was causing Menominee resentment.[61] Indian workers had the further problem of paying for a house in Neopit in addition to still supporting their families in their homes elsewhere on the reservation.

Federal officials simply believed that they should house the "more responsible" workers in better quarters. James Carroll, the agent in charge of the Menominee mill, wrote to the commissioner of Indian affairs in 1909, "It must be admitted that those employees that hold the more responsible positions, and who have families, should be provided with individual quarters; but such consideration should not extend to laborers, teamsters and itinerant artisans whose places may be easily supplied." The latter were the only jobs allowed to Menominees.[62]

Agency officials inadequately addressed Menominee grievances over this issue. A town developed around the mill in which the white mill employees, who generally held the higher managerial positions, lived in an area with respectable housing, known locally as White City, while the Indians who worked in the mill lived in an area with run-down and unimproved shacks, known as Dogtown or Shanty Town. A federal inspector described Dogtown as consisting of "small paper covered shacks and not fit to be occupied for living quarters by either whites or Indians." Due to open privies and drainage into this section of town "during heavy rains or in the spring of the year," both typhoid fever and diphtheria were recurring problems.[63]

The relatively minor nature of the dispute between Wilson and Braniff underscored the larger issue of jurisdictional control. Braniff appears to have been power hungry, but he may merely have been driven by the desire to prove himself. He had no management experience when hired for this job.[64] Yet Wilson soon heard that Braniff was indeed in charge of the whole reservation. Wilson also heard that Braniff "swore he was going to have me removed and some one put in charge here that would do things as he, Braniff, wanted them done."[65]

The Indian Department began to develop its own Forestry Division when the cooperative agreement between the Forest Service and the Indian Department ended in July 1909, but Braniff agreed to continue working. He now reported directly to the commissioner of Indian affairs. On 28 August 1909 Braniff wrote to the commissioner of Indian affairs to outline all the problems that he had previously reported but that the department had failed to address. The issue of jurisdiction, he claimed, had caused great difficulties between himself and Wilson. Braniff had drafted a set of instructions dividing the jurisdiction, but they had not been acted upon.[66]

A month later, with these issues still pending, Braniff wrote a lengthy letter in which he stated that, if the commissioner of Indian affairs did not take actions to provide him with both authority and funds, he would resign. [67] According to one source, he resigned in October 1909. According to another source, he was fired in 1910. [68] In fairness to Braniff, an Indian Department official later remarked of Braniff's duties both to open sawmill operations and to clear up timber from the 1905 blowdown in a profitable way, "A more difficult assignment was never given an American forester."[69] Unfortunately, he proved himself unequal to the task.

Braniff's skills and knowledge in forestry did not match the needs the Menominee had defined for their forest resource. His struggles with the Indian Department created a situation in which Menominees could not be proactive in protecting their resources but rather only reactive to prevent any further undermining of them. They were so far removed from self-governance in these circumstances that it almost disappeared entirely just when the law indicated it should be emerging from hibernation. The promise of both the 1904 constitution and the 1908 LaFollette Act dissipated so rapidly that they seem scarcely to have existed.

Then in 1912 the Menominee leader Neopit, who was the strongest connection to the old generation of leaders, died. Also in the 1910s white policemen replaced the Indian police force.[70] Federal officials now assumed almost complete control of tribal governance and economics. Tribal members, reeling from the rapid changes, had to find ways to persevere.

CHAPTER SIX

The Weight of Federal Wardship

During the years from 1908 until 1924 the Menominee reached the nadir of their ability to govern themselves. Ironically, this adversity occurred following the enactment of the 1908 LaFollette Act, which called not only for the employment of tribal members but also for their training to take over Menominee business affairs. Unfortunately, the federal government under the LaFollette Act ran the tribe's business as a paternalistic wardship, virtually without input from the tribe.

Since agency officials constantly thwarted the Menominee, the tribe's only alternative was to appeal directly to Washington, either to the commissioner of Indian affairs or to Congress. Thus they sent delegations to Washington as they had done since the 1850s. The makeup of these delegations and their success or failure were always controversial issues in tribal politics and manifested themselves in an ambivalence toward the delegates themselves. The agency superintendents compounded the problem: they were quick to vilify any Menominees who opposed them and sometimes successfully convinced tribal members that these delegates were agitators and greedy, lazy, self-interested people. When delegations returned from Washington without success, Menominees were inclined to believe that they had wasted their efforts. In most cases these charges lacked truth. The problem was that bureaucracies in government are notorious for moving ever so slowly. As longtime tribal leader Gordon Dickie described the problem many years later, "I've done a lot of lobbying for the tribe. And this is one thing that I haven't been able to get across to tribal members or even the [tribal] legislature. You don't just go up and ask Congress to appropriate money. You've got to be able to sell it to key members of the committee before and after the hearings. So you've got to be able to have a personal contact with those people. And this isn't done overnight, this has taken years."[1] Thus, sometimes lobbying trips were brief, while other times they lasted from several weeks to months.

One tribal member who frequently made such trips to Washington was Mitchell Oshkenaniew. The tribe's ambivalence toward his role is instructive, since delegates before and since him had similar experiences. The tribe censured Oshkenaniew for his role as secretary of the Business Committee, and in 1908 the tribe in council banned him for life from speaking for the tribe. In 1913, however, the tribal council in meeting officially lifted this ban.[2] Agency Superintendent Angus Nicholson called Oshkenaniew a man "whom this office has had more trouble with than perhaps anyone else."[3] On the other hand, Oshkenaniew and other delegates knew how to work the system in Washington.

When the federal government refused to finance delegations from tribal funds, the delegates went anyway, paying their own expenses and hoping for remuneration later. One inspector reported that Oshkenaniew tried to collect a dollar from each tribal member at annuity time to pay for his trips to Washington.[4]

Menominee efforts at gaining control were largely reactive, however. Despite tribal efforts, the federal officials controlled nearly all aspects of tribal life. Local federal officials not only clamped down in the political and economic realms but attempted to control the social realm as well. To make matters worse, government control was generally accompanied by mismanagement. Though the real U.S. focus seemed to be the forest, the notion of training Indians to be American-style citizens remained a core foundation of U.S. policy. Intimidation continued, therefore, on the religious front as well.

PEYOTISM

In 1914 Peyotism arrived on the Menominee reservation in much the same way as the Dream Dance had some three and a half decades earlier. A Native American Church member later recalled, "I respect . . . the Indian religion"—meaning the Mitāēwin, to which he had once belonged—but he believed it had become corrupted when practitioners forgot parts of the ritual and ceremony or when others disrespected the ceremonies themselves. As a result, the tribal leader Neconish led several families in an out-migration from the Zoar community. They founded an even more isolated community, the Neconish settlement, and attempted to establish new religious rites there. Neconish's father, in 1912, "had a revelational dream in which the arrival of a new religion was announced." In 1914 "a Peyote missionary," Nah-qua-tah-tuck, or Mitchell Neck, a Potawatomi relative of Neconish's wife, visited the family and remained for several years. He introduced the use of peyote and the rites of the Cross Fire Way to the residents of the Neconish settlement. Many of those who began to follow the newly introduced religion were closely related to Ho Chunks and Potawatomis through intermarriage.[5]

Peyotism was a relatively new religion in the United States that developed in part from traditions with a much longer history in Mexico. For thousands of years peyote, a type of cactus, has been harvested, dried, and ingested to be used for sacraments and for other purposes by Indian tribes along the Rio Grande River and south. The Carrizo are credited as the likely "originators of the peyote ceremony in the United States" in the late nineteenth century, but the Lipan Apache "were undoubtedly the principal purveyors of the ritual" to tribes in the United States. Oklahoma, then known as Indian Territory, became the "Cradle of Peyotism" in the United States in the 1880s. There the religion developed as a multitribal movement that made a place for traditional faiths within the rapidly changing world. Each tribe that accepted Peyotism did so in its own way, adapting rituals, ceremonies, and doctrines that were consistent with its people's own traditional beliefs. By the early twentieth century, Peyotism had spread north.[6]

The new rites introduced to the Menominee included an infusion of both Christianity and traditional Mitāēwin religious beliefs into the services in which peyote served as a sacrament. The Peyotists, like the traditional Menominees who followed the Mitāēwin or the Dream Dance religions, believed that the supernatural world contained powers that helped people to be "effective and strong" but remained inaccessible to most humans without aid. For the Menominee three interchangeable words represented this power: *tatāhkesī-wen*, that which has energy or life; *meskōwesen*, that which has strength; and *ahpēhtesēwen*, that which is valuable. These powers were accessible through Māēc Awāētok, the supreme power. The Peyotists also referred to Māēc Awāē-tok as "our father." Practitioners took peyote because Māēc Awāētok would speak to them through the plant. In that way peyote was considered stronger than the Bible, which aside from direct quotations from Jesus was considered to, at least arguably, consist only of the words of men. Jesus could also communicate with Peyotists, most often through visions, and could provide instructions on proper living. Specifically prescribed rituals had to be carefully followed in order for Māēc Awāētok to bring power to followers through peyote.[7]

Agency officials reacted to the introduction of Peyotism with alarm and hostility. Neconish's son, Theodore Neconish, later recalled that anti-peyote Menominees approached Agency Superintendent Nicholson, and "they squeal[ed]"; as a result, Nicholson sent the police to arrest Nah-qua-tah-tuck.

Nah-qua-tah-tuck was arrested under the 1897 Indian Prohibition Act, which outlawed the distribution of intoxicating beverages in Indian country. Congress had unsuccessfully attempted to include peyote in the law in 1913. Witnesses at Nah-qua-tah-tuck's trial testified that the peyote was used as part of religious services, and "[t]he defendant was acquitted on the ground that the meeting was one of a religious nature."[8]

Nicholson, however, accepted the unfounded prevailing beliefs of the larger society that peyote was a heavy intoxicant and that religion was used as a mask for taking illicit drugs. In 1916 a sensationalistic article entitled "Peyote Replaces Whisky on Reservation" appeared in the *Denver Times* in which the reporter misstated the results of the Menominee trial. He wrote, "The judge and jury were quite convinced that peyote was a good substitute for common booze."[9] This observer and others confused peyote with a strong intoxicant, the mescal bean, which is native to the same region in Mexico. Also in 1916 a federal inspector who visited the reservation reported that peyote users "are similar to the cases of opium addicts." He added, however, that the farmer and doctor claimed that peyote's "effect on the Indians is not so obviously bad as alcohol."[10] In fact, according to Theodore Neconish, at least some of the peyote practitioners were recovering alcoholics. Their religious faith and practices helped them overcome their addiction.[11]

Nicholson, whose informants included Peter LaMotte, reported his own or his informants' understanding of peyote ceremonies to Samuel A. Barrett of the Milwaukee Public Museum, who recorded these observations in 1917. Barrett wrote that the use of the Bible in services served as a subterfuge "for the sole purpose of proving that the ceremony is a strictly religious rite." He added that the ingestion of peyote "produce[s] a distinctly exhilarating, intoxicating effect" and leaves the participant in "a distinct stupor" afterward.[12]

In 1917 Inspector W. S. Coleman visited the reservation, and he too commented on peyote. The use of it was increasing, he observed, despite Nicholson's efforts to oppose it. He wrote, "The Superintendent is exerting active means to suppress this evil, and is endeavoring to break it up by handling the users for neglect of family, lack of industry, or any other grounds."[13]

The next year the Indian Department sent a list of nineteen questions to reservations throughout the United States to conduct its own study of peyote. Nicholson's successor, Agent Edgar A. Allen, wrote to the commissioner of Indian affairs in 1919, "The claim is made of course, here as elsewhere, that the use of this drug is in connection with religious observances, but the claim is not well founded."[14] The agent then attempted to cast aspersions on the Peyotists: "The users are the less industrious and less progressive of the Menominees, although the persons charged with the responsibility of introduction here, the

Neconishes, are really a fairly industrious family, though thoroughly Indian and rather adverse to taking on the way of civilization."[15]

By contrast, the agency farmer, who worked more closely with tribal members distant from agency headquarters in Keshena, reported that Peyotists were more industrious than other tribal members. "They do better farming, more of it and make effort at self-support and get along harmoniously with Government employees, complying with rules and regulations," he wrote to the superintendent. He also reported that he had never known harm to come from the use of peyote, adding that "members ate and prayed all [Saturday] night long and part of the following Sunday with no noticeable effects and on following Monday morning went to work as usual on their logging contracts." He estimated that approximately 3 percent of the Menominee population, slightly more than fifty tribal members, followed the religion, an approximation supported by others.[16]

The families that lived in the region of the reservation where Peyotism was practiced were not of the original farming bands but had taken up some agriculture after their settlement there. They could also be branded as religious conservatives. They had not taken up Catholicism, but they believed the Mitāēwin's power to be diminishing. Their own lives reflected the social upheaval accompanied by the new economic system on the reservation. Instead of turning to Christianity to help them cope, they turned to what they believed to be a purer form of religious power, found in Peyotism. Their religious conservatism did not keep them from adapting to changing social and economic conditions, however. In fact, it is likely that this religious basis provided them an anchor in the adaptive process, which would help explain the observations that they made such reliable farmers and loggers and had given up drink.

Despite harassment, Menominee Peyotists eventually established a Native American Church chapter, providing tribal members who did not follow Catholicism, the Mitāēwin, or the Dream Dance with another religious option.[17] In Menominee country, as elsewhere in Indian country, religious freedom was something for which tribal practitioners had to battle. For the Menominee, the prejudices of successive agents and the standards of federal policy toward tribal religious beliefs blinded officials to the reality of the religious movement. Federal officials branded even tribal members who successfully farmed and logged as backward due to their religious practices. Though the United States continued to attack Menominee culture in a variety of ways, the major federal efforts during this time continued to revolve around the forest.

Angus Nicholson replaced Thomas Wilson as agency superintendent in late 1909. After Edward Braniff left, Nicholson took on the forester's responsibility also. Having been a civil servant in the Customs Service, he had no forestry experience.[18] In 1910 the Indian Department officially created an Indian Forest Service, which took charge of Menominee and other tribes' forests.[19] Ironically, 1910 also marked the year in which blatant disregard of the LaFollette Act began to cause gross mismanagement of the tribe's forest, which led to the "Ballinger-Gifford" congressional investigation. In this investigation, the Indian Department blamed Braniff for all the problems, while Braniff blamed the Indian Department. A forestry expert later laid the blame on intransigent, obstructionist Menominees.[20] Under Nicholson (1909–18) and his successor, Edgar A. Allen (1918–25), the federal government supervised the clear-cutting of Menominee forests, which diminished rather than preserved the timber resource.[21]

Nicholson actually supported selective cutting. However, after a 1910 forest fire that covered tens of thousands of acres in the eastern part of the reservation, he concentrated efforts on clearing the burned-over area, even to the extent of taking less valuable burned wood to the mill. In 1911 the mill began to run railroad lines to that burned-over area, where logging operations were concentrated until the mid-1930s.

The Menominee, many of whom were experienced woodsmen and understood the intent of the 1908 LaFollette Act, readily recognized the mismanagement of their resource. They protested practically from the time the law passed, but to no avail. Their first protests were related to the changing conditions caused by the 1908 law, which ended the old logging contract system wherein an individual was responsible for his own logging. The new system regularized labor under the United States' direction. This led to dissatisfaction, as Menominees were forced to neglect farms in order to keep their jobs in the mill, which unlike logging was more regular, less seasonal work.[22] The tribe met in council on 5 March 1910 and voted to reestablish the Business Committee to help deal with such matters. The agency superintendent wrote the commissioner of Indian affairs opposing that step, and the commissioner concurred in a letter to the secretary of the interior. By April the department sent a letter prohibiting the reestablishment of the committee, which essentially froze the tribe out of decision making in the political arena.[23]

The only tribal government the superintendent would recognize was one styled after an American system. He generally ignored the actions of the General Council, a body consisting of all adult tribal members who made decisions much as they had for centuries. Unfortunately, their decisions had no authority behind them.

Nicholson made a feeble attempt in 1911 to create a town-board form of government for the town of Neopit. It was to consist of seven Menominee members and seven white members, who would train the former to run the town. It is noteworthy that, of the Menominees, at least four were former members of the Business Committee.[24] A fire protection committee reported to the board several times that the tarpaper shacks the Indians lived in needed chimneys instead of stovepipes, but apparently nothing was done about the problem. A law and order committee recommended to the board that alcohol-related trials be held in Neopit as well as Keshena. Interest in the board diminished rapidly, and little was accomplished. No board meetings are recorded except from April to July 1911, although a 1915 election is mentioned.[25]

This board failed because it did not adequately address tribal needs. The agent thought of solutions in terms of educating the tribe toward white-conceived notions of advancement, but even in those terms Menominee concerns were not dealt with properly. To be effective, governance would have to respect traditional roles and solutions and to provide for the people. The tribe viewed gaining control of the timber resource as its first need; other concerns were secondary. The Menominee thought in terms of independence and self-governance, while the federal government thought in terms of wardship. The Menominee wanted to control their own affairs, but the federal government thwarted their efforts.

Things were no better on the economic side. Problems occurred because the foresters assigned to the reservation, as they themselves later testified in the tribe's lawsuit against the federal government, were unaware of the purposes of the 1908 law. Nearly everyone assigned to the reservation who had forestry backgrounds had experience in clear-cutting, not in conservation-based silvacultural methods. The logging superintendents built their reputations on keeping costs low, not on practicing conservation for the future. This met with the desire of agency superintendents to show immediate profits, but profits were difficult to achieve because Braniff's large mill in Neopit was very costly to build and run, which increased the tendency toward clear-cutting.[26]

Under the LaFollette law, the Menominee began to demand a role in the mill management. In 1912 twenty-four members of the tribe, including several former members of the Business Committee (Mitchell Oshkenaniew, Mose Tucker, Weiskesit, George McCall, John Grignon, and Thomas LaBell), "called on Nicholson 'to appoint . . . Reginald Oshkosh'" to manage the timber resource. Oshkosh was Neopit's son and had been trained in government schools. He thus crossed over the old and new leadership categories. When Nicholson refused, the tribe sent delegations to Washington, but still no action was taken. Finally, several Menominees, including Mitchell Oshkenaniew, hired outside attorneys to investigate official misconduct of Menominee affairs on the reservation. They brought mismanagement charges to Congress that led to a BIC investigation conducted in 1913 and reported in 1914 by Edward E. Ayer, a Chicago businessman and member of the BIC.[27]

The Menominee told investigators they were unhappy because, though work was available, Menominees still lived in substandard housing and people were hungry. As one Menominee said, the white people were the ones "who have good things to eat."[28] The Menominee, through their attorneys, charged that Nicholson used a system that allowed white workers to get the best jobs, at the expense of Menominees who were capable of doing the same work. The tribe requested that Nicholson be immediately removed from office. According to the historian Brian Hosmer, however, "Ayer virtually ignored these charges and limited his investigation to debunking charges of waste and mismanagement."[29] To counter Menominee claims that the mill was financially unsound, Ayer told tribal members that the mill had added $444,000 to the Menominee fund in the federal treasury.[30]

Ayer also strongly supported the goal of agriculturalizing the Menominee economy. He began his investigation report with a pastoral description of the area surrounding Keshena: "Radiating out from Keshena for a distance of twelve miles is a scene of agricultural progress, Indian farmers cultivating farms of 5 to 80 acres, cleared, fenced and in various stages of improvement." In his interviews with Menominees, Ayer urged individuals to accept his views on farming and to request individual allotments. Some farmers, such as Mose Tucker, enjoyed enough success growing corn, potatoes, beans, and hay that they had no need to work in the lumber industry. Others, living in the Zoar area, for example, observed that their land was good timberland, but not good farmland. Weiskesit told Ayer that there was "[g]ood land, timber land; but how am I going to use the farm?" Peter LaMotte said the millwork disrupted farmwork. Individuals in the past could log during the winter and farm the rest of the year, but millworkers could not do so. "[N]ow you have to go to work every day and you have nothing to farm with, and if you stop work for a week you are going to starve."[31]

Wage labor seemed to diminish the quality of life, and several Menominees recognized this. It also reflected a non-Menominee value placed on the resource and on the work itself. Hosmer describes Frank Waubano's response to the situation: "Waubano denounced 'the way the white man works to earn money.' . . . The white man, so Waubano argued before a 1915 council meeting, 'steals money from other people, and murders and gambles to earn it. There is no Menominee here that will do that.'"[32] Neither farming nor logging was inherently good or bad; in fact, many tribal members needed both to provide a living. They recognized the utility of both resources. They also wanted their livelihood to support them without keeping them on the brink of starvation.

Ayer seemed to view the forest resource as a support to the development of agriculture. More of his recommendations related to farming than to the forest. He even suggested allotting farms to those who wanted them; paying a per capita bonus of several hundred dollars to farmers; sending several of the Menominee's brightest young men to Madison to be trained in the agricultural school so they could help educate Menominee farmers; and establishing a herd of a thousand cattle.[33]

Nicholson, though also a proponent of allotment, was more cautious. He believed that allotments would be counterproductive until the tribe had profited from the timber, so that they could divide tribal funds to support allotment. An allotment survey had not yet been conducted, and Nicholson's superiors in the OIA did not intend to make one. It was the policy of the OIA throughout Nicholson's tenure not to support "legislature to provide allotments for the Menominee until the sale of the tribal timber is completed." Nonetheless, the government position clearly seemed to equate farming via allotment, not exploitation of the forest resource, as the long-term foundation of a successful tribal economy. Nicholson, with support of his superiors, began a book in which Menominees staked claims to land in case of future allotments.[34]

Ayer's only recommendations for logging and the mill—ostensibly the reason for the visit—were to bring a railroad to Neopit from the south, to cruise the forest to gain an accurate estimate of its volume, and to hire a timber salesman at the mill.[35] Some tribal members, such as storekeepers Peter Lookaround and C. A. Tourtillot, supported the work of the agent.[36] However, the tribe at large apparently viewed Ayer's report as a whitewash. In November 1914 an anonymous individual who called herself "A Menominee Indian Woman in Distress" wrote to President Woodrow Wilson regarding continuing dissatisfaction with the federal government's handling of reservation issues. Her letter captures the glum mood of tribal members: "I am writing this letter in the hopes that it might help a down trodden and very much abused race the Menominee indians. Our propery is being wasted by incompetant officals, we are refused work at our own mill, our doctor has left indians crippled for life through neglect and our agent up holds him, they do this for no reason other than his hatred for an indian, he is against our religious belief. . . . There was inspectors here they lied to us and lied to Washington we can prove it if given a chance. One man was Mr. Ayer of Chicago."[37]

A General Council held on 16 January 1915 voted 56–5 to demand Nicholson's resignation. Unfortunately, some of the proceedings conducted in Menominee were not translated for the record, but anger at Nicholson surfaced in the recorded statements of several people. Mitchell Komanekin began the council by saying, "I wish to state the purpose for which we Menominees have come here to-day. It is the wish of this tribe. We hereby remove our agent from the service here to-day. What we try to do in Washington our agent here thwarts." The resolution began by remembering that Superintendent Nicholson had told the Menominee in 1910 that, if they were dissatisfied with the way he ran their affairs, he would resign. The next seven paragraphs detailed why they were unhappy with his tenure. The document finished by stating that, if Nicholson refused to resign, "the tribe [would] pledge itself to use all efforts to compel his removal."[38]

Nicholson forwarded the minutes to the commissioner of Indian affairs with an eighteen-page letter denouncing the resolution and the Menominees responsible for it. He said they were merely the agitators who did not like to work. They were mad because the Ayer report negatively reflected on them for this very reason, he argued, and so they took the opportunity to foment trouble. He pointed out that the tribe had 575 males over eighteen years of age, all eligible for participation in council, but only fifty-six voted for the resolution. He added that Shawano attorneys had prepared the resolution. He also angrily stated that the council refused to discuss "the business of the tribe," which included agriculture and applications for enrollment or membership, focusing instead on agitation. "Many tribal members" in attendance left in disgust, others remained but did not participate, while still others voted with the majority to avoid the "ill feelings" of their fellows. Nicholson then listed twenty-one Menominees and stated why twenty of them were not trustworthy to make these decisions. The reasons varied from drunkenness to agitation. Some he accused of being "sadly misled" pagans, others of being "always against agency officials." One was "a good Indian who does not understand," another a disgruntled former employee. Though Joe Longley invited Nicholson to defend himself during the council, the superintendent felt no need to do so. Besides, he pointed out, many of the accusations were made in Menominee, so he did not know all of them.[39]

Mill and forest management were key issues for tribal members and served as the basis of their discontent. The jurisdictional battle between OIA foresters and Forest Service employees in Nicholson's early years exacerbated the troubles. Forest Service employees were assigned to the reservation until 1918, but Indian Department officials refused to work with them. The law required Forest Service employees to mark trees for cutting, but after 1912 the Indian Department entirely ignored the forestry employees, so they lost their function. In an atmosphere of enmity these employees could not be effective anyway. In fact, due to clumsy bureaucracy they did not even realize until 1924 that they had been relieved of duty in 1918![40] At the same time, both of these federal factions effectively barred Menominees from participation in decision making.

During the years before 1918, Indian agency officials ignored foresters' tree marks so that the Menominee could clear-cut under the mistaken assumption that the mill, with a capacity of forty million feet per year, should be supplied with at least thirty-five million. All the cutting took place on a twenty-three-hundred-acre tract, and loggers found that if they were to take thirty-five million feet they would have to cut nearly all the trees. This obviated the need for marking. The government, when the tribe later sued for mismanagement, argued that the law did not require the marking of trees. The Court of Claims concurred but decided that this reasoning did not provide an excuse to manage the forest so it would fail to perpetuate itself. During the hearings on the 1908 law, Congressman Morse had testified that trees should be marked and that tree marking was ostensibly the purpose of the Forest Service officials assigned to the reservation.[41]

During Nicholson's reign, Menominees continually pressured the Indian Bureau to investigate their claims of federal forest and mill mismanagement. The department sent another inspector, E. B. Linnen, to the reservation in the fall of 1915. In a conference with various agency officials and 263 adult male Menominees, tribal member Charles Chickeney indicated to Linnen the level of frustration Menominees felt at federal micromanagement: "We just get one set of regulations learned when they are changed and we have to leanr another. One cannot cut wood for his fire without a permit. One cannot even visit relatives at their homes without first reporting to Assistant Superintendent Marble his whereabouts. One cannot have time to dig a grave for his dead without being ordered to bury same within twenty-four hours."[42]

Linnen noted both Nicholson's lack of experience with the timber business and his failure to get along with Menominees. He recommended that "Superintendent A. S. Nicholson be promptly transferred to some position not requiring the supervision and handling of Indians, or requiring knowledge of lumber operations." The tribe passed a second resolution requesting Nicholson's removal from office, voting 249–1.[43]

In 1916 another inspector sent to study Menominee dissent blamed the agency doctor and one of the agency clerks for tribal unrest.[44] As tribal dissension continued, the United States dispatched yet another inspector, W. S. Coleman, to review the situation in the fall of 1917. Coleman's investigation lasted six weeks. He too concluded that the chasm between Nicholson and his assistant, on the one side, and the Menominee, on the other, was so great

> that the present status between these two officials and these Indians is absolutely hopeless; that there is no hope of palliation or reconciliation; that the gulf between them is impassable; that the hope of the future readjustment and satisfactory reconciliation is absolutely impossible; and that the spirit of antagonism and cross-purposes has reached the acute stage that may possibly lead to personal violence or a probable tragedy; that there is a declared purpose on the part of these Indians to continue the fight to the bitter end in their desire and efforts to have removed these two officials.[45]

This aspect of the conflict ended in early 1918. A 1917 forest fire had hastened the deterioration of Nicholson's already failing health when he suffered exposure and overexertion while helping fight it; he resigned in March of 1918 and died two months later.[46]

RESOURCE MISMANAGEMENT AFTER NICHOLSON

Federal control did not diminish and federal management did not improve after Nicholson's departure. It continued unabated, quashing Menominee attempts at self-determination in economic, political, and social terms. In the forest, under federal direction, temporary railroad spurs were run into timbered areas. On these, the Menominee could transport hemlock and hardwood, as well as pine, to the mill even from areas where no rivers ran. The federal government established logging camps and built bunkhouses, barns, sheds, and cook shanties similar to those in the larger camps before the passage of the 1908 law. Several of these camps operated each winter. When the loggers cut them clean, they abandoned them for new camps.[47]

A less than sympathetic observer said that under Nicholson there existed "a pretense of regulated cutting." Under his successor, Edgar A. Allen, even this pretense disappeared.[48] Allen "was a strong advocate of allotments for the Menominee, maintaining that he accepted the position of Superinten-

dent there with the distinct understanding that allotments would be made."
He continued the process of recording future allotment claims in the book
that Nicholson had opened. To clear land for these allotments, he supervised the clear-cutting of Menominee timber without any plans for regen-
eration.

Although clear-cutting was illegal, Allen wanted to clear land for allotment
and actually went about trying to do it. J. P. Kinney, forest supervisor for the
OIA, conducted a study in the summer of 1918 with two other professionals
and recommended making forty-acre allotments in the eastern portion of the
reservation. They could make allotments this size and in this region "without
injuring or taking from the forest area" in the western portion of the reservation. Kinney later said that he "was strongly opposed to the allotment of
forested lands that were not clearly of high agricultural value" but that the
Indian Office and the Department of the Interior accepted Allen's recommendations over his.[49]

After Nicholson resigned and Allen took over, the Indian Forest Service
appointed a mill manager, George A. Gutches, who took on some of the major
logging responsibilities formerly held by the agency superintendent. Gutches's
primary motive was profit for the tribe. He clear-cut lands with a vengeance,
refusing to restock from seedlings, with the support of Allen and over the
opposition of his boss, J. P. Kinney.[50]

Allen, who like Nicholson lacked any forest experience before this job, also
believed the forest would rapidly regenerate itself after clear-cutting. He saw
no reason to plant young trees, let alone to cut selectively. Kinney later said
that, in step with fairly common practices in the 1910s, he did not believe
that selective cutting was viable but instead believed in "clear cutting and
subsequent planting." In his own memoranda, however, introduced in the
Court of Claims case, Kinney advocated selective cutting, clearly contradicting
his later justifications. Besides, as H. H. Chapman has pointed out, Europeans
had practiced selective cutting successfully for a thousand years. It had also
worked on the Menominee reservation in 1909 and 1910. Allen openly ignored
orders from his superiors. Indeed, Kinney observed that all efforts at selective
cutting were consistently undermined. In the fall of 1919 full-fledged clear-
cutting of green pine began. It had the advantage of being the most efficient
and profitable method available in railroad logging, and there was no threat
of fire loss to young timber since none was left behind.[51]

Under neither Nicholson nor Allen and Gutches did any planning for the
future take place. Even with this wasteful cutting, the tribe derived no extra
income than it would have generated under sustained-yield logging.[52] The

forest suffered in this period not only from clear-cutting but also from the government's failure to clear the slash, or waste, which led to conditions in which only popple (aspen) and a few birch trees could grow, and these not healthily.[53] A significant foundation of the lawsuits the tribe would successfully initiate against the U.S. government in 1935 was based in this mismanagement under Nicholson and Allen. The tribe sustained a net loss of half a billion board feet of timber between 1908 and 1934.[54]

The forest resource was not the only thing the federal government mismanaged at the time; it also mismanaged the mill. The mill account books provided a constant source of consternation to the tribe. They were closed, and the Menominee time and again demanded an audit. Menominees were dissatisfied with the losses charged against their account in the U.S. Treasury and were fed up with white managers who, the Menominee correctly charged, had little or no previous experience in the logging business.[55]

The unwieldy size of the mill caused further complications. At a 1919 General Council meeting, tribal members demanded participation in the control of the mill, but Superintendent Allen denied it and instead called for them to allot their lands. An audit conducted by the OIA in 1925 found the accounting system at Neopit atrocious, opposed to government methods, and below standards. Property was no longer being transferred from one agent to another, though this had been the practice since the early nineteenth century; federal officials apparently no longer made inventories; and accounting was done with improper classification according to forestry employees at this highly valuable Menominee plant.[56]

In addition to mismanagement of the forest resource, from the woods to the mill, the tribe also suffered mismanagement of the human resource. Braniff had known the forest business, but his grating personality caused Indians to quit their jobs. His successors, on the other hand, often lacked knowledge of the forest business. The Menominee not only believed many of their bosses to be incompetent but also strongly resented the white practice of ignoring Menominees in filling higher-level positions. The federal officials established a hierarchy from the beginning and tried to enforce it. This was done politically, economically, and socially.

Mill supervisors regularly bypassed Menominees in promotion, even though they protested against this discrimination in council meetings from 1912 into the 1930s. Menominees approached work from a different perspective than the white government officials. Work was only a part, not the center, of their lives, unlike the case for many Americans. For Mitāēwin and Dream Dance practitioners, for instance, their religious ceremonies took precedence over work, which could lead to absenteeism.[57] Those Menominees trained for and placed in higher level positions were especially doomed to failure. Instead of bringing Menominee values to the workplace, they "were expected to act like white managers or lose their positions," the anthropologist Nancy O. Lurie has observed. For that reason, combined with federal reluctance to give up any form of control, Menominees remained in the lowest positions.[58]

It is little wonder that Menominees looked back in fondness on the pre-1908 logging years. After 1908 they lost not only their forest but also the little independence they had retained or regained. They were forced to work within the faulty system created by the federal government, sometimes even acknowledged in government reports, yet the government failed to solve the problems. One observer, forester J. P. Kinney, blamed the Menominee for much of the failure to protect the forest. He said that they did not fully support government actions but wanted to run the forest in the old ways and that they opposed change for the better.[59] Faced with the conditions imposed upon them, however, how could the Menominee have acted or believed differently?

The Menominee tried to blunt the mismanagement of their forest, mill, and human resources through actions and criticisms made at tribal council. Their agents, however, belittled the role of the council. Allen, for example, often refused to call council meetings because he believed that only the Menominee whom he viewed as agitators and idlers had interest in attending.[60] Federal refusal to acknowledge the council blocked the only local voice the Menominee had in the governance of their affairs. When the tribal council met, the agents ignored or disparaged it and stripped it of its power.

In desperation the tribe continued to support delegations to the nation's capital. In November 1921, for example, the General Council voted on several matters, all of which they could only resolve by sending a delegation to Washington. The council voted to seek to rewrite the LaFollette law to read that Menominees should be given such executive positions at the mill as they could handle. Not only should the tribe in council select a board to run the mill, they proposed, but it should also oversee appropriation of tribal funds. Mitchell Oshkenaniew asked for a resolution to give the tribe a voice in the management of its affairs. The council decided to send a delegation to Washington to address these issues, but before it could be selected the meeting broke up in disorder.[61]

During the first quarter of the twentieth century the weight of federal wardship was at its peak, both locally and nationally. Federal policies in this period were aimed at eradicating tribal governance, religion, and culture and brought long-term destruction to many tribal communities. Across the United States, tribes attempted to maintain control of governing systems, economic systems, family structure, and religious systems, but often with little success. Tribes and Indians fought to maintain or to reduce federal control in various ways. For the Menominee, unlike many other tribes, the law was specifically on their side. Unfortunately, that did not seem to make their fight any easier.

CHAPTER SEVEN

From Allotment to Incorporation

Federal mismanagement and control over Menominee resources only served to increase Menominee resentment of U.S. oversight and to strengthen tribal resolve to do something about it. The 1920s proved to be a crucial decade in the history of Menominee political resistance and self-determination. During the 1920s the tribe attempted to hold the United States to its major responsibility—directing tribal development under the 1908 law. Instead of fulfilling this duty, federal officials attempted to make one after another astonishing changes that, in the federal view, would bring the tribe to self-sufficiency. Though the Menominee also desired self-sufficiency, they were unwilling to permit the United States to relinquish its trust-based responsibility to the tribe. Although the Menominee considered all of the federal proposals and made some proposals of their own, tribal leaders could not come to an agreement with federal officials on how they should be carried out, and eventually they rejected them. The outcome of two key issues, allotment and incorporation, helped shape modern Menominee governance.

ALLOTMENT

Despite the tribe's rich forest resource, the Indian Service continued to hope to individualize Menominee holdings and to turn tribal members into farmers. The Menominee accepted the concept of allotment in 1919 under Superintendent Edgar A. Allen, a strong supporter of allotment as a method to end federal supervision of Indians, but they did not accept it under the terms Allen proposed. Not until the late 1920s would the fundamental differences between the Menominee and federal definitions of allotment become fully crystallized.

Allen pushed the Menominee to allot because it would be a first step toward removing Indians from federal responsibility, toward providing "equal rights and equal opportunity" for all races.[1] Allen, according to J. P. Kinney, "never regarded seriously the provisions of the act of March 28, 1908 . . . requiring that the Menominee timber be cut under conservative principles. He was very strongly of the opinion that the said legislation was a great mistake, against the best interests of the Menominee, and that such legislation and forestry practice should not for a moment stand in the way of his plan to individualize the holdings of the Menominees at the earliest possible date."[2]

The Menominee supported the concept of diminished federal oversight. However, in 1920 they reversed the 1919 vote that had accepted allotment.[3] The issue remained contentious. A week later Allen sent a copy of the allotment bill, which was pending before both houses of Congress, to every adult tribal member with instructions to discuss the issue with their families. He sent about 900 letters and received 538 replies, with 482 in favor of and 56 in opposition to allotment.[4] The tribe was on record again in support of the allotment policy.

Allen believed that tribal opposition to allotment would not exist at all if it were not for Mitchell Oshkenaniew. Oshkenaniew came into prominence within the tribe as a member of the new leadership that developed as a result of logging. While he hailed from a long-standing family of leaders, his role was nonetheless a new one. The new economic climate caused a development of greater sophistication in tribal leadership and brought new styles of leadership into the tribe as business-savvy tribal members established a constitutional form of government that gave them a significant role in tribal decision making.[5] The new system both reinforced and challenged the old tribal governing system that derived from family and band membership. That system had already been undergoing change as federal officials worked to disempower tribal leadership. Tribal leaders used new systems in an attempt to regain tribal control.

Despite his entrepreneurial bent, Oshkenaniew made decisions based not on what would be best for his pocketbook but on what would be best for the tribe as a whole. In this way he followed a longstanding tradition by which tribal leaders took on new roles defined by their relationship to the changing world—a world that increasingly impinged on tribal society—all the while keeping tribal needs at the forefront in their decision making.[6]

Allen believed he knew better than Oshkenaniew what was good for the tribe. He warned the commissioner of Indian affairs about Oshkenaniew: "He is an inveterate enemy of the Indian Office and all connected therewith although when he appears at your office he will endeavor to lead you to believe that he is working in harmony with the Department. There is no other single influence on the Reservation that works so much harm to these Indians because he puts in all his time spreading discontent among the illiterate and superstitious, who have been taught to be fearful of every measure proposed by a white man."[7] Allen seems to have been out of step with the commissioner's office at this point in time, however. Despite Allen's support of allotment, the department made no plans to proceed with it. Assistant Commissioner of Indian Affairs E. B. Merritt wrote to tribal member Louis LaFrombois in 1921, "The Office does not contemplate allotting the lands at Menominee in the immediate future."[8]

Allen did not give up, and the allotment issue reared its head again in 1925. That year Congressman Edward E. Browne of Wisconsin's Eighth District, which included Shawano County and therefore a portion of the Menominee reservation, brought a bill to authorize Menominee allotment before the House of Representatives. In House and Senate reports accompanying the bill, Congressman Browne said he introduced it at the request of a Menominee delegation that "had been sent to Washington by the tribe and instructed by the tribe to request that such a bill be introduced." Allen informed Browne that the tribe had voted 482–56 in favor of the bill, reporting the vote from five years previous. Allen also told Browne that those who opposed the bill were merely "some discontented Indians who oppose all progress." Oshkenaniew was doubtless one of these malcontents: his opposition continued to thwart Allen's plans. This time there was support from higher up the federal hierarchy. Charles Henry Burke, a strong supporter of allotment, was now the commissioner of Indian affairs. His boss, Secretary of the Interior Hubert Work, a 1923 Coolidge appointee, supported the bill. Work believed it had support of a "majority of the Indians of the Menominee Reservation."[9] This statement was likely based on the disputed five-year-old vote.

Events at a two-day General Council meeting in May 1925 made the secretary's contention questionable, however. U.S. forester J. P. Kinney, who attended the meeting, reported that tribal leaders denounced the balloting process that had led to the favorable revote in 1920.[10] Dr. Samuel Blair, sent by the secretary of the interior on an inspection of the reservation, convened the council to discuss both the mill operation and allotment. Wisconsin congressman George Schneider, a state senator, the Wisconsin attorney general, and other dignitaries attended the meeting, prompting Blair to observe that "this is really the greatest Indian Council Meeting that I have ever attended."[11] It occurred at the height of federal mismanagement of the Menominee forest. Tribal leaders worked hard locally and in Washington to put an end to this mismanagement, which formed the basis of discussion at numerous tribal council proceedings in this era.[12] Nonetheless, allotment was important enough to the tribe to warrant discussion during a large portion of this two-day council.

The meetings began Saturday morning with a discussion of allotment. Congressman Schneider of the Ninth District, which included Oconto County and therefore a portion of the Menominee reservation, began by speaking in opposition to the allotment bill. Several Menominees followed suit. Most cited the cases of both the Oneida and Stockbridge, Menominee neighbors who had been allotted on ceded Menominee lands some twenty years previously. They "are now poor Indians," Peter Pamonicutt said. "I know where to go when I want to go home; those Indians . . . have no homes to go to. That is why I oppose allotment." Another man pointed out that "After twenty years, you can go there [to Stockbridge land] and you will not see a Stockbridge there, they are all white men. That is my view of allotment." Still another pointed out that Menominees had served to protect the United States during the world war; the United States should stand by its treaty promises to protect the Menominee on their land. [13]

Pamonicutt concluded his talk by refusing to trade away his children's most important physical inheritance, Menominee land. Alluding to the schoolhouse in which they were meeting, he said, "Here is where [Indian children] receive educations to compete with White people. There are different institutions all over the country filled with Indian children learning the ways of White people. I leave it to this new generation to break up this reservation when they see fit. If I take this allotment, I am going to cut my own throat." [14]

In this statement, Pamonicutt both rejects American cultural values, in which individual enterprise and ownership play the primary role, and affirms Menominee cultural values, in which tribal control of the resources is a right of the future generations and a responsibility of the present generation. It is interesting to note that, although he rejects American values, he accepts the advantages of the white education system as a way to improve quality of life— but in a tribally defined way. Allotment as defined by the United States simply did not provide the necessary mechanism for tribal control.

Before the Saturday morning meeting adjourned two Menominees, both in the employ of Agency Superintendent Allen, spoke in favor of allotment. Dr. Blair also expressed his opinion, supporting Allen:

As it stands today, you have . . . [t]wo hundred and thirty two thousand acres [of land] within the bounds of this reservation. This really is owned by all the members of this Tribe. It is owned by 1800 Indians who are enrolled as members of the Tribe, yet no one Indian owns a single foot of land. The land that you have where you live and where you have your home is not yours. That land belongs to the Tribe as a whole. If you have built for yourself a house and are living within that house today, the land on which that house stands does not belong to you.[15]

Blair did not recognize that to many Menominees this arrangement was the proper order of things. He simply failed to comprehend the value of tribal land control as opposed to individual land ownership.

After taking Sunday off, the council took up allotment again on Monday. By then the federal forester and most of the dignitaries had departed. Mitchell Oshkenaniew challenged the government's opinion that the tribe supported allotment. He read a document that apparently disputed Agent Allen's contention that the 1919 vote of the tribe supported allotment. Unfortunately, he failed to submit that document to the secretary, so it went unrecorded in the minutes. Oshkenaniew opened the floor up to comments, and one tribal member accused a government employee of threatening both him and his father that the government would not disburse individual Indian money unless they agreed to allotment. Agent Allen denied any knowledge of this and said he had expressly forbidden the accused employee "to exert . . . influence . . . for or against the measure." Several other Menominees, however, charged that government officials used coercion.[16] Dr. Blair, probably because he favored allotment, refused to call for a vote on the issue at the council meeting.

Like most officials of his day, Blair could not believe Indians were competent to make their own decisions. He believed Congressman Schneider may have "influenced" tribal members to vote against the bill. Congressman Schneider himself, Blair believed, had been influenced by Mitchell Oshkenaniew, "who seemed to be opposed to everything advocated by either the Superintendent of the Agency or the Indian Bureau in Washington." According to Blair, Oshkenaniew had spoken against allotment at a Chamber of Commerce meeting in Appleton the previous winter, "and as a result of that address many of the citizens in Appleton had brought pressure to bear upon Congressman Schneider and evidently had induced him to champion the cause of Oshkenaniew and other Indians on the floor of Congress."[17] Schneider was from Appleton; Browne, who introduced the bill, was from Waupaca. Both were Republicans who lived almost equidistant from the reservation, the former in the southeast, the latter in the southwest; both of their jurisdictions included portions of the reservation.

Blair believed that the other Menominees who spoke against allotment were under both Schneider's and Oshkenaniew's influence. He added, "These Indians gave no logical reason for their opposition to the allotment."[18] A sympathetic reading of the evidence, however, especially in the context of the experiences of other tribes, reveals these Menominee concerns to be both logical and relevant. A closer look at the allotment bill and Menominee responses to it shows even greater logic in the Menominee opposition to allotment.

The bill called for distribution of Menominee land in eighty-acre lots to heads of household, with the United States holding the land in trust for twenty-five years and then turning it over to the individual owners in land patents. The federal government could cut the merchantable timber on the allotments for the tribe's benefit, but the rights to any other timber would pass to the allottee. The secretary of the interior reserved the right to hold back valuable timberlands from allotment but recognized that allotment would require more than 147,000 of the tribe's total of approximately 232,000 acres.

The bill made no mention of the disposition of the remaining 85,000 acres of land, nor of how the proposed law affected the requirements of the LaFollette law, which stipulated that the federal government manage the tribe's forest in perpetuity. Allotment would break up the tribal land base and destroy the economic foundation of the tribal resource. Though this foundation had already been diminished by mismanagement, it was still salvageable. Tribal members hoped to retain the forest and to farm their own small plots. They wanted their individual plots of land recognized but not at the expense of losing the forest, which they understood to be their key resource.

The bill implied that, during the twenty-five-year trust period, the United States would manage the forest for the tribe. However, at that time, the state laid claim to more than 26,000 acres, and some 30,000 acres were unsuitable to forestry or farming, according to J. P. Kinney. This would leave virtually no forest land to be managed after allotment. The bill permitted the United States to grant land for schools, for the agency, and for religious purposes in tracts of up to ten acres and also to set aside townsites.[19] After twenty-five years, all allotted lands would somehow be privately owned.

At this point, in October 1925, the Menominee League of Women Voters proposed several amendments to the bill in a resolution presented to the Menominee Advisory Council. The league consisted of a group of women, including Lily Oshkosh, Rhoda House, and Susan Corn, who had organized to become a political force to advocate on behalf of tribal interests. Their amendments delineated the problems tribal members saw with the way the bill was written. The league suggested, for example, that section 2 of the bill be amended to read "All unallotted lands shall be held for subsequent allotment" instead of "That the Secretary of the Interior may, in his discretion, reserve from allotment lands chiefly valuable for the timber thereon, or that may, in his opinion, be needed for reforestation." The league also suggested amending section 3 from saying that minerals would be reserved as common tribal property "during the period of trust" to saying that these would be "reserved perpetually as the common property of the Tribe." Another recommended change would have required the appointment of a three-person board to adjudicate conflicting allotment claims, with one person appointed by the agency superintendent, one by the governor of Wisconsin, and one by the Menominee tribe. Such a board, if implemented, would give the tribe more control in the distribution of its land.[20] All the information regarding the allotment bill indicates that the United States intended to remove itself from tribal oversight after the twenty-five-year trust period and to immediately remove the tribe's government from any governing role. The United States envisioned individualizing the resources, while the Menominee intended to strengthen communal or tribal control.

Agent Allen left the reservation in 1925, but the issue of allotment remained. In 1926 Flora Warren Seymour—an assimilationist, author of children's books about Indians, and former Indian Service employee—visited the reservation on behalf of the BIC to report on conditions.[21] The BIC, established as a watchdog for the Indian Service, generally served in a supportive rather than oversight role. Seymour referred to allotment, rather than the forest, as "the fundamental question with the Menominee Indians." She believed that allotment would be successful so long as it drew on lessons from the past. She argued that land patents should be made available in ten years instead of twenty-five, so that tribal members could sell them more quickly if they failed at farming. She also supported immediately selling the other tribal resources, including the forest. Her views simply mirrored those of Agency Superintendent William Donner, Allen's replacement.[22]

Donner's supervisor, District Superintendent Peyton Carter, who worked out of the Minneapolis office, also supported allotment. In October 1927 he wrote, "I am convinced that there is nothing of more importance to the general welfare of the Menominie Indians than that their reservation be allotted. . . . [T]he Office should energetically and enthusiastically promote the plan and see that it is actually accomplished during the coming season of Congress." It was Carter's view that the Menominee land was only fair farmland, which made it ideal for allotment. He believed it would attract "courageous . . . sturdy and thrifty" non-Indian farmers, whose presence would help wean Indians from their "primitive state" by "bring[ing] roads, town governments, and public schools." A "liberal selling plan" would be necessary so that tribal members could sell most of their land to these white pioneers.[23]

There was now increasing debate at the higher policymaking level regarding the efficacy of allotment. By this time both outside scholars and some American policymakers had begun to view allotment as the wrong answer to tribal needs. Though Commissioner of Indian Affairs Burke supported allotment, Secretary of the Interior Work in 1926 commissioned a study of problems and recommendations of solutions under the direction of Lewis Meriam of the Institute for Government Research, now known as the Brookings Institution. The resulting 1928 Meriam Report viewed allotment as a debilitating policy for Indian tribes in general and predicted for the Menominee that it would be an outright disaster.[24] Nonetheless, in 1930 Agency Superintendent W. R. Beyer, Donner's successor, urged immediate allotment. At that time Menominees were abandoning their farms, and OIA officials argued that failure to allot was the cause. Yet non-Indians surrounding the reservation in all directions but east were also abandoning their farms in the 1920s due to lack of productivity.[25]

Considering the strong support of the agency superintendents and the strong federal push to allot Indian lands, it seems astonishing that this fate did not befall the Menominee. Aside from Congressman Schneider, the tribe had little support from outsiders to defeat allotment. That they succeeded can be attributed to the battles fought off the reservation by Mitchell Oshkenaniew and others on the tribe's behalf and to the clear understanding that a significant portion of the tribe's members had of the *Menominee* definition of allotment, a definition from which the tribe never faltered. Despite the Menominee practice of avoiding council meetings and votes when an individual opposed an issue, enough opposition arose to prevent the federal government from allotting the Menominee during these years. The Menominee, by tying tribal retention of the resource base into any allotment agreements, nullified the purpose of the bill, which was to end tribal control, to force individual Indians to support themselves without tribal connections, and to allow white entrepreneurs to seize many of these resources.

THE TRIBAL ECONOMY

The Menominee, after they were unable to define allotment in tribal terms, began to reconsider how best to utilize the forest as a resource base for the tribal economy. Federal mismanagement was so blatant and discouraging that they began to consider how to get out from under federal control altogether, as well as how to make the United States pay for its mistakes. These efforts would become the new focus of tribal leaders, even as federal officials continued to lay waste to tribal resources.

Menominee frustration with federal oversight built to a crescendo in the late

1920s. While they pushed for allotment, agent after agent continued to favor non-Menominees in logging and millwork. Agency Superintendent Shepard Freeman had argued at his hearing in 1908 that he let Indians lose money on contracts without intervening because he wanted them to learn the lessons of business.[26] The agents who succeeded him, however, did not even pay lip service to teaching the Menominee how to run their business; they believed instead that the tribe needed further education in civilization before the government should allow them to run their own affairs, and they believed that the forest would not provide for the tribe forever.

Agency Superintendent William Donner, appointed in 1925, followed the pattern of his predecessors and refused to allow Menominee participation in decision making. When he arrived the tribe met in General Council to take up such issues as allotment, inequality of pay in logging and millwork, and the rescission of a 1925 amendment to the 1908 law that allowed white people to do some of the logging on the reservation. But Donner put off these issues until more of the tribe could be there to discuss them and argued that the superintendent was not a "cure all."[27]

Donner openly opposed the tribe's desire to govern itself. He told the Menominee, before the council's conclusion, "I will say that if the Department withdrew the employees from this reservation and turned it over to you, you wouldn't last six months. You know that you have vultures on every side that would flock in. The employees are here for your protection, the education of your children and your welfare. It may be that some of them are not serving to full capacity that is also the case among some of your own people; you do just as little as you can for the money."[28] Donner defended incompetent federal employees by accusing Menominees of loafing on the job!

In reality, the Indian Service had done a poor job protecting Menominee interests. Some twenty thousand acres had been clear-cut under Donner's predecessors, and he continued the practice. Unfortunately, this area of the forest would not regenerate for generations. Donner, who lacked forest experience, sarcastically stated that trying to perpetuate the Menominee forest after all the clear-cutting that had been done was like "locking the barn door after the horse is stolen."[29] He also believed that other materials would soon replace wood as an important building material, rendering the Menominee forest relatively valueless, an idea that he used to justify clear-cutting.[30]

Not all federal employees were so myopic. A case in point is Lloyd O. Grapp, whom the Department of the Interior had assigned to oversee forestry operations on the Menominee reservation in 1922. The agents ignored Grapp's advice and excluded him from participation in planning meetings until 1925.

Up to that point he confined his efforts to creating a tree nursery. In 1926 he introduced the idea of selective cutting.[31] After Donner left in 1927 the federal government under Grapp's direction instituted a plan of selective cutting, harvesting 70 percent of mature trees in 1927. In 1934 they would reduce this to 50 percent and in 1938 to 30 percent, which allowed the forest to regenerate more quickly. The Menominee were convinced that this method would provide the tribe with a perpetual forest harvest.[32] Seeing the results, the Menominee recognized within two years that selective cutting was a superior method of forest management. The federal officials in Washington recognized it quickly too. Had Grapp been involved sooner, no doubt some of the waste could have been avoided.

In direct opposition to the employees of the OIA stood Menominee tribal leadership, which acted in two ways: either in an advisory role to the agency superintendent or in a protest role, generally through petitions or delegations sent to Washington. Both methods, however, were reactive. Federal officials did not permit Menominees to develop their own initiatives (though sometimes they did so anyway); they were only allowed to exert their political influence in the hope of reshaping federal decisions and actions. The Menominee restructured their government and created an Advisory Council in a new constitution approved by the commissioner of Indian affairs in 1924, but they still used the General Council for tribal decision making.[33] Although the commissioner of Indian affairs had requested the formation of the Advisory Council to avoid strife, he refused to relinquish any control, since ultimately he would be held responsible for the fate of the Menominee.[34] Because of this, much of the authority vested in the councils was merely theoretical.

As a result, in the late 1920s the General Council and the Advisory Council, both long ignored by the federal officials on the reservation, began to work to expand their spheres of influence. In 1928 the tribe reestablished the Advisory Council that forms the general basis for today's Menominee tribal government. The General Council, which consisted of all adult members of the tribe, in theory served to provide oversight for Advisory Council decisions. Political scientist Nicholas Peroff has pointed out that the General Council, being an inefficient decision-making body based on consensus that rarely met, did not serve as much of a check on the Advisory Council, which in actuality would eventually come to direct tribal affairs.[35] The General Council could be effective, however. Menominees had long left decision making to a small group; they had also long used the adult community as a whole through their General Council to empower or disempower that group, as they had done with the Business Committee in early logging years, for example.

Two issues brought federal management and the reasons for Menominee opposition to it into stark relief: the definition of economy and job discrimination. These two issues were connected to twin federal efforts to streamline operations and to make the economy more "efficient," both of which tribal members opposed. The first effort was the addition of a second band saw to the mill in Neopit; the second was the extension of the railroad across the Wolf River into the northeast section of the reservation, into the vicinity of the South Branch community. Federal officials had proposed both efforts as early as 1912, but they came to a head in the late 1920s.

The addition of another saw at the mill would double the output and put an end to nighttime shift work. Agent after agent supported another saw, and Seymour reported on it favorably after her 1926 visit. The Menominee opposed it because it would permit the mill manager to hire more white workers and because those Menominees who worked the night shift would lose their jobs.[36]

The railroad spur would run into land that remained largely uncut due to its distance from the market. The track would run from the mill in Neopit directly to the South Branch region. South Branch families especially opposed this extension. Numerous families in this area, many of mixed blood, were largely farmers who supplemented their income with some logging. Individuals hauled their timber to market. They lived too far from Neopit to both maintain their farms and work in the mill, so they preferred the status quo. Though their logging was small-scale and inefficient by American standards, it served to supply the families with enough support to earn a living. They feared for their future if large-scale logging laid waste to the forest in their homeland as it had done in other parts of the reservation.[37]

These two proposals reflect very different conceptions of the purpose of the forest and the mill and ultimately the definition of economy. The United States viewed these resources in terms of potential profit. The Menominee, on the other hand, viewed them as sources of work, often to supplement other sources of income. At this time people also supplemented their income by making baskets and reed mats for the tourist trade, by picking berries, and by gathering ferns, for which florists paid ninety cents per thousand leaves. Individuals also hunted, fished, and gathered to put food on the table and collected their own medicinal plants, as tribal members long had done.[38] The timber sources were best exploited a little at a time, and certainly not by non-Indians, who added nothing to the welfare of the tribe.

Non-Indians and squatters were indeed a problem frequently remarked on by tribal members.[39] One tribal member, voicing common concerns, wrote to

the commissioner of Indian affairs in frustration about the issues of employment, job discrimination, and white encroachment on the reservation:

> The Tribe owns all this property, and should have all the benefits from it, and
> members of the tribe should be given first chance to be employed at anything
> that which he can do on the Reservation, there are at the present time a lot
> of white persons employed on the reservation at jobs which any Menominee,
> and member of the tribe can perform, but those places are filled by white men,
> which should be given to members of the tribe. . . . [T]hey hunt and fish on the
> reservation, others bring cattle here and pasture them on the reservation free,
> besides getting away from paying taxes, there is the police department, [white]
> people are drunk most every night on our streets, why not give these jobs to an
> Indian? he can do as well as a whiteman, at that job, it is his money, he needs it.[40]

MENOMINEE INCORPORATION

The heightening tribal frustrations regarding forest mismanagement issues,
the fight over railroad expansion and the double band saw, the drawn-out
battle over allotment, and their lack of allies in these fights increasingly led
tribal leaders to the conclusion that they needed to gain greater control of
the management of both their economic resources and their political affairs.
Many of the new tribal leaders, including Mitchell Oshkenaniew and Reginald
Oshkosh, not only were members of old leading families but had also received
boarding school education.[41] They believed that the purpose of their training
was to help them fulfill the requirements of the LaFollette Act in preparing
tribal members for leadership positions.

The reservation was still divided into communities based on band affiliation
and religion, as it had been since its establishment. Catholic families lived
in places such as Keshena and South Branch, practitioners of the traditional
religion had moved west to Zoar, and the small Native American Church group
lived in their own area. The new mill town of Neopit drew people from across
the reservation, although men sometimes came alone and set up a second
residence there, while their families remained in their old homes. Catholic
tribal members, who as children were more likely to gain a formal U.S.-style
education, more often, though not exclusively, filled formal leadership positions. To some extent tribal roles were still defined by the band affiliations that
had determined original settlement patterns on the reservation. But despite
the social and economic divisions that resulted from this separation, tribal
members from all areas of the reservation had a common understanding that

the forest needed to provide for them, and they recognized the problems in federal management of their resource.

John Collier, executive secretary of the American Indian Defense Association, first articulated the idea of incorporation to the tribe in a speech he made to a small crowd at Keshena Falls in about June 1926. He told tribal members that a bill before Congress might soon turn management of tribal affairs over to the tribe. BIC inspector Flora Warren Seymour scoffed at Collier's idea, probably reflecting the opinions of many white officials: "Such a proposition implies that while Menominees are not to be trusted individually with a farm apiece, for fear they will lose it, they can collectively be given not only the land, but the management of large power and timber interests, the running of a big sawmill, with the railroad and other activities it entails. Out of nineteen hundred incapacities is to arise a great super-capacity. The whole is to be several times the sum of its parts. The mere statement of this proposition indicates its impractionbility."[42]

In 1928, at the height of forest and agricultural conflict, the Meriam Report echoed Collier's idea and suggested incorporation as a solution to Menominee problems. The recommendations in the Meriam Report surprisingly foreshadowed the next half-century of the tribe's history. Incorporation became the second great ancillary battleground of the 1920s and 1930s.

For the Menominee, the Meriam Report served as an important symbol of the future. Its recommendations, which both the tribe and the federal government attempted to implement, shaped Menominee political and economic history. The report suggested that the United States use the Menominee tribe and another timber-rich tribe, the Klamath of Oregon, to test incorporation as a plan for meeting the economic future of tribes. Because of their timber resources, both the Menominee and the Klamath were wealthier than most tribes. Incorporation, as envisioned in the report, would "individualiz[e] the holdings of the Klamath and Menominee Indians without allotting their timber lands."[43]

Federal purposes had not changed—the United States still intended for individual Menominees to make it on their own. But tribal purposes had not changed either. The Menominee were unwilling to sacrifice group welfare for individual advancement. The result was continuing conflict. The proposal to form an economic corporation to replace both the reservation as a federal trust–managed land base and the tribal government became part of the continuous struggle for control between the tribe and the federal government that had gone on since the establishment of the reservation. This incorporation intended to give control of the Menominee forest to adult members of the tribe as corporate shareholders.

As had happened twice already—with the introduction of U.S.-planned farming in the 1850s and with the creation of the logging business in 1890—the tribe and the United States both proposed to use the same means but to different ends. As before, the tribe and the federal government agreed on the actions needed to improve the Menominee future, but again the two sides differed in the definition of that future. The federal government, as always, wanted Menominees to meet the future as individuals by individualizing property holdings. The Menominee tenaciously insisted they do so as a tribe. Both sides agreed, however, that the key to the Menominee future was control of both the timber resource and tribal affairs.

The Meriam Report suggested a conservative approach to incorporation for the Menominee. It would mean ending the federal wardship by creating a corporation to oversee the tribal resource. A group whom the Meriam commissioners identified as the "intelligent progressive Indians" among the Klamath told the investigators they wanted to liquidate resources immediately and pay individual tribal members the money for them; they did not want the forest land.[44] The Menominee, by contrast, refused to sell their forest; they wanted to manage it themselves. A board of directors made up of Menominees and a majority of federal government officials would administer the exploitation of the timber. Each tribal member would receive a share either to work or to sell.[45] The latter method was similar to the one used on the Menominee reservation between 1890 and 1908. The key to incorporation, however, according to the Meriam Report, was to detribalize the resource so that individual Indians could get the capital to run their own farms or to "improve" themselves in whatever way they saw fit. Eventually, the goal was for the Indians to control the board of directors. The Meriam Report presented the Klamath as more intelligent and advanced than the Menominee, probably because of their desire to distribute the tribe's wealth individually.[46]

The Menominee, who had refused to accept allotment except on a tribal basis, responded similarly to incorporation. They were willing to try it but only on Menominee terms, not on those suggested in the Meriam Report. A fervent supporter of Menominee incorporation was the author Phebe Jewell Nichols, who had prepared a socioeconomic report on behalf of the Meriam commissioners in 1928.[47] Nichols was married to a Menominee man, Angus Lookaround, and they lived on the Menominee reservation until his death. Many of her writings, even her highly romanticized fiction, accurately portray some aspects of Menominee history and conditions on the reservation. One of her romance novels, *Sunrise of the Menominees*, includes a thinly fictionalized description of Menominee efforts to achieve incorporation against the opposition of local government agents. For her discussion of tribal governance and incorporation, she relied heavily on the journals of Ralph Fredenberg, a leader of the Menominee protest against conditions on the reservation and a frequent member of the delegations to Washington. The description of the tribe's frustrations rings true until Nichols predicts the future by finishing her novel with a semiutopian description of life on the reservation after incorporation.[48]

Nichols wrote in a small pamphlet on incorporation, "Indian Bureau control has brought the Menominee Indians not a satisfactory adjustment to the white man's progress but years of maladjustment," even though the tribe had eleven million dollars in assets and resources worth more than thirty million dollars. From its own money, the tribe paid for all of the federal services it received. Commissioner of Indian Affairs Burke once said, "Not one cent of government money is spent on the Menominee Reservation." Yet although the Menominee provided all this funding, they had almost no voice in how the government spent it.[49]

Part of the reason why incorporation seemed so promising was the tribe's increasing anger over federal mismanagement of the Menominee forest and sawmill. According to Nichols, when Advisory Council members traveled to Washington to protest this mismanagement, they were discriminated against in their jobs back home. This is possible since the government agent and the government-employed mill agent controlled most of the jobs on the reservation. After the harsh winter of 1928–29, a Menominee delegate traveled to Washington to obtain a special investigation of affairs on the reservation.[50]

In April 1929 Mitchell Oshkenaniew charged that Ralph Fredenberg was fired from his job for his role as a critic and delegate. Fredenberg had demanded evidence of blacklisting and firings of tribal members from mill manager George C. Hammer. Hammer responded that the firings, including Fredenberg's, were reasonable. He went on to proclaim, "It is time to call a halt to the 'horseplay' as conducted by these so-called leaders of the Menominees. They are not interested in the welfare of the Tribe, but are willing to sacrifice the Tribe at any time to further their own interests."[51]

Fredenberg then wrote Senator Robert M. LaFollette Jr., Fighting Bob's son, in May 1929, requesting that he instigate an investigation.

I finally mention the systematic policy of the Indian Bureau Forestry Service to disregard the requirements of the Act of 1908 with respect to giving Indians preference in employment. Indians are consistently discriminated against in employment, and, in addition, we assert that members of the Menominee Tribe, heretofore employed in milling operations, have been and are blacklisted for no other alleged offense except that they have tried to call the attention of the Secretary of Interior to glaring abuses. These abuses are so glaring that they are a matter of common knowledge and of joking among the lumbering concerns of Wisconsin.

This letter prompted LaFollette to pressure Secretary of the Interior Roy Lyman Wilbur to dispatch another team of special investigators. Fredenberg requested that they be appointed from outside the Department of the Interior, preferably from the Department of Agriculture's forestry programs. Wilbur insisted he had competent men he could send. The lead investigator was Ernest P. Rands of the General Land Office. His final report became known as the "Rands Report."[52]

In the report Rands took testimony regarding job discrimination and forest and mill mismanagement. He recommended the firing of Hammer, whom he called incompetent but honest. He pointed out that the employment policy permitted 420 whites and only 330 Indians—including non-Menominee Indians—to work in the forest and the mill. This was "certainly not in compliance with either the letter or intent of the [1908] law." He also recommended against both the addition of a second band saw and the building of the railroad spur to the northeast, both of which he believed would have negative impacts on Menominee employment.[53] Menominee supporters of incorporation hoped that greater tribal control of the economy would correct this.

In September 1929 the Advisory Council, together with William Kershaw, a Menominee attorney who practiced in Milwaukee, brought the first mismanagement suit by the tribe in federal court. Kershaw believed the Indian Bureau "was made up of incompetents." The council used the suit in an attempt to block a logging road that accessed ninety million feet of pine along the Wolf River. In part, they feared the new road would be too efficient—thus putting tribal members who hauled logs by team out of work. The petitioners included Mitchell Oshkenaniew, James Caldwell, Ralph Fredenberg, and Charles Frechette, among others. "We charge gross mismanagement and waste," the Advisory Council said in a statement. They charged that agency officials had depleted tribal funds and destroyed the tribal resource, and they demanded an audit of the Neopit mill. The Indian Bureau fought the charges by having the venue moved from federal court in Milwaukee, which was an easy travel distance for tribal members, to Washington.[54]

In October, incensed at federal obstruction, the tribe in council voted to incorporate and to send a delegation to Washington to "register their claims of millions of dollars of loss."[55] The commissioner of Indian affairs was inclined to allow the tribe to investigate the idea of incorporation, but local federal officials opposed it entirely, believing tribal members to be incompetent to run their own affairs.[56]

Local officials also continued to deny any culpability in mismanagement. Agency Superintendent William Beyer attempted to placate the Menominee by appointing Fredenberg as personnel officer to assure that Menominees were hired at the mill. The position lacked authority, however, and conditions failed to improve.[57] Beyer, who served from 1928 to 1934, favored allotment as the only answer for the Menominee. He reasoned, "History has proven the communal life does not tend to progress, either industrially or financially."[58]

The Menominee protesters, however, persevered. The tribe sent a three-member delegation to Washington in 1930—this time consisting of Fredenberg, Charles Frechette, and Peter LaMotte—to hire attorneys and to seek incorporation. Fredenberg traveled to New York first and employed the law firm of Hughes, Schurman, and Dwight. Richard E. Dwight, a topnotch legal mind who served pro bono until Congress would permit the tribe to hire attorneys, met with the three delegates in Washington. He believed the tribe could make a claim against the United States for both "illegal cutting of timber and maladministration of the Menominee Mills." Congressman Browne brought two bills before Congress on behalf of the Menominee—one to allow them to file in the Court of Claims, the other to allow them to hire attorneys.[59]

The latter bill also accused the federal government of mismanaging tribal resources and called for an investigation of the possibility of tribal incorporation to gain control of their resources. The secretary of the interior's office defended its timber management and opposed the tribe's attempts to hire attorneys. The Department of the Interior also suggested the possibility of establishing a "joint-stock association" modeled after the Osages, rather than incorporation.[60] The tribe and the federal government continued to disagree on what incorporation should look like.

Hughes, Schurman, and Dwight drafted an act to incorporate that would be presented to Congress in May 1930. This bill was apparently presented to Congress but not brought to the floor. It clearly stated tribal hopes in relation to control of the resource: "The purposes of incorporation of the Menominee Tribe of Indians into Menominee Indian Corporation are to enable the Menominee Indians to preserve and maintain their own peculiar traditions and habits of life by ordinances of their own making and officers of their own choice and to enable them to take, hold, control and administer, manage, operate and dispose of the assets and property of the tribe and to exercise such powers and functions as are delegated to it by Congress." The corporation membership would consist of all enrolled tribal members, and a nine-member board of directors selected by the membership would govern it. The tribe's property would be held by the corporation in trust; the tribe's affairs would be managed by the corporation. The trust relationship would remain in place, and the tribe would control corporate directorship. After fifty years there would be the possibility of changing assets from trust to fee patent.[61] Fredenberg warned tribal members, however: "You understand that when this incorporation bill goes through the Department of the Interior will have nothing more to do with your business."[62]

The bills to allow the tribe to file in the Court of Claims and to hire attorneys did not pass at this session, in part due to opposition from Congressman Schneider, but both the OIA and Vice President Charles Curtis approved of the Menominee's choice of attorneys as members of a reputable law firm.[63] "We found that we assumed the right attitude with the Indian Bureau and with the Secretary's office," Fredenberg reported to the General Council. "Instead of trying to tear things down we tried to help them build things up. The Commissioner has said at various times in meetings where I happened to be present that he considered the Menominee Tribe one of the most highly advanced tribe of Indians in the United States. I have heard him also make the statement that the Menominee Tribe had gone ahead ten years this past winter as against other tribes dropping back ten years. Now what we must do is to keep going ahead. We daren't drop back."[64]

Incorporation and the tribal claim against the government were two faces of the same issue: federal control of Menominee resources had cost the tribe dearly and continued to do so. The Menominee attempted one method after the next to gain some semblance of control. Ralph Fredenberg, seeking outside allies, spoke to the Milwaukee League of Women Voters in November 1930. He stated Menominee concerns concisely: "We do not want charity. . . . All we ask is the support of citizens to obtain legislation that will give us the right to administer our own affairs and in this way solve the problems that beset us."[65]

In the Menominee view several issues were interconnected. The *Milwaukee Journal* reported, "The Indians declare that they do not want an allotment of lands, that they are in favor of selective logging and are willing to do all logging under the supervision of agents of the United States forestry service. They simply want to form a corporation similar to that of the Klamath Indians of Oregon, in which each adult Indian owns an equal share. They exhibit a petition asking for an accounting since 1908 and other relief."[66] The OIA now opposed incorporation, however, believing the Menominee to be incompetent to manage their own affairs. On 17 March 1931 District Superintendent Peyton Carter wrote the commissioner of Indian affairs that the plan to incorporate was unconstitutional, would be a disaster, and only gave tribal members false hopes.[67]

The issue of incorporation did not die here. Indeed, it helped define tribal politics for more than a decade to come. The Menominee had to find a way to gain control of their most valuable resources. The Rands Report would become a useful tool for tribal members hoping to bring about change. Meanwhile, even while the Menominee were defeating the push for allotment, fighting federal mismanagement, and taking the concept of incorporation under consideration, they were also fighting new battles over another valuable natural resource on the reservation, the Wolf River.

CHAPTER EIGHT

Illusory Control

In the late 1920s and early 1930s the tribal-federal battle over resources extended beyond allotment, incorporation, and mill and forest mismanagement. In this crucial decade in the history of Menominee political resistance, the tribe faced two new threats. First, Wisconsin Power and Light Company (WPL) attempted to gain authorization to dam the Wolf River to build commercial hydroelectric plants. Second, as a result of the opposition to this plan, Congressman George Schneider proposed purchasing that portion of the reservation along the Wolf River for the creation of a national park. A plethora of local interests attempted to sway the tribe, Congress, and the OIA on these two issues. Throughout the ensuing battles, the tribe continued in its efforts both to fight off outsiders attempting to define their future and to gain a modicum of control. A hopeful change would occur in 1934, after John Collier took over as commissioner of Indian affairs, when for the first time the Indian Bureau assigned a Menominee as agency superintendent. For an illusory moment it appeared that the tribe may actually be able to gain some control of its destiny.

HYDROELECTRIC POWER AND A MENOMINEE NATIONAL PARK

In April 1926 WPL, a corporation under the influence of Samuel Insull, applied to the Federal Power Commission (FPC) for a permit to build a hydroelectric dam on the Wolf River where it ran through the Menominee reservation. The next month WPL amended its application, this time seeking authorization to build six hydroelectric dams on the Wolf River, five on the reservation and one just below, near Shawano. The latter would flood river water back onto reservation lands. The other five would be located at Keshena Falls, Big Eddy Falls, Smoky Falls, the Dalles, and Sullivan Rapids and would flood a good portion of the river valley on the reservation.[1]

The tribe itself had sought congressional permission to build commercial hydroelectric dams. Agency Superintendent Donner commented to Congress, "It would probably be impossible for private corporations to get the Indians consent to develop this power" commercially, since they wanted to do it themselves. In the summer of 1926 the tribe built one dam for local needs, near Keshena Falls, which powered the town of Keshena. [2] Donner, an engineer, supported the development of commercial power on the reservation. So did riparian landowners downriver, who saw it as an opportunity to provide flood control for their property along the Wolf River. Donner, in commenting on their concerns, said at a public hearing in Milwaukee, "To me it is purely a commercial proposition for the benefit of the Indian. If it is going to benefit the riparians below the reservation, as the gentleman said it would, they owe us an additional million dollars, and they ought to pay it." At this, members of the audience applauded. He added, "We want to develop this power. It will perhaps ruin a few beauty spots, but I believe the majority of the Indians are in favor of the development of this water for commercial resources." He believed that there was one or two million dollars' worth of development and that it would create one or two million dollars' worth of lake frontage as well. [3]

Local sportsmen and sporting organizations, such as the Izaak Walton League, on the other hand, opposed the damming for the damage it would do to the fishery. Tribal member Frank Gauthier responded to their concerns:

> As far as the natural beauty of the Wolf River is concerned I am pretty sure that the Menominee Indians can handle that part in a manner to suit themselves. The Menominees are looking forward so as to realize some benefit from those power sites. . . . Furthermore, if the Wisconsin Power & Light Co. offers to buy the power sites, the Menominees are ready to consider such a deal. If the members of the Izaak Walton league or any organization which wants to save the natural beauty of the Wolf River, comes across with a few million dollars, the Menominees are ready to consider such a deal. [4]

The state of Wisconsin opposed the building of the dams as well. Attorney General John W. Reynolds believed incorrectly that Wisconsin, not the FPC, controlled all rivers and streams in the state. In fact, the FPC had authority over such waterways in Indian country, because Congress specifically granted it when it created the FPC. And Congress maintained plenary power over issues related to Indian country, as the Supreme Court had determined in *Lone Wolf v. Hitchcock*. [5]

By May 1927 Donner reported,

> The Indians almost unanimously are in favor of water power development, but their idea of the development has become somewhat conflicting because of the misrepresentation imposed upon them by the whites, instigated principally by the Isaak Walton League, and the Wisconsin Federated Band of Women's Clubs.

Both of these organizations are opposed to any development at all, their idea being to conserve the reservation in its natural state, with a primitive Indian here and there in the back ground to complete the setting for the thousands of tourists who are flocking to the reservation every summer. . . . This reservation favors the development of water power by the Indians, or rather through the Indians without the supervision of the Federal Power Commission.[6]

The tribe was not thrilled with the idea of the U.S. Indian Service supervising exploitation of the sites, either. Charles Chickeny said in an April 1927 General Council meeting, "If the dams are built they will stand for three or four generations and the money will be placed in the Treasury, so that the Bureau can spend it for us. That is what experience has shown." Another tribal member pointed out "[t]hat the reservation belongs to the tribe and the Menominee should be able to do as they liked about the question." Albert A. Grorud, an attorney who at one time served as a staffer on the Senate Indian affairs committee, observed that the Menominee should not try to control the project. He believed control would by default fall to the bureau, which would inevitably mismanage the project. Mitchell Oshkenaniew, on the other hand, encouraged tribal members to support the dam, out of a sense of desperation: "The resources are being wasted now," he said. "If the Indians do not get the money they will go hungry. Get some benefit out of it now."[7]

Eventually, the Shawano Dam was built, flooding 127 acres on the reservation, from which the tribe received fifteen hundred dollars annually. However, tribal opposition to the other dams steadily increased. Peyton Carter, the OIA district superintendent from Minneapolis, blamed the opposition on "10,000 outside friends," who he said were trying to protect the river for tourists.[8]

Nonetheless, the *Milwaukee Journal* reported dam construction by Insull's company on the reservation's portion of the river as a "certainty" on 15 September 1929. However, the FPC "agreed to leave the decision as to whether the river shall be dammed to the Indians." The Menominee in council had voted to give the General Council veto power over the Advisory Council to maintain control over this specific issue, among others.[9]

Only ten days later Reginald Oshkosh made the news with yet another proposal: that the OIA fund the Menominee to establish recreational parks along the Wolf River for use by the general public. Oshkosh said, "Menominees will resist to the last any attempt by individual corporations to destroy the reservation for power." The *Milwaukee Journal* reported on 25 September 1929, "The Indians, retaining title to the land, would exploit the Keshena area themselves for resort purposes rather than have power interests destroy its beauty by exploiting it for water power." Calling the tribe's lakes and streams "as pretty as paradise," Oshkosh said the Menominee would build and maintain roads, log cabins, and a fish hatchery to stock the waters with trout. Indeed, the Menominee reservation was already an attractive tourist area. Agency Super-intendent Donner reported, perhaps with some exaggeration, that some five thousand visitors from as far away as Chicago visited on summer weekends and that "almost as many people visited the Menominee Reservation during the summer as visited Yellowstone National Park."[10]

The tribe was trying desperately on several fronts now to gain control of its resources. It was not able to gain funding to establish a park, however. At the same time Congressman Schneider, probably spurred by Reginald Oshkosh's efforts, proposed a bill to turn six of the reservation's ten townships into a national park. Schneider argued that the tourist trade was an economic boon to tribal members. Advisory Council member Al Gauthier disputed this argument in a letter to Senator LaFollette: "When Mr. Schneider said that the Indians received substantial sums from the tourists who journey through our reservation, the most I know I got out of tourists, up until now is a lot of dust. There are . . . confectionery stands, we call them, that run during the summer months. No doubt they receive a few nickels from the tourists, but that does not benefit the Indians as a whole."[11] Here again is an example of the government trumpeting the success of the individual, while the tribe is more concerned with community-wide welfare.

Local newspapers supported Schneider's bill enthusiastically in early 1930, since it would help sustain local economics in areas surrounding the reserva-tion through the tourist trade. The *Antigo Journal* dubbed it "A Worthy Bill" and gushed, "Wisconsin has no national park. What better selection for such a park could be made than part of the Menominee reservation? Its timber surpasses in beauty anything to be found in the Yellowstone. It has an inter-esting Indian population that the Yellowstone does not have. The Wolf river is the wildest and most picturesque stream in the Middle West, and all of this is within a day's drive from Chicago and its metropolitan area." Regarding the Indian population, the paper also said, "There is plenty of room for the Indians, the entire reservation does not need to be placed in the proposed national park, and the Indians would prove an additional attraction. Many can be used as guides, boatmen, rangers, and in other occupations. Their basketry and handicrafts would be in great demand by national park visitors." The Menominee would be ideal tourist attractions for a society still enthralled by the "myth of the vanishing race."[12]

The *Wausau Herald Record* pointed out that the Schneider bill could pre-serve the Wolf River for tourists. Appleton and Green Bay papers published identical articles pointing out that the dam leases were based on pure greed and that individual Menominees would benefit to the tune of merely thirty dollars per person per year from the dams. Schneider estimated that, based on the value of the forest, each Menominee was worth twenty-seven thousand dollars. The newspapers opined, "Something is wrong when Indians so favorably situated feel compelled to submit to the exploitation of water power in the Wolf river for [such] a paltry return." The story went national when the *Washington Star* picked up an article and reported that the bill "would be a solution, eventually, of the mixed question of water power. . . . We should preserve this acreage of landscape and woodland, the singing river and the symphony of trees, for all time and all generations."[13]

Congressman Schneider's bill passed the House. Menominee tribal delegate Ralph Fredenberg followed the movement of this bill through the Committee on Public Lands and Parks. After it passed the House, he wrote Senator Gerald Nye of North Dakota, who chaired the Senate Committee on Public Lands and Grounds, lobbying against the bill. Commissioner of Indian Affairs Charles Rhoads observed, "This bill . . . was not introduced at the suggestion of the Indian Service, nor apparently on the suggestion of any one connected with the Department of the Interior." He added that the Menominee delegation to Washington strongly opposed the bill. A month's worth of hard work paid off with success: the bill failed to pass the Senate.[14] This was a victory for the tribe—a national park would not meet the Menominee needs of preserving tribal control of the resources.

Another success soon followed. In April 1930 the *Oshkosh Northwestern* reported, "Persistent and extensive opposition to waterpower development plans for the Menominee Indian reservation . . . has caused the Insull power people to announce they have no desire to press their proposition, if the public wants a park made of the Wolf river beauty spot."[15] The national park issue did not die, however. The Menominee League of Women Voters a year later passed a strongly worded resolution opposing creation of a national park on Menominee land, and the tribe voted to oppose it unanimously in council. In June 1932 Fredenberg observed that Schneider seemed to be using the bill as a tool to gain popularity in an election year, since it enjoyed little support among his colleagues.[16] It demanded considerable time and energy from Menominee leadership, however.

CONTINUING DISSATISFACTION

With the power and park threats behind them, the Menominee intended to continue to log their forest to provide themselves an economic foundation. Mismanagement of logging remained a primary tribal concern. A 9 August 1930 General Council meeting is especially revealing of the tribe's mood regarding this concern, because even statements made in Menominee were translated into English and recorded in the minutes. Often the assigned secretary failed to translate the Menominee-language statements, merely pointing out that someone spoke in Menominee rather than recording what that person said.

After the delegation members reported on business in Washington, the meeting moved on to the logging business. One resolution, which passed 169–0, proposed decreasing the annual cut to ten million feet. This would preserve the forest and allow Menominee loggers to do more of the work. The tribe viewed non-Indian laborers who logged on the reservation under the amended LaFollette law as a drain on tribal resources. According to the delegation, the commissioner of Indian affairs had agreed to allow Menominees to do a larger portion of the work supplying their mill. This plan, which did not actually go into effect, would have achieved that goal by reducing the amount of lumber cut and thus the extent of the need for outside labor.

Another resolution, which passed 141–0, called for the discontinuation of the policy of renting houses to Menominees in Neopit, allowing them to purchase them instead. Edwin Warrington argued that if all Menominees made homes for their families, the white "supervisors will begin to hold us in higher esteem."

> It will be so in time that, with the discontinuance of rented houses in Neopit, that there will be nothing but Menominees living up there. We will be able to work in that mill without being ousted out by some white man. There are a lot of jobs there in that mill that Indians have worked and taken care of like they should have, but there seems to be friction somewhere whereby he can't hold that job. If they don't get him out of there by bucking him out, they will pay him lower wages to get him out of there. If you are looking to better yourself I think it would be a good plan to support the resolution that has been presented.

Reginald Oshkosh spoke in Menominee of the sacrifices the tribe had made to keep its resources: "A lot of our old people now have passed away, those who have worked hard in order to save our properties, especially the timber. We can see now what the old people used to tell us, that some day the people would see how we have sacrificed many things in order to save our resources, i.e., the timber particularly." This was apparently meant as encouragement in the tribe's efforts to gain control of the logging.

Charles Chickeney ended the meeting by lamenting the apparent failure of the LaFollette law. Under the old 1890 law, he said, using "a dull axe, a dull saw and muskrat ponies," the Menominee had put aside nearly three million dollars. Under the LaFollette law, the Menominee were being told they were incompetent to manage their affairs.[17] Unfortunately, U.S. administration of the LaFollette law had thus far failed in the two major goals of perpetuating the forest and of training Menominees to manage the forest and the mill. Logging did provide employment and brought some returns to the tribe, however: in 1925, for instance, only thirty-nine Menominees—"all of whom were either mentally or physically incapacitated," in the words of the commissioner of Indian affairs—had received free rations, since logging provided support for so many tribal members.[18] Yet, it failed to add greatly to Menominee wealth. The tribe's nest egg had remained virtually unchanged since the passage of the law.

In 1931 the Menominee received congressional approval to hire the law firm of Hughes, Schurman, and Dwight. The lawyers reported in July 1932 that the tribe had substantial claims against the government. Again the OIA denied any culpability, countering with a report from an assistant forester in the U.S. Indian Service who refuted the Hughes report point by point.[19] Yet the tribe continued to protest, sending delegations to Washington and voting in council to oppose agency officials.

When the mill began sawing less timber, Fredenberg proposed running it ten hours a day, five days a week, until all the pine permitted for that season was processed. The mill manager, George C. Hammer, proposed running it three days a week to extend the number of weeks. Under Hammer's plan the white civil service employees could continue to draw their paychecks. Under Fredenberg's proposal the entire mill could be closed for part of the year, and a number of the supervisory positions could be eliminated, steps unanimously approved in General Council in June 1932.[20]

Fredenberg continued to lead delegations to Washington, despite opposition of agency officials, of officials in Washington, and of some tribal members. He claimed that the tribe had chosen him for the task. He spoke eloquently at a General Council meeting in 1933 about the difficult role of the tribal delegate-lobbyist in Washington. After three years, he observed, he found that his hide was no longer thick enough for the job. While a white man who does this kind of work for his community is respected, Fredenberg suggested, an Indian "immediately becomes [seen as] a crook, an agitator, and a kicker," in his view probably by both federal officials and fellow Menominees. He asked the elders to recall the stories about those who went to Washington as tribal delegates in the past. Yet the tribe had always been judicious in selecting people who looked after its interests in Washington, and he added that he was willing to go again if the tribe so decided. "I do not want to hide myself and I don't want to refuse the tribe if they call on me." The council then chose Fredenberg, James Caldwell, and Aloysius Dodge as the delegates.[21]

The year 1933 set the stage for improved Menominee-federal relations. President Franklin D. Roosevelt appointed John Collier as commissioner of Indian affairs, and Collier initiated the "Indian New Deal." This policy shift formally recognized the failure of allotment and the assimilation it was supposed to bring. The Menominee delegation in Washington at the time of Collier's appointment lent him its support. The tribe voted in council to support the Indian Reorganization Act (IRA), a law intending to recognize some inherent rights of tribal self-rule, before it passed Congress. The Indian Office soon replaced the mill manager and promised to support the tribe's efforts to press logging and mill mismanagement charges against the government in the Court of Claims.[22]

The tribe's attorneys commissioned the Sterling Report, which was completed in February 1935 and showed gross federal mismanagement of the Menominee forest. The Sterling Report pointed out that, while 10.1 percent of the reservation had been clear-cut by 1934, 9.7 percent had been selectively cut, 30.7 percent consisted of old growth, and 17.6 percent remained as virgin forest. It concluded that the forest could still be maintained. The Menominee made claims to damages on 20,486 acres, and the government was eventually found responsible for the mismanagement of 20,326 acres.[23] Such a loss was significant, but thanks to the perseverance of the Menominee, their attorneys, and the change in federal policy, the damage was still reparable.

In September 1935 Congress passed a law allowing the tribe to seek restitution in the Court of Claims. The law said nothing regarding incorporation.[24] The Menominee initiated a suit that was dismissed, then initiated thirteen separate suits. Four of these were dismissed, and one, which provided for the purchase of swamp lands on the reservation from the state, was decided in the tribe's favor in the mid-1940s.[25] Several others were eventually heard together and resolved favorably to the tribe in 1951.[26]

In the meantime, the situation on the reservation took an odd twist. Although the Keshena agency remained subsidiary in importance to the Neopit Mills agency, the Keshena agency superintendent still exerted some authority over the tribe. In the tribe's view, this dominance often damaged rather than helped tribal interests. In 1934 the Collier administration secured the IRA. That same year the Indian Department appointed its longtime critic, Ralph Fredenberg, as Keshena agency superintendent. Fredenberg stressed to the tribe that even Collier's predecessors in the office of the commissioner of Indian affairs believed the Menominee to be among the "most highly advanced" tribes, probably because of their wealth in assets.[27]

Collier himself told the tribe in General Council, "In the case of the Menominee Tribe, your problem of instituting real self-government is an easier problem than it would be in a tribe whose lands have been all broken up by the allotment system. You have this great advantage, that your property, your important resources, are common resources, and that gives you a tremendous send-off towards a real and successful self-government."[28] The honeymoon proved to be short, however. Collier's view of tribal self-governance was unfortunately infused with a heavy dose of paternalism. This was something in which the Menominee had no interest.

Fredenberg's appointment proved both an opportunity and a danger. With one of their own within the bureaucracy, the Menominee perspective on problems and solutions could receive real recognition. But since the Keshena agency's role—overseeing education and internal affairs unrelated to the lumber business—was relatively inconsequential, it left plenty of room for disappointment and disillusion.

The tribe voted 596–15 to accept the IRA in 1934.[29] They paid their attorneys to write a constitution that would lead to incorporation. This time they had the support of the Indian Department. But the tribe rejected the new charter in council in 1935.[30] Nonetheless, the Menominee perceived themselves to be in the process of reorganizing. For example, Al Dodge, Advisory Council chairman, wrote to Collier in August 1935 requesting that he attend a summer event. The commissioner indicated that he would be unable to attend, so Dodge urged him to send a representative. "It is extremely important that one of the Commissioners attend, in order that the interests of the Menominee Tribe may be protected in this period of reorganization," Dodge wrote. "Plans on self government have been submitted to your office," he reminded Collier.[31] These plans were based on the tribe's definitions of self-governance, not on Collier's.

In an eerie presaging of events that actually occurred later under termination, the tribe rejected incorporation out of fear that it would change Menominee legal status by eliminating their trust relationship with the federal government. The Menominee realized that without this trust relationship their wealth could easily prove illusory. Tribal members believed the mill should be run to maximize Menominee employment and benefits, not to maximize profits. Such profit-driven management policy could destroy the tribe's economy in a more conventional system. Taxation, for instance, would take a large bite out of the tribe's funds. In response to these concerns, the incorporation charter as originally drawn up by the tribe's attorneys would reverse the tribe's loss of status and retain the trust relationship. The OIA, however, struck this provision. In addition, the tribe sent a delegation to visit other tribes that had reorganized under Collier's authority and found them in terrible circumstances. Although these other tribes lacked the resources the Menominee held, it made the latter more cautious.[32]

Even Fredenberg, the early leader of the fight for incorporation, now opposed it, as did Menominees at all levels throughout the reservation. They feared that liberal self-government coupled with loss of the trust relationship would lead to a rapid loss of resources. Fredenberg wrote to Collier, expressing his opposition: "If the tribe were given the powers and rights asked for under their charter and constitution, would it not be possible that outside sources could come in and exploit the reservation, disorganize its membership and bring shame upon your administration because of its liberal and sympathetic attitude in allowing the Indians to control their very complicated problem? I am sorry to say it, but I actually believe that self-government to the degree that such exploiting of tribal property could follow would be dangerous and unwise and therefore premature."[33] The Menominee rejected incorporation and accepted the IRA, but they never governed themselves under its auspices. This issue would drive a wedge between the OIA and the tribe for years to come.

Meanwhile, management of the forest resource also continued to cause conflict between the United States and the Menominee. Tribal member James Caldwell was appointed logging superintendent, but during his appointment the mill manager held ultimate authority. No Menominees held the latter position, which effectively froze tribal members out of positions of power in the logging business. In 1934, desperate to gain some control, the tribe brought about congressional amendment of the LaFollette Act. The amendment gave the Advisory Council the power of approval over the mill's budget. Council oversight led to either the dismissal or the resignation of several mill managers, who, in turn, accused the tribe of placing them in impossible situations.[34]

The dispute over the purpose of the Menominee resource and the employment of outsiders continued to rage as well. In 1933 Forest Supervisor Lloyd Grapp had outlined a plan for truck logging that essentially became the first well-organized plan the government followed in the Menominee logging business. Roads proved more economical and practical to build than railroads, and by 1936 the use of railroads to haul logs to Neopit had ended. Truck logging made selective cutting more economical, which meant the government would firmly support it as a viable method since it did not conflict with efficiency. Indians could cut lumber and haul it to Neopit in small trucks, a process that needed not only loggers but drivers. This plan theoretically met the tribal need of providing widespread employment.[35]

In 1937 Roy Oshkosh brought a motion before the General Council that Menominee truckers be given hiring preference to haul Menominee logs and that others be hired only when necessary. Of forty-seven truckers, only twenty-three—less than half—were Menominees. Peter White lamented, "We know the Menominees have very poor representation in their own enterprise. Our business is alienated to the extent where white people monopolize our business."[36]

Fredenberg was unable to exert much influence on the mill, and the promises of a Menominee-run administration turned somewhat sour. As superintendent he could be blamed for not solving the problems he had previously so desperately denounced; he now found that he could do little to resolve them, due to both his weak position and the unwieldy bureaucracy, which in the final analysis was not sympathetic to Menominee solutions.

Even those areas over which Fredenberg clearly had jurisdiction proved difficult for him to manage. He believed strongly in educating children in the American system, for example, and attempted to achieve various types of educational reform but without success. Time and again, Fredenberg lobbied the Indian Office to close the large and costly boarding school in Keshena and to open day schools in towns throughout the reservation in order to cut costs and to allow children to live with their parents.[37]

Neopit was the only outlying community in which schools operated at this time, the schools in South Branch and West Branch having closed when St. Joseph's opened in Keshena. The agency had never established a school in Zoar, despite strong community support there for an institution in which the Zoar children could be educated without having to move to Keshena.[38] Soon after Neopit's founding, the tribe had voted in council to grant three acres to the Catholic Church and one-half acre to the government to build schools there.[39] Shortly thereafter, however, the tribe voted twice to oppose the Catholic Church's building of a schoolhouse in Neopit, since St. Joseph's in Keshena was being enlarged.[40] However, St. Anthony's Day School and a government day school were both established in Neopit. The need for students there touched off a competition in the late 1930s that mirrored the competitions in Keshena more than a half-century earlier. The government day school brought in new leadership, and Father Virgil Benzman and government school superintendent Jerry Thompson clashed over enrolling students. Superintendent Thompson was a strong-willed man, and Father Virgil could be downright caustic.

The newly invigorated government school lacked support in the Neopit community. Fredenberg commented to Thompson, "The Neopit Day School . . . was established only under great protest by a majority of the Menominee Indians."[41] This put the government at such a disadvantage that it did little but verbally condemn some of the abuses of the church school's administrators.

Father Virgil, like his predecessors in Keshena a half-century earlier, used threats against parents and children to encourage attendance. He told parents, for example, that he would not confirm their boys; he threatened "dire calamity"; and he "preached a sermon on the evil of pupils attending the day school." Some students and their parents wished for the children to attend the government school but felt threatened enough to register their children at or to transfer them into the Catholic school.[42]

In one case, "Father Virgil suffered a spasm of 'RIGHTEOUS WRATH,'" according to Thompson, and beat a student. The father precipitated the incident by accusing the student's mother of being lax in her church attendance. Against federal rules, Thompson permitted this student to transfer to the government school. This brought an investigation from Washington in which the federal Indian education officials recognized the priest's abuses but warned that the need for peace between the mission and government schools superceded an individual student's welfare. Director of Indian Education Willard Beatty began his cautionary warning by admitting, "It appears to me that there has been undue coercion of certain pupils by men in charge of the mission schools." But then he added,

> I think it unfortunate in the present instance that [the student] has been permitted to sit in on classes at the Neopit day school, and I believe the matter should have been referred to this office for general discussion with Father Tennelly while the youngster was excluded from the mission school and on the basis of his parents' appeal for admission to the government school. After all, the amount of instructional loss to [the student] by being out of school for a

semester is not tremendously serious, and certainly is not as important as the establishment of sound relationships between both groups of schools on the reservation.[43]

Fredenberg, a Menominee who put a high value on Menominee education in the American system and perhaps succeeded better in shaping educational policy in the reservation's schools than in anything else during his tenure as agency superintendent, had already begun to recognize that Thompson and his teachers did a quality job of providing innovative education in Neopit. As a result, he offered Thompson any support his office could provide.[44] In Fredenberg's view, education for Menominee children was the most important tribal issue. He had once stated, "A Menominee child is entitled to have a better education than a white man, because he must make himself better than a white man so he can hold his own."[45] Yet federal regulations and the tension-filled nature of the government-church relations caused Menominee children to suffer, for which the federal government and the Catholic Church share the blame.

While Father Virgil and Superintendent Thompson battled for Menominee children, many in the tribe strongly supported St. Joseph's boarding school in Keshena. The priest there, Father Englehard Troeskin, known as Father Englehard, had begun work on the reservation in 1907 and became *praeses*, or leader of the Franciscans, on the reservation in 1914 or 1915. He was a popular, well-liked, selfless servant of the church.[46] Under his guidance, conflicts in Keshena were largely avoided. Indeed, in 1933 "the General Council . . . unanimously passed a resolution, requesting the government to turn over [its boarding] school to the Franciscan Fathers."[47] Soon thereafter St. Joseph's became the sole boarding school on the reservation.

The tribe supported education in the government or mission school systems when tribal members believed it would be to their children's advantage. Even though Fredenberg supported ultimately closing St. Joseph's boarding school, when he became agency superintendent he worked hard to improve access of children living outside of Keshena to all of the schools and to improve their experiences once they arrived.[48]

Although many in the community accepted the Catholic Church and knew the importance of educating Menominee children in American terms, the experiences of the children in the reservation boarding schools crossed a broad range. For some the boarding schools meant full meals three times a day and new clothing annually, including a new pair of shoes for the Corpus Christi celebration at St. Joseph's. But others resented the forced loss of culture: children were not permitted to speak Menominee, and at most times none of the St. Joseph's schoolteachers spoke or understood Menominee.[49] The impact on the community was arguably more deleterious than that on the individual.

Disappointment with Fredenberg's failure to solve all the tribe's problems flared up at a General Council meeting in early 1938. James Frechette, Al Dodge, and Fredenberg had been the delegation to Washington in 1934 when the Collier administration asked Fredenberg to serve as an agent on a reservation of his choice. Frechette and Dodge, with the backing of the Advisory Council by telephone from Keshena, had urged Fredenberg to accept the position on the Menominee reservation so he could work for his own people. Frechette reiterated these facts at the General Council meeting and urged Fredenberg to act in order to regain the confidence of the tribe. Dodge in turn urged the tribe to renew its support for Fredenberg. He stressed that under Fredenberg the tribe had gained concessions from Washington as never before, that Fredenberg's education plans made a higher educational level possible for more Menominees, and that the agency took better care of elders under Fredenberg's administration than it ever had done under previous agency superintendents. He also reminded the tribe that Fredenberg—who had started working as a dishwasher in the Neopit hotel, an establishment that roomed and boarded single Menominee men who worked the mill; who had worked in the lumber industry; and who had an understanding of tribal affairs at all levels—was largely responsible for initiating the timber lawsuit.[50]

Fredenberg was in a nearly impossible position, however. He was not in control of Menominee affairs because the mill superintendent controlled affairs related to Neopit and the timber industry. With his scant authority, and without support from the OIA, he could do little more than try to humanize part of the bureaucracy and approach problems from a Menominee rather than a federal perspective; he could not effect real change, and to some degree he became part of the bureaucracy. Charges of misconduct against Fredenberg led to two federal investigations, both of which exonerated him, and allegations of scandal caused Fredenberg to leave office in 1940. He took a superintendent's position on a reservation in the Pacific Northwest, "after bitter attacks from his erstwhile colleagues and convinced that the tribe was unable to manage its own affairs."[51] Fredenberg had not damaged the tribe's affairs, as had so many of his predecessors, but he was unable to accomplish the good for which he and others in the tribe had hoped.

The major conflict between the Menominee and the United States in their battles over the forest and over the ancillary initiatives of the 1920s and 1930s was a philosophical one. The Menominee viewed the forest resource as belonging to the tribe as a whole and believed that exploitation of it should benefit all Menominees. Primary among tribal values was the sharing of resources, which dated to the tribe's earliest history.[52] This core value put the Menominee at odds with the American individualistic philosophy. It meant that the tribe would attempt to hold the resources communally instead of parceling them out to individuals, and it meant that the optimal exploitation of those resources would be for the best good of the whole instead of the best good of the individual.

The United States, on the other hand, desired individual Menominees to succeed on their own. Indian Service and other federal officials therefore worked hard to separate the individual from the tribe and the tribe from its resource base. They equated progress with individual effort divorced from the community. The two cultures simply defined success in radically different ways. So while both sides seemed to have the same goals—Menominee success in a modern American culture—their definitions of success differed so drastically that they were constantly at loggerheads with each other. In other words, two different processes were now in conflict.

Ironically, tribal leaders and federal officials often thought that the same methods might lead to success, and so at times the Menominee embraced federal initiatives; at other times the tribe itself proposed initiatives that turned out differently than they had hoped and that in the end the Menominee would have to fight off. Tribal goals generally centered around maintaining the tribal way of life and establishing a high quality of life for tribal members. They hoped to accomplish these goals within an evolving economic and political system that was largely driven by their forest resource. Over the years, federal goals were generally to find ways to abandon their trust responsibility and to encourage individual Menominees to enter into a vaguely elaborated, idealized, and unrealistic representation of the larger society.

The late 1920s and early 1930s served as a prelude to termination for the Menominee in key ways. Both incorporation and the notion of individualization served as precursors to the heart-wrenching era that followed. Ironically, the success the Menominee achieved in banding together to fight off deleterious initiatives of the federal government ultimately proved to be destructive to them. The Menominee resistance was so successful that the federal government would eventually decide that their success was good reason in itself to end its trust responsibility to the tribe.

Four men on loaded logging sleigh. Courtesy
Menominee Historic Preservation Department.

John V. Satterlee. These two photos capture John Satterlee's playful nature. Courtesy Milwaukee Public Museum, negative no. 45580 and no. 105078.

Log jam on Little West Branch of Wolf River, 1886. Courtesy Menominee Historic Preservation Department.

A hi up in the port
Arrs
Dells Dam
on the
Wolf River

Top left: Three Menominee loggers. From left to right, Fred Seymour, Jerry Grignon, and John Fossum. Courtesy Menominee Historic Preservation Department.

Bottom left: White City in Neopit. Courtesy Menominee Historic Preservation Department.

Above: River drivers at Wolf River Dells Dam. Courtesy Menominee Historic Preservation Department.

Top: Council meeting. Courtesy Milwaukee
Public Museum, negative no. 2744.

Bottom: St. Mary's Church in Kinepoway.
Courtesy Marquette University Archives.

Top: Corpus Christi celebration, St. Joseph's school, Keshena. Courtesy Marquette University Archives.

Bottom: Boys of St. Joseph's school, Keshena. Courtesy Marquette University Archives.

Above: Sewing class at St. Joseph's school, Keshena. Top row: Mary Jane Matchapatow, Sister Blase, Theresa Wolf, Evelyn Fish. Bottom row: Betty Frechette, Cordelia Beauprey, Isabel "Tippy" Sackatook. Courtesy Marquette University Archives.

Top right: St. Joseph's carpentry shop. Courtesy Marquette University Archives.

Bottom right: Brother David's shoe shop, St. Joseph's school, Keshena. Courtesy Marquette University Archives.

St. Joseph's Industrial School, Keshena Wis.
The Carpenter Shop.

Above: Nellie Wishkeno driving truck. Menominee women went to work in the forest during World War II. Courtesy Menominee Historic Preservation Department.

Top right: DRUMS leader James Washinawatok at a demonstration. Courtesy Menominee Historic Preservation Department.

Bottom right: Menominee language class. Words on wall translate as "books" and "war bonnet." Courtesy Menominee Historic Preservation Department.

mēkaehsēhsak   mēkon-wiahkwan

Left and right: Menominee Tribal Enterprises, Neopit. Photos by the author.

The Wolf River on the Menominee
reservation. Photo by the author.

CHAPTER NINE

Termination

Federal mismanagement of their affairs and their own lack of voice in them frustrated the Menominee. They interpreted the 1908 LaFollette Act as requiring that Menominees be trained to run the mill, for example, and were increasingly angered at being passed over for leadership positions. They used the little power they had to run bad managers out of the reservation. Agency superintendents and managers at the mill were forced to leave office in succession, including three of the latter who held tenure during Fredenberg's reign from 1934 to 1940. The Advisory Council disapproved mill budgets time and again, believing that their resources were being mismanaged.

When a new mill manager arrived again in 1940, the tribe's attorneys warned the Menominee that the government was using tribal interference in the government's running of Menominee affairs as an excuse for federal mismanagement in the court claims. After a short grace period, the tribe nevertheless rejected this new manager's budget and asked that he be replaced. After the manager got into a fistfight with a Menominee in a nearby tavern, he attacked the honesty and integrity of the Menominee opposition leader. Tribal members shouted him down in a General Council meeting, "and in a dramatic outburst he resigned and left the hall." He left at the same time as Fredenberg's successor, Earl Woolridge, who had not enraged the tribe but had clashed with the mill manager.[1] At this point, the Indian Bureau combined the agency superintendent's and mill manager's jobs and jurisdictions.

In 1940 the Menominee proposed an amendment to the 1908 law that would permit the tribe to manage the mill over a ten-year period under the secretary of the interior's supervision. If their management was deemed successful, at the end of the ten years the tribe would be placed completely in charge. Some of the elders believed this plan did not go far enough in terms of self-governance, but the tribe generally believed this to be a move in the right direction.[2]

The Menominee had no interest, however, in absolving the United States of its trust responsibilities. Tribal governance remained disorganized without federal support of a tribal constitution. The OIA withheld this support as Collier continued to wrangle with the Menominee over acceptance of an IRA government. In April 1941 a tribal delegation reminded the Senate Committee on Indian Affairs, "We desire to state very emphatically that the Tribe has been on record for the past several years not to change their present status or to be included under the Reorganization Act."[3]

The IRA was a broad law that dealt with a myriad of issues. Perhaps its most important feature was that it "permitted Indian tribes to organize a local government to provide for the general welfare of the Indian community."[4] While tribes could establish governments outside the purview of the IRA, IRA governments were on a fast track to approval and authorization under the guidance of the Collier administration. Ironically, the law intended to recognize powers the tribes already had. The Menominee became suspicious of federal intentions, especially when they saw that tribes accepting the IRA did not immediately see political and economic independence.[5]

In May 1941 Jim Frechette, acting on instructions from the tribal council, wrote Collier to reiterate that the tribe would not bring in a new constitution under the IRA. Though the tribe had accepted the IRA, it never organized under it. In part, he said, this was because tribal members feared that acceptance of an IRA government would eventually lead to taxation of their resources and even loss of them. Tribal members Neil Gauthier and Margaret Wilber testified at a 7 May council meeting that people were "terribly afraid" of the IRA. Wilber said she opposed it from the beginning because other tribal members "thought they could use anything on our farm"—that all property would belong to all or any tribal members. Tribal members feared trespass on the farm plots they had established. Menominee hopes for allotment had been little more than hopes to protect these farm plots for their families while still maintaining the forest as a tribal resource; tribal farmers feared that organization under an IRA government would provide the mechanism for their dispossession of these plots. They also feared taxation.[6]

Frechette suggested that it would be a quicker solution for Congress to pass a separate law accepting the new Menominee constitution and bylaws. Agency Superintendent Woolridge voiced the same opinion. Assistant Commissioner William Zimmerman Jr. responded in July that he disagreed. He felt it would be easier for the tribe to accept its constitution under the 1934 reorganization law.[7]

Zimmerman's solution indeed would have been easier for the United States, since congressional approval already existed through the IRA, but the tribe still wanted no part of the IRA. The absence of a ratified constitution hampered the tribe's ability to govern itself and to act in an advisory capacity to agency officials. The Indian Office was only willing to turn control over to the Menominee on terms defined by the United States. Tribal leaders refused to accept this responsibility without the power of control.

Meanwhile, the agency governing structure again underwent changes. In the 1940s, after the agency superintendent in Keshena again became the single most powerful Indian Department official on the reservation, Menominees ironically finally gained top positions in the logging operations, as both logging and mill superintendents. As with Fredenberg, however, they were not the highest-ranking employees on the reservation; now Fredenberg's old position held that responsibility. These two superintendents earned the same sort of criticism from their fellow Menominees as had Fredenberg.

The agency superintendent who succeeded Woolridge, J. Lyle Cunningham, quickly alienated the tribe by ignoring Advisory Council advice and then by challenging the Menominee's rights to reject the mill budget. The tribe refused to accept the budget unless Cunningham fired certain employees, which Cunningham refused to do. Soon neither Cunningham nor the Advisory Council were communicating with each other.[8]

The Indian Department then prepared legislation to transfer all responsibility of the mill and the agency to the tribe. Cunningham ignored the Advisory Council and appealed directly to the tribe through a newsletter, warning tribal members of the potential results of this bill: "If such legislation is presented and passed by Congress, it means that the Government would step out, and the Menominees themselves would be responsible for the entire Reservation's operations. This matter has been discussed with the Tribal delegation which went to Chicago in March and I am informed that the Advisory Council has been told this information, but I am not sure that all members of the Tribe are aware of it." The tribe in General Council then voted to refuse this transfer of responsibility, in part because the Menominee had not prepared the bill. Cunningham soon left the reservation.[9]

His successor, Daniel E. Murphy, quickly recognized that tribal wishes conflicted with federal purposes. He proposed that the Indian Bureau simply ignore the wishes of the Menominee General Council and negotiate strictly with the Advisory Council. Yet the IRA protected the tribe from this type of situation. Even though the Menominee had never organized under the IRA, the fact that they had accepted it led Assistant Commissioner Zimmerman to write that, short of a change adopted by the U.S. Congress through legislation, powers could not be shifted among Menominee governing bodies unless the Menominee adopted a constitution under the IRA.[10]

The agency superintendent may have wanted to remove the authority of the tribe over budget issues, but the overall goal of the Indian Office was for the tribe to take over the management of all operations as expeditiously as possible so that federal supervision could be withdrawn. On 1 April 1946 Zimmerman wrote to Murphy, "The Council should continue to take an active interest in the affairs of the Tribe so that the Tribe will be able, in the not too distant future, to take over and manage its own affairs."[11]

The constant upheaval in mill management frustrated the Indian Department, which viewed it as the result of the Menominee having power without responsibility.[12] But the reverse can be argued. The federal government failed because it had the power to make decisions but did not have to pay the price or suffer the consequences of those decisions. After all, the tribe paid the expenses of federal services from its own funds, essentially providing the financial basis for the United States to uphold its trust responsibilities to the Menominee.

WITHDRAWAL OF FEDERAL SUPERVISION

The OIA more than ever looked to the Menominee as a tribe that needed to make the transition from wardship to independence, even though the OIA in the early 1930s and the Menominee in the late 1930s had refused to support incorporation. The Menominee remained adamant that they wanted to increase their control but under the protection of the trust relationship. The United States, on the other hand, still hoped to end its treaty-based relationships with Indians. Because of the tribe's timber wealth the Menominee were among those at the top of the list.

Superintendent Murphy, whose tenure lasted barely a year, worked in this direction. "The outstanding characteristic of his administration was emphasis on advisory council assumption of Mills management and de-emphasis of the authority-responsibility correlation," according to the anthropologist Rachel Reese Sady. Both his goal and the tribe's seemed to be the eventual assumption of Menominee-run governance. Both sides had the same basic goal in mind, but their philosophical reasons for it differed greatly. The Advisory Council gained influence so quickly that it became cautious in its role, its members fearful of making decisions beyond their understanding of the details. This earned the disapproval of the General Council.[13] Then Murphy left the job in May 1946, and the OIA did not appoint a permanent replacement until December.

The federal government soon resumed its support of the authority-responsibility paradigm. The heavy hand of paternalism that infused Indian policy complicated federal efforts at defining this paradigm. Collier's experiment of establishing tribal governments based on American models was failing tribes, in part because tribal economies still languished miserably and in part because federal bureaucrats insisted on thwarting self-rule almost wherever it appeared. The OIA itself had fallen into further disarray during World War II, when it moved its operations to Chicago to make room for the war effort in Washington and then moved back after the war.[14] During this time, the Menominee future became increasingly bound by national policy.

In 1934, when Collier first took office, the solicitor Nathan Margold had written an opinion on tribal sovereignty for him. In it he recognized that tribes retained inherent sovereignty on a wide variety of fronts. The Indian Bureau ignored Margold's opinion in its actions. In response, a coalition of tribal governments formed an organization that would become a leading voice in Indian America. The National Congress of American Indians (NCAI), founded in 1944, called for the gradual dissolution of the OIA at its first meeting. NCAI especially opposed paternalism, but it supported maintenance of the trust relationship.[15]

Then in 1946 the Association on American Indian Affairs (AAIA), a non-Indian organization, issued a report recommending against cure-all programs like the New Deal and calling for the Indian Bureau to liquidate itself. This report recommended a study be made to determine which tribes might be ready for what it termed "freedom from federal supervision."[16]

At the same time as these calls for the federal government to get out of the Indian business occurred, Congress hoped to downscale big government. To senators and congressmen, these two goals dovetailed neatly. Collier resigned in 1945. In 1946 both the House and Senate subsumed their Committees on Indian Affairs into larger Department of the Interior committees, whose venues included lands and resources. This change relegated Indian affairs to the level of unenticing subcommittees.[17] Also in 1946 Congress created the Indian Claims Commission, with the aim of settling all Indian claims against the United States once and for all in order to save money over time.[18] This commission was established under the administration of the new commissioner of Indian affairs, William A. Brophy. When he became ill, Zimmerman became acting commissioner of Indian affairs and, at its insistence, presented to Congress the plan on which termination would be based.

Zimmerman declared the Menominee to be one of several tribes ready for immediate termination of federal supervision because they were self-supportive and, according to federal officials, an ideal case.[19] Federal officials saw termination as an opportunity to sever the trust relationship completely, leaving the tribe to fend for itself in both political and economic terms. The Menominee supported a more cautious approach to withdrawal of federal supervision.

The Menominee had a strong economic base in the mill and forest, despite the problems the tribe had with Indian Service management. The logging industry had become institutionalized almost as a social service agency for the tribe. Dating to the 1890 law, profits had supported the hospital and had provided services to the elderly, the incapacitated, and the ill. Profits had also been paid to tribal members in annuities, providing small amounts of much needed cash that many people used for subsistence items such as food and clothing. The logging camps, the transportation system, and the mill all provided employment. Nearly all Menominee men worked in one way or another for the lumbering industry at some point during the year.[20]

Together with the hunting, fishing, and gathering and help from the stump- age fund, most Menominees, though economically impoverished, nonetheless were self-sufficient. The tribe paid the costs of federal employees stationed on the reservation as well. In addition, in the late 1940s the tribe established a loan program to support small businesses. A garment factory was established in Keshena, and within five years "there were a number of privately owned gift shops, gas stations, restaurants, cabin rentals and a horse riding academy. More than twenty small businesses existed" on the reservation "during this era of heightened economic development," according to one observer.[21]

The congressional committee to which Zimmerman submitted his report on termination in 1947 asked him how much money the government would save by instituting termination. He replied that fifty-eight federal employees served the Menominee. This was a disingenuous response since, as Stephen J. Herzberg has pointed out, Zimmerman "failed to tell the committee that the Menominee, not the government, paid the salaries of these fifty-eight federal employees."[22]

Zimmerman was only telling Congress what it wanted to hear. By 1948 a group of Republican congressmen had compiled a list of ten tribes that were "ready for release" from trusteeship; the Menominee were one of the ten.[23] Gordon Dickie, reelected chairman of the Advisory Council in 1946 after his return from military service, had to face the increasing pressures from Congress: "What people don't fully realize was that we had warnings ahead of time but we really didn't take them seriously. In . . . 1947 Senator Hugh Butler of Nebraska introduced a bill to make a National park on the Menominee Reservation. Well, we blocked that, it never got out of committee. Then in 1948 the acting commissioner of Indian Affairs testifying before the Civil Service

Commission was asked what tribes could run their own business, and then the first two tribes that were mentioned were the Menominees and Klamaths."[24] Dickie opposed the federal concept of termination. In a letter to Utah senator Arthur V. Watkins in June 1949, Dickie wrote, "We are proud of the progress made by our people but wish to reiterate that we have not, in my opinion, reached the point of assuming full responsibility of our own affairs."[25]

In 1951 the Menominee finally won an $8.5 million judgment in the timber lawsuit. The Court of Claims ruled that the LaFollette Act had required the federal government to manage the Menominee forest on a basis that would preserve rather than diminish its value, since, as Congress recognized, the Menominee would "in all probability . . . have to remain on the reservation indefinitely." The United States supported its decision to clear-cut in a variety of arguments, all of which the Court of Claims rejected. When the government decided to appeal the decision to the Supreme Court, "the parties agreed to settle five of the claims filed by the tribe under the enabling legislation for a lump sum of $8.5 million."[26]

Officials within Congress and the Bureau of Indian Affairs (BIA) not only believed the Menominee were ready to be cut loose from federal wardship, but they also strongly resented the tribe's successful lawsuit. Federal officials supporting termination argued that, if the Menominee were smart enough to sue the government, they were smart enough to run their own affairs. They feared the tribe might sue them for mismanagement again in the future if the federal government did not stop managing tribal affairs. Watkins vacillated between calling the policy a "freedom" policy for Indians and a "decontrol" policy for the federal government.[27]

Watkins was driven not only by his role as senator but by his Mormon beliefs as well. According to Mormon doctrine, Lamanites "are the principle ancestors of American Indians," although the latter had fallen away from God's grace and become spiritually "dark and loathesome." Mormonism, according to one scholar, "is the only [Western] faith in which North American Indians are featured in the holy scripture."[28] Mormons feel duty-bound to lead Indians back to the light. In writing about the Menominee, Watkins blamed Catholics for tribal unrest. In a letter to the First Presidency of his church, Watkins said of the Catholics, "These people have recently stirred up the Indians on the Menominee reservation as well as other places." He then went on to justify his work as a terminationist: "The more I go into this terrible Indian problem the more I am convinced that we have made some terrible mistakes in the past. It seems to me that the time has come for us to correct some of these mistakes and help the Indians stand on their own feet and become a white and delightsome people as the Book of Mormon prophecied they would become."[29]

After the settlement award from the successful lawsuit, which left the tribe with $7.65 million after attorney fees, the Menominee voted to award each member of the tribe a one-time payment of $1,500 and to use the rest of the money for various social services.[30] Since the original enabling legislation for the claims suit did not allow any claims received by the tribe to be paid out to individuals in per capita payments, Wisconsin congressman Melvin Laird, on behalf of the tribe, introduced legislation in Congress in 1952 to allow the payment.

At the end of February a Menominee delegation consisting of Gordon Dickie, Jim Frechette, John Fossum, Lester Dickie, and Al Dodge held a series of meetings with Commissioner of Indian Affairs Dillon Myer to discuss how the tribe would spend the judgment money. According to notes from the meeting, Myer broached the topic of termination at this time.

> In a conference with Commissioner Myer on February 28, the Commissioner indicated that he felt the tribe should be giving careful and thorough consideration to the possibility of taking over all its operations, thus relieving the federal government of the responsibility it now has. He discussed in some detail the plan worked out by the Osage Tribe under which its members, pursuant to a closed roll, distributed the tribal assets in headrights which were inheritable. Such a plan would of course require the closing of the Menominee rolls. No commitments were made by the Menominee delegation, but it was assumed by all that the delegates would recommend consideration of future handling of Menominee business. There was some indication that because of the decreasing percentage of Menominee blood in enrolled members of the Menominee Tribe, that the problem of the increase in the tribal enrollment might work itself out without any artificial breaking-off point.[31]

In March the House Subcommittee on Indian Affairs held a hearing on the per capita payment. In that hearing the tribe's attorney, Glen Wilkinson, indicated that tribal leaders had a continuing interest in replacing federal leadership with tribal leadership. He indicated that Jim Frechette, Gordon Dickie, and Al Dodge "are unanimously agreed that they will recommend to the General Council that a good portion of the functions now supervised by the Department of Interior be taken over by the Tribe within two or three years."[32]

The tribe knew that the risk of complete self-governance was potentially high, however. Gordon Dickie clarified that these Menominee hopes were long-term goals and that they needed to plan carefully:

[T]he Menominee Tribe has recognized the fact that it cannot expect to go on indefinitely under the supervision of the Federal Government. They have over a period of years worked out a plan of operation that is far from being perfect as yet, but they are in the process of learning. I think the members of the delegation and I are all in agreement that we are not as yet prepared to assume full responsibility, and it may be several years hence before we can possibly absorb additional authority. . . . [W]e are attempting to learn to handle our own business. We are being cautious about assuming additional authority until such time as we ourselves are satisfied we have the ability to handle our business. There is so much at stake.[33]

The solution, tribal leaders believed, was to act slowly, and it ultimately depended on a combination of education and experience. Dickie explained, "[O]ur answer is the promotion of educational programs." He continued, "Some discussion has already taken place about increasing the number of scholarships with the idea in mind that some day the Congress will look to the Menominees to assume responsibility, and until we can put these programs into operation to assist these students, carrying them onto higher education, we are not going to be able to assume the responsibilities. But we do recognize the fact that we cannot just sit back and expect to carry on the way we are now, indefinitely."[34]

Washington, on the other hand, decided to go full bore ahead. On 8 May 1952 a Menominee delegation consisting of Al Dodge, Jim Frechette, Gordon Dickie, and others met with Commissioner of Indian Affairs Dillon Myer, Minneapolis area director Don C. Foster, and BIA program officers in Washington about hospital and school construction issues. As the discussion turned to oversight of the mill, "[t]he Commissioner stated that the Bureau was willing to turn the whole operation over to the tribe so that they could manage it to their satisfaction," according to program officer John B. Keliiaa, who attended the meeting. The tribal delegates immediately responded with caution, but the BIA officials urged them to consider the commissioner's suggestions. Al Dodge said point-blank that the government still held responsibility for tribal operations. According to Keliiaa, "The Commissioner stated that we do have the responsibility, but we are not sure we should have. In the meantime, we want the tribe to get the experience of acting as a board of directors." Bureau officials left the meeting under the impression that the Menominee were willing to work with the bureau "in commencing studies designed to free the Federal Government of responsibility for supervision of the Menominee Reservation and the Menominee Indians."[35]

If tribal members had any doubts regarding the commissioner's intentions after this meeting, they should have dissipated in June after Keliiaa visited the reservation. He came as part of a BIA delegation to urge the Menominee to accept the inevitability of termination, or "withdrawal of federal supervision," as they called it. On 3 June Keliiaa flew to Milwaukee and commenced a trip to the reservation with two other BIA employees. Over the next three weeks, they attended council meetings, held community meetings in Zoar and South Branch, and met with individual tribal members to urge them to plan for termination. Gordon Dickie announced that he was planning to run for Congress but abruptly changed his mind when he realized federal intentions and recognized the fight in which the tribe would be involved.[36] The tribe's hope for a long-term withdrawal plan based on education of tribal members was not part of these discussions.

Menominees resisted the idea of withdrawal of federal supervision, but Keliiaa and the others ignored them: "They will probably be much more interested in the whole programming effort after they have given more thought to the matter." While the bureau officials spoke in terms of withdrawal, the Menominee spoke in terms of self-government. Their definitions were worlds apart, since self-government in the minds of Menominees would occur under the protection of the federal trust relationship. Keliiaa commented after the meeting at South Branch, "I think that the comment of one of the members to th[e] effect that they were somewhat stunned is an apt characterization of the meeting, if slightly exaggerated."[37] The Advisory Council was reluctant to begin a program of withdrawal. Keliiaa believed this to be due to tribal political concerns rather than opposition to the "program," as he referred to termination.[38]

In November 1952 the Republican Party gained control of both the presidency and the Congress. Senator Watkins took over the Senate Subcommittee on Indian Affairs and ardently pushed for withdrawal of federal services from tribes. Watkins argued before Congress that the Indians should be freed from federal control. This freedom theme worked well with senators from both sides of the aisle, most of whom knew and cared little about the details of Indian affairs anyway.[39] Both Republican and Democratic Party platforms in 1952 included language supporting termination.[40] The Menominee fell victim to a governmental crusade carried out by Congress and the executive branch in which the main advocates of the new policy were the commissioners of Indian Affairs and Senator Watkins.

THE TERMINATION BILL

In 1953, when the House passed legislation to release per capita money to the Menominee, Senator Watkins rewrote the Senate version of the bill entirely, making payment contingent on the Menominee's acceptance of termination. The new bill was "To provide for a per capita distribution of Menominee tribal funds and authorize the withdrawal of the Menominee Tribe from Federal jurisdiction." When tribal members protested in Washington, Watkins agreed to visit the reservation.[41]

At a tribal council meeting on 20 June 1953, Watkins informed the Menominee that, if they did not agree to termination, the government would not release the claims money. Dr. David W. Ames later wrote, "Most Menominees I have spoken with say . . . that the per capita payment was an 'outright bribe' or 'stick' by which they were 'forced' to accept termination."[42] One tribal member, William Grignon, exclaimed in anger, "We were bribed with our own money!"[43]

Coercing tribes with their own money was, if not official federal policy, at least a not unknown practice. Vine Deloria Jr. pointed out in the late 1960s that "Rarely does a judgement bill come before the termination committee but what [James] Gamble [a Senate Interior Committee staffer] tries to have a termination rider attached."[44] The methods and plans Congress attempted to use against other tribes—including the Three Affiliated Tribes at Fort Berthold, the Colville, the Utes, the Klamath, and the Allegheny Seneca—are so similar to those used on the Menominee as to suggest that these methods may have been part of a larger federal plan. At the very least, the government seemed willing to pursue any methods to accomplish its mission of ending federal supervision of Indian nations.[45]

Ada Deer, in testimony before the Senate on behalf of a number of tribal members, later described Watkins's motivations: "Senator Watkins badly wanted our termination. He was firmly convinced that factors such as our status as Reservation Indians, our tribal ownership of land, and our tax exemption were blocking our initiative, our freedom, and our development of private enterprise. He wished to see us rapidly assimilated into the mainstream of American society—as tax paying, hard working, 'emancipated' citizens. Senator Watkins did *not* believe that *our* consent to termination was necessary for its enactment. Yet he knew that his cause would be helped if he could persuade us to agree to termination."[46]

Deer was correct. Watkins compared termination policy to the Emancipation Proclamation: "I see the following words emblazoned in letters of fire above the heads of Indians—THESE PEOPLE SHALL BE FREE!" He also believed that "the matter of freeing the Indians from wardship status is not rightfully a subject to debate in academic fashion. . . . Much more I see this as an ideal or universal truth, to which all men subscribe."[47]

At the 20 June meeting the Menominee, with barely 10 percent of eligible voters participating, accepted Watkins's resolution, 169–5. To this day much confusion surrounds that meeting. Though Watkins knew that many of the Menominees at the meeting spoke only the Menominee language and had little understanding of English, he refused to allow interpreters to fully translate the proceedings. Several Menominees voted with the understanding that they were accepting the per capita payout. Others thought they were voting to accept a "principle of termination," as the anthropologist Nancy Lurie has observed. Some probably supported the resolution to show respect for the visiting dignitary, since courtesy remained fundamental to Menominee culture, not only in the social and economic realm but also in the political one. This also served as appeasement, since in the Menominee system the tribe could revote and reverse earlier decisions, as had been done with the 1848 treaty, allotment, incorporation, and reorganization under the IRA.

According to the tribe's official history, the vote "was done with a show of hands. . . . An important issue such as this . . . should have been done by a 'referendum vote' for all adult Menominees to vote on it but instead the Senator chose to use a show of hands." The history also says that Watkins "did not believe our consent was necessary." Indeed, Watkins said so himself both in hearings and in a televised debate on the termination issue.[48]

Many Menominees who opposed the idea avoided the meeting altogether, in the traditional Menominee way of showing disapproval of the topic under debate or discussion. No one knew what would follow for the tribe, or they would not have supported the idea. Few, if any, believed the vote to be binding. The tribe often voted one way and then another, changing positions, before finalizing a decision. Some believed that they could appease Watkins now but that the tribe could reverse the decision and avoid termination.[49] The headline of a Shawano newspaper captured the outside world's view of events, however: "Menominees' Full Freedom Assured at General Council."[50]

Less than a month later, on 17 July the tribe held another council, rejecting the earlier vote by 197–0. They agreed to give up their $8.5 million claim settlement if it meant they had to accept termination. Again, a large number of non-supporters of termination probably avoided the meeting entirely. Nonetheless, Watkins used the earlier vote to convince the Senate to pass the Menominee termination bill. He conveniently failed to mention that he had pressured the tribe into supporting it or that the Menominee had later repudiated their decision.[51]

Gordon Dickie described the situation succinctly: "In 1953 is when Arthur Watkins, Senator from Utah, pushed termination. And one thing that I've always taken exception to is the accusation or allegation that the Menominee tribe sold out for the per capita payment. That is not true. Absolutely false. Because I presided at the meeting in July of 1953 when they voted 197 to zero to drop the per capita payment rather than accept Watkins' proposal on termination. But Watkins went ahead and pushed it anyway."[52] Nancy Lurie, an anthropologist who worked extensively with the Menominee, has observed, "All Menominees, whatever their social status, opposed termination, which they denounced as an unjust and capricious policy experiment that treated them as 'government guinea pigs.'"[53]

The cavalier attitude with which Watkins and the BIA viewed the Menominee political system is not remarkable; the purpose of "freeing" the Indians from federal wardship, after all, was to help them modernize in the American, not the Menominee, cultural context. Watkins ran roughshod over established tribal government procedure and ignored tribal convention in gaining the tribe's 20 June vote to accept termination. He then misinformed Congress regarding the proceedings in order to get the bill passed and signed.

Two conventional Menominee methods of political participation clashed with the U.S. methods to such an extent that, when the United States ignored these, the tribe suffered for it: the Menominee practice of avoiding meetings that deal with issues people oppose and the practice of voting by consensus. In the American system of democracy, majority rules. The Menominee system was based on consensus-based voting. At their council meetings, members often discussed issues at great length, hearing everyone's opinion spoken in either Menominee or English and then translated. Then, when the meeting participants had a feel for how the majority thought, nearly all voted together. These two factors—the absence of much of the strongest opposition at meetings and consensus-based voting—led to the often lopsided vote totals.[54]

Watkins and the federal government in general ignored all these factors, especially the fact that the Menominee opposed termination but still wanted more control over the governance of tribal affairs. Yet federal officials successfully convinced the Menominee that termination was inevitable. In actions reminiscent of the 1848 treaty negotiations, federal officials lied to the tribe, misrepresenting Congress's actions. Ada Deer described Watkins's behavior at the General Council meeting: "On June 20, 1953, Senator Watkins spoke for 45 minutes to our General Council. He told us that Congress had already decided on terminating us, and that at most we could have three years before our 'affairs would be turned over to us'—and that we would not receive our per capitas until *after* termination."[55]

At legislative committee hearings before the bill's passage, Menominees failed to oppose termination. They concentrated their efforts instead on pushing back the date when it would take effect, even though other tribes named in the pending legislation successfully opposed the idea. When tribes and their corresponding state officials both opposed termination, those tribes were stricken from the list. Yet neither the Menominee nor officials of the state of Wisconsin voiced opposition to termination at these meetings. Both merely asked for more time to plan it. In an indication of how trapped the Menominee must have felt, NCAI—the premier national tribal advocacy organization of the time—in its report on the Eighty-third Congress, noted the Menominee termination bill as a *victory* for Indians. NCAI said the Menominee had "requested" it. But what they requested was not what Congress gave them.[56]

Menominee termination occurred because federal officials like Senator Watkins, Congressman Laird, and Commissioner of Indian Affairs Glenn L. Emmons convinced the tribe of its inevitability. Laird, who represented the district in which the Menominee lived, and Emmons visited the reservation and urged the General Council in September 1953 to accept termination. Emmons "told the Menominee that termination was inevitable and that they had better plan for it."[57] Emmons later told NCAI delegates at their 1954 annual convention, "The termination legislation affecting this tribe . . . was the end product of discussions and consultations held with these Indians by Bureau representatives and by key Congressional members over a period of many months. In fact, the general principle of a termination program for the Menominees was approved in a tribal resolution adopted as far back as June 1953."[58] General Council approval for the Menominee was a political requirement in a major decision such as this. The tribe's "consent" in the matter was largely a sham.

Menominees later said they had hoped to avoid deciding about termination until a more sympathetic Democratic Congress might be elected. Gordon Dickie explained:

> So then our strategy for that was okay, we set up a commission. I was a member of that commission, to work on plans for termination. And our strategy that we couldn't make public was that we would push for five years. The first year, one more year and Watkins would be out as chairman of the Indian committee. So we'd have two years of a new chairman. And that covered three years. And if that didn't work out we'd still have a third chairman, would run up to five

years. Hopefully between the three we'd find one favorable chairman. It didn't work out that way.[59]

As S. Lyman Tyler pointed out, the termination program "is a good example of how nonpartisan Indian legislation is. The policy and program of one administration is carried over almost without change to the next. The change from Democrat to Republican made almost no difference."[60]

Tribal frustration and anger built over the issue. With the tribe's support Congressman Laird submitted a bill calling for termination but requesting more time for implementation. The BIA supported Watkins's bill in the Senate. The committees compromised, giving the tribe until 31 December 1958 in the bill that passed. Stephen J. Herzberg, in a history of the events, argues that the Menominee could not have hoped to oppose termination without the support of the state or the federal government, especially after tribal repudiation of termination was entirely ignored and the plan was pushed forward anyway. He lays much of the blame on the state of Wisconsin.[61]

On 17 June 1954 President Eisenhower visited the greatest modern disaster upon the Menominee by signing the termination bill into law. That day the federal government released the per capita payment and closed the Menominee tribal rolls. No Menominees born after 17 June 1954 would be considered Indians by the United States. The new law charged the tribe with formulating a plan to take over federal responsibilities.[62]

FIGHTING CHANGE

According to Zimmerman, former assistant commissioner of Indian affairs, "The Menominee Termination Act was barely signed . . . when differences arose between the Indians and the Bureau." Some were procedural, some were economic, and some related to law enforcement. For example, bureau officials began to adopt implementation plans without consulting tribal leaders. Rancor immediately arose over the per capita distribution as well. Bureau officials had told the tribe that they would pay children's funds to parents, except in unusual circumstances, but the legislation was changed unbeknown to the tribe so that the United States held onto the money. Tribal leaders and family members steamed over this problem, as they saw their interest money being lost to the federal government. A dispute also arose over hunting and fishing rights.[63]

In 1955 the state of Wisconsin established the Menominee Indian Study Committee (MISC) to aid the state legislature in preparing for Wisconsin's responsibilities under termination. Although membership in the committee included not only state and local county representatives but also tribal members, MISC worked to protect the state's interests, not the tribe's. The state desired above all to protect the future of the Menominee forest, since the forest would be the base for the state's future tax income. Although MISC commissioned studies from the University of Wisconsin in Madison, these proved to be of little help to the tribe; MISC's work only supported tribal interests when they coincided with state interests.[64]

The burden of preparing a plan for termination, or for the assumption of governing responsibilities, fell to the tribe. After a century of reservation wardship, in which the tribe's governing system played only advisory, domestic, or reactive roles, the tribe was ill-prepared for this task. The BIA refused to help with the planning.[65] The problems the tribe faced were of immense scale. We can glimpse the complexities of the new situation in the way the tribe dealt with law-and-order issues after 1954.

The enactment of termination immediately created jurisdictional confusion for the Menominee. It established a transitional period, originally set to end 31 December 1958 but later extended to end 31 December 1960. During that time BIA officials remained on the reservation, and the Menominee land remained in trust until the turnover dates, but management of tribal affairs fell into a kind of limbo while the Menominee developed their termination plan. The Menominee had initially opposed participation in Public Law (PL) 280, a federal law that shifted civil and criminal jurisdiction over Indian country from the federal government to the state government in several states, including Wisconsin. In 1953, when Congress passed the law, the Menominee declined to participate, and an exception was written into the legislation.[66]

In April 1954 the tribe reversed its position on the law in General Council, wishing to come under the jurisdiction of the Wisconsin state government. Four months later Congress amended PL-280, extending its provisions to the Menominee. The tribe then needed to plan how to come under state jurisdiction, since the reservation was located in two counties. Until that plan could be effected, federal law enforcement officials remained in place but applied state and county law, not federal law. The BIA found this situation unacceptable and demanded that the tribe replace these law officers by 1 January 1955. Although its officers were employed with tribal funds, the Department of the Interior feared it was operating outside the authority granted by the appropriation act that had authorized the spending in the first place. Also, the assistant secretary of the interior pointed out to tribal members that the officers were employed to enforce departmental regulations and federal code, not state law.

Tribal members protested that the BIA had not fully informed them of the consequences of coming under PL-280. The bureau responded that it had provided a report to the Advisory Council, which had presented it into the records of a General Council meeting on 9 October 1954. At that meeting, a resolution asking Congress again to reverse itself and to repeal PL-280's application to the Menominee passed unanimously. Congress chose to ignore this revote. The tribe invited bureau officials to a 30 October General Council meeting to describe the changes but did not call upon them to speak at the meeting.[67]

Events were transpiring so quickly at this point that it would have been all but impossible for tribal leaders to educate tribal members on the intricacies of these legal changes while in the midst of negotiating the changes. The tribe's Law and Order Committee negotiated with Oconto and Shawano Counties. The committee, chaired by Hilary "Sparky" Waukau, met on 26 January 1955 and assigned tribal law enforcement officials to six policing positions, including police chief, regular police officers, and a juvenile officer, and also appointed a conservation warden. The tribe paid for these positions. The *Menominee News* described their role as follows:

> In enforcing the laws of the State of Wisconsin the officers duties are about the same as those of a Wisconsin County Sheriff in the prosecution of criminal cases on the reservation. They must attend court sessions as needed, coordinate the Tribal Law and Order Program with that of the State of Wisconsin and Shawano and Oconto Counties in particular. They will work under the technical direction of the Sheriff of Shawano County and work under the legal guidance of the Shawano and Oconto County District Attorneys. As deputies to the Sheriff of Shawano County, they are still under the responsibility of the Menominee Advisory Council for administrative purposes.[68]

Law enforcement was but one area of rapid change brought about by the passage of the termination act; the tribal leaders were also dealing with the economy, forest management issues, resource management issues, education, healthcare, governance, the establishment of a separate county, and various other challenges all at once. In an issue that foreshadowed a significant future dispute, the Menominee refused to accept state jurisdiction over hunting and fishing. Tribal member Thomas Oshkosh reflected Menominee sentiment when he said, "It isn't freedom. Now, when I want a deer I can go into the woods and hunt any time. I can fish when I please and take as many fish as I can get. So we get what they call freedom and I have a game warden pointing a gun in my back when I go out to pick a few berries. Is that freedom?"[69]

The Menominee attempted to establish a tribal court to monitor hunting and fishing activities, "but as the Solicitor for the Department [of the Interior] held that the tribe had no authority to set up such a court, the Bureau of Indian Affairs opposed its establishment and refused to release tribal money asked for this purpose."[70] This legal arrangement would of course become void on the date of actual termination, because the Menominee would no longer have the status of a tribe. At that point their law enforcement issues would be the same as other Wisconsin citizens, at least as anticipated by state officials, who did not realize such rights were inherent, not delegated.

The tribe was originally required to develop a plan by the end of 1957 for termination at the end of 1958. By the end of 1958 the secretary of the interior had already begun to oppose the concept of termination. But, as the political scientist Nicholas Peroff points out, "political inertia"—the slow pace of policy change within the federal bureaucracy—prevented the Menominee from escaping this fate.[71] Though the final dates were pushed back, the United States never relented, and it slowly became clear to the Menominee that termination would be put into effect. Many of the tribe's members began to believe that their own leaders had sold out. [72] This belief led to a steady decline in the influence of the Advisory Council between 1954 and 1961 and an intensification of political factionalism.

Incivility entered tribal politics at this time, because the stakes were so high and the potential losses so great. Disagreement and division had been part of Menominee politics for a long time. Some divisions dated to the split between Catholic and non-Catholic bands, others to the Business Committee established at the turn of the century. Family connections often defined where people stood in relation to these politics. But the termination era initiated a quarter-century of political division that would test the Menominee ability to survive. One observer, a youth at the time, later recalled, "The confusion led to misunderstandings and led to shouting matches at Council meetings. I'd never seen that before; that was the beginning of the end."[73]

The Advisory Council admitted its inability to resolve the tribe's problems and asked the General Council to select a three-member Coordinating and Negotiating Committee (CNC) to formulate an implementation plan, which it did. George Kenote, a Menominee who worked for the BIA in Washington DC, was chosen to head the committee, after he actively sought the position at the General Council meeting. He had cut his political teeth in the reservation bureaucracy but since 1930 had worked for the BIA among other Indian peoples. Kenote was chosen because he was not connected to any political group within the tribe. The BIA gave him leave from his position as assistant director of law and order to lead the CNC, which began its work on 20 January 1958 and had less than a year to create a workable plan. Many Menominees still view him as a villain who sold out his own people; he spent much effort toward the end of his life attempting to clear his name.[74]

With the help of attorneys, the state of Wisconsin's MISC, the University of Wisconsin, and state and federal officials, the CNC created an implementation plan. The General Council repeatedly urged the CNC to push for the post-ponement of termination but was eventually forced into deciding whether to accept the implementation plan or to let the secretary of the interior appoint a trustee. The Menominee had little choice but to accept the plan devised by the CNC, which met the deadline by only a week.[75]

The plan led to the creation of two forms of governance: the first was a corporation, Menominee Enterprises, Inc. (MEI), to oversee the timber and sawmill operations, and the second was Menominee County as a separate county. The new county's boundaries were contiguous with those of the reservation.[76] Tribal members, all of whom received stocks and bonds, owned MEI. A nine-person board of directors, chosen by a seven-person voting trust, ran MEI operations. The board consisted of five non-Indian and four Menominee members, by decision of the General Council.[77]

Shareholders, in theory consisting of all Menominees who were on the roll before 1954, selected the voting trust, which elected the board. But the First Wisconsin Trust Company, which acted as a trustee, held all the voting shares for minors. Menominee parents were deemed incompetent to vote their children's shares, no matter what their educational background. The tribe's lawyer advised that it would simply be easier to have First Wisconsin Trust vote these shares in a block rather than dividing the votes among some fourteen hundred guardians. First Wisconsin Trust thus held 44 percent of the vote at termination in 1961. This in essence gave First Wisconsin Trust a controlling share, because Menominee voter turnout ranged from a high of 17.8 percent to a low of 3 percent at the annual shareholders' meetings. The historian Blue Clark has pointed out that, after the U.S. Supreme Court's *Lone Wolf v. Hitchcock* ruling, no Indians could expect to claim competency.[78]

Menominees served on both the voting trust (later expanded to eleven members) and the board of directors. The entire process lay outside the provenance of the General Council and of the control of the tribe as a whole. The tribe lost the power of approval or disapproval it had always held over the Advisory Council and its predecessors, the Business Committee and band leaders.

The creation of the county, meanwhile, was the tribe's chosen method for coming under state jurisdiction. On 9 September 1958 the General Council voted 622–99 in favor of establishing a separate county. The county was established in 1961 on a ten-year trial basis. The counties of which the reservation was part, Oconto and Shawano, coveted the Menominee forest. However, the non-Indian residents of these counties feared that the Menominee would become a financial burden to their counties through the welfare system. So they did not attempt to prevent the establishment of a separate county. The Menominee believed that a separate county would provide them with the powers and protections of their own decision-making authority. The largest threat was the cost of paying for services, including social services, which had to be paid from MEI profits and from taxes in the new county, the poorest in Wisconsin from its inception into the twenty-first century. As these costs mounted and important services were cut, the tribe approached financial ruin.[79]

The Menominee could hold back the dam no longer, and termination rushed into effect on 1 January 1961. Even after it occurred Menominees could scarcely believe it. They held a General Council meeting on 9 January to establish time lines and rules for elections of representatives to county committees—to begin the actual process of governing under the new political conditions. George Kenote proposed the enabling resolution, which Gordon Dickie amended as follows: "the election of the provisional town and county board shall not constitute an agreement between the Menominee Tribe and the Secretary of the Interior to terminate Federal jurisdiction over the Menominee Tribe and Reservation." The tribe discussed sending a delegation to Washington in part to protest termination, to ask the federal government to study it, and to test its legality.[80] A study of the potential impact of termination had never been done.[81] These efforts proved futile, however, and termination remained in effect.

In another setback for the tribe, the newly established Menominee County lacked some powers that most Wisconsin counties held. For example, the Wisconsin enabling legislation for the establishment of the county provided that Shawano County oversee juvenile court services, since the Menominee lacked attorneys, and that both the school superintendent and the district attorney of Shawano County have jurisdiction over Menominee County.[82]

Now the interests of three jurisdictional bodies potentially conflicted with each other: MEI, the county, and the tribe. The latter, however, had lost its authority. MEI held the power because it controlled the resources. MEI had to prove Menominee County a success by 1971, or it would not receive final approval from the state to remain as a county. But the economy, destroyed at the onset of termination, progressively worsened as costs increased. The Menominee desperately needed their own county, even though it was a financial disaster. If the state chose to break up the county, this would create an intense threat to the tribal culture. As Nancy Lurie put it at the time, "Division means certain oblivion of the Menominee as a people, since their corporation holding their assets would be torn between white interest groups from all sides, all of which outnumbered the Menominee tribal population."[83] Most Menominees felt helpless to resolve the problems facing them.

Ironically, the Menominee now theoretically had what they had desired for several decades—control over their resources. Yet they had also lost their trust status and the "protection" of the U.S. government. While that protection had proven flimsy time and again, tribal leaders knew it to be necessary to ensure tribal survival. Not since the loss of their land base during the treaty years had the Menominee faced such a struggle to survive both politically and culturally.

CHAPTER TEN

The Road to Restoration

Termination immediately brought financial crisis to both the tribe and individual Menominees.[1] It also destroyed the political base of the tribe. It placed the Menominee cultural and social fabric under siege. In economic, political, and sociocultural terms, termination visited an unmitigated disaster on the tribe, comparable only to the land losses associated with the nineteenth-century treaty era.

Even before termination went into effect the Menominee assets diminished rapidly. They used nearly half of the $10 million tribal nest egg for the per capita payment of $1,500 to each of the 3,270 tribal members. The tribe was forced to spend another $2 million in dividends to make up for a shortfall caused by BIA underpayment on the stumpage fund. With the costs of renovations to the hospital in Keshena and the church in Neopit, the tribal accounts fell below $2 million. In testimony before Congress a decade later, Ada Deer and others said, "[B]y 1960 our tribe was operating at a $250,000 annual deficit."[2]

Under termination the Menominee "freedom" from governmental oversight actually diminished. George Kenote observed that termination "*did not end* government supervision. The immediate experience was that we immediately became subject to about twenty-seven other federal or state regulatory or investigative agencies."[3] Termination failed in its most basic aim, since the removal of the BIA actually led to an increase in federal oversight.

At the same time, the cost to the federal government increased markedly. For example, in the year preceding termination the tribal budget for services stood at over $500,000. The tribe paid most of this from its own funds. According to the tribe's official history, "The Federal Government, which was obligated to provide all these services, actually spent only . . . $144,000." Over the next five years the federal government spent some $5 million in aid to the Menominee, an annual increase of some sevenfold, in an attempt to help the tribal members survive termination.[4]

Termination led to a reorganization of the logging business, a fight over control of natural resources and land, crises in healthcare management and education, a diminution of tribal governance authority, and ultimately a threat to the survival of the Menominee as a people. It struck a vicious blow to tribal identity in general, causing individuals to suffer in terms of both physical and mental health.

The reorganization of the logging business damaged the tribe economically, both by diminishing the profits from the mill and by destroying the social service nature of the operations. At the time of termination the mill was found to violate state code in 132 instances; the tribe paid one hundred thousand dollars to correct these violations. MEI ran the mill under termination. Because federal officials had never trained Menominees to take over mill operations, the tribe was forced to hire outsiders. Of the first six presidents of MEI only one was Menominee.[5] The new mill leadership, largely ignorant of or unsympathetic to the role of the mill in Menominee culture and society and needing to bring large profits to support the tribe in its new status, tried to modernize mill operations.

Their attempts proved disastrous. The managers, unlike early twentieth-century government officials on the reservation, had logging experience. Unfortunately, it was large-scale, clear-cut logging in the western United States they knew best, and these "West Coast cowboys" tried to import their methods to the Menominee reservation. For example, they purchased larger, more efficient trucks to haul lumber, which put the small tribal truckers out of work. Stephen J. Herzberg, in an article on the effects of termination, described what happened when these large trucks came to the reservation: "It was not until after the new trucks were delivered that the managers found that they were too wide for the reservation roads. Undaunted, they had the roads widened. But the trucks still could not be used; when loaded to near capacity, they were so heavy they sank into the roads. Similar attempts at innovation failed."[6] As with other facilities on the reservation, the Menominee logging facilities and the infrastructure were not up to modern U.S. standards.

"Not able to improve the efficiency of the operation with physical changes," Herzberg continued, "the management attempted to increase the productivity of the work force." This too was done in an attempt to "maximize profit." Managers held workers more accountable in their jobs and fired them for things that they would not previously have fired them for. Yet all these changes failed to increase profits. During this time the mill lost money, in part due to the upheaval of the termination process, in part due to a decreasing demand for mill products.[7]

Gordon Dickie, who served on the MEI board of directors, later recalled,

> I had worked out west enough in my early days to know the difference between the two operations. . . . But we had some pretty rough times then. . . . I was reprimanded a number of times by management because I took opposition to some of their proposals. So we started out a million seven-hundred and fifty thousand dollars in the treasury in the bank, twenty million feet of lumber in the yard, all our bills were paid up, and they blew the million seven-hundred fifty thousand working at the mill, they liquidated the inventory, they sold the power line, they sold the telephone system, they sold everything they could possibly sell in order to try to show a profit. It never worked.[8]

Resources failed to provide the economic base on which everyone had counted.

Yet the Menominee never wavered from the belief that the forest was tribal property. "Most of us felt that to liquidate [the forest] would destroy the tribe entirely," Gordon Dickie explained.[9] The tribe had not permitted a parceling of the resource or individual ownership. In creating their plan for termination, the Menominee never considered dividing or selling the forest. They merely sought a viable method for managing it. The forest was inseparable from the tribe's identity. It had sustained Menominees since time immemorial. They had logged it to provide for individuals and the tribe as a whole since 1871, with ever so slowly increasing control. The disaster of termination proved to be one more in a long line of setbacks in the tribe's relentless efforts to gain control of the management of its resource.

Meanwhile, mill improvements aimed to increase safety, to improve productivity, and to expand product lines. Management added safety devices to existing machines, purchased safer machines, and added updated equipment such as new large-capacity kilns.[10] Some of these costs legitimately added value to the mill. Other expenses, however, were directly related to previous mill mismanagement that had not kept the mill up to standards and code.

The deleterious impacts of termination on the tribal economy were felt at both the tribal and individual levels. In terms of resources, the state stepped in immediately to take control of hunting and fishing rights in Menominee County. The state of Wisconsin arrested Joseph L. Sanapaw and two others for "jacklighting deer" on 8 and 9 September 1962. According to the attorney Charles A. Hobbs, Sanapaw "admitted the offense, but claimed he had hunting rights under the [1854] Menominee Treaty." That treaty did not specifically delineate hunting rights but did direct that reservation lands "be held as Indian lands are held."[11]

Judge R. H. Fischer of the County Court of Shawano-Menominee Counties ruled in favor of the defendants. However, the Wisconsin Supreme Court ruled that the Termination Act abrogated treaty-based rights because "upon termination of federal supervision . . . enrolled members of the tribe and their land became subject to same Wisconsin game laws as other persons and lands within the state."[12]

The impacts of termination on the community extended even beyond the threats to the forest and the loss of subsistence hunting and fishing rights. Healthcare was immediately affected. In 1961, for example, the old hospital in Keshena was closed for failure to meet state standards even after the tribe spent three hundred thousand dollars to upgrade it. The federal government refused to kick in the final fifty thousand dollars needed. Few tribal members owned cars, and even when they did "many could not depend upon them for a 20 mile trip to a clinic in the neighboring Shawano County," according to a tribal source.[13]

Ten years later tribal leaders summarized the healthcare disaster: "With the closing of the BIA hospital, we lost most of our health services, and most Menominee continue to suffer from lack of medical care. There have been no full-time doctors or dentists in Menominee County since termination. Shortly after termination, our people were stricken by a TB epidemic which caused great suffering and hardship because of the lack of local medical facilities."[14]

The same group of leaders summarized the impact of termination on education. The St. Joseph's Catholic boarding school in Keshena had closed its dormitories in 1952 and become a day school. At this time approximately 80 percent of Menominee children attended Catholic schools. That percentage began a steady decline as parents moved more children into the public school system. Termination brought the end of funding to help parents send their children to parochial schools.[15] The leaders testified:

Education in Menominee County—which theoretically should offer our people a hope of future advancement—has also suffered because of termination. The loss of the BIA school required that our youth be sent to Shawano County for their high school training. The Shawano school system has assumed that Menominee children possess the same cultural and historical background as a middle-class white family community. Consequently, the school system has shown insensitivity to the cultural background and the special needs of *our* children. In many cases, our children find themselves objects of rejection and discrimination. Since 1961, our high school drop-out rates have increased substantially, absenteeism has soared, and our children apparently are suffering a downward trend in achievement. Comparisons based on educational achievement tests show that Menominee children fall significantly below district and national norms.[16]

Taxes as well proved to be an enormous burden, both on the tribe and on individuals. Although Menominee County was Wisconsin's poorest, the state required a higher percentage of payments from the county—providing less help than to almost any other county in the state. The political scientist Nicholas C. Peroff observed, "The state of Wisconsin was extremely reluctant to grant special aid to Menominee County. State officials argued that, since termination was the idea of Congress, it was the responsibility of the federal government to provide the necessary funds to bring Menominee County up to state standards for government services."[17] The cost of taxes in addition to the cost of improvements to the mill proved crippling to the tribe. By 1967 these costs were "more than double MEI's net income."[18]

Menominee individuals did not qualify for welfare payments as long as they held the "income bonds" issued on termination, which provided a small stumpage income. But with high unemployment and without federal aid, welfare became a necessity for many Menominees. In addition, they were forced to purchase the land on which they lived and to pay taxes on it. Many people, probably a majority of the tribe, thus lost their income bonds, either as collateral for land purchase or as collateral to the state for welfare payments. As Peroff points out, the state thus used Menominee money to subsidize its welfare payments to tribal members—a practice reminiscent of the nineteenth-century use of forest monies to pay for treaty annuities. Homeowners who could not pay taxes lost their land; others were unable to pay for home repairs and upkeep now that individual money rather than tribal funds paid for these things.[19]

The Menominee had difficulty responding to these problems, since their tribal government had ceased to exist and governance now occurred through MEI and the county. Both of these institutions had different purposes and aspirations than the tribe itself. The federal government recognized the financial crisis to some degree. On 10 and 11 November 1965 Senator Gaylord Nelson of Wisconsin conducted public hearings at St. Anthony's gym in Neopit. An impressive array of witnesses turned out to testify to the high financial costs of termination to the Menominee people and Menominee County. A bill before the Senate and the House proposed to provide nearly three million dollars in grants and up to five million dollars in loans over a ten-year period to support the schools, public welfare, health, sanitation, and the economy. Some of the grant money would be spread over five to ten years, while some would be expended immediately.[20] Just five years after the implementation of termination, federal officials were ready to admit that the Menominee had fallen far from the state of self-sufficiency that had been the reason for their termination in the first place. The grim testimony at these hearings bolstered this interpretation.

Yet government assistance would only begin to resolve the problems. By 1968 the official Menominee unemployment rate reached 24.4 percent. MEI, in search of sources of income to ease its financial problems, began to consider the option of selling Menominee land to outsiders, who could build summer and retirement homes in the beautiful Menominee forest. In 1967 a Washington firm, Ernst and Ernst, using federal money but at the request of the MEI board of directors, conducted a study of the tourism and development potential for the reservation.[21] MEI had already leased public campsites along the Wolf River to the state and summer home lots on the Wolf River and on small reservation lakes to non-Indians. "MEI then quietly sold these plots outright to increase the number of county taxpayers."[22] Voters approved land sales at a meeting of 253 stockholders, although the language of the proposal was stated so generally that most of those voting did not realize what they had agreed to.[23]

This led to an agreement between the MEI board and the developer N. E. Isaacson, Inc. In 1968 they formed a partnership to flood a series of small reservation lakes to create one large lake, called Legend Lake or Lake of the Menominees. In July 1968 sale of individual lake lots to non-Menominees began. Within three years, thirteen hundred lots were sold; eventually, some two thousand were sold.[24] Non-Indians began to build homes and move onto Menominee land for the first time.

The force of all these changes weighed heavily on the Menominee—economically, politically, and psychologically. In the words of the anthropologist Katherine Hall, "For the Menominee under Termination, there was an abrupt and far-reaching change in every cultural institution simultaneously, and in a manner found only in the dislocation or the devastation of war victims which had been unprecedented in 'peace time'. Between 1954 and 1973, a massive shift of Menominee relationships with social institutions occurred in every sociocultural category. Subsistence, allocation of land, political system, law enforcement, economic resources, education, health care, and family were drastically changed; thus, affecting cultural values and belief systems." Menominee children raised during this period after the closing of the tribal rolls have been called "the lost generation" due to these factors and the breakdown of the tribal language and other cultural practices that accompanied them.[25]

THE TRIBE FIGHTS BACK

The sale of Menominee land and the threat to Menominee identity and existence galvanized public opinion within the tribe and served as a catalyst for change. At the same time as things were falling apart, positive change began to occur on several fronts. Tribal members had been working to reverse termination and its impacts since before it went into effect. From the beginning of termination a variety of tribal leaders, those with governing experience as well as those with a grassroots background, opposed it in multiple ways.

Though the Termination Act effectively legislated the tribal government out of existence, a number of the old-time tribal leaders banded together in an attempt to maintain a recognition of the tribe itself. They formed the Council of Chiefs, which they incorporated as a not-for-profit organization in 1962. Years later Al Dodge recalled this step as an attempt "to redeem ourselves to a degree . . . to organize a respected government, a respected organization." According to the tribe's official history, "The main purpose of the organization was . . . to preserve our name as a tribe." Gordon Dickie explained that "that's one thing we were very, very cautious about." They incorporated with the state as the "Menominee Indian Tribe of Wisconsin, Inc." The key members were Alex Frechette, Atlee Dodge, Gordon Dickie, Al Dodge, Jim Frechette, Sparky Waukau, and Wayne Chevalier.[26]

This effort not only gave a boost to morale within the community, but it also signaled to the outside world that the Menominee still considered themselves a tribal nation. The tribe's legal entanglements with the state and federal governments also reflected this self-view. In 1967 the Menominee sued the United States, "alleging mismanagement of tribal assets by the Bureau of Indian Affairs."[27] This lawsuit became the basis for tribal claims against the United States in relation to termination.

Meanwhile, the U.S. Supreme Court refused to accept the Sanapaw hunting case on its docket in 1964, so the tribe turned to the Court of Claims. Gordon Dickie later recalled what happened then:

> And this is one of the things that happens that is just good fortune I guess or maybe the Great Spirit is watching over us or something. Years, many years ago when I was chairman [of the Advisory Council] we invited and gave guest permits to three gentlemen out of Madison. One was Chairman of the . . .

Public Service Commission. He and his buddies came up and they really enjoyed themselves camping out and fishing on the reservation. Eisenhower then appointed him . . . as Chairman of the Civil Aeronautics Board. From there he was then nominated to the Court of Claims, in Justice. So when our fishing and hunting suit went up and we wanted the Supreme Court to handle it and the Supreme Court decided not to . . . it automatically went before the Court of Claims. And Judge Jim Durfee, our old friend wrote the majority decision that we . . . were not entitled to damages because we had not lost the hunting and fishing rights. So that forced the issue into the Supreme Court. The Supreme Court then had to settle it. Here's the state saying we did lose it, here's the U.S. Court of Claims in Washington saying we didn't. The only possible solution was for the Supreme Court to take it up. And the Supreme Court ruled in our favor, that we retained our hunting and fishing rights.[28]

Actually, Durfee wrote the dissenting opinion for the Court of Claims, concluding, "Therefore, rather than reach a decision on the merits of the case at this time, I would have certified the following question to the Supreme Court: Did the Menominee Termination Act of 1954 cancel the hunting and fishing rights of plaintiffs on their reservation and thereby subject them to the game laws of the State of Wisconsin as if they were non-Indian citizens of the state?"[29] The Supreme Court did indeed take the case and address that very issue.

In 1968 the U.S. Supreme Court recognized the tribe's hunting and fishing rights as still existing despite the extension of state jurisdiction over the former reservation. The 1854 treaty did not specifically mention hunting and fishing rights, but the Supreme Court decided that these were inherent Menominee treaty rights and, furthermore, that termination did not abrogate any treaty rights except those specifically spelled out in the act.[30]

Justice William O. Douglas wrote in the majority opinion, "The essence of the Treaty of Wolf River was that the Indians were authorized to maintain on the new lands ceded to them as a reservation their way of life which included hunting and fishing." He also said, "We decline to construe the Termination Act as a backhanded way of abrogating the hunting and fishing rights of these Indians." He finished by quoting Senator Watkins, "who stated upon the occasion of the signing of the bill that it 'in no way violates a treaty obligation with this tribe.'"[31]

The Menominee's attorneys, Wilkinson, Cragun, and Barker, wrote to the Council of Chiefs, "The rights will exist as long as the tribe exists. This means the tribe must remain active in supervising these rights. Otherwise the rights may be held to be abandoned."[32] The tribe's refusal to accede to state law proved fortuitous. The outcome of this case affected federal Indian policy nationwide. The fact that the tribe retained treaty rights gave added impetus to the opposition to termination.[33]

At about this time, parents frustrated with the education system took action. Menominee schools had been incorporated into Shawano Joint School District No. 8 at termination. While grade schools had remained open in Keshena and Neopit, the district bussed middle school and high school students to Shawano. In addition, parents lost other schooling options, since the federal government no longer paid tuition at parochial or boarding schools. The primary schools on the reservation lagged behind the rest in the district. The middle school segregated Menominee students almost immediately upon entering through a system that tracked many of them into classes for underachievers—a typical segregation tactic in public schools. The schools provided no culture-based education in the district curriculum to Indian students and no cultural sensitivity training to teachers who suddenly faced large numbers of Indian children in the classroom. In addition, Menominee children were punished more often and more severely than non-Indian children in the schools. Whereas many Menominee children had enjoyed a good experience in Shawano schools before termination, the added pressure in schools after termination built up, until serious problems began to surface. Between sixth grade and the end of high school, some 50 percent of Menominee children dropped out of the school system during this time.[34]

In 1969 parents began to organize action committees to challenge the administration to deal with the issues of prejudice and violence against Indian students. Students themselves began to demonstrate. As the situation "became increasingly tense" in 1971 community members established the Menominee County Education Committee, with Andre LeMay as president and Atlee Dodge as chair. The committee immediately initiated an "Indian control philosophy." In April it "forced [a] referendum on a reluctant County government" that called for Menominee County to split from Shawano and establish its own school system. The referendum passed in Menominee County, but the Wisconsin Department of Public Instruction (DPI) failed to support it.[35]

In May 1972 the parents and students filed a federal lawsuit against the school district charging discrimination. In July 1972 the DPI completed a study showing that Menominee children earned deficient scores on standardized achievement tests but concluding that Menominee students had good opportunities in Shawano. At this point the education committee turned its efforts to establishing a community school in Keshena, modeled on successful programs elsewhere in Indian country. The school opened with its first seven students and began steadily to build from there.[36]

Meanwhile, tribal members began to respond to an even more serious threat, the sale of the land base to nontribal members. The words of several tribal leaders reflected the general feelings of the tribe. Three spoke at an MEI board of directors meeting in 1965. Sparky Waukau said, "I have to say that I am opposed to the sale of these lake lots by warranty deed." James Frechette added, "I believe the majority of the Menominee Indians are interested in holding onto whatever land they still have title to. . . . I am not in favor of letting go of one foot of our country." Gordon Dickie said, "We are now down to the last things we have—the lake lots. My vote is NO."[37]

Ernest Neconish, speaking through the interpreter Louise P. Fowler to a Senate Indian Affairs subcommittee in 1973, when the impetus for restoration had gained momentum, lamented on the current affairs in the Menominee world. "I told Menominee Indians years ago to block off our roads so no white people could come in and make trouble for us. That's what's happening today."[38] None of the groups that blossomed in the early 1960s succeeded in mobilizing enough support to bring about change, however. A feeling of gloom had descended upon the tribe, bringing with it an attitude that conditions were beyond tribal control.

When outsiders began to purchase Menominee land, effective anger at the leadership arose throughout the reservation and among Menominees living in the nearby cities of Milwaukee and Chicago. A group of tribal leaders likened "selling our land to generate cash for payment of community services" to "burning down your house to keep warm in a blizzard."[39] A well-organized opposition developed in a group called DRUMS, an acronym for Determination of Rights and Unity for Menominee Shareholders, founded in 1970. DRUMS listed eight goals from the time of its inception, including restoring tribal control of the timber resource, ending the sale of tribal lands to nonmembers, reopening the tribal rolls, and protecting treaty rights.[40]

THE RISE OF DRUMS

On a small budget but with high enthusiasm fueled by deep anger, DRUMS was determined to attack the tribe's problems at the seat of power: the MEI voting trust. At the same time, they took their fight to the outside world—to state officials, federal officials, and the American public. Among Menominees, DRUMS members first sought greater understanding of MEI's finances and decision making and eventually decided to mobilize shareholders to elect new leadership to the MEI voting trust. DRUMS organized less easily in Menominee County than it did in the other areas, due to natural resistance within Menominee County.[41]

DRUMS borrowed tactics from the burgeoning civil rights movement. Their tactics included direct action and angry public accusation, picketing of the First Wisconsin Trust Company offices in Milwaukee, and public marches. These tactics were bolder and more divisive than many Menominees would generally support. Many tribal members in Menominee County depended on MEI for their jobs. However, given the divisive intransigence of those in charge of MEI, DRUMS steadily grew in influence in Menominee County.[42]

As DRUMS brought attention surrounding the Menominee plight to the outside world, anger at termination was increasing even among non-Menominees and non-Indians. In 1965 Congressman Melvin Laird of Wisconsin and others began speaking against it; in 1968 President Lyndon Johnson added his voice to the opposition. Arthur Watkins stubbornly insisted that Congress had made the proper policy choices: "It was an experiment worth trying. The Indians had been critical of all government agencies but they found out that running a government agency was a real task." But few others agreed. President Richard Nixon publicly denounced termination in July 1970 when he put forth the new federal policy of self-determination.[43] DRUMS began focusing its attention not only on overthrowing MEI (and county) leadership but on reversing Menominee termination entirely. This idea was not even considered as an option by most people at this time. Wisconsin state senator Reuben LaFave said in 1971, for example, "For the Menominees there is no turning back. But what happened to the Menominees should and cannot happen to the other Indian tribes of America."[44]

DRUMS's actions led to bitter conflict on the reservation between the "governing elites," or the Menominee leaders who supported or were part of MEI, and DRUMS members and followers. Longstanding political factions dating to the old Catholic-traditional religious divisions and the Advisory Council–General Council divisions that followed the establishment of logging burst into full flower, creating an ever more divisive subtext within community politics.

Though Menominee tribal members each owned MEI voting certificates, which they could use in decision making at annual meetings, the First Wisconsin Trust Company held and voted all shares of minors and those deemed incompetent. With low voter turnout among Menominees deemed competent, First Wisconsin Trust voted between 80 and 93 percent of the annual vote.[45]

The role that urban Indians played in helping their home reservation communities proved critical. They not only sent aid in whatever form they could, but they also advocated to the larger public on their peoples' behalf. For example, Jim and Gwen Washinawatok had moved to Chicago in 1956 and stayed for nearly twenty years. The Washinawatoks, like many Menominees, were angry about termination. The sale of Menominee land to non-Indians for recreational use catalyzed that anger to action.[46]

Jim Washinawatok brought together the core group that established the DRUMS organization. Joan Harte, a key member of that core group, later recalled, "The truth of the matter is that Jim was the visionary and if it weren't for him restoration would not have happened."[47] Washinawatok himself recalled the early meetings in which Menominees from Chicago and Milwaukee would gather at his house on the north side of Chicago. Throughout these efforts the core of the DRUMS group retained its base in both Chicago and Milwaukee. The important work they did carried on longstanding Menominee traditions and longstanding customs within the urban Indian community as well. These activities provide a valuable historical picture of cooperation between urban and reservation communities and of the too often ignored connections between tribal members who have left home and those who have stayed. The Menominee restoration effort could not have succeeded without significant contributions from both groups of people.

"We would just sit around and talk about things that were happening up on the reservation," Washinawatok said.

> We were all concerned about the destruction that was going on, and the development of what they called Legend Lake, or Lake of the Menominees. . . . And we would come up here [to the reservation] and visit our parents and they would take us out to the area where this was being developed and we would see the bulldozers out there knocking down trees, and scraping and digging up . . . our old springs, which our old people considered sacred. . . . And we were especially disturbed by [the developer's] motto which said, "Another improvement on nature." . . . And they kept referring to this land as substandard and of marginal value, that it was nothing but scrub oak growing out there, and the land was of little value. And . . . that disturbed us, because all our land was valuable to us, it was land that our ancestors . . . had fought very, very hard for, and sacrificed many years of their lives. So that, when you'd go to these old council meetings, you would always hear these people get up and say that they . . . had to think of their grandchildren and their great grandchildren of future years and have a place where they could always call home. . . . And that's why we used to sit down in Chicago and Milwaukee and talk about these things and wondered what we could do about it.[48]

Every member of that group lacked political sophistication, savvy, or know-how, however. Although they felt overwhelmed at first, they began two courses of action that would become the foundations of their movement: they began to visit the reservation and organize protest meetings there, and they sought the help of outside groups and individuals with vast experience in community organizing and action. These outsiders included Saul Alinsky's Industrial Areas Foundation; the musician Buffy Sainte-Marie; LaDonna Harris's Americans for Indian Opportunity (AIO); the Center for Community Change; and Wisconsin Judicare, which provided legal advice. Judicare, supported by U.S. Office of Economic Opportunity (OEO) money, also brought in the Native American Rights Fund (NARF), a newly formed Indian-run legal organization based in Boulder, Colorado, and Washington DC. The Center for Community Change provided funding for transportation to Washington DC in early efforts to lobby Congress. AIO provided the connections to enable those efforts to be successful. Harris and her husband, Senator Fred Harris, opened their home, their offices, and their services to Menominee tribal members, first Jim Washinawatok and later Ada Deer, and provided a base for the Menominee lobbying effort.[49]

Nevertheless, the most important work focused on the reservation and the state of Wisconsin. Many of the state's newspapers reported that the Menominee were eager to sell their land. Washinawatok described DRUMS's goals in relation to public sentiment within Wisconsin: "*The Milwaukee Journal*, and *The Milwaukee Sentinel*, and *The Green Bay Press-Gazette* were producing propaganda . . . to the state of Wisconsin public that we wanted to sell this land. And that . . . all these big organizations were doing this to help the poor Menominees survive termination. . . . [T]hat was the picture that was being presented to the public in the state of Wisconsin. And we wanted the state of Wisconsin to know that this was not true, that we did not want to sell our land."[50]

DRUMS members received little help from tribal members on the reservation at first. Established leaders told them that the land sales simply could not be stopped and that termination could not be reversed. If potential allies on the reservation protested against the Legend Lake project, they would be jeopardizing their jobs with MEI or the tribe and thus their own families' welfare. The first times DRUMS members traveled home they were unable to secure meeting rooms, but nonetheless they began to demonstrate at the site of the new development. Washinawatok recalled,

[M]y family and I drove up every weekend. If we missed a weekend it was so insignificant I can't even remember it now. . . . And it was through those demonstrations . . . that we were able to stop the Legend Lake Project. . . . I told our people in the organization many times, if we quit and we do not follow up on what we're doing, I said the Menominees will never ever recover from that. So I said once we commit ourselves to doing this we've got to fight it right out to the end. And no matter what happens if we do our best and fight it out to the end and not give up we'll stop the sale of land. And we did that through our demonstrations. And we were consistent, we never missed unless it was an emergency, and we'd come up here every weekend and we'd demonstrate out at the project to let these people know we didn't want to sell our land. And eventually the land developer, it affected the land sales, and the project. We had them dissolve the partnership between Menominee Enterprises, Incorporated and the land developer, and the project was dissolved.[51]

This was done with the legal help of Wisconsin Judicare and with increasing support of tribal members. In October 1972 tribal members staged a ten-day march from the reservation in Keshena to the state capitol in Madison. They stopped to demonstrate in the hometown of the Lake Project developer along the way. This march culminated on Columbus Day and garnered support from non-Indians throughout the state.

DRUMS publicly attacked the opposition, using sometimes bitter personal invective. For example, the DRUMS newsletter named a person that DRUMS considered as a traitor to the Menominee people as "Apple of the Month."[52] DRUMS's opponents included the Menominee County Shareholders and Tax-payers Alliance, the Council of Chiefs, and Menominees for Progress. One individual charged that DRUMS had created "a wide division among the Menominee people. Brother against brother, children against parents. . . . Many of those now called 'drums' do not live in Menominee County. Many are too young to know the trouble we've seen."[53] George Kenote, also a strong opponent of DRUMS, wrote that the organization was established and controlled by the white allies. Those allies included the attorney Joe Preloznik of Judicare and the anthropologist Nancy Lurie, outsiders to the tribe whom Kenote accused of having communist or red-tinged motivations.[54] DRUMS, with the help of Preloznik and Judicare, took MEI to court to open its books, to block land sales, and to free the bonds from First Wisconsin Trust. All of these suits were unsuccessful but were costly to MEI.[55]

The success at ending the land sales spurred DRUMS members and other tribal members to begin to push for a restoration of tribal rights through a congressional overturn of termination. This too was a slow, difficult process in which tribal members and the numerous allies of the tribe worked together in a remarkable effort that has been credited with playing a significant role in moving federal policy in the direction of tribal self-determination.

In 1971 DRUMS forced a vote to dissolve the MEI board and "obtained a majority of the shares voted." However, First Wisconsin Trust voted its shares in opposition and defeated the attempt. DRUMS then changed tactics, running candidates for positions in the voting trust as they became open. "The new strategy was a spectacular success," such that by the end of 1972 DRUMS controlled a majority of MEI's board of directors.[56]

Meanwhile, non-Indian opposition to termination mounted, and DRUMS began demanding restoration of federally recognized status. In the words of Nancy Lurie, "While [Washinawatok] united the Menominee people in mass public expressions of their opposition to MEI and termination itself, Ada [Deer] appealed to the American public to right this great wrong."[57] Following a long-established pattern among tribal leaders, dating back over a century, Deer traveled to Washington to lobby Congress and the Nixon administration for restoration. She successfully gained support of the Democratic Party and rallied non-Indian public opinion in favor of the Menominee. In a statement that became a hallmark of her professional career, Deer told a reporter, "Mainly I want to show people who say nothing can be done in this society that it just isn't so. You don't have to collapse just because there's a federal law in your way. Change it!"[58] Key Republicans also supported the tribe. Bradley Patterson and Melvin Laird worked in the White House to ensure Nixon's support of restoration, for example.[59]

Deer's popularity with the media led to a falling out with DRUMS founders. Jim Washinawatok resigned as president, the original incarnation of DRUMS dissolved, and those members who would eventually become the Menominee Restoration Committee (MRC) took over the organization. This broadened the political factionalism among Menominees but did not diminish tribal members' efforts to end termination.[60]

With the clear voice of the Menominee rising in opposition to continued existence as a federally unrecognized tribe, Congress held hearings in Keshena and Washington in May and June 1973. Both Menominee and non-Indian experts testified to the destructive effects of termination.[61] Even George Kenote spoke strongly in favor of restoration, although he believed that termination failed because it was forced too quickly on the tribe. He believed the process should have been more gradual—a belief among Menominee leadership that predated termination. Kenote also strongly supported the sale of Legend Lake lots for financial reasons.[62]

Momentum increased for passage of the restoration bill but ran into a snag with the proposed amendments of Republican congressman Harold Froehlich of Appleton, who represented the Menominee's district. Froehlich had purchased a lot at Legend Lake, and he insisted that the law protect the rights of non-Indian landowners. When his proposal to create a separate county failed, and when DRUMS agreed to compromise with him, the final bill, including the protections, was brought to Congress.[63]

Congress passed the Restoration Act, and President Nixon signed it into law on 22 December 1973.[64] Nixon reasoned that the Menominee had retained their cultural identity and thus deserved to have their tribal status restored: "Because the Menominee People have seen their tribal status involuntarily terminated but had nonetheless kept their land and their tribal structure together, the Congress enacted and I signed the bill which restored the Menominee tribe to trust status." In a verbal slap at the more radical and flamboyant American Indian Movement (AIM) organization, Nixon also praised the Menominee "for their persuasiveness and perseverance in using the tools of the political process to bring about peaceful change."[65]

Menominees are quick to note that DRUMS achieved restoration through the work of a number of leaders, not just one or two.[66] DRUMS's success on a variety of fronts—taking over MEI, gaining support throughout the county, gaining support throughout the state, and forcing change on Capitol Hill—testifies to this notion. As with other important political battles against the federal government also won by the tribe—such as the creation of the reservation in 1854, the rejection of land sales in the 1870s and 1920s, and the rejection of allotment—Menominee leaders led the fight, but they were also willing to rely on non-Menominee aid. For example, NARF donated more than fourteen hundred man-hours of legal help in the fight for restoration; allies in the anthropological community and legal system helped popularize the tribe's cause outside of Menominee County; and sympathetic government officials lent their help in Washington and Madison.[67] But Menominees did most of the work. Many DRUMS members and leaders went on to leadership positions within the tribe after restoration, continuing to the present.[68] Their involvement was critical, because the difficult task of building a tribally controlled community and reestablishing the reservation lay ahead.

CHAPTER ELEVEN

Restoration

The Menominee victory over termination provided a surge of hope on the reservation. James Washinawatok described perhaps the biggest barrier that the activists had overcome: hopelessness. "I'd have to say . . . that when we first started out, that if we'd have listened to people . . . that were very knowledgeable in politics, local people I'm talking about, and people we'd known all our lives, . . . this would have never come about, because every time we talked to them, they told us that this would never ever happen. . . . And even other people . . . off the reservation told us that we'd never be able to do this. And even some of the politicians, the professional politicians were very skeptical about how we would be able to do this."[1]

The Restoration Act officially granted federal recognition to the Menominee tribe, while repealing the Termination Act and reextending "all rights and privileges of the tribe on its members." The act authorized the Department of the Interior and the Department of Health, Education, and Welfare (HEW) to provide grants to the Menominee. It established a nine-person interim governing body, the MRC, to be elected by the General Council. This committee was to draft the tribe's constitution and bylaws, to create the new governing system, and to develop a plan for the resumption of federal trust status.[2] These tasks created a whole new set of challenges for the Menominee.

GROWING PAINS

The initial problem related to the MRC election was the fact that the Termination Act had closed tribal rolls on 17 June 1954. The new restoration law therefore established eligibility standards that applied only to the election of the MRC. The electorate included all members who were listed on the 1954 tribal roll and eighteen-year-old descendants who were at least one-fourth-blood Menominee. The secretary of the interior was charged with overseeing all these stipulations.[3]

On 2 March 1974 tribal members voted at polling places in Neopit, Keshena,

South Branch, and Zoar to elect the MRC. In a field of forty-five candidates, Ada Deer heavily outpolled the rest. The top nine vote-getters were already politically active in the reservation community on a variety of fronts. Several had represented the tribe in Washington regarding restoration, while others were active in MEI, the voting trust, DRUMS, the Council of Chiefs, the Education Committee, the Woodworker's Union, and county politics. A mere seven votes separated the eighth- through twelfth-place candidates.[4] This close vote led to two recounts in which the ninth-place position ended in a tie between John Peters and Sarah Skubitz. Both offered to withdraw so as not to delay the process of restoration. Skubitz was seated as the ninth member of the committee, but Robert Grignon resigned, and Peters replaced him.[5]

The newly elected MRC became certified on 6 May, with Ada Deer as chair. Nancy Lurie observed, "Ada's election as chair of the committee, in effect making her the head of the restored Menominee tribe, demonstrated that she still had the confidence of a majority of her people." Deer later recalled, "Both men and women said, 'We don't know about this. We've never had a woman at the head of our tribe.' The men have always been in charge and I said, 'Well that could be *part* of the problem.' You have to change. You have to change people's thinking."[6]

The role of the MRC would be to guide the tribe as it reestablished a tribally controlled government, its first step toward self-determination. The MRC thus had to govern the tribe and to pave the way for the new Menominee leadership during this transition period. To accomplish this end, the MRC was charged first with revising the newly reopened tribal roll, both deleting names of those tribal members who had passed on during termination and adding the names of those who had been born. The law established one-quarter-blood quantum as the minimum standard for membership.[7]

While the roll was being finalized, the MRC was charged with drafting a constitution and bylaws, in consultation with those who would be eligible to vote. After the secretary of the interior approved finalization of the roll, eligible voters would vote to approve the constitution. The MRC then would have some four months to hold elections for the tribal officials whose positions the constitution would create. These elections, both on the constitution and on the governing body, would require a minimum participation of 30 percent of eligible voters, and then a simple majority vote would determine the result.[8]

The restoration law authorized the MRC and the state of Wisconsin to establish governing bodies to provide state and local services within Menominee County.[9] This paved the way for the reestablishment of a reservation but with governance controls divided between the tribe and Menominee County. The

MRC established several committees—a Constitution Committee, an Enroll-ment Committee, and a Contracted Services Committee—and began the work of establishing a tribal government. The MRC also had to deal with an eight-million-dollar debt that occurred as a result of termination.[10]

The law also established a method for returning tribal assets to the United States to hold "in trust for the tribe." This included assets and land of MEI and any land held by individual Menominees who desired to have that land placed back into trust. The law did not take private land from nontribal members who had moved onto the reservation.[11] The transfer of land back into trust was to occur based on a plan developed by the MEI voting trust and board of directors. NARF drafted the final version of the plan, "incorporating the suggestions of the BIA and the tribe." The plan would remove the corporation from the tax rolls, leading to a boost in its economic base. It would also protect the Menominee from land sales.[12] At the same time, the MRC began to develop a management plan for the land and resources after MEI's upcoming dissolution. In addition, MEI borrowed $1.2 million to repurchase 334 Legend Lake lots from the developer.[13]

The MRC was officially designated as the recipient of federal grants from the Comprehensive Employment and Training Act (CETA), which provided com-munity health representatives (CHRs) and other services to the reservation. Several CHRs were trained to work within the community under one grant. Other grants provided for the payment of medical bills incurred by tribal members and for a feasibility study for the establishment of an in-patient/out-patient health facility to be built in Keshena.[14]

In the midst of all this work on various fronts, a crisis broke out and at-tracted the national news media. Just after midnight on New Year's Day in 1975, an armed group of disaffected dissidents calling themselves the Menom-inee Warrior Society joined with members of AIM and burst into caretaker Joe Plonka's home at the Alexian Brothers Novitiate in Gresham. They took Plonka and his family and guests hostage.[15] Apesanahkwat, who later became tribal chairman of the Menominee, was one of the first warriors into the house that night, following John Waubanascum Jr., one of the key leaders. Ape-sanahkwat later recalled, "When Joe Plonka opened the door and we moved into the house, he reached in his back pocket for a two shot derringer. . . . John Waubanascum let go one round into the ceiling of his armor piercing weapon, a thirty ought six or a thirty ought eight, and I was so afraid to look at where he shot." The warriors wanted the Alexian Brothers to turn the novitiate over to the tribe since it was no longer in use as a religious training center. After two tense hours in which the hostages said the warriors threatened their lives several times, the Alexian Brothers agreed to negotiate. The warriors then freed the Plonkas and their guests. "We released them," Apesanahkwat remembered. "In fact, they got stuck in the snow and we helped push them out."[16]

The media portrayed the Menominee Warrior Society as made up primarily of young men, many Vietnam veterans, but a significant number of women were involved as well.[17] They demanded that the Alexian Brothers give the novitiate to the tribe for use as a healthcare facility. They also expressed dissatisfaction with tribal leadership, which they viewed as female dominated. Their motto, "deed or death," signified the serious nature of their action.[18]

The warriors were well armed. Shawano County police arrived on the scene, but the warriors easily held them at bay with their firepower. Apesanahkwat explained, "Because we were predominantly all Vietnam veterans we divided people into killer teams, fire teams if you will, and we assigned them to various strategic locations with rifles, some of them with pistols. That first week was constant shooting and firefighting. . . . And a lot of these guys were just itching for a firefight. They just loved it when the cops were there because we got to shoot at them every night. How people weren't killed I'll never know."[19]

On 5 January the MRC issued a press release aimed at state officials, tribal members, and the warriors. In this statement, they, "as the elected tribal governing body, request[ed] to be allowed to intervene and offer . . . assistance for a quick and just solution to the situation." They especially wanted "to insure the safety of all involved," since "[h]uman life is sacred—Menominee lives to us cannot be replaced."[20]

However, they strongly denounced both the tactics and the goals of the Menominee Warrior Society. "[W]e the Menominee Restoration Committee have been elected . . . to act as the official governing body of the Menominee Indian Tribe," they began. This election showed "overwhelming support of tribal leaders," they continued. "Tribal actions thus far have produced dramatic accomplishments. We have used Indian tradition and worked quietly, diligently and progressively. . . . This historic accomplishment was obtained by working through the system. Militancy and violence were not utilized nor attempted." Finally, they said, "Indian people hurt themselves with jealousy and greed. When there is disunity on important major issues and this disunity is promoted by self-interest and greed, Indian people lose, white society gains. . . . We deplore the tactic of placing the lives of women and children in jeopardy in order to achieve an unethical goal. We call upon those people in the novitiate to leave peacefully or to at least send the children to a place of safety."[21]

The Menominee Warrior Society, the county, and the state all ignored the

MRC. Shawano County responded to the takeover with an illegal wiretap and shortly thereafter requested support from the National Guard. Governor Patrick Lucey ordered the guard deployed on 6 January. He also asked that they attempt to oversee a peaceful solution to the standoff and protect the warriors from harm. The guard's numbers grew to 350 and then to 750 by the end of the siege.[22] Governor Lucey also appointed Artley Skenandore, an Oneida man, as a mediator on behalf of the state. Skenandore had recently been forced to resign from his position as executive director of the Minnesota Indian Affairs Commission. In addition, although AIM was involved from the beginning, national figures Russell Means and Dennis Banks arrived on the scene. The actor Marlon Brando and the activist Father James Groppi of Milwaukee also eventually joined the list of celebrities in attendance.[23] The negotiations proceeded in fits and starts.

Reaction on the reservation was mixed, with some people supporting the warriors, others opposing them, and still others primarily concerned that the standoff end safely. Gordon Dickie represented the latter group and later recalled, "It wasn't a question of whether they were right or wrong then, that wasn't for us to decide anyhow. You know, the whole thing was how do we get them out without somebody getting killed or hurt. So in the meantime the Restoration Committee had some pretty rough language about the young folks, the young people. And I never like to talk about it, because my position is right or wrong they're still young Menominees, and they need help, and if we can help them we will."[24]

On 10 January the MRC issued a detailed response to the events that, among other things, expressed anger at state actions. "It should be noted that at the beginning of the occupation the Menominee Restoration Committee was not consulted by anyone in these matters," the MRC stated in its newsletter. "Governor Lucey appointed Artley Skenandore to be his official mediator without consulting the Menominee Restoration Committee, and the American Indian Movement officials also came to have a part in the negotiations without first consulting the Tribe's governing body."[25]

The MRC established a Menominee Negotiating Committee, consisting of three tribal members, and called on several national Indian organizations—the National Tribal Chairman's Association, the NCAI, and the National Indian Youth Council—and local organizations such as the Great Lakes Inter Tribal Council to help with the negotiations. The MRC proposed that the Alexian Brothers turn the facility over to a multitribal group with an all-Indian board of directors, to be used for educational purposes.[26]

On 19 January Ada Deer, as chair of the MRC, issued another press release in which she softened her rhetoric aimed at the warriors. "It is time to speak out bluntly on the root causes of the occupation" of the novitiate, she began. "We Menominees, and all other Indian Tribes, are engulfed by racism. This is one of the chief causes of the occupation, which has been conducted by frustrated Indian people with the best of motives." She outlined several examples of ways in which racism scarred and impacted Menominees and other Indian people, especially in relation to legal justice.[27]

The issue had deeper ramifications for the tribe. It established the battle lines between the Menominee and the state of Wisconsin over law enforcement on the reservation and threatened to undermine tribal hopes for self-governance. MRC representative Al Fowler expressed concern about the impact of state actions in relation to PL-280. Since restoration, the state believed it had criminal and civil jurisdiction over the Menominee based on that law, but the tribe disagreed. "Tribal officials feel that the Governor and the Am[e]rican Indian Movement showed no respect for the tribe's right to tribal sovereignty," Fowler wrote. "Both of these outside forces acted in a manner contrary to their previous statements concerning tribal sovereignty."[28]

Ada Deer spoke out as well. She called for the repeal of PL-280. "The State of Wisconsin must publicly state its position that the Menominee Tribe is free of P.L. 280 jurisdiction and that we are entitled to maintain our own system of justice. The Federal Government has agreed with our position on this issue and we call on Governor Lucey and Attorney General La Follette to follow suit immediately." She also called on the state and federal governments to repeal PL-280 statewide and noted that NCAI would soon convene a discussion of the issue on the Menominee reservation.[29]

Finally, Deer reminded people that the MRC was "but an interim governing committee with the specific task of developing a government and an election process that will establish a tribal council to solve problems." She called on the warriors to participate in the process of tribal government after they ended their siege.[30]

The days of the takeover dragged on with relatively few incidents until the end of the month. The white population in Shawano, including law enforcement officials, became increasingly angered at the state's handling of the situation. By the end of the month reactionaries had established a Concerned Citizens Committee (CCC). On 25 January the National Guard met with between two hundred and three hundred non-Indian citizens who opposed the Menominee Warrior Society. That day the CCC issued an ultimatum to Governor Lucey in which it charged that "the Wisconsin National Guard have neglected to enforce the law." They demanded that the state cease negotiations

Figure 2. Novitiate takeover. January 1975 cartoon by Bill Sanders, from *The Milwaukee Journal*, © 2004 Journal Sentinel Inc., reproduced with permission.

with the militants, cut off utilities and food supplies, and evict the warriors and turn them over to the Shawano police. Racial hostilities increased both at the site and in general. White snowmobilers buzzed the novitiate, exchanging shots with the warriors; in Shawano white merchants began to refuse service to Menominees in their stores.[31]

The National Guard ignored the demands of the CCC but took the committee itself seriously. The guard brought in fourteen armed personnel carriers, purportedly to protect the warriors from the angry non-Indian mobs. Finally, after several days of a rumored agreement, the Alexian Brothers and the warriors signed a settlement on 2 February that would allow for the Menominee purchase of the novitiate and the surrender of the warriors to authorities. That night heavy gunfire erupted in what the FBI believed to be an effort by the warriors to rid themselves of their ammunition before surrender. On the night of 3 February the warriors surrendered peacefully, "leaving the novitiate in something of a shambles."[32] The five warriors identified as leaders were charged with felonies, the other thirty-four occupants with misdemeanors.

The MRC was unhappy with the agreement, which would add a financial burden that the tribe could not afford. Indeed, later when the Alexian Brothers offered the novitiate deed to the tribe for one dollar, the Menominee turned them down, due to the potential costs of restoration and upkeep.[33]

Local non-Indians were upset as well. The Minneapolis office of the FBI reported that one of their sources "reportedly learned 'white action groups' at Gresham are outraged over settlement and have threatened to 'blow up' ABN [Alexian Brothers Novitiate] rather than see it go to Indians. Local whites fear eventual loss of Legend Lake, Wisconsin, resort area to Indians through court action, since Menominees believe reexamination of treaties might assist them in showing claim to that area."[34] Relations within the tribe and between the Menominee and the non-Indians in the border towns remained strained over this issue for a long time.

TAKING CONTROL

Meanwhile, in preparation for the official restoration of powers and authority to the tribe, the secretary of the interior's office worked with the MRC and MEI to effectuate an orderly transfer.[35] As in the past, tribal members set aside factionalism to be certain they controlled their own future. On the eve of restoration, the *Milwaukee Sentinel* reported a story headlined "Tribe Agrees on Restoration." In it the newspaper observed, "[A]t a time when the tribe is divided on political views, everyone seems to agree that the restoration of the

Menominee Indian Reservation is essential."[36] Restoration officially occurred on 23 April 1975. Secretary of the Interior Rogers C. B. Morton presided over a short ceremony in his office in which he signed the legal documents that restored trust status to the Menominee. Ada Deer proclaimed that, in reestablishing their relationship with the federal government, the Menominee desired "Federal protection, not Federal domination." Morton said the act gave the tribe the "freedom of opportunity to pursue their culture."[37]

As part of the transfer, the secretary of the interior approved a "Management Plan for Menominee Enterprises" dated 22 April. Both the tribe and the Department of the Interior recognized that termination had repealed the 1908 and 1934 laws regarding the Menominee forest and logging and that they remained so despite restoration. This was "fully consistent with the intent of Congress," which was "to give the Tribe maximum self-determination over its own affairs." This provided added importance to the management plan.[38]

The management plan stipulated that "[t]he primary duties of the tribal enterprise shall be to log, manage, and reforest the tribal forest land, and to manufacture, market, sell, and distribute timber, forest products, and related products." The plan established and named a twelve-person board of directors with rotating three-year terms.[39] Attached to the management plan was a "Trust and Management Agreement" negotiated by the MRC and the secretary of the interior. This document, developed under the auspices of the Menominee Restoration Act, "recognize[d] that the tribal governing body, rather than the Menominee Restoration Committee, should negotiate with the Secretary." However, in the meantime, this plan established a working arrangement that "intended to provide maximum self-determination to the Tribe" until the tribal government would become established. This document suggested that Menominee self-governance be modeled on the U.S. contract with the Zuni tribe, apparently the most far-reaching of its time.[40]

The agreement stipulated that the tribe should continue to manage the forest based on the plan under which MEI had operated it, including retaining the plan of managing it on a sustained-yield basis, unless the tribe modified that plan. It also stipulated that the tribe would develop a new plan before the current plan expired and that the tribe should "manage, operate, and control the tribal business." The MRC received authority to oversee this process until the establishment of the new tribal government. Finally, the agreement provided that, upon transfer, "all tribal assets . . . be exempt from all local, State and Federal taxation."[41]

Things were changing in a positive way on the education front as well. In May 1975 the state finally approved the establishment of a separate public school district for Menominee County and the reservation. That fall, on 7 September, the district began operation with 734 students enrolled.[42]

On the healthcare front the tribe succeeded in establishing the first Indian-controlled clinic in the United States. Construction began in 1976, and the facility, which provided medical, dental, and eye care, opened in 1977. It has been a source of tribal pride ever since. The Menominee Health Board was established to provide oversight, and the numbers of patients steadily grew.[43]

Then, on 4 February 1976, exactly one year after the novitiate siege had ended, Menominee County Sheriff's Department employees killed John Waubanascum Jr. and Arlin Pamanet at Waubanascum's house outside of Neopit. The U.S. Department of Justice and the BIA were involved in a dispute over jurisdiction on the reservation in the wake of restoration, which left Ken "Paddo" Fish as the county sheriff in charge of law enforcement. The Department of the Interior believed the Restoration Act voided PL-280 and removed jurisdiction of law enforcement from the state, because the amendments to the law were made during termination, when the United States did not consider the Menominee to be a tribe. The Department of Justice, however, disagreed, and the state continued to maintain jurisdiction instead of turning it over on 1 January 1976, or the extended date of 1 February, as planned.[44]

During the year since the novitiate takeover, the law enforcement department had grown considerably. The growth brought with it allegations of "police brutality" and of the development of a "goon squad," at the encouragement of the MRC, that was used to intimidate political opponents.[45] Sheriff Fish responded to criticism that he hired and deputized criminals by commenting, "If I couldn't use anyone who has a record, we wouldn't have a sheriff's department."[46]

Waubanascum was one of five members of the Menominee Warrior Society set to go on trial for the novitiate takeover, and he was also wanted for traffic violations. When the Sheriff's Department arrived at his home on the night of 4 February he was intoxicated. What occurred next is unclear in its entirety, but some things are known. Sheriff Fish stated that his officers tried to arrest Waubanascum peacefully, but when Waubanascum began to fire at the officers, Fish shot him. The autopsy report somewhat contradicted Fish's account, indicating that Waubanascum was shot in the back, but in a direction "much more side-to-side than back-to-front." A deputy was shot in the finger, which Fish used to lay responsibility on Waubanascum and Pamanet, but later investigation showed he was shot by his own weapon. Fish said Pamanet also shot at officers, but other witnesses said Pamanet was unarmed. The deputy reported he had urged Fish not to shoot; Fish said he shot to defend the deputy.[47]

Waubanascum was driven to the hospital immediately after the shooting, where he died. Pamanet was "shot and killed by two blasts from Sheriff Fish's weapon" and then left in the woods to die. Robert W. Huntington III, the forensic pathologist who conducted the autopsy, reported, "I believe [Pamanet] lived longer than Waubanascum." As it turns out, Pamanet probably would have died anyway, even if he had received immediate medical attention. One of the shotgun pellets entered his heart, but that was not known at the scene. Huntington contributed to a paid advertisement urging the suspension of Fish but said he did so based on his Quaker religion, not the autopsy itself.[48] The whole story remained clouded in a shroud of confusion.

Tribal members protested the law enforcement actions surrounding the event and were joined by the American Friends Service Committee, a state senator, and Madison residents in calling on Governor Lucey to investigate and suspend Fish over the incident. The governor had previously investigated Fish for using undue force but had exonerated him. The protesters also encouraged Lucey to turn tribal jurisdiction over to the United States.[49] This change occurred relatively quickly. On 1 March "law enforcement jurisdiction on the Menominee Reservation was transferred from the state of Wisconsin to the federal government."[50] The Menominee thus again became the only tribe in the state not subject to PL-280.

The Menominee began to achieve self-governance in other areas as well. The tribal rolls had been reopened on 16 May 1975, and soon thereafter the Menominee gained control of several important areas of government. In November 1975 the federal government authorized tribal establishment of a police force; in March 1976, when the state returned jurisdiction to the Menominee, the tribe was permitted to create the Court of Indian Offenses.[51] Unlike their pretermination predecessors, the police force and the court system were controlled by the tribe, not the BIA. In fact, the BIA assigned no agency superintendent to the tribe, which would elect its own legislature and legislative chair or tribal chair under the new constitution. Until the constitution went into effect, the MRC ran tribal affairs.[52]

The process of electing a new government dragged on longer than expected. NARF helped draft the constitution, a lengthy document that tribal voters ratified on 12 November 1976. In January 1977 the Department of the Interior approved it. Then began the contentious process of electing the new government. Disagreements, charges of abuse of power, name-calling, and occasional violence had become an increasingly common part of Menominee politics, and it continued here.[53]

After passage of the constitution, Ada Deer stepped down from the MRC, saying she believed that the most difficult time was over and that it was time for her to step aside. Shirley Daly, Al Fowler, and Sylvia Wilber were among those who took on expanded leadership roles in the MRC. Various factors held up elections, including inadequate percentages of votes to elect candidates and a lawsuit filed against MRC. In February 1978, on a fifth attempt and after a year of campaigning, the tribe elected the first three of nine legislators.[54]

A year later, in January and February 1979, the tribe again held elections in Zoar, South Branch, Neopit, and Keshena. This time everything worked out. A nine-person legislature was elected and began work on 5 May. The new leadership was a mix of people. Gordon Dickie Sr., the old-time political leader, was elected as the first chair. Lucille Chapman, long a mill and MEI employee, was secretary. Ken "Bum Bum" Fish, who had been part of the novitiate takeover, served as chair of the Judiciary Committee, which oversaw the establishment of the tribal courts. The creation of the legislature paved the way for Menominee governance under the constitution. The tribal courts, for example, had operated under direct federal authorization; now the tribe would take control of them. Gordon Dickie Sr. later described the newness of the experience: "In '79 when we took over we had to start right from scratch. We had no inner organization or anything, it was a difficult year. That's why it's so hard to compare that one with . . . the years following. Because you weren't faced with all the same kind of problems you did the first year, this was entirely something new."[55] This new government was a far cry from pretermination tribal governing systems. Tribal self-determination reached a high point not matched since the early nineteenth century.

In the end the tribe succeeded in gaining more control than it previously had in governing Menominee affairs. Secretary of the Interior Morton also recognized the significance of the Restoration Act for federal Indian policy nationally. He portrayed the changing policy as a "new dawning of the nation's responsibilities to the Indian people—not in a custodial sense." Indeed, he was correct. In many ways the cornerstones of the incipient policy of self-determination for tribes were the Menominee Restoration Act, the return of Blue Lake to the Taos Pueblo in 1970, and, ironically, the Alaska Native Claims Settlement Act, which though couched in the language of self-determination was in many ways a continuation of the termination policy.[56] The Menominee, as the first tribe to successfully beat back termination, led the way for others to receive restoration over the next decade.[57]

This was a time of great conflict and turmoil for the Menominee reservation but also a time of great growth. For the first time in over a century, the Menominee would have a great deal of control in governing themselves. Arriving at this point after suffering under the heavy weight of colonialist federal wardship, which had stymied and stunted the development of tribal leadership for generations, was both triumphal and painful. The exciting and daunting task of rebuilding their tribal nation on their own terms now lay ahead for the Menominee.

CHAPTER TWELVE

Tribal Self-Determination and Sovereignty Today

The Menominee have turned their worst modern experience, the largest single threat to the tribe since removal in the 1840s and 1850s, into an opportunity. The Menominee response to termination has led to a renewed hope in the tribal future. Restoration has seen a burst of development in the economic, political, social, and cultural realms of tribal life. The development of the tribal economy and tribal governance systems is perhaps most important, for they can provide a foundation for cultural and social revitalization. Yet all these things are occurring simultaneously, in fits and spurts. At the same time, the Menominee continue to struggle with pressures from federal and state government and local non-Indian populations, which are attempting to weaken or eliminate the hard-won gains of the restoration era.

INSTITUTION BUILDING

A series of developments in the 1980s and 1990s led to the reestablishment of old institutions and the creation of new ones. In 1980 ground was broken for an elderly housing facility in Keshena. In 1987 a "new million dollar addition to the Clinic was dedicated." Another million-dollar addition, which included a wellness center, was added in 1993. Under Jerry Waukau's direction beginning in the mid-1980s, the clinic made a concerted effort to professionalize its work.[1]

Two schools were soon under construction as well: an elementary school in Neopit and the combined junior and senior high school in Keshena. The schools opened 16 September 1982, but the district continued to face a series of ongoing problems. It was not until the 2003–4 school year that for the first time a Menominee, Wendell Waukau, took over as superintendent of schools. This was significant because Waukau, a principal of the high school, had brought Menominee dropouts back into the system and also had worked to establish a cooperative program with the Historic Preservation Department to bring tribal language trainees into the school.[2]

In 1997 the tribal legislature strengthened the educational oversight of the tribe by creating the Menominee Language and Culture Code. Menominee culture and language were deemed a key part of educational development. The new code established a commission to oversee curriculum issues for kindergarten through postsecondary education in reservation-based schools.[3]

The tribe recognized the threat of language loss as a critical community issue. Whereas in the 1950s all council proceedings involving outsiders had to be translated by an interpreter into the Menominee and English languages, by the late 1990s the tribe counted only seventy-two fluent Menominee speakers. The language programs now emphasize family involvement at the multigenerational level and training young adults.[4] Only time will tell whether these efforts will be able to save the language. The development of coordinated programming with broad community support and support within the educational system is an important first step, but the most successful Native language revitalization programs in the United States are based on the full immersion model, which by 2004 the Menominee had yet to implement.[5]

Higher education came to the reservation during the 1980s and 1990s as well. In 1989 tribal members asked NAES College (Native American Educational Services), a private, Indian-controlled college, to establish a campus on the reservation. This innovative institution, the only college of its kind to survive the 1980s, was known for its community-based bachelor's curriculum and its small size. It filled a need for older students who wanted to stay close to home and learn in a curriculum specifically designed to train community members to be effective leaders in their fields. NAES alumni have gone on to serve on the tribal council, to serve as campus dean, and to work in such areas as education, historic preservation, language preservation, and resource management.[6]

In 1993 a much larger institution was founded in Keshena, the College of the Menominee Nation (CMN). CMN became a land-grant institution in 1994 and earned accreditation in 1998. It is part of the national tribal college movement that provides basic higher education needs to tribal communities in culturally sensitive ways. Like NAES College, CMN was designed to allow students to live at home, to continue to work and meet family and community obligations, and to attend college at the same time. In 2002 CMN entered into an articulation agreement with the University of Wisconsin-Madison that established a program for CMN students who have earned an associate's degree in sustainable development to matriculate into a program leading to a doctorate at the university.[7]

ECONOMIC DEVELOPMENT AND GOVERNANCE

The Menominee have long recognized education as an important key in protecting tribal sovereign rights, but self-governance is at best difficult and tenuous without an economic base. At the same time as the healthcare and education developments occurred, the tribe needed to stabilize its economy. With the establishment of Menominee Tribal Enterprises (MTE) Menominees now manage the tribe's lumber business. The business has expanded, including the production of veneers. It is again a positive economic force on the reservation, even more so since it is more responsive to tribal demands than it was when the federal government ran it. It was the largest employer on the reservation before gaming was introduced, although in 1986 the Menominee unemployment rate stood at 39 percent.[8]

Finally, under tribal management, the forest is fulfilling the hopes set forth in Senator LaFollette's plan: to provide the tribe with a perpetual rich resource that the Menominee manage themselves. Dating to the 1890 and the 1908 logging acts, the tribal governance and the resource governance are divided: MTE now runs the forest and sawmill operations, with a board elected independently of the tribal legislature. This division of business and government provides an interesting contrast to the U.S. system. Outsiders now recognize the Menominee forest as an international model for a commercially viable, sustained production forest.[9] Businesses purchasing environmentally sensitive wood products procure them from MTE. Marshall Pecore, the forest manager, said in 1992 that the tribe's forest had already produced more than two billion board feet of wood, "the entire forest has been harvested two times," and the forest nonetheless contains more timber now than it did in the nineteenth century.[10]

Some tribal members have disagreed on whether the forest is being optimally managed, however. A group of ten Menominee loggers wrote the tribal newspaper in June 1999 to chastise MTE and the BIA for what they viewed as poor forest management practices.[11] Other tribal members are concerned that logging practices undermine the forest's health by diminishing the biodiversity of plant life that is not commercially grown. They express their concern for future generations of Menominee.[12] The fact that this healthy debate is occurring is due in part to the tribe's success at establishing control over its forest economy.

That control is still periodically threatened. In the early 1980s, for example, the U.S. Department of Energy (DOE) identified the Menominee reservation as one of twelve potential U.S. sites for the establishment of a nuclear waste depository. While such an arrangement could provide the tribe with a long-term source of income, tribal members and the tribal government strongly opposed it, because of the potential environmental damage and for reasons of sovereignty. The DOE did not consult with the Menominee prior to including them in the plan.

In February 1983 Lucille Chapman, as tribal council chair, signed a resolution opposing the establishment of a nuclear waste site on the reservation. In 1986 Gordon Dickie, then current tribal council chair, testified against the plan in both congressional and DOE hearings. He pointed out that the long-term economic consequences could be devastating, both because timberland would be lost to production with the creation of the site and because there would be a high potential for accidents. He concluded by commenting, "We are supposed to be a sovereign government. . . . I don't see why, the Federal Government cannot recognize this." The DOE abandoned the plan in 1986.[13]

The tribe turned its attention to another source for economic development instead. In the mid-1980s, the Menominee further stabilized their economy and finances with the development of gaming, first bingo and then casino gambling. According to a fact sheet put out by the tribe, although the tribal budget grew almost fivefold between 1986 and 1991, gaming revenues increased more than twenty times, considerably outpacing the tribal budget. The unemployment rate on the reservation dropped from 39 percent to 23.9 percent, remarkably low for Indian country in those five years, although tribal membership actually rose. For the first time unemployment dropped to the rate of pretermination years. By 1991 gaming revenues helped fund some sixty programs on the reservation, including social programs (powwows, logging museum, recreation), social service programs (day care, elderly care, housing, parent support group, substance abuse treatment), educational programs (scholarships, library building construction), land acquisition, and more. Menominee gaming has also provided an economic boost to non-Indian communities surrounding the reservation, in restaurant and motel businesses, for instance.[14]

With economic development have come outside pressures to diminish tribal sovereignty. When the American economy reached a downturn in both the early and late 1990s, resentment of Indian economic development increased in surrounding non-Indian communities. Although some Shawano residents recognize the economic boom that the Menominee casino has brought to their town—finally beginning to ease tensions that came to a head in the 1970s—the state has opposed Menominee casino development off the reservation. As the twenty-first century opened, the tribe and state struggled over the establishment of a Menominee casino in the potentially lucrative market of Kenosha, located between Milwaukee and Chicago.[15]

As of the 1990 census, Menominee County remained the poorest county in Wisconsin and the thirteenth poorest in the entire nation. A 2002 study showed that, although the casino and forest provided employment and had significantly increased the average income levels on the reservation, Menominee County remained the poorest in the state.[16] Other social ills rampant in American society also challenge the tribe. A 2004 report found people living in Menominee County to be the least healthy in the state of Wisconsin.[17] The Menominee's rich history of political strength is helping the tribe to face this challenge, but such strength still lacks the financial base necessary for solving many of its problems.

Unfortunately, this economic hardship means the tribe is forced to develop political leadership in less than ideal conditions. A weak economy both diminishes the tribal capacity to problem solve and increases dependency on outside support. Yet, the Menominee political condition has certainly benefited from restoration. Indeed, the tribe effectively used its authority to create a constitution to go further than mere reinstatement. Restoration gave the tribe more control of its governance than it had before termination. The tribe now governs itself more freely of BIA control than do most Indian nations within the United States. This control reflects what the Menominee had hoped for with the incorporation plans of the 1930s and the termination plans of the 1950s: to shift the focus of federal trust to tribal rather than federal bureaucratic governance.

The ratification of the constitution and the establishment of a new government ushered in a new era in Menominee history. The constitution determined the power of the tribal legislature and the judiciary, providing at least in theory for separations of power. It delineated individual tribal members' rights. It limited the power of the tribal government to dispose of tribal lands and defined the legal uses of tribal lands. The constitution also created a separate business arm of the tribe, over which the tribal legislature has little authority, to manage the tribal forests and business. Finally, the bylaws created a General Council open to all members, which the tribal legislature must call into session annually and whose concerns the tribal legislature must answer in writing.[18] Such input by the General Council into tribal leaders' decision making dates to the earliest Menominee records. At the present time the General Council reviews tribal governance and makes recommendations for change, but its advice is not binding on the tribal legislature.[19]

The constitution, a document numbering some fifty pages, has been the subject of lively debate, but it has also laid the basis for the Menominee style of self-governance. The present governing system—a "muddle," as one observer has put it—derives from a combination of factors based on traditional Menominee governance, on nineteenth-century changes, on further changes caused by the 1908 logging act, and on termination and restoration. The entire system is further complicated by the fact that, dating to termination, the tribe and the county have separate but overlapping jurisdiction. Therefore, the non-Indians who bought Menominee land during termination participate directly in the county government but not in the tribal government.

The BIA, however, has little jurisdiction over Menominee internal affairs. In fact, when the Minneapolis area office, as a matter of routine, requested copies of the tribe's minutes and motions, the tribe refused to supply them. The BIA insisted but then backed down. The tribe does have to clear certain decisions with the BIA and does so through the area office in Minneapolis. These decisions include amendments to the constitution; compacts with the state, for example, the gaming compact between the tribe and the state signed in May 1992; and approval of contracts the tribe makes for services that take the place of a federal agency on the reservation.[20]

The federal courts are now beginning to recognize the authority vested in the tribe through its constitution. In March 2003 the Seventh Circuit Court of Appeals ruled that "The Menominee Restoration Act . . . makes clear that Congress intended to . . . restore the Menominee tribe to its pre-'termination' status" and that "Courts have construed the Restoration Act to effect a full restoration of the Menominee Tribe's pre-Termination powers." The court clarified that Congress " 'reinstated' " the tribe's powers in relation to criminal jurisdiction and that these powers were not delegated. This is a recognition of the inherent powers of law enforcement.[21] In essence, the tribe theoretically always held the power over law enforcement, but whereas the federal government, as part of its trust responsibilities, oversaw its enactment previous to termination, the tribal legislature has assumed that authority since restoration. These institutions lack independence and depend on the goodwill of the tribal legislature; before restoration they depended on the goodwill of the federal government.

ISSUES OF SOVEREIGNTY

In the late twentieth century the tribe not only developed internal self-governance but also faced external threats to Menominee sovereignty. Several of these issues help define the ambiguous relationship between the tribe, the state, the federal government, and the surrounding communities. The negotiation with the state for the return of sturgeon to the Menominee reservation is a success story, as is the tribe's attempt to repatriate the remains of Menominee ancestors to the reservation under the 1990 Native American Graves Protection and Repatriation Act (NAGPRA). A lawsuit against the state attempting to secure off-reservation hunting and fishing rights failed in federal court, while the tribe finally succeeded in gaining a settlement in its suit against the federal government for damages caused by termination.

On 17 April 1993 the Menominee celebrated the return of the sturgeon to *namāēw uskiwamit*, or Sturgeon Spawning Place, the name the tribe has used for Keshena Falls on the Wolf River since before the creation of the reservation. After several years of pressure from tribal members and after months of negotiations with the Wisconsin Department of Natural Resources (DNR), the state agreed to provide the Menominee with the sturgeon required for the renewal of this celebration, a part of the tribe's heritage dating to its earliest history. The state also agreed to formulate a plan for reintroducing the sturgeon into Menominee waters.[22]

At that celebration in 1993, after the traditional opening ceremonies and welcoming, tribal elders and members spoke about the historical and cultural significance of sturgeon to the tribe. Recognition was given to the family that had continued to offer prayers and ceremonies to the sturgeon despite a decades-long absence of the fish in tribal waters. David J. Grignon (Nahwahquaw), the director of the Menominee Historic Preservation Department (MHPD), led dancers in performing the Fish Dance. Afterward, the tribe fed nearly five hundred people in a feast that included sturgeon and wild rice.

Tribal members viewed this celebration as a beginning point in the cultural revival of this ancient practice. Meanwhile, non-Indians both on and off the reservation feared that expanding Menominee control over the sturgeon resource would threaten their own interests. So a broad coalition of both tribal officials and non-Indian representatives joined together, hoping to establish a mutually beneficial cooperative plan for sturgeon management and reintroduction on the reservation. This meant developing and implementing plans for the resource management of both the fish and their aquatic environment, legal regulations, educational programs, and the continued revitalization and evolution of cultural tradition relating to the sturgeon.[23]

The coalition achieved success in all of these areas. By 2001 both hatchery-raised and Wolf River sturgeon had been stocked in reservation waters in a successful effort that culminated in the opening of a sturgeon spearing and fishing season on Legend Lake in February and April 2005. Tribal members have served as biologists and coordinators in the program. Both the tribe and the state have established regulations to protect the newly introduced fish.[24] And the state continues to provide sturgeon for the annual spring celebration. The tribe continues this celebration, with some members even referring to the tenth anniversary celebration as the "ten thousand and tenth."

Meanwhile, after the passage of NAGPRA, tribal culture leaders, through the MHPD, began a study of how to bring the remains of lost ancestors back to the reservation. David Grignon became active in a statewide multitribal repatriation committee in Wisconsin. Tribal researchers began to track down all the places that hold remains. At the end of a decade-long process, tribal leaders finally believed themselves prepared to take on this task, though potentially fraught with land mines.

Museums and collectors had disturbed graves to acquire the remains, an issue for which the tribe had no traditional remedies. Conducting proper ceremonies that honor the supernatural world in an appropriate way was extremely important to the tribe. With the aid of eminent elders, veterans, and tribal historians, officials chose a burial site on the reservation and planned ceremonies. In 1999 tribal leaders began the systematic task of securing the return of the ancestors and conducting reburial ceremonies under the direction of Dewey Thunder Sr., an eminent elder from Zoar.[25]

During this same period, on the heels of successful attempts by the Ojibwes to secure their off-reservation hunting and fishing rights, as well as their own on-reservation successes first with the Sanapaw hunting case and then (outside the courtroom) with the sturgeon, the Menominee sued the state of Wisconsin on 13 January 1995 for off-reservation hunting and fishing rights they had retained in their nineteenth-century treaty negotiations. Under judicial interpretations of treaty rights, often referred to as the canons of construction, any ratified treaty, no matter how deceitfully negotiated, is considered law. But treaties must also be interpreted as the Indians who signed the agreement understood them.

In a 17 September 1996 decision, Judge Barbara Crabb ruled that the Menominee failed to prove their interpretation of the treaty. Ken "Bum Bum" Fish, the Menominee director of treaty rights, pointed out afterward that "the

Menominee nation did not read or speak English, and the terminology was not being translated to the best understanding of the Menominee." Tribal chair John Teller said, "Contrary to Judge Crabb's opinion, we don't believe the treaty language [was] clear to the chiefs who signed the treaties." Teller and Fish were correct, as a look at how the Menominee understood the treaties from a tribal perspective makes clear. However, the judge did not consider it proven in court. The tribe unsuccessfully appealed the case in the Seventh Circuit Court of Appeals in Chicago, which upheld Judge Crabb's decision on 17 November 1998.[26]

The Menominee had greater success with their lawsuit against the United States for damages caused by termination. The suit, filed in the Court of Claims, included complaints regarding the restrictions placed on the forest, mismanagement claims on both the forest and the mill between 1951 and 1961, highway right of way, tax exemption, power line right of way, water and sewage system claims, and litigation claims. The tribe charged the federal government with breach of its fiduciary responsibility. In 1981 the Court of Claims ruled in the tribe's favor in both the highway and power line right-of-way claims, as well as in the reimbursement of the expenses of termination. The Menominee remained uncompensated, however, so the tribe turned to Congress for relief. In August 1999 President William Jefferson Clinton signed a bill brought by Congress to provide the tribe twenty-seven million dollars in damages caused by termination.[27]

At the dawn of the twenty-first century, tribal sovereignty in the United States again came under heavy governmental assault, particularly from state governments and the U.S. Congress and even in the courts. As a small minority of tribes began to establish a viable financial base through gaming, political opportunists saw an opening to deny treaty rights and to eliminate the federal trust relationship for all tribes. The Indian Gaming Regulatory Act was used to diminish tribal sovereignty, for example.[28] The late 1990s also brought another attempt at downsizing the federal government, which meant turning funding control of social programs over to states. This gave states more power in their attempts to squeeze tribal sovereign rights.

Tribes like the Menominee continue to fight for those rights on a variety of fronts: social, cultural, educational, economic, and political. In the words of Edgar Bowen, a Coos tribal leader from Oregon who devoted most of his career to a successful fight to bring restoration to his tribe after Congress terminated it, "The price of maintaining our sovereignty is eternal vigilance."[29] Menominee leaders have followed that precept since the establishment of the reservation, such that, despite sometimes vast differences of opinion among tribal members, the leadership has accomplished a startling feat in modern America: shaping a separate existence, tribally defined, in an ever more global world.

The essence of survival for the Menominee tribe meant retaining control of the definition of their identity. A strong identification with their environment helped them through some of the worst threats of the American period, including allotment, agricultural policy, and termination. Just as important during this period was the tribe's leadership, which time and again set aside factionalism to respond successfully to American threats. Throughout all of this turmoil, the tribal economy remained the key. From the sturgeon and the wild rice of the early years to the reservation forest, their natural resources have remained an important part of the essence of being Menominee.[30] Their resources have shaped not only economic but political and social roles as well. Tribal leaders, in responding to outside threats, have stubbornly insisted that Menominee welfare has always depended on these resources. The forest is indeed, as Senator LaFollette recognized and as Menominees have known all along, the base of the Menominee heritage. As Reginald Oshkosh observed in 1930, many Menominees have sacrificed much in their lives in their efforts to maintain this heritage for the tribe. The forest is a tribute to these sacrifices and a visible symbol, a visible recognition, of the successful fight for survival and self-determination of the Menominee people.

Appendix

Table 1. Agents among the Menominee, 1849–1958

1837–55	Green Bay subagency
1855–1910	Green Bay agency
1909–43	Keshena agency or Keshena Indian School
1927–43	Neopit Mills agency
1943–61	Menominee agency
1849–51	William H. Bruce (appointed 2 April 1849)
1851–53	George Lawe (appointed 28 March 1851)
1853–54/55?	John V. Suydam (appointed 11 May 1853)
1855	Ephraim Shaler (appointed 21 February 1855)
1855–57	Benjamin Hunkins (appointed 8 May 1855)
1857	Frederick Moscowitt (appointed 16 February 1857)
1857–61	Augustus D. Bonesteel (appointed 23 September 1857)
1861–65	Moses M. Davis (appointed 1 April 1861)
1866–69	Morgan L. Martin (appointed 8 May 1866)
1869	A. H. Read (appointed 9 April 1869, did not serve)
1869–70	Lt. John A. Manley (appointed 24 June 1869)
1870	Lt. W. R. Bourne (appointed 10 February 1870)
1870–73	William T. Richardson (appointed 8 September 1870)
1873	Isaac W. Hutchins (appointed 3 March 1873, did not serve)
1873–74	Thomas N. Chase (appointed 31 May 1873)
1874–79	Joseph C. Bridgeman (appointed 22 August 1874)
1879–82	Ebenezer Stephens (appointed 3 March 1879)
1883–85	D. P. Andrews
1885–90	Thomas Jennings
1890–93	Charles S. Kelsey
1893–96	Thomas H. Savage
1897–1902	Dewey H. George (sworn in 17 April 1899, term expired September 1902)

Table 1, continued

1902–08	Shepard Freeman (began 30 September 1902)
1908–09	Edgar A. Allen
1909	Thomas B. Wilson (superintendent of school, 1909–10)
1909–18	Angus S. Nicholson
1918–25	Edgar A. Allen (began 1 April 1918)
1925–27	William Donner (superintendent of Neopit Mills/Keshena agency)
1928–34	W. R. Beyer
1934	Lloyd S. Andrews (acting July–August)
1934–40	Ralph Fredenberg (ca. August 1934–June 1940)
1940–42	Earl Woolridge (ca. July 1940–26 March 1942)
1942–45	J. Lyle Cunningham (began ca. May 1942)
1945	Mr. Allen (acting, previous to Murphy)
1945–46	Daniel E. Murphy (until May 1946)
1946	R. M. Allen (acting, July–December)
1946–54	James Arentson (ca. December 1946 to May 1954)
1954–55	Raymond H. Bitney (began June 6 1954)
1955–58	Melvin L. Robertson (began 14 July 1955)

Sources: Hill, *Historical Sketches*; *Letters Received by the Office of Indian Affairs, 1824–81*, Microcopy 234; Letters Received, 1881–1907, RG 75, NARA-DC; Central Classified Files Green Bay and Keshena, RG 75, NARA-DC; Records of the Keshena/Menominee Agency, 1892–1961, NARA-GLR.

Table 2. Missionaries and priests among the Menominee, 1853–1980

Catholic Missions

1853–57	Fr. Otto Skolla, OSF
1857–66	Four priests visit with interruption
1859–62	Rev. Anthony Maria Gachet, OM Capuchin
1860–61	Menard Stern
1863	Rev. Mignault (3 months of service)
1864–65	Rev. A. M. Mazeaud, French (1 year of service)
?	Rev. Godhart, from Netherlands
?	Rev. van den Huevel, from Netherlands
1866–68/69	*Capuchin Fathers of Calvary, Wisconsin, in charge*
1866–67, 1868	Fr. Cajetan Krauthahn
1867–68	Fr. Solanus Fedderman (during Father Cajetan's illness)
1869	Fr. Fidelis Steinauer (January–November)
1870s	*Agents in collusion with Protestants; no resident priest after Capuchins abandoned mission; several visited it off and on*
1870–71	Rev. Vermare of Oconto City
1872	Rev. Drerus or Daems
1873	Rev. Bayerle of Duck Creek
1873–74	Fr. J. Chebul (also a few days in 1872)
1874	Rev. Bayerle (also served by Rev. Chr. Verwyst from Lake Superior Missions)
1875–80	Fr. Amandus Masschelein, Franco-Belgian
1880	*Franciscan Brothers of St. Louis take over*
1881	*Sisters of St. Joseph take charge of schools*
1880	Fr. Arnold Wilnus
1880–82	Fr. Servatius Altmicks (*praeses*)
1880–85	Fr. Zephyrin Englehardt (*praeses*, 1882–85)
1881–83	Fr. Marianus Glahu
1882–1914/15	Fr. Blaze Krake (*praeses*, 1897–1914/15)

Table 2, continued

1883	Fr. Justinian(?) (Kinepoway and Little Oconto)
1883–85	Fr. Hugo Fessler (*praeses*, 1885)
1885–87	Fr. Norbert Wilhelm
1885–97	Fr. Oderic Derenthal (*praeses*)
1887–88	Fr. Pius Niermann
1897–1914+	Rev. Simon Schwartz
1907–42	Fr. Englehard Troeskin (*praeses*, 1914/15–42)
19??-50	Fr. Virgil Benzman (Neopit)
1942–50	Fr. Benno Tushaus, OFM (*praeses*)
1951–53	Fr. Bede Middendorf
1951–52	Fr. Lucien Trosy(sp?), OFM (*praeses*)
1952–55	Fr. Landelin Belker, OFM (*praeses*)
1955	Fr. Hildebart
1956	Oscar Rascher (Neopit)
1955–60+	Fr. Floribert Veverka, OFM
1968	Fr. Alexis Preumer, OFM
1976	Cyril J. Wagner
1980	*Transferred to Diocesan priests*
1980	Joseph Benedict Hagen, OFM

Lutheran Mission

1903	Robert Kreutzman attempts to found Lutheran mission in Zoar, abandoned by 1914

Lutheran Church, Neopit

1908–13?	Largely for non-Indian millworkers

Sources: *Sacred Heart Franciscan Provincial Indian Records,* microfilm, Marquette University Archives; *Letters Received by the Office of Indian Affairs, 1824–81,* Microcopy 234; Letters Received, 1881–1907, RG 75, NARA-DC; Central Classified Files Green Bay and Keshena, RG 75, NARA-DC; Bittle, *A Romance of Lady Poverty;* Habig, *Heralds of the King;* Rosholt and Gehl, *Florimond J. Bonduel.*

Table 3. Menominee population estimates and figures, 1852–2004

Year	Value	Year	Value	Year	Value
1852	2,002[1]	1879	1,460	1908	1,464
1855	1,930	1880	1,450	1909	1,487
1857	1,697	1881	1,450	1910	1,509[5]
1862	1,748	1882	1,500	1916	1,736
1863	1,724	1883	1,392	1917	1,745
1864	1,864	1884	1,400	1919	1,733
1865	1,879	1885	1,308	1922	1,819
1866	1,376	1886	1,306	1927	1,940
1867	1,393	1887	1,632[2]	1929	1,939[6]
1868	1,418	1888	1,442	1935	2,112[7]
1870	1,336	1889	1,469[3]	1952	3,059[8]
1871	1,348	1890	1,311	1957	3,270
1872	1,362	1891	1,318	1971	2,242[9]
1873	1,480	1892	1,335	1994	7,409
1874	1,480	1893	1,286[4]	2000	7,883[10]
1875	1,522	1894	1,302	2004	8,189[11]
1876	1,522	1895	1,286		
1877	1,368	1907	1,375		

Sources: *Reports of Indian Affairs*, 1854–1910; Keesing, *The Menomini Indians*; Rosholt and Gehl, *Florimond J. Bonduel*; Peroff, *Menominee Drums*; *1994 Annual Report*, Menominee Indian Tribe of Wisconsin; U.S. Census 2000; *Menominee Nation News*.

1. This number of Menominees removed to Falls of Wolf River.
2. Three hundred of this number lived off the reservation.
3. The total population, including those living off the reservation, was 1,761.
4. In addition, ca. three hundred Menominees lived near Marinette.
5. The census counted 1,422 this year.
6. During the period 1902–29, 202 were admitted to the roll.
7. Of this number 1,998 lived on the reservation.
8. Ca. 80 percent lived on tribal lands.
9. This number reflect shareholders accounted for (Peroff, *Menominee Drums*, 167).
10. Including those who identified themselves with other tribes or races, the 2000 census count was 9,840.
11. Tribal Enrollment Office figure.

Table 4. Mill and forest management until 1950

Mill Managers

1908–09	Edward A. Braniff, manager
1909	James A. Carroll, agent in charge
1909–10	A. M. Riley, manager
1910–18	Angus S. Nicholson, no manager employed
1918–22	George A. Gutches, manager
1922–25	Edgar A. Allen ("L. P. Johnson designated as Manager, but not in control.")
1925–27	William Donner
1927–33	George C. Hammer, manager
1933	Robert Allen, chief clerk
1933–34	E. H. Mullan, manager
1934–35	Robert Allen, chief clerk
1935–39	Hermann W. Johannes, manager
1939	George G. Robson, sales manager
1939–40	John V. Quinlan, manager
1940–42	Harold E. Holman, manager
1942–44	J. Lyle Cunningham, no manager
1945–46	Daniel E. Murphy, no manager
1946	Robert Allen, chief clerk
1946–47	James Arentson, no manager
1947-[1949]	R. Dickinson, manager

Superintendents of Logging

1903?-04	James T. Chase
1904–08?	William Farr
1909–10	Robert Riley
1910–13	Charles H. Woodcock (woods foreman in 1910)
1913–16	Ernest J. Brigham

Table 4, continued

1916–20	William Gardner
1920–26	Lawrence P. Johnson
1926–33	Tom C. White
1934-[1949]	James Caldwell

Source: Except for Chase and Farr, list is from Kinney, *Indian Forest and Range*, 328–29. See those pages for exact dates.

NOTES

ABBREVIATIONS

AFSC	American Friends Service Committee
AMA	American Missionary Association
CCF	Central Classified Files
DRUMS	Determination of Rights and Unity for Menominee Shareholders
Ex. Doc. No.	Executive Document Number
FBI-FOIA	Federal Bureau of Investigation-Freedom of Information Act
FPC	Federal Power Commission
GBARC	Green Bay Area Research Center
HR	House of Representatives
LR	Letters Received
M234	Microcopy 234, National Archives Microfilm
MRC	Menominee Restoration Committee
MTE	Menominee Tribal Enterprises
NAES	Native American Educational Services
NARA-DC	National Archives and Records Administration, Washington DC Branch
NARA-GLR	National Archives and Records Administration, Great Lakes Region (Chicago)
NARF	Native American Rights Fund
NCAI	National Congress of American Indians
RG	Record Group
SC	Special Case
SHFR	Sacred Heart Provincial Franciscan Indian Records
UPI	United Press International
WDOJ-DCI	Wisconsin Department of Justice-Division of Criminal Investigation

PREFACE

1. Dr. Tax is known for developing action anthropology, a method that encourages both students of anthropology and scholars to interact with and make positive contributions to the communities they study.

2. According to the Menominee Historic Preservation Department, the plural of Menominee is Menominee when referring to the tribe and is Menominees when referring to individuals. This is based on the translation of the tribe's name for itself from the Menominee language.

3. This is more true of Pacific Island studies than of North American Indian

studies; see Smith, *Decolonizing Methodologies*, for example. However, for examples of more nuanced scholarly research that speaks to critical issues in Native American communities today, see Basso, *Wisdom Sits in Places*; Metcalf, *Termination's Legacy*; and Clow and Sutton, eds., *Trusteeship in Change*.

4. Dening is writing about Pacific Islands history, so I have adapted some of his language to reflect Native American history within the United States. See Dening, "History 'in' the Pacific," 136.

5. This quote and variations of it appear in Barry, *Dave Barry Slept Here*, 28, 52, 64, 78, for example.

6. Rosaldo, *Culture and Truth*, 87.

7. Smith, *Decolonizing Methodologies*, 1, 28–30.

8. Hau'ofa, "Epilogue," 456–57.

9. Keesing, "Applied Anthropology," 379–80.

INTRODUCTION

Most of this introduction is a synopsis of Beck, *Siege and Survival*.

The epigraph that begins the introduction is from Sho-no-niew in Council, as reported in Francis Huebschmann to Charles E. Mix, 28 September 1855, in U.S. Congress, Senate, Ex. Doc. No. 72 (hereafter Ex. Doc. No. 72, Senate), 226–27.

1. Americans for Indian Opportunity has articulated the concept of core cultural values among tribal people of North America. Harris and Wasilewski, "This Is What We Want to Share: Core Cultural Values."

2. Carl "Chummy" Maskewit, interview, Menominee Tribal Historic Preservation Department. The interviews conducted by the Menominee Historic Preservation Department are identified as such, and those citations include names of interviewees.

3. Quoted in "Squaws Rule Wigwam Now."

1. THE EARLY RESERVATION YEARS

1. Keesing, *The Menomini Indians*, 150–52. Besides those in the Marinette-Menominee area, photographer Roland Reed recorded that in 1871 a Menominee band headed by Thundercloud " 'lived on the north shore of Lake Poygan directly across from my home.' " Quoted in Meier, "A Photographic Treasure Reappears," 7–8. For an analysis of diversity in band-based societies, see Binnema, *Common and Contested Ground*. His work relates to the northwest plains but suggests intriguing lines of analysis for the Upper Great Lakes as well.

2. Beck, *Siege and Survival*, 168–200.

3. Map 2 is created from a hand-drawn map of the fifteen townships set aside for

the Menominee based on the Joint Resolution by the State of Wisconsin Legislature, *Letters Received by the Office of Indian Affairs, 1824–1881*, M234, reel 322, frame 172, and Huebschmann to Commissioner of Indian Affairs Manypenny, 7 March 1854, M234–322, frames 372–73; "Joint Resolution Concerning the Menominee Tribe of Indians, Resolved by the Senate and Assembly of the state of Wisconsin," 1 February 1853, Edward E. Ayer Collection, The Newberry Library; Newman, "The Menominee Forest," 11; Huebschmann to Charles E. Mix, 13 April 1857, M234–323, frames 318–19; Thomsen, Neumann, and Schuttler, *The Forests of the Menominee*, 12–13, Menominee Historic Preservation Department.

4. Newman "The Menominee Forest," 9–11.

5. Nesbit, *Wisconsin*, 280.

6. Newman, "The Menominee Forest," 15–18.

7. Beck, "Return to *Namä'o Uskíwämît*," 44–45; Keesing, *The Menomini Indians*, 152–53; interviews with Menominee people. As noted in the bibliography, I offered anonymity to interviewees I deposed myself.

8. Treaty with the Stockbridge Tribe, 1848; Treaty with the Stockbridge and Munsee, 1856; Treaty with the Menominee, 1856, all in Kappler, *Indian Treaties*, 574–82, 742–55, and 755–56; "Protest of A. Miller," 4–7.

9. Beck, *Siege and Survival*, 108, 122–24, 140, 142–43.

10. Letter from 46 Menominees, including Carron, LaMotte, Aiometah, Oshkehenaniew and Komanikin or Little Wave to Supt. E. Murray, 6 December 1852, M234–322, frames 186–88.

11. Results of Menominee Tribal Council, 21 April, 12 May, and 15 May 1856, reported by Agent Hunkins, M234–323, frames 57–63.

12. Results of Menominee Tribal Council, 21 April, 12 May, and 15 May, 1856, reported by Agent Hunkins, M234–323, frames 57–63. On Wayka, see Keesing, "Leaders of the Menomini Tribe," 11–12, Wisconsin Historical Society Archives.

13. Results of Menominee Tribal Council, 21 April, 12 May, and 15 May 1856, reported by Agent Hunkins, M234–323, frames 57–63.

14. Hunkins to Huebschmann, 12 July 1856, M234–323, frame 163.

15. Report of Menominee Council, 4 July 1856, reported by Agent Hunkins, M234–323, frame 165. See also Speech of I ya ma taw (Aiometah), 13 October 1835 Annuity, M234–316, frame 292; 1855 Memorial to President Franklin Pierce from 117 Menominee chiefs and young men, M234–322, frames 601–2; and Sho-no-niew in Council, 8 September 1855, in Huebschmann to Mix, 28 September 1855, in Ex. Doc. No. 72, Senate, 226–27.

16. Report of Menominee Council, 4 July 1856, M234–323, frames 166–68.

17. Report of Benjamin Hunkins, 30 September 1856, in *Report of the Commissioner of Indian Affairs*, 1856, 42.

18. Report of Farmer Friederich Haas, in *Report of the Commissioner of Indian*

Affairs, 1858, 33; Report of Rosalie Dousman, Teacher, Report of Friederich Haas, Farmer, in *Report of the Commissioner of Indian Affairs*, 1859, 38–47; Nesbit, *Wisconsin*, 280–82.

19. Treaty with the Menominee, 1854, and Treaty with the Menominee, 1856, in Kappler, *Indian Treaties*, 626–27, 755–56; Article 3, Treaty with the Stockbridge and Munsee, 1856, in Kappler, *Indian Treaties*, 744. On the treaties of the 1850s, see Prucha, *American Indian Treaties*, 235–60. He discusses the Manypenny treaties at 241–42. On reservation policy, see Trennert, *Alternative to Extinction*.

20. Report of Green Bay Agent A. D. Bonesteel, 25 October 1860, in *Report of the Commissioner of Indian Affairs*, 1860, 35.

21. Report of A. D. Bonesteel, Agent, in *Report of the Commissioner of Indian Affairs*, 1859, 38–47.

22. Charles C. Cotton, Deputy Marshall, Milwaukee, to Robert McClelland, Secretary of the Interior, 23 March 1854, M234–322, frame 317; Report of Senate Committee on Indian Affairs, 14 February 1853, in Report of the President regarding "information relative to the appropriation in the civil and diplomatic bill of March 3, 1855, for Richard W. Thompson, on account of alleged services to the Menominee Indians," Ex. Doc. No. 72, Senate, 67; Chas. A. Grignon to G. W. Ewing, 27 June 1853, in George W. Ewing Collection, Indiana State Library; Report of Commissioner Geo. W. Manypenny to Secretary of the Interior Hon. R. McClelland, in *Report of the Commissioner of Indian Affairs*, 1854, 21; McClelland to Commissioner of Indian Affairs, 20 February 1855, M234–322, frame 810.

23. Report of A. D. Bonesteel; Report of Orlin Andrews, Teacher; Report of Friederich Haas, Farmer; Report of Rosalie Dousman, Teacher, all in *Report of the Commissioner of Indian Affairs*, 1859, 38–47; Gachet, "Journal of a Missionary," 204.

24. Before the Office of Indian Affairs was renamed the Bureau of Indian Affairs in the late 1940s, both employees and tribal members referred to the office as the Indian Department, the Indian Service, the Indian Bureau, and the Indian Office. Those terms are used interchangeably in this book when discussing the years before the change.

25. Report of James W. Howe, 6 December 1860, in U.S. Congress, Ex. Doc. No. 4, 2–8.

26. Interviews with Menominee people; Report of Kintzing Pritchette, 8 June 1860, Ex. Doc. No. 4, 40.

27. Howe's report, Ex. Doc. No. 4, 3.

28. Deposition of Ke-she-na, Ex. Doc. No. 4, 80–82; Howe's Report, Ex. Doc. No. 4, 3, 6; Deposition of William Powell, Ex. Doc. No. 4, 120.

29. *Report of the Commissioner of Indian Affairs*, 1860, 12–13.

30. Huebschmann to Manypenny, 16 August 1853, M234–322, frame 110. See paragraph 9, article 4, Treaty with the Menominee, 1848, in Kappler, *Indian Treaties*, 573.

31. Howe's Report, Ex. Doc. No. 4, 5.

32. Deposition of LaMotte, Ex. Doc. No. 4, 88–90.

33. Beck, *Siege and Survival*, 185, 195–96; Deposition of Sho-no-nee, Ex. Doc. No. 4, 65–66.

34. Bourne to Commissioner of Indian Affairs E. S. Parker, 25 July 1870; Manley to Parker, 22 January 1870; Manley to Parker, 1 March 1870; Manley to Parker, 4 March 1870, including affidavits in his support; Philetus Sawyer to Parker, 15 January 1870; and Sawyer to Secretary of the Interior J. D. Cox, 19 February 1870, accompanied by four affidavits sworn out against Manley, M234–327, frames 231, 521–22, 596, 621–46, 758–59, and 782–87. A. H. Read was appointed between Martin and Manley but did not serve.

35. Report of Commissioner of Indian Affairs Wm. P. Dole and Report of Green Bay Agent M. M. Davis, in *Report of the Commissioner of Indian Affairs*, 1862, 42, 331.

36. Report of Commissioner of Indian Affairs William P. Dole and Report of Green Bay Agent M. M. Davis, in *Report of the Commissioner of Indian Affairs*, 1863, 33, 348–350; Report of Commissioner of Indian Affairs William P. Dole and Report of Green Bay Agent M. M. Davis, in *Report of the Commissioner of Indian Affairs*, 1864, 42–43, 437.

37. Petition from Menominees to Secretary of the Interior or Commissioner of Indian Affairs, 5 April 1865. Witnessed by J. D. Grignon as interpreter and Joseph M. Ostroph, Clerk. Signed by Acco na may Oshkosh, Osh ke e neh new, Me teh we nah new, Wau kah chune, Lammote, Way keh, Ko man ne kin, Pe quo ca nah, Shaw pwa tuck and Mau kah teh pe nas as head chief and chiefs of bands, followed by 8 sub-chiefs and 71 warriors, M234–325, frames 199–208. Davis's response is found at frame 236. On the history of the northern superintendency, see Hill, *Guide to Records*, 139–40.

38. Keesing, *The Menomini Indians*, 157; Gachet, "Journal of a Missionary," 191, 358. On Oshkosh genealogy, see Hoffman, *The Menomini Indians*, 52.

39. Krautbauer, "Missions Among the Menominee in Wisconsin," 157, Wisconsin Historical Society Library; Gachet, "Journal of a Missionary," 192.

40. Gachet, "Journal of a Missionary," 74, 192, 347. This number is corroborated in Report of Green Bay Agent Martin, in *Report of the Commissioner of Indian Affairs* 1868, 292.

41. Gachet, "Journal of a Missionary," 72–75, 195.

42. Gachet, "Journal of a Missionary," 72–75, 195, 350.

43. Report of M. M. Davis, in *Report of the Commissioner of Indian Affairs*, 1864, 438; Habig, *Heralds of the King*, 522.

44. Report of Rosalie Dousman, 19 September 1864; Report of Kate Dousman, 17 September 1864; Report of M. M. Davis, 26 September 1864, all in *Report of the Commissioner of Indian Affairs*, 1864, 438–41.

45. Report of Kate Dousman, Teacher, 11 September 1865; Report of Samuel A. Miller, Farmer, 18 September 1865, both in *Report of the Commissioner of Indian Affairs*, 1865, 439–40.

46. Report of Commissioner of Indian Affairs D. N. Cooley, 31 October 1865, and Report of Agent M. M. Davis, 25 September 1865, in *Report of the Commissioner of Indian Affairs*, 1865, 4, 437; Menominee Indian Tribe of Wisconsin, *Menominee Tribal History Guide*, 61.

47. Report of Commissioner Cooley, 31 October 1865, and Report of Agent Davis, 25 September 1865, in *Report of the Commissioner of Indian Affairs*, 1865, 52, 438; Davis to Commissioner of Indian Affairs Wm. P. Dole, 10 June 1865, M234-325, frames 57–58.

48. Davis to Dole, 10 June 1865, M234-325, frames 58–59.

49. Davis to Dole, 10 June 1865, M234-325, frame 60; Report of Commissioner of Indian Affairs Cooley, in *Report of the Commissioner of Indian Affairs*, 1865, 4.

50. Chronicle of the "History of the Catholic Mission Among the Menominee Indians," from information collected by Bishop Francis Xavier Krautbauer, 1889, in SHFR microfilm, reel 13, frame 490, Marquette University Archives.

51. Habig, *Heralds of the King*, 521–32; Bittle, *A Romance of Lady Poverty*, 177–79.

52. Chronicle of the "History of the Catholic Mission Among the Menominee Indians," from information collected by Bishop Francis Xavier Krautbauer, 1889, in SHFR, reel 13, frame 474.

53. Report of Agent Martin, in *Report of the Commissioner of Indian Affairs*, 1866, 288; Wm. T. Richardson to Commissioner of Indian Affairs Walker, 22 February 1872, M234-328, frames 136–37.

54. Report of Agent Martin, 1 August 1869, in *Report of the Commissioner of Indian Affairs*, 1869, 438.

55. Rosholt and Gehl, *Florimond J. Bonduel*, 146; *Report of the Commissioner of Indian Affairs*, 1871, 614. See appendix, table 3.

2. THE PIVOTAL DIVIDE OF 1871

1. *Report of the Commissioner of Indian Affairs*, 1855, 41; *Report of the Commissioner of Indian Affairs*, 1862, 332; Thomsen, Neumann, and Schuttler, *The Forests of the Menominee*, 59, in Menominee Tribal Historic Preservation Department.

2. Beck, *Siege and Survival*, 160–62, 191; Clow, "The Indian Yeoman," 5.

3. Thomsen, Neumann, and Schuttler, *The Forests of the Menominee*, 58, Menominee Tribal Historic Preservation Department; Huebschmann to Commissioner of Indian Affairs Mix, 13 April 1857, M234-323, frame 318.

4. Davis to Cooley, 3 October 1865, M234-325, frames 134–35.

5. Much of Bourne's 1870 correspondence with the commissioner of Indian af-

fairs deals with timber trespass. See M234–327, frames 6–8, 17, 20–22, 197, 199–203, 229, 266, 544, 565, 652–54, and 1100–1101.

6. Keesing, *The Menomini Indians*, 168–69.

7. Davis to Cooley, 1 November 1865 and 28 December 1865, M234–325, frames 164–66, 303.

8. Hurst, *Law and Economic Growth*, 119.

9. Bourne to Parker, 7 March 1870, M234–327, 20–22; Chas. Bagley and Dan'l Crawford to "Sir," 10 February 1870, M234–327, frames 6–8.

10. Current, *Pine Logs and Politics*, 113–16.

11. Cronon, *Nature's Metropolis*, 155.

12. Hurst, *Law and Economic Growth*, 2–3.

13. Current, *Pine Logs and Politics*, 71–72.

14. For copies of the advertisement of these sales, dated in the text as 27 September 1870, as it appeared in the *Milwaukee Sentinel*, the *Chicago Evening Post*, and the *New York Standard*, see M234–327, frames 296–97, 376, and 1356. It was probably advertised locally as well. On 27 September 1870, Buckstaff Bros. Lumber, Lath, and Shingles of Oshkosh wrote to Secretary of the Interior J. D. Cox inquiring whether it was "a fixed fact" that the Menominee reservation would be sold that fall. M234–327, frame 283.

15. Cox to Acting Commissioner of Indian Affairs, 19 August 1870, M234–327, frame 367.

16. Current, *Pine Logs and Politics*, 72–73; for instructions to suspend action regarding the sale, see Cox to Acting Commissioner of Indian Affairs, 12 October 1870, M234–327, frame 490.

17. Letter from 11 Menominee chiefs (Ah-ko-ne-may, La Motte, Ne-yah-tah-wah-po-ma, Wau-ke-che-on, Ke-ne-boy-wa, Wy-tah-sah, Kay-so, Wish-co-by, Ne-o-pet, Wah-pe-nah-nosh, O-ho-pa-sha) to Lt. Bourne, 30 July 1870. Witnessed by Joseph Gauthier, Interpreter, and Z. C. Colborn; Bourne to Parker, 11 August 1870; M234–327, frames 245–247.

18. Petition signed by 76 Menominees, including Carow, Keshena, Wayka, Mi-tay-mi-ni-ni, A-go-ma-ni-ken, Shawano pi-nince and Matcho-kineo, all listed as band chiefs, and 7 second chiefs, 14 February 1870, M234–327, frame 581.

19. Petition from 25 "Chiefs" of the Menominee tribe to Commissioner of Indian Affairs Parker, 29 January 1870. Signers include Ah co ne may, La Motte, Oho pa sha, I ah shien, Jo Osh ke he nah niew, Wish co ba, Wah ke chon, Ne o pet, and others. Witnessed by Joseph Gauthier, U.S. Interpreter. M234–327, frames 630–31.

20. Bourne to Parker, 31 March 1870; Bourne to Parker, 30 July 1870; Bourne to Parker, 30 August 1870; Bourne to Parker, 2 October 1870; Bourne to Parker, 2 November 1870, all in M234–327, frames 64, 236, 251, 293, 308–9. On the ongoing problems with late annuity payments, see Beck, *Siege and Survival*, 149–56.

21. Report of Wm. T. Richardson, in *Report of the Commissioner of Indian Affairs*, 1871, 512. See also statistics, 634. *Report of the Commissioner of Indian Affairs*, 1867, statistics, 391; Richardson to E. S. Parker, 23 February 1871, M234–327, frame 1103. The hay and probably some of the corn, rye, and oats went to feed the stock.

22. "An Act to Authorize the Sale of Certain Lands."

23. See correspondence and petitions regarding this in M234–327, frames 106, 208–9, 211, 220–21, 222, 465, 581–88, 668, 800–822, 1088–90, and 1243–45.

24. Richardson to Parker, 30 March 1871, M234–327, frames 1115–16. Emphasis in original.

25. Neopit Oshkosh, 20 February 1882, letter to editor in the *Milwaukee Republican and News*, reprinted in the *Shawano County Advocate*, 16 March 1882. This letter is partially quoted in Keesing, *The Menomini Indians*, 183, although it is not quite accurately transcribed there.

26. Statement of Menominee Tribe, 27 March 1871, signed by Ahconemay, La Motte, Nah-yah-tah-wah-po-may, Waukechon, Carron, Komanekin, Wah-we-na-niew, Keshena, Shawanopenass, and Ohopasha, M234–327, frames 1120–22.

27. "An Act for the relief of the Stockbridge and Munsee tribe of Indians, in the State of Wisconsin," 6 February 1871, in Kappler, *Indian Affairs*, 128–31; "Protest of A. Miller," 9–11.

28. This would be a large proportion of the male adult population, if that is the number to which Richardson referred. The tribe's population, including men, women, and children, was officially 1,348 that year. *Report of the Commissioner of Indian Affairs*, 1871, 685.

29. Richardson to Parker, 9 June 1871, M234–327, frames 1175–77.

30. Petition to Parker from Menominee Chiefs and Headmen in Council assembled in Keshena, 31 May 1871, M234–327, frames 1179–83.

31. Report of W. T. Richardson, 14 September 1871, in *Report of the Commissioner of Indian Affairs*, 1871, 512; Richardson to Parker, 9 June 1871, M234–327, frames 1175–77.

32. This caused Sawyer to try to have Manley fired. On timber sale, see Affidavit from Charles Bagley and Daniel Crawford, 8 June 1870, M234–327, frame 201. On the Sawyer-Manley conflict, see Manley to Commissioner of Indian Affairs E. S. Parker, 14 January 1870, and Sawyer to Parker, 15 January 1870, M234–327, frames 572–74 and 758–59.

33. Kinney, *Indian Forest and Range*, 8–9; Report of Wm. T. Richardson, 18 October 1872, in *Report of the Commissioner of Indian Affairs*, 1872, 204. See also correspondence between Richardson and the commissioner of Indian affairs, 9 June 1871, M234–327, frames 1175–82, and 15 January 1872, 17 February 1872, 1 July 1872, and 12 August 1872, M234–328, frames 111–12, 132–33, 214–15, and 224–25.

34. Report of N. J. Turney, Board of Indian Commissioners, to Commissioner of Indian Affairs Walker, 6 March 1872, M234–328, frames 364–79.

35. Report of N. J. Turney, Board of Indian Commissioners, to Commissioner of Indian Affairs Walker, 6 March 1872, M234–328, frames 364–79.

36. Clow, "The Indian Yeoman," 9–12.

37. Kinney, *Indian Forest and Range*, 9.

38. *Report of the Commissioner of Indian Affairs*, 1874, 146.

39. Report of N. J. Turney, M234–328, frame 370.

40. Annual Report of the Commissioner of Indian Affairs Edw. P. Smith, and Report of Jos. C. Bridgeman, 18 September 1875, in *Report of the Commissioner of Indian Affairs*, 1875, 68, 369–70; Hosmer, *American Indians in the Marketplace*, 30.

41. Receipts of 1888–89 in "Records of Logs Purchased from Indians," Records of the Menominee Indian Mills, 1900–1961, RG 75, Records of the Bureau of Indian Affairs, NARA-GLR. Hosmer, *American Indians in the Marketplace*, 31. Cutting was stopped again briefly in 1885–86 and 1888. See also Kinney, *Indian Forest and Range*, 24; and Hosmer, "Creating Indian Entrepreneurs," 3. Hosmer gives the final date of the longest hiatus as 1882; Kinney says 1881. Perhaps it was the winter of 1881–82.

42. Bourne to Parker, 11 April 1870, M234–327, frame 107.

43. Head Chief Neopit and Chiefs Chickanay, Neyahtowaupomay, and Moses Ohopasha and Mitchell Oshkenaniew to Commissioner of Indian Affairs Hiram Price, 4 December 1884, LR 1881–1907, 1884:23614, RG 75, NARA-DC.

44. Sam. Ryan to Hon. S. J. Kirkwood, Secretary of the Interior, 1 September 1881, LR 1881–1907, 1881:15782, RG 75, NARA-DC.

45. Beck, *Siege and Survival*, 104; Richardson to Commissioner of Indian Affairs F. A. Walker, 2 November 1872, M234–328, frames 267–68; Bridgeman, Alfred F., NAA-SI; Hoffman, *The Menomini Indians*, 48; Keesing, *The Menomini Indians*, 175.

3. GOVERNMENT AND RELIGION

1. Prucha, *The Churches and the Indian Schools*, 1.

2. Report of the Indian School Superintendent, in *Report of the Commissioner of Indian Affairs*, 1885, lxxxix.

3. Keller, *American Protestantism*, 63–64; Beck, *Siege and Survival*, 91; Loew, *Indian Nations of Wisconsin*, 115–19.

4. Chronicle of the "History of the Catholic Mission Among the Menominee Indians," from information collected by Bishop Francis Xavier Krautbauer, 1889, in SHFR, reel 13, frame 474. For discussion of Catholic-Protestant conflicts in Menominee country in the 1820s and 1830s, see Beck, *Siege and Survival*, 124–40.

5. Richardson to Commissioner of Indian Affairs E. S. Parker, 15 April 1871, 9 May 1871, and 9 June 1871, in M234–327, frames 1129–33, 1154–58, and 1177.

6. Report of Commissioner of Indian Affairs Edw. P. Smith, in *Report of the Commissioner of Indian Affairs*, 1873, 8–9.

7. Report of Jos. C. Bridgeman, 18 September 1875, in *Report of the Commissioner of Indian Affairs*, 1875, 370.

8. Letter of Jos. C. Bridgeman, 16 November 1875, in *Report of the Board of Indian Commissioners*, 1875, 106; Report from Agent Joseph C. Bridgeman, in *Report of the Board of Indian Commissioners*, 1876, 92; Report of Agent Jos. C. Bridgeman, 20 August 1877, in *Report of the Commissioner of Indian Affairs*, 1877, 203–4.

9. Chronicle of the "History of the Catholic Mission Among the Menominee Indians," from information collected by Bishop Francis Xavier Krautbauer, 1889, in SHFR, reel 13, frame 492.

10. Most Rev. Fr. Augustine Sepinski, O.F.M., Foreword to Habig, *Heralds of the King*, v; Habig, *Heralds of the King*, 1, 495–561.

11. Habig, *Heralds of the King*, 521–32; Chronicle of the "History of the Catholic Mission Among the Menominee Indians," from information collected by Bishop Francis Xavier Krautbauer, 1889, in SHFR, reel 13, frame 501; Krautbauer, "Short Sketch," 158.

12. Habig, *Heralds of the King*, 521–32; Chronicle of the "History of the Catholic Mission Among the Menominee Indians," from information collected by Bishop Francis Xavier Krautbauer, 1889, in SHFR, reel 13, frame 501.

13. Glaher to Halbfas, 28 October 1881, SHFR, reel 12, frames 87–89. Parentheses in original. The priest's last name is alternately recorded as Glahu, Glaher, and Glahn in various sources.

14. Krake to Very Reverend Provincial, 22 February 1883, and Jennings to Father Bles, n.d., SHFR, reel 12. The last AMA appointee at Green Bay, Agent Stephens, served until 1882: Keller, *American Protestantism*, 1, 234.

15. Bridgeman, Alfred F., NAA-SI, reported that Father Derenthal in 1885 estimated two-thirds of Menominees to be Catholic; Agent Thomas Jennings in his annual reports to the commissioner of Indian affairs from 1886 to 1889 estimated that between 67.8 percent and 83.2 percent of Menominees were Catholic. Percentages calculated from Jennings's reports, in *Report of the Commissioner of Indian Affairs*, 1886, 248; *Report of the Commissioner of Indian Affairs*, 1887, 225; *Report of the Commissioner of Indian Affairs*, 1888, 237; *Report of the Commissioner of Indian Affairs*, 1889, 297.

16. Interviews with Menominee people. Keesing, *The Menomini Indians*, 179–80, indicates that the dance came to Wisconsin in 1880 and to the Menominee reservation in 1881. Hoffman, *The Menomini Indians*, 157, writing in the early 1890s, indicates that it arrived among the Menominee in the fall of 1880.

17. Keesing, *The Menomini Indians*, 179–80.

18. Stephens to Commissioner of Indian Affairs, 23 August 1881, LR 1881–1907, 1881:15282, RG 75, NARA-DC.

19. Stephens to Commissioner of Indian Affairs, 23 August 1881, LR 1881–1907, 1881:15282, RG 75, NARA-DC; Keesing, *The Menomini Indians*, 181; Hoffman, *The Menomini Indians*, 157–58.

20. Spindler, "Menominee," 716.

21. Barrett, "The Dream Dance," 256–57. For an ethnological description and sources, see Spindler, "Menominee," 716. Metchikeni to Reverend Clay McCauley, 1880, in McCauley, "The Dreamers," 339. Part of McCauley's speech is reproduced in Hoffman, *The Menomini Indians*, 161.

22. Metchikeni to Reverend Clay McCauley, 1880, in McCauley, "The Dreamers," 339; Spindler, "Menominee," 715–16; statistics from Bridgeman, Alfred F., NAA-SI; Agent Thomas Jennings, annual reports to the Commissioner of Indian Affairs, in *Report of the Commissioner of Indian Affairs*, 1886, 248; *Report of the Commissioner of Indian Affairs*, 1887, 225; *Report of the Commissioner of Indian Affairs*, 1888, 237; *Report of the Commissioner of Indian Affairs*, 1889, 297.

23. Beck, *Siege and Survival*, 36–37, 47.

24. Metchikeni to Reverend Clay McCauley, 1880, in McCauley, "The Dreamers," 339.

25. Metchikeni to Reverend Clay McCauley, 1880, in McCauley, "The Dreamers," 339.

26. Metchikeni to Reverend Clay McCauley, 1880, in McCauley, "The Dreamers," 339–40.

27. Hosmer, *American Indians in the Marketplace*, 33.

28. Stephens to Commissioner of Indian Affairs, 23 August 1881; Stephens to Commissioner of Indian Affairs, 6 September 1881, LR 1881–1907, 1881:15283, 1881:16039, RG 75, NARA-DC.

29. Telegram from Stephens, 25 August 1881, LR 1881–1907, 1881:15033, RG 75, NARA-DC.

30. Report of Agent E. Stephens, 1 September 1879, in *Report of Commissioner of Indian Affairs*, 1879, 160–61; "No. 2, Green Bay Agency 1880–81, 1881–82," 76, Rosters of Indian Police, RG 75, NARA-DC.

31. Telegram from Stephens, 26 August 1881; Stephens to Commissioner of Indian Affairs, 26 August 1881, LR 1881–1907, 1881:15132, 1881:15491, RG 75, NARA-DC.

32. Stephens to Commissioner of Indian Affairs, 27 August 1881; Secretary of War to Secretary of the Interior, 30 August 1881; Nyahtowahpomy, Marchekanin, Ohopasha, Waukeech, LaMotte, Shawanopenah, and Ahconemay to Commissioner of Indian Affairs, 27 August 1881; LR 1881–1907, 1881:15219, 1881:15363, 1881:15220, RG 75, NARA-DC.

33. Stephens to Commissioner of Indian Affairs, 1 September 1881; Stephens to

Commissioner of Indian Affairs, 2 September 1881; Stephens to Commissioner of Indian Affairs, 6 September 1881; Major D. W. Benham, Keshena, to Adjutant General, Fort Snelling, 1 September 1881, LR 1881–1907, 1881:15516, 1881:15743, 1881:16038, 1881:16243, RG 75, NARA-DC.

34. Stephens to Commissioner of Indian Affairs, 2 September 1881; D. W. Benham to Assistant Adjutant General of Fort Snelling, 20 October 1881; LR 1881–1907, 1881:15743; 1881:22534, RG 75, NARA-DC.

35. Keesing, *The Menomini Indians*, 181, states it is the other way around: that the founders of Zoar "claimed that [the Dream Dance] would wholly supersede the older religious system." Interviews with Menominee people.

36. Stephens to Commissioner of Indian Affairs, 2 September 1881, LR 1881–1907, 1881:15743, RG 75, NARA-DC; Keesing, *The Menomini Indians*, 181. A small core of Catholic Menominees, led by Ahconemay, vehemently disaffiliated themselves from the Dream Dance. A group of thirty met with McCauley in 1880: McCauley, "The Dreamers," 339.

37. Father Zepheryn to Very Rev. Provincial, 30 August 1883 and 13 September 1883, translated from the German by Franciscan Fathers St. Roch's Friary, SHFR, reel 12. One of these people might have been John Satterlee, who was thirty-one years old at the time.

38. He was known as Father Zephyrin, who served on the Menominee reservation from 1880 to 1885 (as *praeses,* the leader of the Franciscans on the reservation, from 1882 to 1885). He should not be confused with Father Englehard Troeskin, known as Father Englehard, who served among the Menominees from 1907 to 1942 (as *praeses* from 1914 or 1915 to 1942).

39. Halbfas to very Rev. Brousillet [May 1883], and Fr. Vincentius to the most Rev. Bishop, 9 September 1883, the latter translated from the German by Franciscan Fathers St. Roch's Friary, SHFR, reel 12, between frame 238 and 261, and frame 272.

40. Father Zephyrin to Very Rev. Provincial, 30 August 1883, SHFR, reel 12.

41. Father Vincentius, Prolis, in St. Louis, to Rev. Fr. Praeses [Zephyrin], 9 September 1883, translated from the German by Franciscan Fathers St. Roch's Friary, SHFR, reel 12, frame 269. Nonetheless, Father Vincent supported Father Zephyrin when writing to the Bishop. Fr. Vincentius to Most Rev. Bishop, 9 September 1883, reel 12, frame 269.

42. Andrews to Commissioner of Indian Affairs, 13 February 1884, and H. Price, Commissioner of Indian Affairs, to Capt. John Mullan, Catholic Indian Commissioner, 26 February 1884 (copy), SHFR, reel 12, frames 366–68.

43. Father Zephyrin to Charles Lusk, Secretary of Catholic Indian Mission, 13 March 1884 (copy), SHFR, reel 12, frames 388–91; Father Zephyrin to Captain John Mullan, 17 March 1884, SHFR, reel 12, frames 382–83, 391–92, and 397.

44. Father Zephyrin to Charles Lusk, 13 March 1884 (copy), SHFR, reel 12, frames 383–86; religious statistics in Bridgeman, Alfred F., NAA-SI.

45. Father Zephyrin to Charles Lusk, 13 March 1884 (copy), SHFR, reel 12, frames 383–86; religious statistics in Bridgeman, Alfred F., NAA-SI.

46. Father Zephyrin to Charles Lusk, 13 March 1884 (copy), SHFR, reel 12, frames 383–86.

47. Thompson, "John D. C. Atkins, 1885–88," 181–84.

48. Atkins to Agent Andrews, 1 May 1885, SHFR, reel 12, frames 558–60. Atkins demanded from Andrews a report not "of what is talked about at the Agency," but with sworn evidence. The conflict involved vouchers that Andrews refused to forward and inspections he attempted to make in a vindictive manner.

49. Father Zephyrin to Very Rev. Provincial, 7 January 1885, translated from the German by Franciscan Fathers St. Roch's Friary, SHFR, reel 12, frame 473.

50. Chas. S. Kelsey to Commissioner of Indian Affairs, 3 June 1891, 20735, SC 143, RG 75, NARA-DC.

51. Father Oderic to P. Provincial, 2 January 1885; Fr. Zephyrin to Bishop Krautbauer, 21 April 1885; Father Anselm to Very Rev. Provincial, 31 August 1885, translated from the German by Franciscan Fathers St. Roch's Friary; and Father Blase to Very Rev. Mauritius Klosterman, 6 November 1885; SHFR, reel 12, frames 460–62, 528–29, 615–16, and 671–73.

4. TWENTY MILLION FEET A YEAR

1. Richardson to Parker, 9 June 1871, M234–327, frames 1175–77. See also, for example, Report of Thomas Jennings, 24 August 1889, in *Report of the Commissioner of Indian Affairs*, 1889, 298–99.

2. Report of Agent E. Stephens, in *Report of the Commissioner of Indian Affairs*, 1880, 170. In 1869 Agent Martin had proposed allotment, adding that its enactment would have the advantage of diminishing the role of traditional tribal leaders: Report of M. L. Martin, 1 August 1869, in *Report of the Commissioner of Indian Affairs*, 1869, 438. In 1874 Commissioner of Indian Affairs Edward P. Smith had written in his annual report that Menominees wanted to be allotted: Report of Commissioner of Indian Affairs Edward P. Smith, in *Report of the Commissioner of Indian Affairs*, 1874, 25.

3. Report of Agent E. Stephens, in *Report of the Commissioner of Indian Affairs*, 1881, 177; Kinney, *Indian Forest and Range*, 9, 24; Report of Agent E. Stephens, in *Report of the Commissioner of Indian Affairs*, 1882, 172.

4. Neopit Oshkosh, 20 February 1882, letter to the editor in the *Milwaukee Republican and News*, reprinted in the *Shawano County Advocate*, 16 March 1882.

5. Hosmer, *American Indians in the Marketplace*, 40–41; Hosmer, "Reflections," 499.

6. Hosmer, *American Indians in the Marketplace*, 42.

7. Hosmer, *American Indians in the Marketplace*, 43–45; Keesing, *The Menomini Indians*, 183–84; Report of Agent Andrews, 1884, in *Report of the Commissioner of Indian Affairs*, 1884, 178.

8. Kinney, *Indian Forest and Range*, 9, 24; Report of Agent E. Stephens, in *Report of the Commissioner of Indian Affairs*, 1882, 172; Hosmer, "Experiments in Capitalism," 162–63; Report of Commissioner of Indian Affairs J. D. C. Atkins, in *Report of the Commissioner of Indian Affairs*, 1887, xlvii–xlviii.

9. Report of Agent Thomas Jennings, in *Report of the Commissioner of Indian Affairs*, 1887, 226.

10. "An Act to Provide for the Allotment of Lands in Severalty"; *Annual Report of the Board of Indian Commissioners*, 1900, 7.

11. McDonnell, *The Dispossession of the American Indian*; Spicer, "American Indians," 115; Deloria and Lytle, *American Indians, American Justice*, 8–10; Cohen, *A Handbook of Federal Indian Law*, 208, 216. For studies of another forest-rich Upper Midwestern tribe's devastating long-term experience with allotment, see Meyer, *White Earth Tragedy*; Weil, "Destroying a Homeland"; Youngbear-Tibbets, "Without Due Process"; and Beaulieu, "Curly Hair and Big Feet."

12. Report of Commissioner of Indian Affairs J. D. C. Atkins, in *Report of the Commissioner of Indian Affairs*, 1887, xlviii; Report of Agent Thomas Jennings, in *Report of the Commissioner of Indian Affairs*, 1887, 225.

13. Tribal Council proceedings, 14 October 1887, and Jennings to Commissioner of Indian Affairs, 14 October 1887, SC 147, RG 75, NARA-DC.

14. Interviews with Menominee people.

15. Jennings to Commissioner of Indian Affairs, 14 October 1887, SC 147, RG 75, NARA-DC.

16. Jennings to Commissioner of Indian Affairs, 14 October 1887, SC 147, RG 75, NARA-DC.

17. Report of Commissioner of Indian Affairs John. H. Oberly, in *Report of the Commissioner of Indian Affairs*, 1888, xliii.

18. Letter from the Chiefs, Headmen, and Members of the Menomonee Tribe of Indians in General Council, 15 October 1888. 139 signatures, beginning with Neoh Pet (Neopit), Neah ta wa pa ne (Niaqtawāpomi), Chickeney (Mahchakeniew); witnessed by Joseph Gauthier, F. S. Gauthier, J. A. Venus[?], and Mitchell Oshkenaniew. Referred to the Department by C. C. Painter. LR 1881–1907, 1889:13559, RG 75, NARA-DC.

19. Report of Agent Jennings, in *Report of the Commissioner of Indian Affairs*, 1886, 248.

20. Jennings to Commissioner of Indian Affairs, 14 October 1887, SC 147, RG 75, NARA-DC.

21. Report of Wm. H. Waldby and E. Whittlesey, in *Annual Report of the Board of Indian Commissioners*, 1889, 26.

22. Quotation from Hosmer, *American Indians in the Marketplace*, 62.

23. Current, *Pine Logs and Politics*, 217–18.

24. Hosmer, "Experiments in Capitalism," 168–80.

25. Kinney, *Indian Forest and Range*, 24–25; Attorney General A. H. Garland to Secretary of the Interior, 20 November 1888, reprinted in Report of Commissioner of Indian Affairs John. H. Oberly, in *Report of the Commissioner of Indian Affairs*, 1888, xlv–vi; Clow, "The Indian Yeoman," 16. The Supreme Court actually reinforced this ruling in 1902; it was not overturned until the Court of Claims in 1937 and 1938 decided the government had to compensate the Shoshone Indians not only for land the United States had taken but for the value of the timber on the land. Since the trust land granted to Indians was not simply to be held for a person's lifetime but in perpetuity, the Indians held the rights to the timber. Cohen, *A Handbook of Federal Indian Law*, 313–15.

26. Kinney, *Indian Forest and Range*, 25, 27n33, 87; Clow, "The Indian Yeoman," 16.

27. Cohen, *A Handbook of Federal Indian Law*, 314.

28. Receipts of 1888–89 in "Records of Logs Purchased from Indians," Records of the Menominee Indian Mills, 1900–1961, RG 75, NARA-GLR.

29. Report of Commissioner of Indian Affairs T. J. Morgan, 1 October 1889, in *Report of the Commissioner of Indian Affairs*, 1889, 89–91.

30. Hurst, *Law and Economic Growth*, 3–4.

31. Fries, *Empire in Pine*, 84–92; Cronon, *Nature's Metropolis*, 152–53.

32. Fries, *Empire in Pine*, 41, 49; Cronon, *Nature's Metropolis*, 158–59.

33. Keesing, *The Menomini Indians*, 185.

34. Report of Thomas Jennings, 24 August 1889, in *Report of the Commissioner of Indian Affairs*, 1889, 298–99; Hosmer, "Experiments in Capitalism," 170–71.

35. Report of Green Bay Agent Thomas Jennings, Agent, 24 August 1889, in *Report of the Commissioner of Indian Affairs*, 1889, 299; and Report of Green Bay Agent Chas. S. Kelsey, 23 August 1890, in *Report of the Commissioner of Indian Affairs*, 1890, 236; Keesing, *The Menomini Indians*, 192.

36. See Report of Thomas Jennings, 24 August 1889, in *Report of the Commissioner of Indian Affairs*, 1889, 299; and Report of Chas. A. Kelsey, 23 August 1890, in *Report of the Commissioner of Indian Affairs*, 1890, 236, for descriptions of the court in its first two years.

37. Hosmer, *American Indians in the Marketplace*, 51.

38. On Thompson, see Beck, *Siege and Survival*, 179.

39. Hosmer, *American Indians in the Marketplace*, 54–55.

40. Keesing, *The Menomini Indians*, 186.

41. Report of E. Whittlesey, 15 October 1890, in *Annual Report of the Board of Indian Commissioners*, 1890, 15–16.

42. "An act to authorize the sale of timber on certain lands."

43. LR 1881–1907, 1892:46114, RG 75, NARA-DC.

44. "An act to authorize the sale of timber on certain lands."

45. Acting Commissioner of Indian Affairs to Superintendent of Green Bay Agency, 31 December 1907, CCF 1907–1909 Green Bay 339, RG 75, NARA-DC; Accounts of Traders, CCF 1907–1909 Green Bay 253, RG 75, NARA-DC.

46. Report of Commissioner of Indian Affairs T. J. Morgan, in *Report of the Commissioner of Indian Affairs*, 1891, vol. 1, 91, 93.

47. An in-depth discussion of the politics and economics of logging under the 1890 law can be found in Hosmer, *American Indians in the Marketplace*, 58–78.

48. Report from J. A. H. [J. A. Howarth] Jr. to E. M. Griffith, State Forester, 24 December 1907, 10–11; Report on Logging in Recent Years on the Menominee Indian Reservation, Wisconsin, by J. A. H. Jr., 14 February 1907, 2–5, both in Reports, Memoranda + Letters of J. A. Howarth Jr. 1906–1909 folder, Miscellaneous Records of Forest Supervisor, 1905–1955, Records of the Menominee Indian Mills, 1900–1961, RG 75, NARA-GLR; Second Annual Report of Green Bay Agent Thomas H. Savage, in *Report of the Commissioner of Indian Affairs*, 1895, 325; Hosmer, "Experiments in Capitalism," 148.

49. For a history of these dams, see Alegria, "Historic River Drive Sites"; and Seymour Hollister (a frequent purchaser by bid of Menominee timber in the late nineteenth and early twentieth centuries) to Shepard Freeman, 26 October 1903, accompanying Freeman to Commissioner of Indian Affairs, 1 December 1903, in sheaf titled "Rel to the driving of logs on the Menominee Indian Reservation," in Special Case 202, Menominee Logging, Flat Files (hereafter SC 202), RG 75, NARA-DC.

50. Report from J. A. H. Jr., 14 December 1907, 2; Second Annual Report of Agent Savage, in *Report of the Commissioner of Indian Affairs*, 1895, 325. Copies of the eighty-three logging contracts are in CCF 1907–1909 Green Bay 339, RG 75, NARA-DC. The contracts went to L. Richmond, C. Wychesit, J. F. Gauthier, J. Pecore, John Satterlee, E. Fredenberg, E. Tourtillott, John Moon, F. Kakkak, Joe Akachekum, P. La Motte, J. La Motte, Thos. La Bell Jr., L. Kakkak, F. Waukechon, Geo. McCall, Joe Deer, M. Johnson, R. Heath, M. Tucker, Thos. La Bell Sr., M Wausakokamick, P. Lookaround, W. Dodge, Matchokomow, E. Phalen, W. Heath, C. Fredenberg, Jerome Lawe, B. Stove, P. Whitefish, Joe Sackatook, M. Pecore, M. Waukechon, C. Nahchewishkok, Geo. Neconish, J. Gagnon, P. Shawanokosick, Okanow, John Okachekum, Geo. Irving, Louis Keshena, W. Satterlee, L. Tucker Sr., S. Askewett, M. Brisbois, P. Kauaha, M. Assiscuit, John Amob, Gus Ahyahsha, Jim Blackcloud,

L. Dodge Sr., L. Dodge Jr., M. Dodge, P. Dodge, J. W. Dodge, C. Dutchman, Jim Dixon, J. Feather, M. Kyanamick, M. Komauckin, D. Kaquatosh, Joe Nahwahquaw, J. Oshkosh, M. Okachekum, Jim Sunion, A. Sippesow, Gus Star, Sowahquat, Thos. Tomow, L. P. Towasapon, W. Tucker, M. Ticko, P. Vigue, A. Wayka, B. Washequonott, S. Wynos, Mose Warrington, M. Warrington, H. Lookaround, M. Puckiew, Thos. Wesho, and T. Whitefish, all of them Menominee.

51. Second Annual Report of Agent Savage, in *Report of the Commissioner of Indian Affairs*, 1895, 325.

52. Savage to Commissioner of Indian Affairs, 30 November 1894, LR 1881–1907, 1894:48421, RG 75, NARA-DC; D. H. George to Commissioner of Indian Affairs, 28 December 1899, LR 1881–1907, 1900:159, RG 75, NARA-DC.

53. Report of Logging, 14 February 1907, 4, Miscellaneous Records of Forest Supervisor, 1905–55, Records of the Menominee Indian Mills, 1900–1961, RG 75, NARA-GLR.

54. Report from General Supt. of Logging J. R. F. to Commissioner of Indian Affairs, 13 May 1907, 12, in Copies of Letters Sent and Reports of J. R. Farr (Gen. Supt. of Logging) 1907, Miscellaneous Records of Forest Supervisor, 1905–55, Records of the Menominee Indian Mills, 1900–1961, RG 75, NARA-GLR.

55. Report of Inspector Arthur M. Tinker on purported partnership between Joseph F. Gauthier and August Anderson, mailed 24 May 1907, SC 202, RG 75, NARA-DC.

56. See J. R. Farr to Commissioner of Indian Affairs, 15 November 1907, 12, in Copies of Letters Sent and Reports of J. R. Farr (Gen. Supt. of Logging) 1907, Miscellaneous Records of Forest Supervisor, 1905–55, Records of the Menominee Indian Mills, 1900–1961, RG 75, NARA-GLR, for an example. Anderson later ran cattle on reservation lands from which the trees had been cut—his trespassing was an ongoing concern of the agency. See, for example, Hauke to Nicholson, 30 June 1913, and Rhoads to Beyer, 16 February 1933, CCF 1907–1939 Keshena 308.2, RG 75, NARA-DC.

57. Hosmer, *American Indians in the Marketplace*, 70–71.

58. Hosmer, *American Indians in the Marketplace*, 66.

59. Kinney, *Indian Forest and Range*, 117.

60. Keesing, *The Menomini Indians*, 186; Sady, "The Menominees," 3.

61. From statements at the 1921 Council Meeting, in Keesing, *The Menomini Indians*, 233–34; see also Minutes of Menominee General Council Meeting, 9 August 1930, Menominee Tribal Archives.

62. Hosmer, "Creating Indian Entrepreneurs"; Keesing, *The Menomini Indians*, 189. The practice of educating younger children on the reservation and older children in off-reservation boarding schools was a recommendation of the Meriam Report in 1928. See Szasz, *Education and the American Indian*, 23–24.

63. A copy of that proposed constitution and its signatories can be found in LR 1881–1907, 1892:31904, RG 75, NARA-DC.

64. Hosmer, "Experiments in Capitalism," 226. See also LR 1881–1907, 1892:20153.

65. Hon. S. M. Stephenson to Sawyer and Waite, Attorneys, 3 December 1891; and Kelsey to Commissioner of Indian Affairs, 28 October 1891, LR 1881–1907, 1891:43858, 1891:46114, RG 75, NARA-DC.

66. Kelsey to Commissioner of Indian Affairs, 6 September 1892, containing petition signed by tribal leaders opposing constitution; and Chiefs and Headmen to Secretary of the Interior, 19 May 1892, LR 1881–1907, 1892:32898, 1892:20153, RG 75, NARA-DC; Hosmer, "Experiments in Capitalism," 224–32.

67. Hosmer, *American Indians in the Marketplace*, 80–81.

68. For a comprehensive display of these tools and their use, visit the Menominee Logging Camp Museum outside of Keshena.

69. An example of this is given in Report on Logging, 14 February 1907, 10, Miscellaneous Records of Forest Supervisor, 1905–55, Records of the Menominee Indian Mills, 1900–1961, RG 75, NARA-GLR.

5. THE 1905 BLOWDOWN AND ITS AFTERMATH

1. "Constitution of the Menominee Tribe of Indians of the State of Wisconsin, 1904," CCF 1907–1939 Keshena 054, RG 75, NARA-DC.

2. The documentation refers to the federal agent at the reservation in three different ways: as agent, as agency superintendent, and as superintendent. From here on these terms will be used interchangeably for this government official.

3. Beginning early in the twentieth century, records of the minutes of many council meetings are available. Two major repositories retain these records, and for the most part their holdings do not overlap. The Menominee Tribal Archives has cataloged over 375 council minutes in its collection, beginning in 1920. CCF 1907–1939 Keshena 054, RG 75, NARA-DC, contains many others, beginning earlier and continuing through the same period, and several other CCF files also contain meeting minutes.

4. July 1905, John V. Satterlee, police diaries, Menominee Tribal Archives. Most histories report this to have happened on 16 July. See Chapman, "The Menominee Indian Timber Case," 6–7, Menominee Indian Papers, Wisconsin Historical Society Archives; Ourada, *The Menominee Indians*, 170; Herzberg, "The Menominee Indians: From Treaty to Termination," 284, citing Chapman.

5. J. R. Farr to the Commissioner of Indian Affairs, 14 August 1905, and J. R. Farr to the Commissioner of Indian Affairs, 14 October 1905, SC 202, RG 75, NARA-DC.

6. Hosmer, *American Indians in the Marketplace*, 84.

7. Hosmer, *American Indians in the Marketplace*, 84.

8. Chapman, "The Menominee Indian Timber Case," 1–2, 6, Menominee Indian Papers, Wisconsin Historical Society Archives.

9. James T. Chase preceded William H. Farr as logging superintendent; Chase appears in the records in 1903. See 1903 logging contracts, signed by Chase. William H. Farr was appointed because Chase and Agent Shepard Freeman did not get along. When Chase subsequently left, his position was abolished and Farr served as superintendent of logging on the Menominee reservation. Document 1903:1669 and December 1904 correspondence between General Superintendent of Logging J. R. Farr and the Commissioner of Indian Affairs, SC 202, RG 75, NARA-DC.

10. For correspondence and reports of and about all these people and groups, see Miscellaneous Records of Forest Supervisor, 1905–1955, Records of the Menominee Indian Mills, 1900–1961, RG 75, NARA-GLR.

11. Commissioner of Indian Affairs R. Valentine to Secretary of the Interior, 16 June 1910, CCF 1907–1939 Keshena 339, RG 75, NARA-DC; Report of J. R. Farr, General Superintendent of Logging, to Commissioner of Indian Affairs, 11 December 1906, in "Reports re: Blown-down Timber . . . 1906–1908," 7–8, Miscellaneous Records of Forest Supervisor, 1905–1955, Records of the Menominee Indian Mills, 1900–1961, RG 75, NARA-GLR.

12. Report of J. R. Farr to Commissioner of Indian Affairs, 11 December 1906, in "Reports re: Blown-down Timber . . . 1906–1908," 7–8, Miscellaneous Records of Forest Supervisor, 1905–1955, Records of the Menominee Indian Mills, 1900–1961, RG 75, NARA-GLR.

13. Report of J. R. Farr, 11 December 1906, in "Reports re: Blown-down Timber . . . 1906–1908," Miscellaneous Records of Forest Supervisor, 1905–1955, Records of the Menominee Indian Mills, 1900–1961; Leupp to Superintendent in Charge of Green Bay Agency, 13 September 1906, Bureau of Indian Affairs Field Office Records, Menominee Census Rolls, 1912, 1934, Records of the Keshena/Menominee Agency, 1892–1961, RG 75, NARA-GLR.

14. J. R. Farr to the Commissioner of Indian Affairs, 19 February 1906; J. R. Farr to the Commissioner of Indian Affairs, 6 May 1907, both in SC 202, RG 75, NARA-DC.

15. For the voluminous correspondence and reports regarding this mismanagement, see the folders in Miscellaneous Records of Forest Supervisor, 1905–1955, Records of the Menominee Indian Mills, 1900–1961, RG 75, NARA-GLR; and see the documents contained in CCF 1907–1909 Green Bay 339, RG 75, NARA-DC. See also Commissioner of Indian Affairs R. Valentine to the Secretary of the Interior, 16 June 1910, CCF 1907–1939 Keshena 339, RG 75, NARA-DC.

16. Letter to Honorable Commissioner, 17 December 1907, in "Copies of Letters Sent and Reports of J. R. Farr (General Supt. of Logging) 1907," Miscellaneous Records of Forest Supervisor, 1905–1955, Records of the Menominee Indian Mills, 1900–1961, RG 75, NARA-GLR.

17. Edward A. Braniff to Commissioner of Indian Affairs, 29 September 1909, Misc. Correspondence, 1909–1926, Miscellaneous Records of Forest Supervisor, 1905–1955, Records of the Menominee Indian Mills, 1900–1961, RG 75, NARA-GLR.

18. "An act to authorize the cutting," 1906.

19. Hosmer, "Creating Indian Entrepreneurs," 6–7; Report of J. R. Farr to Commissioner of Indian Affairs, 11 December 1906, in "Reports re: Blown-down Timber . . . Proposed Rules and Regulations for Cutting, 1906–1908," Miscellaneous Records of the Forest Supervisor, 1905–1955, Records of the Menominee Indian Mills, 1900–1916 RG 75, NARA-GLR; Court of Claims of the United States, decision of 17 February 1919, CCF 1907–1939 Keshena 339, RG 75, NARA-DC. This judgment was rendered with no opinion delivered: see "Cases Decided in the Court of Claims," 54 Ct. Cls. 208–11.

20. Kinney, *Indian Forest and Range*, 118, 121.

21. Amounts Determined from Court of Claims of the United States, decision of 17 February 1919, 9–27, CCF 1907–1939 Keshena 339, RG 75, NARA-DC.

22. Letter to Honorable Commissioner, 17 December 1907, 7–8, Copies of Letters Sent and Reports of J.R. Farr 1907, Miscellaneous Records of Forest Supervisor, 1905–1955, Records of the Menominee Indian Mills, 1900–1961, RG 75, NARA-GLR.

23. A. S. Nicholson to Commissioner of Indian Affairs, 23 May 1917, accompanying Minutes of Menominee Council Meeting of 31 March 1917, in CCF 1907–1939 Keshena 054, RG 75, NARA-DC.

24. Minutes of General Council Meeting, 26 June 1908, CCF 1907–1909 Green Bay 339, RG 75, NARA-DC.

25. Aantone [*sic*] Stick to Secretary of the Interior, 30 June 1908, CCF 1907–1909 Green Bay 339, RG 75, NARA-DC.

26. Acting Commissioner of Indian Affairs C. F. Larrabee to Col. Thomas Downs, Special Agent, 7 July 1908, and Larrabee to U.S. Forest Service, 17 July 1908, CCF 1907–1909 Green Bay 339, RG 75, NARA-DC.

27. See carbon copy of hearing transcripts. One day's testimony was taken 13 August 1908. Freeman Hearing, c. 1908, Miscellaneous Records of Forest Supervisor, 1905–1955, Records of the Menominee Indian Mills, 1900–1961, RG 75, NARA-GLR.

28. Freeman Hearing, c. 1908, 1–2, 32–37, Miscellaneous Records of Forest Supervisor, 1905–1955, Records of the Menominee Indian Mills, 1900–1961, RG 75, NARA-GLR.

29. Hosmer, "Experiments in Capitalism," 269–70. By October 1908 Edgar A. Allen began signing correspondence as "superintendent of the agency." See Allen to the Commissioner of Indian Affairs, 10 October 1908, for instance, CCF 1907–1909 Green Bay 339, RG 75, NARA-DC.

30. Edgar A. Allen to Commissioner of Indian Affairs, 26 February 1909, CCF 1907–1939 Keshena 057, RG 75, NARA-DC.

31. Aantone [*sic*] Stick to Secretary of the Interior, 30 June 1908, reports that Anderson and Cook were cheating the tribe. In CCF 1907–1909 Green Bay 339, RG 75, NARA-DC.

32. See 1919 letters and affidavits together with Court of Claims of the United States decision of 17 February 1919, in CCF 1907–1939 Keshena 339, RG 75, NARA-DC.

33. Cronon, *Nature's Metropolis*, 166–69.

34. Cohen, *A Handbook of Federal Indian Law*, 316.

35. Kinney, *Indian Forest and Range*, viii–ix; Runte, *National Parks*, 69–70; Spence, *Dispossessing the Wilderness*; Burnham, *Indian Country, God's Country*. According to Runte, the 1891 Forest Reserve Act had first provided federal protection of forests for purposes of "utlititarian conservation."

36. U.S. Congress, House. Representative Morse, 3411.

37. U.S. Congress, Senate. Report of Senator LaFollette, 1182.

38. U.S. Congress, Senate. Report of Senator LaFollette, 1182.

39. U.S. Congress, Senate. Letter from James Rudolph Garfield, 1183.

40. "An Act to authorize the cutting of timber," 1908.

41. Sections 4 and 5, "An Act to authorize the cutting of timber," 1908.

42. Chapman, "The Menominee Indian Timber Case," 11, Menominee Indian Papers, Wisconsin Historical Society Archives.

43. U.S. Congress, House. Representative Morse, 3411.

44. "An Act to authorize the cutting of timber," 1908.

45. U.S. Congress, Senate. Report of Senator LaFollette, 1182–83.

46. Braniff to Griffith, 24 March 1908, Miscellaneous Records of Forest Supervisor, 1905–1955, Records of the Menominee Indian Mills, 1900–1961, RG 75, NARA-GLR.

47. Chapman, "The Menominee Indian Timber Case," 11–13, 18–19, Menominee Indian Papers, Wisconsin Historical Society Archives; Keesing, *The Menomini Indians*, 230; "An Act to authorize the cutting of timber," 1908. Calculations made based on 1890s mill capacity of twenty thousand to twenty-five thousand feet per ten-hour day figured at six days per week.

48. Keesing, *The Menomini Indians*, 222–23, states 1906 as the year of Neopit's founding, but he later implies 1908 as the year (230). Menominee Indian Tribe of Wisconsin, *Menominee Tribal History Guide*, 71, dates the founding as 1908. On rail lines, see Keesing, *The Menomini Indians*, 231; and the Menominee Reservation Map compiled by James A. Howarth Jr., April 1908, in Maps: Neopit Millsite (incl. one General Map) C. 1908 folder, in Maps and Plats, 1908–1937, Records of the Menominee Indian Mills, 1900–1961, RG 75, NARA-GLR.

49. Allen to Braniff, 1 June 1909; Braniff to Allen, 3 June 1909; Braniff to Allen, 18 June 1909, all in 339. (g) General Correspondence (Forestry, Timber Permits Etc.) Supt. Neopit, 1909- folder, in Miscellaneous Records of Forest Supervisor, 1905–1955, Records of the Menominee Indian Mills, 1900–1961, RG 75, NARA-GLR.

50. See correspondence between Braniff and E. M. Griffith, 15 and 16 July 1909 in Copies of Reports + Letters E. M. Griffith, State Forester, 1905–1907 folder, Miscellaneous Records of Forest Supervisor, 1905–1955, Records of the Menominee Indian Mills, 1900–1961, RG 75, NARA-GLR.

51. Braniff to Commissioner of Indian Affairs, 29 September 1909. Misc. Correspondence, 1909–1926, Miscellaneous Records of Forest Supervisor, 1905–1955, Records of the Menominee Indian Mills, 1900–1961, RG 75, NARA-GLR. This cooperation between the Forest Service and the Indian Department on a nationwide basis lasted from 22 January 1908 until 17 July 1909: Kinney, *Indian Forest and Range*, 85.

52. On how this affected Indian forestry, see Kinney, *Indian Forest and Range*, 84–85, 120–21.

53. "Memoranda for Mr. E. A. Braniff," from J. A. H. Jr., 29 March 1908, in Reports, Memoranda + Letter of J. A. Howarth, Jr. 1906–1909 folder, Miscellaneous Records of Forest Supervisor, 1905–1955, Records of the Menominee Indian Mills, 1900–1961, RG 75, NARA-GLR.

54. Interviews with Menominee people.

55. Sterling, *Report of a Forest Survey and Supplemental Investigations of the Menominee Indian Reservation*, 8 February 1935, 6, Miscellaneous Records of Forest Supervisor, 1905–1955, Records of the Menominee Indian Mills, 1900–1961, RG 75, NARA-GLR.

56. Report of Supervisor [probably the supervisor of Indian work, Charles E. Dagenett], 12 November 1908, CCF 1907–1909 Green Bay 339, RG 75, NARA-DC.

57. See Correspondence regarding creation of position of Local Manager in charge of recruiting Indian labor, 1908–1909, CCF 1907–1909 Green Bay 339, RG 75, NARA-DC.

58. Allen to Commissioner of Indian Affairs, 10 February 1909, CCF 1907–1909 Green Bay 339, RG 75, NARA-DC.

59. Wilson to Commissioner of Indian Affairs, 28 August 1909, CCF 1907–1939 Keshena 816.2, RG 75, NARA-DC.

60. Braniff to the Forester, Washington DC, 24 February 1909, CCF 1907–1909 Green Bay 339, RG 75, NARA-DC.

61. Report of Supervisor, 12 November 1908, CCF 1907–1909 Green Bay 339, RG 75, NARA-DC.

62. Carroll to Commissioner of Indian Affairs, 23 October 1909, CCF 1907–1909 Green Bay 339, RG 75, NARA-DC.

63. Menominee interviewees referred to both Dog Town and White City when describing Neopit; interviews with Menominee people. Felix Keesing and his wife referred to White City and Shantytown in the unpublished volume 2 of Keesing and Keesing, *The Changing American Indian*, 344, Menominee Tribal Archives. Volume 1 of this manuscript is the draft for Keesing's *The Menomini Indians*; they originally

intended to publish volume 2 as a contemporary social study but never did. Description of Dogtown in L. F. Michaels, "Report, Keshena Indian School," 28 April 1913, section 6, 5–6, CCF 1907–1939 Keshena 150, RG 75, NARA-DC.

64. Hosmer, *American Indians in the Marketplace*, 91.

65. Wilson to Commissioner of Indian Affairs, 28 August 1909, CCF 1907–1939 Keshena 816.2, RG 75, NARA-DC.

66. Braniff to Commissioner of Indian Affairs, 28 August 1909, Misc. Correspondence, 1909–1926, Miscellaneous Records of Forest Supervisor, 1905–1955, Records of the Menominee Indian Mills, 1900–1961, RG 75, NARA-GLR.

67. Braniff to Commissioner of Indian Affairs, 29 September 1909, Misc. Correspondence, 1909–1926, Miscellaneous Records of Forest Supervisor, 1905–1955, Records of the Menominee Indian Mills, 1900–1961, RG 75, NARA-GLR.

68. Kinney, *Indian Forest and Range*, 122; Hosmer, *American Indians in the Marketplace*, 92.

69. Kinney, *Indian Forest and Range*, 120.

70. Keesing, *The Menomini Indians*, 237–38.

6. THE WEIGHT OF FEDERAL WARDSHIP

1. Gordon Dickie Sr., interview, Menominee Historic Preservation Department.

2. Minutes of Menominee General Council Meeting, 26 June 1908; Supplementary Minutes of Menominee Council Meeting held 21–22 May 1913, CCF 1907–1939 Keshena 054, RG 75, NARA-DC.

3. Nicholson to Commissioner of Indian Affairs, 25 January 1915, CCF 1907–1939 Keshena 054, RG 75, NARA-DC.

4. Blair to Commissioner of Indian Affairs Charles H. Burke, 10 June 1925, CCF 1907–1939 Keshena 054, RG 75, NARA-DC.

5. Slotkin, *Menomini Peyotism*, 574–76; Dewey Neconish, interview by J. S. Slotkin, in *Menomini Peyotism*, 637; Alanson Buck Skinner to Miss Ruth Schonle, 25 February 1924, 1924 Skinner folder, Anthropology Correspondence, Skinner, McKern, 1921–1927, original box 65, Milwaukee Public Museum Archives; Skinner, *Material Culture*, 24, 42; Keesing and Keesing, *The Changing American Indian*, 354, in Menominee Tribal Archives.

6. Stewart, *Peyote Religion*, 3–18, 45–67.

7. Slotkin, *The Menomini Powwow*, 25; Slotkin, *Menominee Peyotism*, 578–86.

8. Slotkin, *Menomini Peyotism*, 576–77; Theodore Neconish, interview by Slotkin; "Warrant to Apprehend"; and excerpt from W. E. Safford, "An Aztec Narcotic," from *Journal of Heredity* 6, no. 306, all in Slotkin, *Menomini Peyotism*, 676–77; Stewart, *Peyote Religion*, 215.

9. Ray M. Humphreys, "Peyote Replaces Whisky on Reservation, Indians Get

'Jags' with the Mescal Bean," *Denver Times*, 2 December 1916, Box 53, Folder Menominee, Omer C. Stewart Collection, University of Colorado Archives; Stewart, *Peyote Religion*, 4.

10. Report of W. H. Gibbes, Inspector, 28 July 1916, 6–7, CCF 1907–1939 Keshena 150, RG 75, NARA-DC.

11. Slotkin, *Menomini Peyotism*, 677.

12. Barrett quoted in Slotkin, *Menomini Peyotism*, 678.

13. Report of W. S. Coleman, Inspector, 12 November 1917, 49, CCF 1907–1939 Keshena 150, RG 75, NARA-DC.

14. Slotkin, *Menomini Peyotism*, 574–77; Allen to Commissioner of Indian Affairs, 24 April 1919, Box 53, Folder Menominee, Omer C. Stewart Collection, University of Colorado Archives; Stewart, *Peyote Religion*, 17.

15. Slotkin, *Menomini Peyotism*, 574–77; Allen to Commissioner of Indian Affairs, 24 April 1919, Box 53, Folder Menominee, Omer C. Stewart Collection, University of Colorado Archives, reprinted in Slotkin, *Menomini Peyotism*, 679; Stewart, *Peyote Religion*, 17.

16. Frank S. Sloniker to Allen, 22 April 1919, Box 53, Folder Menominee, Omer C. Stewart Collection, University of Colorado Archives, reprinted in Slotkin, *Menomini Peyotism*, 680; Alanson Buck Skinner to Miss Ruth Schonle, 25 February 1924, Anthropology Correspondence, Skinner, McKern, 1921–1927, original box 65, 1924 Skinner folder, Milwaukee Public Museum Archives; Skinner, *Material Culture*, 24, 42.

17. Slotkin, *Menomini Peyotism*, 577.

18. Chapman, "The Menominee Indian Timber Case," 12, Menominee Indian Papers, Wisconsin Historical Society Archives.

19. Keesing, *The Menomini Indians*, 231.

20. Kinney, *Indian Forest and Range*, 120–21.

21. Sterling, *Report of a Forest Survey and Supplemental Investigations of the Menominee Indian Reservation*, 8 February 1935, 7, 14–15, Miscellaneous Records of Forest Supervisor, 1905–1955, Records of the Menominee Indian Mills, 1900–1961, RG 75, NARA-GLR.

22. Keesing, *The Menomini Indians*, 232. See also Ayer, *Report*.

23. Minutes of Menominee Council Meeting, 5 March 1910; Wilson to Commissioner of Indian Affairs, 18 March 1910; Commissioner of Indian Affairs Valentine to Secretary of the Interior, 2 April 1910; John Francis Jr., Acting Chief Land Division, to Wilson, 12 April 1910, all in CCF 1907–1939 Keshena 054, RG 75, NARA-DC.

24. These four were Peter Lookaround, Mitchell Oshkenaniew, Reginald Oshkosh, and George McCall. The other three Menominee members were Peter LaMotte, Bert Chevalier, and John Kaquatosh.

25. Department of the Interior, Minutes of Neopit Town Board, 1911–1915, Records of the Keshena/Menominee Agency, 1892–1961, RG 75, NARA-GLR.

26. Chapman, "The Menominee Indian Timber Case," 11–13, 18–19, Menominee Indian Papers, Wisconsin Historical Society Archives.

27. Nicholson to Commissioner of Indian Affairs, 4 December 1913, CCF 1907–1939 Keshena 174.1, RG 75, NARA-DC; Hosmer, *American Indians in the Marketplace,* 98–101. See also Ayer, *Report.*

28. Keesing, *The Menomini Indians,* 232–33.

29. Hosmer, "Creating Indian Entrepreneurs," 17–18; Hosmer, *American Indians in the Marketplace,* 101.

30. Ayer, *Report,* 80, 82, 84. See also Hosmer, *American Indians in the Marketplace,* 102.

31. Ayer, *Report,* 6, 15–17. Ayer interviews with Mose Tucker, Peter LaMotte, and Wyeskesit, in *Report,* 79–80, 82–83, 83–84.

32. Hosmer, *American Indians in the Marketplace,* 107.

33. Ayer, *Report,* 15–17.

34. Nicholson to Commissioner of Indian Affairs, 10 June 1913; Hauke to Mrs. Jane Jacobs, 9 November 1914; Hauke to Nicholson, 13 April 1915; Assistant Commissioner Merritt to Aug. A. Breuninger, 8 December 1915; and Report of H. M. Creel, Inspector, 10 March 1923, all in CCF 1907–1939 Keshena 313, RG 75, NARA-DC; Merritt to Peter Washinawotoke, 4 April 1914, CCF 1907–1939 Keshena 054, RG 75, NARA-DC.

35. Ayer, *Report,* 15–17.

36. Ayer interviews with Peter Lookaround and C. A. Tourtillot, in *Report,* 67–69, 70–71.

37. A Menominee Indian Woman in Distress to President Woodrow Wilson, 24 November 1914, CCF 1907–1939 Keshena 155, RG 75, NARA-DC.

38. Minutes of the Council Meeting held by the Menominee Indians, Keshena, 16 January 1915, CCF 1907–1939 Keshena 054, RG 75, NARA-DC.

39. Nicholson to Commissioner of Indian Affairs, 25 January 1915, CCF 1907–1939 Keshena 054, RG 75, NARA-DC.

40. Chapman, "The Menominee Indian Timber Case," 19–20, 26, Menominee Indian Papers, Wisconsin Historical Society Archives.

41. Chapman, "The Menominee Indian Timber Case," 19–20, Menominee Indian Papers, Wisconsin Historical Society Archives; *Menominee Tribe of Indians v. United States,* 117 C. Cls. 443, 470, 489–501.

42. Report of E. B. Linnen, 12 October 1915; Minutes of a Conference held at Keshena, 10 September 1915, Exhibit W attached to Linnen Report, CCF 1907–1939 Keshena 150, RG 75, NARA-DC.

43. Report of E. B. Linnen, 12 October 1915, 111; Minutes of a Conference held at

Keshena, 10 September 1915, Exhibit W attached to Linnen Report, CCF 1907–1939 Keshena 150, RG 75, NARA-DC.

44. Addendum to Report of W. H. Gibbes, stamped received by Office of Indian Affairs 31 July 1916, CCF 1907–1939 Keshena 150, RG 75, NARA-DC.

45. Report of W. S. Coleman, 12 November 1917, 62, CCF 1907–1939 Keshena 150, RG 75, NARA-DC.

46. Kinney, *Indian Forest and Range*, 122–23; Sterling, *Report of a Forest Survey and Supplemental Investigations of the Menominee Indian Reservation*, 8 February 1935, 6, Miscellaneous Records of Forest Supervisor, 1905–1955, Records of the Menominee Indian Mills, 1900–1961, RG 75, NARA-GLR; Herzberg, "The Menominee Indians: From Treaty to Termination," 288, 294; Chapman, "The Menominee Indian Timber Case," 3–4, 19–20, Menominee Indian Papers, Wisconsin Historical Society Archives.

47. The government numbered these camps. A map from 1920 or 1921, for example, shows camps 16, 19, and 20 located on railroad spurs. See maps in Railroad Maps (Logging) n. d. folder. Camps number 3 and 8 are identified on maps in Range Maps n. d. folder. Both in Maps and Plats, 1908–1937, Records of the Menominee Indian Mills, 1900–1961, RG 75 NARA-GLR. See also Kinney, *Indian Forest and Range*, 129.

48. Sterling, *Report of a Forest Survey and Supplemental Investigations of the Menominee Indian Reservation*, 8 February 1935, 7, 14–15, Miscellaneous Records of Forest Supervisor, 1905–1955, Records of the Menominee Indian Mills, 1900–1961, RG 75, NARA-GLR.

49. Kinney, *Indian Forest and Range*, 125–27; Report of H. M. Creel, Inspector, 10 March 1923, CCF 1907–1939 Keshena 313, RG 75, NARA-DC; William R. Layne to Commissioner of Indian Affairs Rhoads, 18 February 1930, and J. P. Kinney memorandum, 4 February 1930, both in CCF 1907–1939 Keshena 313, RG 75, NARA-DC.

50. Kinney, *Indian Forest and Range*, 136.

51. Kinney, *Indian Forest and Range*, 132–33, 323; Chapman, "The Menominee Indian Timber Case," 13–14, 41, 54, Menominee Indian Papers, Wisconsin Historical Society Archives.

52. Sterling, *Report of a Forest Survey and Supplemental Investigations of the Menominee Indian Reservation*, 8 February 1935, 4–5, Miscellaneous Records of Forest Supervisor, 1905–1955, Records of the Menominee Indian Mills, 1900–1961, RG 75, NARA-GLR.

53. Chapman, "The Menominee Indian Timber Case," 23–25, Menominee Indian Papers, Wisconsin Historical Society Archives. For the most part this occurred after 1915.

54. Sterling, *Report of a Forest Survey and Supplemental Investigations of the Menominee Indian Reservation*, 8 February 1935, 4, Miscellaneous Records of Forest Supervisor, 1905–1955, Records of the Menominee Indian Mills, 1900–1961, RG 75,

NARA-GLR. Mismanagement of the forest under the 1890 law and mismanagement of the 1905 blowdown were other bases of these lawsuits; Smith, comp., *Indian Tribal Claims*, 61–104.

55. See, for example, text of letters from Ralph Fredenberg, 1929–30, and text of charges brought by the Menominee Indian Advisory Board against the Department of the Interior, 21 September 1929, reprinted in Nichols, *Sunrise of the Menominees*, 283–85, 293–95; "Tribal Fund Depleted."

56. Report attached to Letter from John Pohland, Travelling Auditor, to the Commissioner of Indian Affairs in re Conditions, Neopit Operation, Keshena Agency, Wisconsin in Misc. Correspondence, 1909–1926 folder, Miscellaneous Records of Forest Supervisor, 1905–1955, Records of the Menominee Indian Mills, 1900–1961, RG 75, NARA-GLR; Minutes of a General Council of the Menominee Tribe of Indians, 29 November 1919, CCF 1907–1939 Keshena 054, RG 75, NARA-DC. The status of Menominee records also reflects this. For example, nonoverlapping tribal council minutes are available in NARA-DC, the Menominee Tribal Archives, the Menominee County/Tribal Library and the Green Bay Area Research Center.

57. Today, when Menominees run the business and the government, cultural practice is incorporated into employer policy. When an elder passes on, for example, workers are often granted the option of taking time off to attend funeral services.

58. Lurie, "The Menominee Indians," 38.

59. Kinney, *Indian Forest and Range*, 121.

60. See letters from Allen to Commissioner of Indian Affairs, 1921–1922, in sheaf of correspondence regarding councils held 1922–1942, CCF 1907–1939 Keshena 054, RG 75, NARA-DC.

61. Minutes of Menominee General Council Meeting, 12 November 1921, Menominee Tribal Archives, Keshena; Sady, "The Menominees" 4.

7. FROM ALLOTMENT TO INCORPORATION

1. See Allen, "The Indian," 39–45, for a statement of Allen's philosophy of federal responsibilities toward American Indians. When Allen had previously served as agency superintendent in 1908–9, he reported in a letter to the commissioner of Indian affairs on 11 January 1909 that "a great many of the tribe" favored allotment. Letter accompanying Minutes of General Council Meeting held 31 December 1908, CCF 1907–1939 Keshena 054, RG 75, NARA-DC.

2. J. P. Kinney memorandum, 4 February 1930, CCF 1907–1939 Keshena 313, RG 75, NARA-DC.

3. Minutes of General Council of the Menominee Indian Tribe held at Keshena, Wisconsin, 19 June 1920, Menominee Tribal Archives.

4. Minutes of General Council Meeting held 23 and 25 May 1925, Keshena, CCF 1907–1939 Keshena 054, RG 75, NARA-DC.

5. For a discussion of new tribal leadership roles that developed in the twentieth century, see Hosmer, "Reflections."

6. This is discussed in relation to pretreaty years in Beck, *Siege and Survival*, 202–5. Hosmer also analyzes leadership role change in "Creating Indian Entrepreneurs."

7. Allen to Commissioner of Indian Affairs, 14 August 1920, CCF 1907–1939 Keshena 313, RG 75, NARA-DC.

8. Merritt to LaFrombois, 29 August 1921, CCF 1907–1939 Keshena 313, RG 75, NARA-DC.

9. U.S. Congress, Senate, Report No. 1113. For a description of Wisconsin congressional districts' jurisdictions in the 1920s, see Martis, *The Historical Atlas*, 278.

10. J. P. Kinney memorandum, 4 February 1930, CCF 1907–1939 Keshena 313, RG 75, NARA-DC.

11. Minutes of General Council Meeting held 23 and 25 May 1925, Keshena, CCF 1907–1939 Keshena 054, RG 75, NARA-DC.

12. See, for example, Tribal Resolution, 12 November 1921; Council Minutes, 24 June 1922; General Council, 23 April 1927; Council Minutes, 1 October 1927; and Council Minutes, 15 October 1927, all in CCF 1907–1939 Keshena 054, RG 75, NARA-DC. See also the following General and Advisory Council Meeting Minutes, all in Menominee Tribal Archives: 12 November 1921, 10 December 1921, 5 January 1922, 9 January 1922, 24 March 1925, 19 October 1925, 23 October 1925, 23 April 1927, and others.

13. Minutes of General Council Meeting held 23 and 25 May 1925, Keshena, CCF 1907–1939 Keshena 054, RG 75, NARA-DC.

14. Minutes of General Council Meeting held 23 and 25 May 1925, Keshena, CCF 1907–1939 Keshena 054, RG 75, NARA-DC.

15. Minutes of General Council Meeting held 23 and 25 May 1925, Keshena, CCF 1907–1939 Keshena 054, RG 75, NARA-DC.

16. Minutes of General Council Meeting held 23 and 25 May 1925, Keshena, CCF 1907–1939 Keshena 054, RG 75, NARA-DC.

17. Blair to Commissioner of Indian Affairs Charles H. Burke, 10 June 1925, CCF 1907–1939 Keshena 054, RG 75, NARA-DC.

18. Blair to Commissioner of Indian Affairs Charles H. Burke, 10 June 1925, CCF 1907–1939 Keshena 054, RG 75, NARA-DC.

19. U.S. Congress, Senate, Report No. 1113; U.S. Congress, House, HR 6869, 2234–35; J. P. Kinney memorandum, 4 February 1930, CCF 1907–1939 Keshena 313, RG 75, NARA-DC.

20. Resolution presented by the Menominee League of Women Voters to the Menominee Advisory Council, Minutes of the Menominee Indian Advisory Coun-

cil held at Neopit, Wisconsin, 19 October 1925, Menominee Tribal Archives; U.S. Congress, House, HR 6869, 2234.

21. See Priest, "Biography, Flora Warren Seymour."

22. Flora Warren Seymour, Report on the Menominee Indian Reservation, 30 June 1926, 36–40; Donner to Commissioner of Indian Affairs, 25 July 1927, both in CCF 1907–1939 Keshena 150, RG 75, NARA-DC.

23. Peyton Carter, Inspection Report, 19 October 1927, CCF 1907–1939 Keshena 150; Carter to Commissioner of Indian Affairs, December 1926, CCF 1907–1939 Keshena 313, both in RG 75, NARA-DC. Carter advocated this for both the Menominee and the Red Lake, Minnesota, Chippewa.

24. Meriam, *The Problem of Indian Administration*, 462.

25. J. P. Kinney memorandum, 4 February 1930, CCF 1907–1939 Keshena 313, RG 75, NARA-DC.

26. Freeman Hearing, ca. 1908, in unnumbered pages, Miscellaneous Records of Forest Supervisor, 1905–1955, Records of the Menominee Indian Mills, 1900–1961, RG 75, NARA-GLR.

27. Minutes of Menominee General Council Meeting, 12 September 1925, Menominee Tribal Archives.

28. Minutes of Menominee General Council Meeting, 12 September 1925, Menominee Tribal Archives.

29. Sterling, *Report of a Forest Survey and Supplemental Investigations of the Menominee Indian Reservation*, 8 February 1935, 5, 7, Miscellaneous Records of Forest Supervisor, 1905–1955, Records of the Menominee Indian Mills, 1900–1961, RG 75, NARA-GLR. Kinney, *Indian Forest and Range*, 137; Herzberg, "The Menominee Indians: From Treaty to Termination," 289; Chapman, "The Menominee Indian Timber Case," 15, Menominee Indian Papers, Wisconsin Historical Society Archives.

30. Kinney, *Indian Forest and Range*, 128.

31. Herzberg, "The Menominee Indians: From Treaty to Termination," 289; Chapman, "The Menominee Indian Timber Case," 14, Menominee Indian Papers, Wisconsin Historical Society Archives. Grapp later coauthored a report that the government hoped would preempt a Menominee lawsuit by defending and justifying government actions, the Nicholson-Grapp Survey. See Chapman, "The Menominee Indian Timber Case," 31, for discussion.

32. Chapman, "The Menominee Indian Timber Case," 13, 15, 27–29, 33–34, 38, Menominee Indian Papers, Wisconsin Historical Society Archives; Kinney, *Indian Forest and Range*, 137, 323.

33. Minutes of Menominee General Council Meeting, 5 January 1922; Minutes of Menominee Advisory Council Meeting, 24 March 1925, Menominee Tribal Archives.

34. Sady, "The Menominees," 4.

35. Peroff, *Menominee Drums*, 30–42.

36. Commissioner of Indian Affairs Hubert Work to Congressman James A. Frear, 27 August 1927, Box 136, Special Committee on Indian Affairs, Committee on Interior and Insular Affairs, Sen. 83 A-F9 (70th–82nd), RG 46, NARA-DC; Kinney to Rhoads, 2 July 1927; Minutes of General Council Meeting, 23 April 1927; Report of Ernest P. Rands, General Land Office, June 1929, all in CCF 1907–1939 Keshena 054, RG 75, NARA-DC; Flora Warren Seymour, "Report on the Menominee Indian Reservation," 30 June 1926, 27–28, CCF 1907–1939 Keshena 150, RG 75, NARA-DC.

37. Ralph Fredenberg to Senator Robert M. LaFollette Jr., 2 May 1929, in both Box 136, Special Committee on Indian Affairs, Committee on Interior and Insular Affairs, Sen. 83 A-F9 (70th–82nd), RG 46, and CCF 1907–1939 Keshena 054, RG 75, NARA-DC; Kinney to Rhoads, 2 July 1927; Report of Ernest P. Rands, General Land Office, June 1929, both in CCF 1907–1939 Keshena 054, RG 75, NARA-DC; Nicholson to Commissioner of Indian Affairs, 20 March 1912, CCF 1907–1939 Keshena 056, RG 75, NARA-DC.

38. Flora Warren Seymour, Report on the Menominee Indian Reservation, 30 June 1926, 23–25, CCF 1907–1939 Keshena 150, RG 75, NARA-DC.

39. Nicholson to Commissioner of Indian Affairs, 12 March 1915, CCF 1907–1939 Keshena 308.2, RG 75, NARA-DC; Minutes, Advisory Council Meeting, 8 December 1931; Fredenberg to Commissioner of Indian Affairs, 28 April 1936, both in CCF 1907–1939 Keshena 054, RG 75, NARA-DC; Fredenberg to Commissioner of Indian Affairs, 26 August 1933; Collier to Fredenberg, 2 September 1933, both in CCF 1907–1939 Keshena 155, RG 75, NARA-DC.

40. A Member of the Menominee Tribe to Commissioner of Indian Affairs, 4 August 1926, CCF 1907–1939 Keshena 155, RG 75, NARA-DC.

41. Hosmer, "Reflections."

42. Flora Warren Seymour, Report, 1926, 39; Flora Warren Seymour, Report, 7 November 1932, 30–32, in both CCF 1907–1939 Keshena 150, RG 75, NARA-DC, and Scott, Hugh L., Box 5 (La-Roe), Ms 4525, National Anthropological Archives, Smithsonian Institution.

43. Meriam, *The Problem of Indian Administration*, 42, 462–66, 515–16.

44. Meriam, *The Problem of Indian Administration*, 463.

45. Meriam, *The Problem of Indian Administration*, 42–43, 463–64.

46. This attribution is based on the language used in the passages in Meriam, *The Problem of Indian Administration*, 42–43, 462–66, 515–16.

47. Ourada, *The Menominee Indians*, 180.

48. Nichols, *Sunrise of the Menominees*, 276–349.

49. Nichols, "Stating the Case for the Menominees," Wisconsin Historical Society Library.

50. Nichols, "Stating the Case for the Menominees," Wisconsin Historical Society Library.

51. Oshkenaniew to Secretary of the Interior Roy Lyman Wilbur, 2 April 1929; Hammer to Commissioner of Indian Affairs, 29 April 1929, CCF 1907–1939 Keshena 054, RG 75, NARA-DC.

52. Fredenberg to Lafollette, 2 May 1929, in both Box 136, Special Committee on Indian Affairs, Committee on Interior and Insular Affairs, Sen. 83 A-F9 (70th–82nd), RG 46, and CCF 1907–1939 Keshena 054, RG 75, NARA-DC; Wilbur to LaFollette, 15 May 1929, Box 136, Special Committee on Indian Affairs, Committee on Interior and Insular Affairs, Sen. 83 A-F9 (70th–82nd), RG 46; Report of Ernest P. Rands, General Land Office, June 1929, CCF 1907–1939 Keshena 054, RG 75, NARA-DC.

53. Report of Ernest P. Rands, General Land Office, June 1929, 9, 18–21, 26–27; 6 June 1929 hearings attached to Rands report, 13–14; both in CCF 1907–1939 Keshena 054, RG 75, NARA-DC.

54. "Indians Block U.S. Log Road"; "Indian Road Suit Deferred"; "Tribal Fund Depleted"; Minutes, Indian Welfare Department Meeting, 18 January 1939, Indian Welfare 1936–1947 folder, Illinois Federation of Women's Clubs Papers, Illinois State Historical Society Library Manuscript Collections.

55. Nichols, "Stating the Case for the Menominees," 4–5, Wisconsin Historical Society Library.

56. Carter to Commissioner of Indian Affairs, 17 March 1931, CCF 1907–1939 Keshena 806, RG 75, NARA-DC; Sady, "The Menominees," 5.

57. Nichols, "Stating the Case for the Menominees," 6–7, Wisconsin Historical Society Library.

58. Supt. William R. Beyer, "Annual Narrative Report, 1933," in Ourada, *The Menominee Indians*, 180, 244n27.

59. Report of Delegation, Minutes of Menominee General Council Meeting, 9 August 1930, Menominee Tribal Archives and CCF 1907–1939 Keshena 054, RG 75, NARA-DC; Oral History Interview with Oscar R. Ewing, Harry S. Truman Library.

60. Report of Delegation, Minutes of Menominee General Council Meeting, 9 August 1930, Menominee Tribal Archives and CCF 1907–1939 Keshena 054, RG 75, NARA-DC; U.S. Congress, House, Committee on Indian Affairs, "Menominee Tribe of Indians to Employ General Attorneys"; U.S. Congress, Senate, Committee on Indian Affairs. "Menominee Tribe of Indians to Employ General Attorneys."

61. Hughes, Schurman, and Dwight, "Tentative Draft of Act to Incorporate the Menominee Tribe of Indians," Box 136, Special Committee on Indian Affairs, Committee on Interior and Insular Affairs, Sen. 83 A-F9 (70th–82nd), RG 46, NARA-DC.

62. Report of Delegation, Minutes of Menominee General Council Meeting, 9 August 1930, Menominee Tribal Archives and CCF 1907–1939 Keshena 054, RG 75, NARA-DC.

63. Report of Delegation, Minutes of Menominee General Council Meeting, 9

August 1930, Menominee Tribal Archives and CCF 1907–1939 Keshena 054, RG 75, NARA-DC.

64. Report of Delegation, Minutes of Menominee General Council Meeting, 9 August 1930, Menominee Tribal Archives and CCF 1907–1939 Keshena 054, RG 75, NARA-DC.

65. Nichols, "Stating the Case for the Menominees," Wisconsin Historical Society Library.

66. "Tribal Fund Depleted," 2.

67. Nichols, "Stating the Case for the Menominees," 4–5, Wisconsin Historical Society Library.

8. ILLUSORY CONTROL

1. "Memorandum for Congressman Lampert, Power sites on the Wolf"; "HEAR-ING ON APPLICATION to the Federal Power Commission for a Preliminary Permit for a Water Power Project on the Menominee Indian Reservation on the Wolf River," 16 September 1926 (hereafter FPC Hearing); document labeled Exhibit H, Map, "Drainage Area of the Wolf River above Keshena, Wisconsin Showing Project Boundary. Wisconsin Power and Light Company," all in Box 136, Special Committee on Indian Affairs, Committee on Interior and Insular Affairs, Sen. 83 A-F9 (70th–82nd), RG 46, NARA-DC.

2. Individual Building Report, Office of Indian Affairs, October 1931, Menominee Historic Preservation Department; Donner to Commissioner of Indian Affairs, 14 September 1926, CCF 1907–1939 Keshena 155, RG 75, NARA-DC; Superintendent, Keshena, to Hon. Edward E. Browne, 27 February 1926, in Misc. Correspondence 1909–1926 folder, Miscellaneous Records of Forest Supervisor, 1905–1955, Records of the Menominee Indian Mills, 1900–1961, RG 75, NARA-GLR; interviews with Menominee people.

3. FPC Hearing, 55–59, Box 136, Special Committee on Indian Affairs, Committee on Interior and Insular Affairs, Sen. 83 A-F9 (70th–82nd), RG 46, NARA-DC.

4. Frank S. Gauthier, letter to the editor, *Milwaukee Journal*, 31 July 1927; copy appears to be typed from newspaper copy, Box 136, Special Committee on Indian Affairs, Committee on Interior and Insular Affairs, Sen. 83 A-F9 (70th–82nd), RG 46, NARA-DC.

5. "Menominee Indian Reservation, Wisconsin, Abstract of the Record in the Application for Development of Power," 11–12; Memorandum for Executive Secretary from J. F. Lawson, Attorney, 19 May 1927, both in Box 136, Special Committee on Indian Affairs, Committee on Interior and Insular Affairs, Sen. 83 A-F9 (70th–82nd), RG 46, NARA-DC; *Lone Wolf v. Hitchcock*, 187 U.S. 553.

6. Donner to Commissioner of Indian Affairs, 12 May 1927, CCF 1907–1939 Keshena 054, RG 75, NARA-DC.

7. Minutes of the Menominee General Council Meeting, 23 April 1927, 10; Minutes of the Menominee General Council Meeting, 27 August 1927, 10, both in CCF 1907–1939 Keshena 054, RG 75, NARA-DC; Grorud to Miss G. C. Winslow, Wisconsin Indian Defense Association, Milwaukee, 4 August 1927, Box 136, Special Committee on Indian Affairs, Committee on Interior and Insular Affairs, Sen. 83 A-F9 (70th–82nd), RG 46, NARA-DC.

8. Unpublished hearing, n.d., in Menominee Reservation (Water Power and Timber) folder, Box 136, Special Committee on Indian Affairs, Committee on Interior and Insular Affairs, Sen. 83 A-F9 (70th–82nd), RG 46, NARA-DC; Peyton Carter, Report, Keshena, General Reservation Conditions, 10 February 1928, CCF 1907–1939 Keshena 150, RG 75, NARA-DC.

9. "Wolf River's Beauty Seems Prey to Power"; Minutes of Menominee General Council Meeting, 6 October 1928, Menominee Tribal Archives.

10. "Offers Indians' Land for Park"; U.S. Congress, House, Committee on the Public Lands, "Report."

11. Gauthier to LaFollette, 6 February 1930, Box 136, Special Committee on Indian Affairs, Committee on Interior and Insular Affairs, Sen. 83 A-F9 (70th–82nd), RG 46, NARA-DC.

12. "A Worthy Bill," *Antigo Journal*, 8 January 1930; "No Need to Injure Indians," *Antigo Journal*, 27 January 1930, both in CCF 1907–1939 Keshena 307.2, RG 75, NARA-DC; Beck, "The Myth of the Vanishing Race."

13. "Indian Lands as a National Park," *Wausau Record Herald*, picked up from *Oshkosh Northwestern*, 15 January 1930; "Despoiling the Indians," *Appleton Post-Crescent*, 6 February 1930; "The Menominee and Wolf River, *Green Bay Press Gazette*, 8 February 1930; "Menominee Purchase Would Aid Indians," *Washington Star*, 3 February 1930, all in CCF 1907–1939 Keshena 307.2, RG 75, NARA-DC.

14. Rhoads to Amelia E. White, Secretary, Eastern Association of Indian Affairs, Inc., 8 February 1930, CCF 1907–1939 Keshena 307.2, RG 75, NARA-DC; Report of Delegation, Minutes of Menominee General Council Meeting, 9 August 1930, Menominee Tribal Archives and CCF 1907–1939 Keshena 054, RG 75, NARA-DC. The delegation mistakenly identified Nye as a senator from South Dakota.

15. "Will Not Press Power Development," *Oshkosh Northwestern*, 14 April 1930, CCF 1907–1939 Keshena 307.2, RG 75, NARA-DC.

16. Resolution, Menominee League of Women Voters, 4 February 1931; Beyer to Commissioner of Indian Affairs, 8 September 1930, both in CCF 1907–1939 Keshena 307.2, RG 75, NARA-DC; Minutes of the Menominee General Council Meeting, 2 June 1932, CCF 1907–1939 Keshena 054, RG 75, NARA-DC.

17. Minutes of Meeting of Menominee General Council, 9 August 1930, Me-

nominee Tribal Archives and CCF 1907–1939 Keshena 054, RG 75, NARA-DC. For a discussion of the amendment that allowed white contracts and employment in the Menominee logging business, see CCF 1907–1939 Keshena 054, RG 75, NARA-DC.

18. Burke to Miss Clara R. Brian, Home Adviser, McLean County Home Bureau, Bloomington, Ill., 26 September 1925, CCF 1907–1939 Keshena 810, RG 75, NARA-DC.

19. Ourada, *The Menominee Indians*, 184–85.

20. Minutes of Menominee General Council Meeting, 2 June 1932, Menominee Tribal Archives.

21. Minutes of Menominee General Council Meeting, 15 March 1933, Menominee Tribal Archives.

22. Sady, "The Menominees," 5; Minutes of Menominee General Council Meeting, 16 and 17 March 1934, 21–22, CCF 1907–1939 Keshena 054, RG 75, NARA-DC.

23. Chapman, "The Menominee Indian Timber Case," 13, 15, 27–29, 33–34, 38, Menominee Indian Papers, Wisconsin Historical Society Archives. Percentages apparently are figured by Chapman based on statistics in Sterling, *Report of a Forest Survey and Supplemental Investigations of the Menominee Indian Reservation*, 8 February 1935, 9, Miscellaneous Records of Forest Supervisor, 1905–1955, Records of the Menominee Indian Mills, 1900–1961, RG 75, NARA-GLR.

24. Sterling, *Report of a Forest Survey and Supplemental Investigations of the Menominee Indian Reservation*, 8 February 1935, Miscellaneous Records of Forest Supervisor, 1905–1955, Records of the Menominee Indian Mills, 1900–1961, RG 75, NARA-GLR. "An Act to refer the claim of the Menominee Tribe of Indians to the Court of Claims"; Sady, "The Menominees," 5.

25. Smith, comp., *Indian Tribal Claims*, 61–104; *Menominee Tribe of Indians*, 95 Ct. Cls. 232; *Menominee Tribe of Indians*, 101 Ct. Cls. 863.

26. Ourada, *The Menominee Indians*, 189; *Menominee Tribe of Indians*, 101 Ct. Cls. 10; *Menominee Tribe of Indians*, 101 Ct. Cls. 22; *Menominee Tribe of Indians*, 102 Ct. Cls. 555; *Menominee Tribe of Indians*, 107 Ct. Cls. 23; *Menominee Tribe of Indians*, 117 Ct. Cls. 442; *Menominee Tribe of Indians*, 118 Ct. Cls. 290; *Menominee Tribe of Indians*, 119 Ct. Cls. 832.

27. Minutes of Menominee General Council Meeting, 9 August 1930, Menominee Tribal Archives and CCF 1907–1939 Keshena 054, RG 75, NARA-DC.

28. Minutes of Menominee General Council Meeting, 4–5 December 1933, 27, CCF 1907–1939 Keshena 054, RG 75, NARA-DC.

29. Keesing, *The Menomini Indians*, 247.

30. Sady, "The Menominees," 6.

31. Dodge to Collier, 2 August 1935, CCF 1907–1939 Keshena 047, RG 75, NARA-DC. A copy of the "Charter of the Menominee Tribe of Indians" that circulated within the Department of the Interior ca. 1936 is in Folder 1566, Box 97, Felix S. Cohen Papers, Beinicke Rare Book and Manuscript Library.

32. Sady, "The Menominees," 6–7.

33. Fredenberg to Collier, 3 January 1938, CCF 1907–1939 Keshena 054, RG 75, NARA-DC.

34. Sady, "The Menominees," 6–14; "An Act to amend the law relating to timber operations," 964.

35. Sterling, *Report of a Forest Survey and Supplemental Investigations of the Menominee Indian Reservation*, 8 February 1935, 5, Miscellaneous Records of Forest Supervisor, 1905–1955, Records of the Menominee Indian Mills, 1900–1961, RG 75, NARA-GLR; Kinney, *Indian Forest and Range*, 323; Statements of Al Dodge and Gordon Dickie, U.S. Congress, House, Committee on Interior and Insular Affairs, Subcommittee on Indian Affairs, Hearings on H.R. 7104, 19, 22.

36. Minutes of Menominee General Council Meeting, 10–11 December 1937, 29–40, CCF 1907–1939 Keshena 054, RG 75, NARA-DC.

37. See Minutes of Menominee General Council Meetings, 15 March 1933, 13 May 1933, and 8–10 June 1933, Menominee Tribal Archives; and Fredenberg to William C. Beatty, Director of Education, Office of Indian Affairs, 19 February 1937, CCF 1907–1939 Keshena 806, RG 75, NARA-DC.

38. School Report from A. Nicholson to Commissioner of Indian Affairs, 19 September 1910, CCF 1907–1939 Keshena 150, RG 75, NARA-DC.

39. The vote count supporting the church site totaled 44–19, while the count supporting the government site totaled 34–25. Based on historical Menominee practices regarding attendance at tribal council meetings, these low figures might indicate a strong opposition or indifference to the issue. This was the only topic on the agenda at this council of adult male members of the tribe. Council Minutes, 11 September 1909, CCF 1907–1939 Keshena 816.2, RG 75, NARA-DC; interviews with Menominee people.

40. Minutes of Menominee Tribal Council Meeting, 6 July 1912, and Minutes of Menominee Tribal Council Meeting, 14 November 1912, CCF 1907–1939 Keshena 816.2, RG 75, NARA-DC.

41. Fredenberg to Thompson, 29 January 1939; "Report covering the First Semester of the School Year 1938–1939 at the Neopit Day School, Neopit Wisconsin," 4 February 1939, both in Outgoing Correspondence 1936–1939, Neopit Day School, Records of the Keshena/Menominee Agency, 1892–1961, RG 75, NARA-GLR.

42. Thompson to Mr. Willard W. Beatty, Director of Indian Education, Washington DC, 4 March 1939, and Thompson to Fredenberg, 10 March 1939, both in Outgoing Correspondence 1936–1939, Neopit Day School, Records of the Keshena/Menominee Agency, 1892–1961, RG 75, NARA-GLR.

43. Thompson to Fredenberg, 10 March 1939; Beatty to Fredenberg, 7 June 1939, both in Outgoing Correspondence 1936–1939, Neopit Day School, Records of the Keshena/Menominee Agency, 1892–1961, RG 75, NARA-GLR.

44. Fredenberg to Thompson, 3 February 1939, in Outgoing Correspondence 1936–1939, Neopit Day School, Records of the Keshena/Menominee Agency, 1892–1961, RG 75, NARA-GLR.

45. Minutes of Menominee General Council Meeting, 15 March 1933, Menominee Tribal Archives.

46. Interviews with Menominee people.

47. Habig, *Heralds of the Kings*, 525.

48. See Fredenberg's correspondence in CCF Keshena 1907–1939 806, RG 75, NARA-DC, for example.

49. Interviews with Menominee people. For an oral history of St. Joseph's boarding school, see Shillinger, "'They Never Told Us They Wanted To Help Us.'"

50. Minutes of Menominee General Council Meeting, 25 and 26 February and 5 March 1938, 98–102, CCF 1907–1939 Keshena 053, RG 75, NARA-DC.

51. Sady, "The Menominees," 9.

52. Beck, *Siege and Survival*, 15–16.

9. TERMINATION

Termination is the most-studied aspect of Menominee history. Not only must modern histories of the tribe devote considerable space to this issue (for example, Ourada, in *The Menominee Indians*, consigns her final two chapters to termination and restoration), but virtually any account of modern federal Indian policy must include discussion of Menominee termination and restoration. For general views of termination, see Burt, *Tribalism in Crisis*, which analyzes the conservative ideology and the roles of conservative terminationists in formulating federal policy in the 1950s; Philp, *Termination Revisited*, which analyzes policy from the New Deal through termination and Indian responses to it and views the termination era as providing the seeds for self-determination; and Fixico, *Termination and Relocation*, which provides an overview of the federal policy. The best analysis of Menominee termination remains Orfield's Master's thesis, "Ideology and the Indians." Herzberg, in two lengthy articles, views termination in the perspective of long-term Menominee history and then analyzes the destructive effects of termination: "The Menominee Indians: From Treaty to Termination" and "The Menominee Indians: Termination to Restoration." Several articles written during termination give timely perspectives from those affiliated with DRUMS: Deer, "The Menominee Restoration Act"; Lurie, "The Menominee Indians, Menominee Termination"; and Lurie, "Menominee Termination: From Reservation to Colony" are good examples. After restoration, DRUMS, the group that rallied the tribe and the federal government to accept restoration, presented its own views of both termination and the coming restoration in Shames, ed., *Freedom with Reservation: The Menominee*

Struggle to Save their Land and People. Kalinoski studied federal policy as it related to Menominee termination in "The Termination Crisis." Ray covers the tribe's lack of preparation for termination in a book written for a claims suit, *The Menominee Tribe of Indians, 1940–1970.* Congressional debate on the termination bill can be found in the *Congressional Record* for the Eight-third Congress. Congressional hearings proceedings provide valuable insight into termination: U.S. Congress, Joint, Subcommittees on Interior and Insular Affairs, *Termination of Federal Supervision Over Certain Tribes of Indians.* See also *Congressional Reference to the United States Court of Federal Claims.*

1. Sady, "The Menominees," 11.

2. "Menominees Will Attempt to Settle Their Difficulties With Government."

3. Menominee Delegates, Memorandum for the Senate Committee on Indian Affairs, 5 April 1941, Box 136, Special Committee on Indian Affairs, Committee on Interior and Insular Affairs, Sen. 83 A-F9 (70th–82nd), RG 46, NARA-DC.

4. Deloria and Lytle, *The Nations Within,* 140–53.

5. Deloria and Lytle, *The Nations Within,* 154–57; Sady, "The Menominees," 6–8.

6. Frechette to Collier, 7 May 1941; Minutes of Council Meeting, 7 May 1941, 24–31, Box 136, Special Committee on Indian Affairs, Committee on Interior and Insular Affairs, Sen. 83 A-F9 (70th–82nd), RG 46, NARA-DC.

7. Frechette to Collier, 7 May 1941; Letter from Zimmerman, 10 July 1941, both in CCF 1940–1943 Keshena 066, RG 75, NARA-DC; U.S. Congress, House, Committee on Interior and Insular Affairs, Subcommittee on Indian Affairs, Hearings on H.R. 7104, 4. Frechette letter in both RG 46 and RG 75.

8. Sady, "The Menominees," 9, 11–13.

9. Sady, "The Menominees," 9, 11–13; J. Lyle Cunningham, *Menominee News* 4:6, June 1944, Box 136, Special Committee on Indian Affairs, Committee on Interior and Insular Affairs, Sen. 83 A-F9 (70th–82nd), RG 46, NARA-DC.

10. Murphy to Commissioner of Indian Affairs, 25 September 1945, and Zimmerman to Murphy, 5 November 1945, Decimal Correspondence Files 1934–1961, General Records, Records of the Keshena/Menominee Agency, 1892–1961, RG 75, NARA-GLR.

11. Zimmerman to Murphy, 1 April 1946, General Correspondence 1935–1961, General Records, Records of the Keshena/Menominee Agency, 1892–1961, RG 75, NARA-GLR.

12. This is Sady's interpretation of the problem as well.

13. Sady, "The Menominees," 13.

14. It took thirty-two railroad boxcars to move the agency. "Removal of Indian Office to Chicago," 7.

15. Margold, "Solicitor's Opinion"; Philp, *Termination Revisited,* 2, 13–15; Cowger, *The National Congress of American Indians.*

16. Philp, *Termination Revisited*, 12–13.

17. Burt, *Tribalism in Crisis*, 5.

18. Rosenthal, "Indian Claims," 36; Fixico, *Termination and Relocation*, 26–27.

19. Herzberg, "The Menominee Indians: From Treaty to Termination," 306. Zimmerman named ten groups, one labeled "New York," ready for immediate termination in 1947: Tyler, "Indian Affairs," 32.

20. Sterling, *Report of a Forest Survey and Supplemental Investigations of the Menominee Indian Reservation*, 8 February 1935, 5, Miscellaneous Records of Forest Supervisor, 1905–1955, Records of the Menominee Indian Mills, 1900–1961, RG 75, NARA-GLR; Kinney, *Indian Forest and Range*, 323; Statements of Al Dodge and Gordon Dickie, U.S. Congress, House, Committee on Interior and Insular Affairs, Subcommittee on Indian Affairs, Hearings on H.R. 7104, 19, 22.

21. Gauthier, "Economic Development," 8–9.

22. Herzberg, "The Menominee Indians: From Treaty to Termination," 304.

23. Ourada, *The Menominee Indians*, 190.

24. Gordon Dickie Sr., interview, Menominee Historic Preservation Department. See Mitchell Al Dodge Papers, L. Tom Perry Special Collections, for a copy of the bill, S 1680, 80th Cong., 1st sess., 21 July 1947: "A Bill to remove restrictions on the property and moneys belonging to the individual enrolled members of the Menominee Indian Tribe in Wisconsin, to provide for the liquidation of tribal property and distribution of the proceeds thereof, to confer complete citizenship upon such Indians, and for other purposes." For a contemporary analysis of the situation for these two tribes, see Collier, "The Menominee of Wisconsin."

25. Dickie to Watkins, 14 June 1949, Box 12, Folder 9, Arthur V. Watkins (1866–1973) Papers, L. Tom Perry Special Collections.

26. Herzberg, "The Menominee Indians: From Treaty to Termination," 292–95.

27. Herzberg, "The Menominee Indians: From Treaty to Termination," 310, 318; Watkins, "Termination of Federal Supervision," 47–55.

28. 1 Nephi 12:23, *The Book of Mormon*; Oliver Cowdery, David Whitman, and Martin Harris, "Introduction," in *The Book of Mormon*, page not indicated; Price, "Mormon Missionaries," 461.

29. Watkins to the First Presidency, Church of Jesus Christ of Latter-Day Saints, Salt Lake City, 13 April 1954, Box 12, Folder 9, Arthur V. Watkins (1866–1973) Papers, L. Tom Perry Special Collections.

30. Actually, the tribe first requested one thousand dollars, but it changed to fifteen hundred dollars by the time it becomes pertinent to this story.

31. "Memorandum of Conferences Participated in by Menominee Delegation During the Week of February 25 to March 1 [1952], Inclusive." Mitchell Al Dodge Papers, L. Tom Perry Special Collections.

32. U.S. Congress, House, Committee on Interior and Insular Affairs, Subcommittee on Indian Affairs, Hearings on H.R. 7104, 7.

33. Statement of Gordon Dickie, U.S. Congress, House, Committee on Interior and Insular Affairs, Subcommittee on Indian Affairs, Hearings on H.R. 7104, 27, 28.

34. Statement of Gordon Dickie, U.S. Congress, House, Committee on Interior and Insular Affairs, Subcommittee on Indian Affairs, Hearings on H.R. 7104, 28.

35. File memo by John B. Keliiaa, Program Officer, 16 May 1952, re Conference with Menominee Delegation, 8 May 1952; "Attitude [of] Delegation—extracts from [memo] to Commissioner." n.d. Both in Decimal Correspondence Files 1934–1961, General Records, Records of the Keshena/Menominee Agency, 1892–1961, RG 75, NARA-GLR.

36. Keliiaa, Program Officer, Robert Beasley, Acting Director, Division of Program, 11 June 1952; "Notes—Meeting with Members of the South Branch Community. 6/18/52"; Keliiaa to Beasley, 24 June 1952, Neopit. All in Decimal Correspondence Files 1934–1961, General Records, Records of the Keshena/Menominee Agency, 1892–1961, RG 75, NARA-GLR.

37. "Notes—Meeting with Members of the South Branch Community. 6/18/52," Decimal Correspondence Files 1934–1961, General Records, Records of the Keshena/Menominee Agency, 1892–1961, RG 75, NARA-GLR.

38. Keliiaa to Beasley, 24 June 1952, Neopit, Decimal Correspondence Files 1934–1961, General Records, Records of the Keshena/Menominee Agency, 1892–1961, RG 75, NARA-GLR.

39. Herzberg, "The Menominee Indians: From Treaty to Termination," 319; Peroff, *Menominee Drums*, 62–63.

40. Report to accompany H.R. 444, *Per Capita Distribution—Shoshone and Arapaho Tribes, Wyoming*, 83d Cong., 1st sess., S. Rep. 263, 3. Copy in Mitchell Al Dodge Papers, L. Tom Perry Special Collections.

41. Herzberg, "The Menominee Indians: From Treaty to Termination," 311.

42. Ray, *The Menominee Tribe*, 62.

43. House, "Abandonment or Freedom," 2.

44. Deloria, *Custer Died for Your Sins*, 78.

45. Beck, "'Bribed with Our Own Money;'" Lawson, *Dammed Indians*, 59–63; Meyer, "Fort Berthold and the Garrison Dam," 299–303; Deloria, *Custer Died for Your Sins*, 79–80; Josephy, *Now That the Buffalo's Gone*, 143; Metcalf, *Termination's Legacy*, 85–100, 236–37; Haynal, "From Termination through Restoration," 102; Bilharz, *The Allegheny Senecas*, 99–100.

46. Ada Deer, Laurel Otradovec, Lloyd Powless, James White, and Georgianna Ignace (hereafter Deer et al.), "The Effects of Termination on the Menominee," 7, Gordon S. Dickie Sr. Papers, Menominee Historic Preservation Department and Ada Deer Papers, Folder 7, GBARC.

47. Watkins, "Termination of Federal Supervision," 47, 55.

48. Menominee Indian Tribe of Wisconsin, *Menominee Tribal History Guide*, 83; Peroff, *Menominee Drums*, 67–68; "Should the American Indian Be Given Full Citizenship Responsibility?" transcript of televised debate between Senator George Smathers and Senator Arthur Watkins, 22 April 1954, 544.22.7, Fort Berthold Papers, Robert Rietz Collection, Community Archives of NAES College.

49. Herzberg, "The Menominee Indians: From Treaty to Termination," 311–16; Lurie, "The Menominee Indians," 39; Ray, *The Menominee Tribe of Indians*, 14–21; interviews with Menominee people.

50. "Menominees' Full Freedom Assured." Other area newspaper headlines portrayed the same perspective, for example, "Menominee Indians to Back Three-Year Freedom Plan" and "Freedom Plan Okayed by Menominee Indians."

51. Herzberg, "The Menominee Indians: From Treaty to Termination," 314–16.

52. Gordon Dickie Sr., interview, Menominee Historic Preservation Department.

53. Lurie, "Ada Deer," 228.

54. Herzberg, "The Menominee Indians: From Treaty to Termination," 314–16; Ray, *The Menominee Tribe of Indians*, 38; interviews with Menominee people.

55. Deer et al., "The Effects of Termination on the Menominee," 7, Gordon S. Dickie Sr. Papers, Menominee Historic Preservation Department and Ada Deer Papers, Folder 7, GBARC.

56. Herzberg, "The Menominee Indians: From Treaty to Termination," 306–7, 321; "Indians Came Out Better Than Expected in 83rd Congress," NCAI Report, 1954, 549.22.2–4, Fort Berthold Papers, Robert Rietz Collection, Community Archives of NAES College; Peroff, *Menominee Drums*, 66–67.

57. Herzberg, "The Menominee Indians: From Treaty to Termination," 318–22, 327–29.

58. "Address By Commissioner of Indian Affairs Glenn L. Emmons Before the Annual Convention of the National Congress of American Indians, Omaha, Nebraska, November 19, 1954," 2, 5411.19.2, Fort Berthold Papers, Robert Rietz Collection, Community Archives of NAES College.

59. Gordon Dickie Sr., interview, Menominee Historic Preservation Department.

60. Tyler, "Indian Affairs," 38.

61. Herzberg, "The Menominee Indians: From Treaty to Termination," 318–22, 327–29.

62. Herzberg, "The Menominee Indians: From Treaty to Termination," 323–26.

63. William Zimmerman Jr., "Menominee Termination Problems," June 1955, Box 134, Folder 3: Menominee, Sol Tax Papers, University of Chicago Special Collections.

64. Peroff, *Menominee Drums*, 90–94.

65. Herzberg, "The Menominee Indians: From Treaty to Termination," 323.

66. Assistant Secretary of the Interior Orme Lewis to Members of the Menominee Tribe, 12 November 1954, 4–7, Decimal Correspondence Files 1934–1961, General Records, Records of the Keshena/Menominee Agency, 1892–1961, RG 75, NARA-GLR; "An Act to confer jurisdiction."

67. Assistant Secretary of the Interior Orme Lewis to Members of the Menominee Tribe, 12 November 1954, 4–7, Decimal Correspondence Files 1934–1961, General Records, Records of the Keshena/Menominee Agency, 1892–1961, RG 75, NARA-GLR; Herzberg, "The Menominee Indians: Termination to Restoration," 168.

68. "Menominee Agency Reorganization," *Menominee News* 2:2, 27 January 1955; William Zimmerman Jr., "Menominee Termination Problems," June 1955, Box 134, Folder 3: Menominee, Sol Tax Papers, University of Chicago Special Collections.

69. House, "Freedom or Abandonment?" 1.

70. William Zimmerman Jr., "Menominee Termination Problems," June 1955, Box 134, Folder 3: Menominee, Sol Tax Papers, University of Chicago Special Collections.

71. Peroff, *Menominee Drums*, 6–7.

72. According to Peroff, *Menominee Drums*, over a decade later most Menominees had come to believe their leaders had done what they thought was in the tribe's best interests (105).

73. Anonymous interview in "Report of Dr. Katherine Hall," 44, Menominee Historic Preservation Department.

74. Peroff, *Menominee Drums*, 103–5; interviews with Menominee people; George W. Kenote, Affidavit, Menominee Historic Preservation Department; Kenote, "A Personal Memorandum," Menominee Tribal Archives; Hart, "The Making of Menominee County," 183.

75. Peroff, *Menominee Drums*, 103–5, 121.

76. Lurie, "The Menominee Indians," 40. Peroff, *Menominee Drums*, discusses reasons for and the process of creating the county (107–12). See also Hart, "The Making of Menominee County," which discusses also the role of the state of Wisconsin in the process.

77. Hart, "The Making of Menominee County," 185.

78. Lurie, "The Menominee Indians," 40–41, 44; Peroff, *Menominee Drums*, 120–22; interviews with Menominee people; Hart, "The Making of Menominee County," 185–86; Clark, *Lone Wolf*, 101.

79. Herzberg, "The Menominee Indians: Termination to Restoration," 173; Lurie, "The Menominee Indians," 40–41; Peroff, *Menominee Drums*, 95, 123; Hart, "The Making of Menominee County," 183; Kenote, "A Personal Memorandum," 12, Menominee Tribal Archives; "Poverty Levels, Rates, and Ranks, All Counties"; Sandler and Barrett, "State Median Income."

80. Minutes of General Council Meeting, 9 January 1961, 37–45, George Kenote Papers, Menominee County/Tribal Library.

81. Ray, *The Menominee Tribe*, 29.

82. Hart, "The Making of Menominee County," 186.

83. Lurie, "The Menominee Indians," 41.

10. THE ROAD TO RESTORATION

1. *Menominee Drums*, a political science monograph by Peroff, is the key source on the Menominee restoration. In it he provides a policy theory–based analysis of the enactment of termination and Menominee resistance to it. See also Restoration Bill House Hearings, published in U.S. Congress, House, Subcommittee on Indian Affairs of the Committee on Interior and Insular Affairs, *Menominee Restoration Act, Hearings*.

2. Gordon Dickie Sr., interview, Menominee Historic Preservation Department; Deer et al., "The Effects of Termination on the Menominee," Gordon S. Dickie Sr. Papers, Menominee Historic Preservation Department and Ada Deer Papers, Folder 7, GBARC.

3. Statement of George W. Kenote to the Senate Committee on Interior and Insular Affairs, Washington DC, 21 July 1971, signed as Chairman, Menominee Common Stock and Voting Trust, Box 9, Folder 1: Legislation, Federal, Senate Concurrent Resolution 26, 1971, Menominee Enterprises, Inc. Records, GBARC.

4. Menominee Indian Tribe of Wisconsin, *Menominee Tribal History Guide*, 95–97.

5. Herzberg, "The Menominee Indians: Termination to Restoration," 176.

6. Herzberg, "The Menominee Indians: Termination to Restoration," 177.

7. Herzberg, "The Menominee Indians: Termination to Restoration," 177–78.

8. Gordon Dickie Sr., interview, Menominee Historic Preservation Department.

9. Gordon Dickie Sr., interview, Menominee Historic Preservation Department.

10. Thomsen, Neumann, and Schuttler, *The Forests of the Menominee*, 217–21, Menominee Historic Preservation Department.

11. Hobbs, "Indian Hunting and Fishing Rights II," 1261–63; Preloznik and Felsenthal, "The Menominee Struggle," 58–59; Article 2, Treaty with the Menominee, 1854, in Kappler, *Indian Treaties*, 626.

12. *State v. Sanapaw*, 124 N.W. 2d 41–42; Hobbs, "Indian Hunting and Fishing Rights II," 1262.

13. Herzberg, "The Menominee Indians: Termination to Restoration," 173; [De-Leon], "Menominee Health Care," 1.

14. Deer et al., "The Effects of Termination on the Menominee," 17, Gordon S.

Dickie Sr. Papers, Menominee Historic Preservation Department and Ada Deer Papers, Folder 7, GBARC.

15. Menominee Indian Tribe of Wisconsin, *Menominee Tribal History Guide*, 83; Statement of James Frechette, U.S. Congress, House, Committee on Interior and Insular Affairs, Subcommittee on Indian Affairs, Hearings on H.R. 7104, 14; interviews with Menominee people.

16. Deer et al., "The Effects of Termination on the Menominee," 18, Gordon S. Dickie, Sr. Papers, Menominee Historic Preservation Department and Ada Deer Papers, Folder 7, GBARC.

17. Peroff, *Menominee Drums*, 133.

18. Ray, *The Menominee Tribe*, 87; Preloznik and Felsenthal, "The Menominee Struggle," 64.

19. Deer et al., "The Effects of Termination on the Menominee," 22–23, Gordon S. Dickie Sr. Papers, Menominee Historic Preservation Department and Ada Deer Papers, Folder 7, GBARC; Peroff, *Menominee Drums*, 136; "Report of Dr. Katherine Hall," 27–29, 36, Menominee Historic Preservation Department.

20. U.S. Congress, Senate, Hearings Before the Subcommittee on Employment and Manpower of the Committee on Labor and Public Welfare, "Menominee County Aid Hearings."

21. Menominee Indian Tribe of Wisconsin, *Menominee Tribal History Guide*, 91; Herzberg, "The Menominee Indians: Termination to Restoration," 179, 183.

22. Lurie, "Ada Deer," 233.

23. Herzberg, "The Menominee Indians: Termination to Restoration," 183.

24. Peroff, *Menominee Drums*, 148–52, 175, 182; Preloznik and Felsenthal, "The Menominee Struggle," 64; Menominee Indian Tribe of Wisconsin, *Menominee Tribal History Guide*, 91.

25. "Report of Dr. Katherine Hall," 9–10, 57–60, in Menominee Historic Preservation Department.

26. Mitchel Al Dodge, interviews; Gordon Dickie Sr., interview, both in Menominee Historic Preservation Department; Menominee Indian Tribe of Wisconsin, *Menominee Tribal History Guide*, 91.

27. Aukofer, "$32 Million Settlement."

28. Gordon Dickie Sr., interview, Menominee Historic Preservation Department; certiorari denied in *State v. Sanapaw*, 377 U.S. 991; *Menominee Tribe of Indians*, 179 Ct. Cl. 496. Al Dodge also described Durfee's role, in Mitchell Al Dodge, interview, Mitchell Al Dodge Papers, L. Tom Perry Special Collections.

29. Dissenting Opinion by Judge Durfee, *Menominee Tribe of Indians*, 179 Ct. Cl. 520.

30. *Menominee Tribe of Indians v. United States*, 391 U.S. 404.

31. *Menominee Tribe of Indians v. United States*, 391 U.S. 406, 412–13. A draft of

Douglas's opinion is in container 1419 #187, William O. Douglas collection, Library of Congress.

32. "Report to the Council of Chiefs," 6 June 1968, Menominee Indian Tribe of Wisconsin, Inc., folder, Menominee Tribal Enterprises Records, Menominee Historic Preservation Department.

33. See discussion of *Menominee Tribe of Indians v. United States* in American Indian Resource Institute, *Indian Tribes as Sovereign Governments*, 115–16; Clinton, Newton, and Price, *American Indian Law*, 1184–86; Hobbs, "Indian Hunting and Fishing Rights II," 1268.

34. United States District Court for the Western District of Wisconsin, Complaint, 3–5, Menominee Historic Preservation Department; *The Indian Way to Education*, 3–9, Menominee County/Tribal Library.

35. *The Indian Way to Education*, 6–19, Menominee County/Tribal Library; "Petition Before the State Superintendent of Public Instruction," and affidavits signed February and March 1971 in Menominee Enterprises, Inc. Records, Box 8, Folder 6, GBARC.

36. *The Indian Way to Education*, 17–20, Menominee County/Tribal Library; Menominee Indian Tribe of Wisconsin, *Menominee Tribal History Guide*, 93.

37. "Minutes of Board of Directors Meeting," 2–3, in Menominee Historic Preservation Department.

38. "Indian Witness Raps Land Sales."

39. Deer et al., "The Effects of Termination on the Menominee," 21, Gordon S. Dickie Sr. Papers, Menominee Historic Preservation Department and Ada Deer Papers, Folder 7, GBARC.

40. The eight DRUMS goals as listed in a 1970 newsletter were "1) Restore control over the corporation and its assets to the Menominee. 2) Stop the sale of land to non-Menominee. 3) Build socially and economically sound programs that will not destroy the land and culture of the Menominees. 4) Work to improve educational opportunities for Menominee children. 5) Encourage Menominee to participate in decisions affecting their land, their culture, and their future. 6) Work to keep the treaty rights to hunt, fish, and trap exclusively for Menominee. 7) Elect representative leaders who will be responsive to the needs and desires of the Menominee. 8) Reopen the tribal rolls so that our children will once more belong to the Menominee tribe." In Shames, ed. *Freedom with Reservation*, 77. Also in Peroff, *Menominee Drums*, 178–79.

41. Peroff, *Menominee Drums*, 175–80; Lurie, *Wisconsin Indians*, 53.

42. Peroff, *Menominee Drums*, 175–80; Lurie, *Wisconsin Indians*, 53.

43. Hank Adams, in Philp, ed., *Indian Self-Rule*, 240–41; Lurie, "The Menominee Indians," 43; "Watkins Rebuffs Article," unattributed, undated newspaper article, ca.

1969, apparently in response to Vine Deloria's writings, Box 11, Folder 9, Arthur V. Watkins (1866–1973) Papers, L. Tom Perry Special Collections.

44. Statement of Senator Reuben LaFave to the Senate Committee on Interior and Insular Affairs, Washington DC, 21 July 1971, 4, in Menominee Enterprises, Inc. Records, GBARC.

45. Peroff, *Menominee Drums*, 140–42.

46. James Washinawatok, interview, Menominee Historic Preservation Department. At this time Washinawatok still went by his Americanized name, Jim White. Some of the following narrative is reprinted from Beck, "An Urban Platform."

47. Chapman, "Reflections."

48. James Washinawatok, interview, Menominee Historic Preservation Department.

49. James Washinawatok, interview, Menominee Historic Preservation Department; Lurie, "Ada Deer," 235; Castile, *To Show Heart*, 149; Chapman, "Reflections."

50. James Washinawatok, interview, Menominee Historic Preservation Department.

51. James Washinawatok, interview, Menominee Historic Preservation Department.

52. *DRUMS* newsletters, Menominee Tribal Archives.

53. "A Menominee Tribal Reply to Drums and Judicare," by Mrs. Irene Mack, 3-1-71, Public Relations Folder, Menominee Tribal Enterprises Records, Menominee Historic Preservation Department; Peroff, *Menominee Drums*, 207.

54. Kenote, "A Personal Memorandum for Menominee Youth, 1972," Menominee Tribal Archives.

55. Peroff, *Menominee Drums*, 187–89; Kenote, "A Personal Memorandum for Menominee Youth," 44, Menominee Tribal Archives.

56. Peroff, *Menominee Drums*, 189.

57. Lurie, "Ada Deer," 235.

58. Lurie, "Ada Deer," 236–37; interviews with Menominee people; Patricia L. Raymer, "UW Woman Grad Activist Chief of Menominees," *Capital Times*, 18 April 1973, Menominee Enterprises, Inc. Records, Box 9, Folder 3, GBARC.

59. Castile, *To Show Heart*, 150.

60. Lurie, "Ada Deer," 236–37; interviews with Menominee people.

61. Interviews with Menominee people; U.S. Congress, House, Subcommittee on Indian Affairs of the Committee on Interior and Insular Affairs, *Menominee Restoration Act, Hearings*.

62. Statement of George Kenote, 25 May 1973, in U.S. Congress, House, Subcommittee on Indian Affairs of the Committee on Interior and Insular Affairs, *Menominee Restoration Act, Hearings*, 110; Statement of George W. Kenote to the

Senate Committee on Interior and Insular Affairs, Washington DC, 21 July 1971, 7, 11, in Menominee Enterprises, Inc., Records, Box 9, Folder 1, GBARC.

63. Statement of Hon. Harold V. Froehlich and Statement of Hon. David Obey, U.S. Congress, House, Subcommittee on Indian Affairs of the Committee on Interior and Insular Affairs, *Menominee Restoration Act, Hearings*, 259, 267; Tim Wyngaard, "House OKS Restoration—But Division Lingers," *Green Bay Press Gazette*, 17 October 1973, in Menominee Tribal News Records, GBARC; Peroff, *Menominee Drums*, 209–10.

64. "An Act to repeal the Act terminating Federal supervision."

65. "Annual Message to the Congress on the State of the Union," 30 January 1974, *Public Papers of the Presidents of the United States, Richard Nixon, 1974*, 75; "Statement on Signing the Menominee Restoration Act," 22 December 1973, *Public Papers of the Presidents of the United States, Richard Nixon, 1973*, 1023.

66. Interviews with Menominee people.

67. Peroff, *Menominee Drums*, 201.

68. Jim Washinawatok served on the Tribal Legislative Council and became a tribal judge; Sylvia Wilber, Shirley Daly, Rob Deer, and Lorene Pocan were Menominee Restoration Committee members and became Tribal Legislative Council members; Carol Dodge became director of curriculum for the Menominee Indian School District; Glen Miller became chief of police and later tribal chair; Ada Deer became director of the Menominee Restoration Committee and the first Tribal Legislative Council chair and later was named undersecretary of the interior for Indian affairs, the first woman appointed to run the Indian Bureau.

11. RESTORATION

1. James Washinawatok, interview, Menominee Historic Preservation Department. Some of the text in this chapter is from Beck, "An Urban Platform."

2. "An Act to repeal the Act terminating Federal supervision," 770–72.

3. "An Act to repeal the Act terminating Federal supervision," 771–72.

4. Ada Deer, "Restoration Committee Election March 2," DRUMS 3, no. 3 (1 February 1974): 1; "Restoration Committee Selected" and "Final Restoration Committee Results," DRUMS 3, no. 4 (15 March 1974): 1. Eighth through twelfth place vote tallies were unofficially recorded as follows: Robert Grignon, 293; John Peters, 290; Sarah Skubitz, 289; Ron Tourtillot, 289; Gordon Dickie Sr., 286.

5. "Menominee Restoration Committee Recount," DRUMS 3, no. 6 (15 May 1974): 5; "Menominee Restoration Committee," DRUMS 3, no. 8 (31 July 1974): 4–5.

6. "Menominee Restoration Committee Recount," DRUMS 3, no. 6 (15 May 1974): 5; "Menominee Restoration Committee," DRUMS 3, no. 8 (31 July 1974): 4–5; Lurie, "Ada Deer," 237. Deer quoted in Tabachnick, "Fence of Ownership," 362.

7. "An Act to repeal the Act terminating Federal supervision," 771–72.

8. "An Act to repeal the Act terminating Federal supervision," 772.

9. "An Act to repeal the Act terminating Federal supervision," 770–73.

10. "Menominee Restoration Committee," DRUMS 3, no. 8 (31 July 1974): 4–5; "Statement of Menominee Restoration Committee," 10 January 1975, 3–4, Box 134, Folder 3, Sol Tax Papers, University of Chicago Special Collections.

11. "An Act to repeal the Act terminating Federal supervision," 770–73.

12. Gubbs Boyd, "Restoration Progress," and Al Fowler, "M.E.I. Proposed Transfer Plan," *Aq-Ua-Chamine* 1, no. 2 (16 October 1974): 1, 5–6.

13. "Plan for Transfer of all of the Assets of Menominee Enterprises, Inc.," 19, in Menominee Tribal Enterprises, *Relevant Documents*.

14. "Menominee Restoration Committee," DRUMS 3, no. 8 (31 July 1974): 4–5; "Statement of Menominee Restoration Committee," 10 January 1975, 5–6, Box 134, Folder 3, Sol Tax Papers, University of Chicago Special Collections.

15. "Armed Indians."

16. Apesanahkwat interviewed in Rick, "The Novitiate." John Rogozinski, interview by Herbert Bobeck and John Schultz, 19 January 1975; Barbara N. Rogozinski, interview by Herbert Bobeck and John Schultz, 9 January 1975; Joseph Thomas Plonka, interview by Wendall A. Harker and Ernest V. Smith, 20 January 1975. Except for Apesanahkwat's interview, these interviews are all from WDOJ-DCI file SA-180. In addition to the sources cited in this discussion of the takeover, an overview of the takeover may be found in Tronnes, " 'Where Is John Wayne?' " The *Milwaukee Journal* covered the takeover on an almost daily basis throughout January and into February 1975. A clip file of this event is in Series 1, Box 13, LaDonna Harris Papers, Community Archives of NAES College.

17. An FBI document at the end of the siege indicated that twenty men and nineteen women surrendered to police: Urgent memo Milwaukee to Director, FBI, 4 February 1975, 1:50 a.m., FBI-FOIA.

18. Rick, "The Novitiate."

19. Apesanahkwat interviewed in Rick, "The Novitiate."

20. Menominee Restoration Committee News Release, 5 January 1975, Box 134, Sol Tax Papers, Folder 3, University of Chicago Special Collections.

21. Menominee Restoration Committee News Release, 5 January 1975, Box 134, Folder 3, Sol Tax Papers, University of Chicago Special Collections.

22. United Press International (UPI) Wire Story, Washington Capital News Service, 8 January 1975, FBI-FOIA; Farrell, "Guardsman's Leader," put the number at 350 by 28 January, and FBI intelligence put the number at 750 on 3 February, Nitel, Milwaukee to Director, FBI, 3 February 1975, 10:46 p.m., FBI-FOIA; Martino, "Novitiate Wiretap."

23. UPI Wire Story, Washington Capital News Service, 8 January 1975, FBI-FOIA;

Urgent memo Milwaukee to Director, FBI, 31 January 1975, 7:00 p.m., FBI-FOIA; report of Agent Ernest V. Smith, 10 January 1975, WDOJ-DCI.

24. Gordon Dickie Sr., interview, Menominee Historic Preservation Department.

25. "Novitiate Occupation," in *Aq-Ua-Chamine* 2, no. 1 (19 January 1975), 2.

26. "Novitiate Occupation," in *Aq-Ua-Chamine* 2, no. 1 (19 January 1975), 2–3; "Statement of Menominee Restoration Committee," 10 January 1975, 8–10, Box 134, Folder 3, Sol Tax Papers, University of Chicago Special Collections. The latter is also in Mitchell Al Dodge Papers, L. Tom Perry Special Collections.

27. News Release 19 January 1975, prepared by Ada Deer, Chairperson, Menominee Restoration Committee, Box 134, Folder 3, Sol Tax Papers, University of Chicago Special Collections. Also in Mitchell Al Dodge Papers, L. Tom Perry Special Collections.

28. Al Fowler, "Novituate Agreement Reached (No Victory for Tribe)," *Aq-Ua-Chamine* 2, no. 2 (20 February 1975), 2.

29. News Release 19 January 1975, prepared by Ada Deer, Chairperson, Menominee Restoration Committee, Box 134, Folder 3, Sol Tax Papers, University of Chicago Special Collections. Also in Mitchell Al Dodge Papers, L. Tom Perry Special Collections.

30. News Release 19 January 1975, prepared by Ada Deer, Chairperson, Menominee Restoration Committee, Box 134, Folder 3, Sol Tax Papers, University of Chicago Special Collections. Also in Mitchell Al Dodge Papers, L. Tom Perry Special Collections.

31. Summary, in Informative Note, Intelligence Division, 27 January 1975, FBI-FOIA; Milwaukee to Director, FBI, 25 January 1975, 7:45 p.m., 3–4, FBI-FOIA; memo from special agents John E. Schultz and Herbert Bobeck to file SA-180, 20 January 1975, WDOJ-DCI; Al Fowler, "Novituate Agreement Reached (No Victory for Tribe)," *Aq-Ua-Chamine* 2, no. 2 (20 February 1975): 2.

32. Milwaukee to Director, FBI, 3 February 1975 10:46 p.m., FBI-FOIA; Milwaukee to Director, FBI, 4 February 1975, 1:50 a.m., FBI-FOIA; Lurie, *Wisconsin Indians*, 55.

33. Rick, "The Novitiate." However, when the Alexians disposed of the property in July 1975 without consulting the tribe, it led to anger on the reservation, and violence broke out. See Hensel, "Alexians Halt Deal"; "Fire Bombs, Shots"; Wilk, "Armed Men Patrol at Novitiate"; "On, Wisconsin"; Hensel, "Reservation Area Quiet"; Wilk, "State, Indian Leaders Lash Out at Alexians"; "New Deal Possible"; Hensel, "Arson Suspected"; Wilk, "Novitiate Action"; "Scapegoatism." Several of these articles were either front-page stories or editorials.

34. Summary, in Informative Note, Intelligence Division, 4 February 1975, FBI-FOIA.

35. "Plan for Transfer of all of the Assets of Menominee Enterprises, Inc.," in Menominee Tribal Enterprises, *Relevant Documents*.

36. Wilk, "Tribe Agrees."

37. Lurie, *Wisconsin Indians*, 54; "Government Gives Reservation Back." The quote in the *New York Times* of Ada Deer was part of a larger statement she had previously made, which had appeared on the masthead of the DRUMS newsletter, vol. 3, no. 4 (15 March 1974): "With the passage of the Menominee Restoration Act, the Menominee people have achieved one of the most historic reversals in all of American Indian history. This does not mean we turn the clock back to federal paternalism. We want federal protection and not federal domination." The same language, "federal protection but not federal domination," was written into the "Trust and Management Agreement" between the Menominee Restoration Committee and the secretary of the interior. See p. 37 of that document in Menominee Tribal Enterprises, *Relevant Documents*.

38. "Management Plan for Menominee Enterprises," 22 April 1975; and "Plan for Transfer of all of the Assets of Menominee Enterprises, Inc.," 46–48, both in Menominee Tribal Enterprises, *Relevant Documents*.

39. The first board included four members each who would serve through 1975, 1976, and 1977.

40. "Trust and Management Agreement," 35, in Menominee Tribal Enterprises, *Relevant Documents*; Alexander (Sandy) MacNabb, in Philp, *Indian Self-Rule*, 213.

41. "Trust and Management Agreement," 35, in Menominee Tribal Enterprises, *Relevant Documents*.

42. Menominee Indian Tribe of Wisconsin, *Menominee Tribal History Guide*, 97, 99.

43. Menominee Indian Tribe of Wisconsin, *Menominee Tribal History Guide*, 99; [DeLeon], "Menominee Health Care," 1–2.

44. Bob Mong, "Maybe No Shootout if Feds Ruled Reservation," *Capital Times* (Madison), 5 February 1976, in AFSC Community Relations Division, Native American Affairs, Regional Offices, Midwest (Chicago), (hereafter AFSC Archives).

45. Van Vegten, "Report on the February 3, 1976 Slaying of Two Menominee Warriors," Gordon S. Dickie Sr. Papers, Menominee Historic Preservation Department. Andre van Vegten of the AFSC stated, "Numerous accusations have been made that the present Tribal governing body—the Menominee Restoration Committee—is maintaining a police state. This assertion is give[n] considerable credibility by numerous reports of beatings, harassment, intimidation and midnight raids conducted by the Menominee police force, which has grown from a 5-man department to a force of 60 officers in one year's time." In van Vegten to Senator James Abourezk, 5 March 1976, AFSC Archives.

46. Legro, "Deputy Guilty."

47. Bob Mong, "Trial of Menominees: Clash of Two Cultures," *Capital Times*, 3 December 1975; Bob Mong, "Menominee Shootout Is Mystery," *Capital Times*, 4

February 1976; "News Update on the Menominee Slayings," 2 March 1976; Andre van Vegten, "News Update on the Menominee Slayings," 5 March 1976, all in AFSC Archives. Van Vegten, "Report on the February 3, 1976 Slaying of Two Menominee Warriors," Gordon S. Dickie Sr. Papers, Menominee Historic Preservation Department. Autopsy 76:25, University of Wisconsin, Medical School, Department of Pathology.

48. Bob Mong, "Trial of Menominees: Clash of Two Cultures," *Capital Times*, 3 December 1975; Bob Mong, "Menominee Shootout Is Mystery," *Capital Times*, 4 February 1976; "News Update on the Menominee Slayings," 2 March 1976; Andre van Vegten, "News Update on the Menominee Slayings," 2 March 1976, all in AFSC Archives. Van Vegten, "Report on the February 3, 1976 Slaying of Two Menominee Warriors," Gordon S. Dickie Sr. Papers, Menominee Historic Preservation Department. Huntington to Richard Stadleman, 10 February 1976; and Autopsy 76:26, both in University of Wisconsin, Medical School, Department of Pathology.

49. Don Mertic, Executive Secretary, and Andre van Vegten, Program Assistant, Native American Affairs, AFSC, to Governor Patrick J. Lucey, 10 February 1976; Bob Mong, "Menominee Group Schedules Reply to Fish's Version," *Capital Times*, 6 February 1976; Bob Mong, "Lucey Will Look into Slayings," *Capital Times*, 7 February 1976, all in AFSC Archives.

50. Van Vegten to Abourezk, 5 March 1976, AFSC Archives.

51. Menominee Indian Tribe of Wisconsin, *Menominee Tribal History Guide*, 97; Ourada, *The Menominee Indians*, 221–22.

52. Ourada, *The Menominee Indians*, 221; Lurie, *Wisconsin Indians*, 55.

53. "NARF Attorney on Constitution," *Menominee Tribal News* 1, no. 2 (November 1976); "Constitution Passes," *Menominee Tribal News* 1, no. 3 (December 1976); Luke E. Beauprey, "Constitution OK'd by Interior," *Menominee Tribal News* 2, no. 2 (February 1977); "Tribal Education Director Speaks Out," *Menominee Tribal News* 1, no. 3 (December 1976), all in Menominee County/Tribal Library. "MRC Leaders in Scuffle Leaving Keshena Meeting." Report of Tribal Investigating Committee, Menominee Tribal Meeting, 25 September 1976, Gordon Dickie Sr. Papers, Menominee Historic Preservation Department. "What's Happening at Menominee Clinic"; Gary Matthews, "Resignation Focusses Attention," and Gary Matthews, "What MRC Says," all from *Shawano Evening Leader*, ca. April 1978, in Scrapbook 1977–1978, Menominee County/Tribal Library.

54. "Ada Deer Resigns from MRC," *Menominee Tribal News* 1, no. 3 (December 1976); "Tribe Elects 3," *Menominee Tribal News* (February 1978), in Menominee County/Tribal Library; Greg Matthews, " 'General Council' Candidates Dominate Menominee Primary," *Shawano Evening Leader*, n.d., and "Fifth election try," n.d., paper unidentified, in Scrapbook 1977–1978, Menominee County/Tribal Library.

55. Election announcements in *Menominee Tribal News* 4, no. 1 (January 1979); "First Menominee General Council, *Menominee Tribal News* 4, no. 4 (April 1979);

"Tribal Judge Deadline Extended," *Menominee Tribal News* 4, no. 6 (June 1979), all in Menominee County/Tribal Library; Menominee Indian Tribe of Wisconsin, *Menominee Tribal History Guide*, 99; Gordon Dickie Sr., interview, Menominee Historic Preservation Department.

56. "Government Gives Reservation Back." See Gordon-McCutchan and Waters, *The Taos Indians*, for a discussion of the return of Blue Lake to the Taos, and Thompson, "The De Facto Termination," for a discussion of the impacts of the Alaska Native Claims Settlement Act.

57. This was not the first case of termination and restoration, however. The earliest case of restoration, according to Charles Wilkinson, occurred in 1868, when the Wyandottes, terminated by an 1855 treaty, regained recognition. The Wyandottes went through the process of termination and restoration again in the 1930s. Wilkinson, "The Passage of Termination Legislation," 1649.

12. TRIBAL SELF-DETERMINATION AND SOVEREIGNTY TODAY

1. Menominee Indian Tribe of Wisconsin, *Menominee Tribal History Guide*, 103–7; [DeLeon], "Menominee Health Care," 1–2; [DeLeon], "Waukau," 1–2.

2. Caldwell, "Wendell Waukau."

3. "Menominee Nation Language and Culture Code."

4. Menominee Indian Tribe of Wisconsin, *Menominee Tribal History Guide*, 103–7; Washinawatok and Wayka, "Status of the Menominee Language," 74–77; Grignon, "New Certified Menominee Language and Culture Teacher"; Alegria, "Menominee Language."

5. The two primary examples of success are the Native Hawaiian Aha Punana Leo schools and the Nizi puh wah sin Center of the Piegan Institute on the Blackfeet reservation in Browning, Montana.

6. NAES College Catalog.

7. "CMN History"; "CMN Scores a First."

8. Menominee Indian Tribe of Wisconsin, "Fact Sheet, Menominee Casino and Bingo," 1991. Thirty-nine percent unemployment is a relatively low number in Indian country.

9. Since at least 1925, even at the height of federal mismanagement, the Menominee forest has been recognized as the finest in the state. Minutes of Council Meeting, 23 May 1925, CCF 1907–1939 Keshena 054, RG 75, NARA-DC.

10. "Menominee Nation Recognized."

11. Letter from August L. Corn Sr. et al, "'MTE practices unacceptable' say Menominee loggers," *Menominee Nation News* 23, no. 12 (17 June 1999): 3. See also letter from Tony Wilbur, "White Oak Has More Value than Market Value," *Menominee Nation News* 28, no. 4 (23 February 2004): 3.

12. Interviews with Menominee people.

13. Gordon Dickie testimony, "Transcript of Proceedings"; Menominee Historic Preservation Department. "Statement of Gordon Dickie, Chairman, Menominee Tribal Legislature, Before United States Senate Committee on Energy and Natural Resources Subcommittee on Energy Research and Development, 16 June 1986, and Dickie to Secretary of Energy, 16 April 1986," Gordon S. Dickie Sr. Papers, Menominee Historic Preservation Department.

14. Menominee Indian Tribe of Wisconsin, "Fact Sheet, Menominee Nation Casino and Bingo," 1991.

15. Dickenson, "Anniversary"; Stockes, "HHS Nominee."

16. "Poverty Levels, Rates, and Ranks, All Counties"; Sandler and Barrett, "State Median Income."

17. "Public Health."

18. "Constitution and Bylaws."

19. Chapman, "The Menominee Constitution"; Beck, "Historical Overview." Some of the text in the following paragraphs is from the latter source.

20. Interviews with Menominee people.

21. *United States of America v. Frank Long.*

22. Some of the text in the section on sturgeon is from Beck, "Return to *Namä'o Uskíwämît*"; interviews with Menominee people.

23. Runstrom, Bruch, Reiter, and Cox, "Lake Sturgeon," 481–83.

24. Runstrom, Bruch, Reiter, and Cox, "Lake Sturgeon," 481, 483–84; "Biologists Will Sample Legend Lake"; Reiter, "1st Annual Lake Sturgeon Fishery."

25. Beck, "Collecting"; "Ancestors Repatriated"; Grignon, "Menominee Ancestors Repatriated"; "Repatriation Notice," Menominee Historic Preservation Department; interviews with Menominee people.

26. *Menominee Indian Tribe of Wisconsin v. Tommy G. Thompson, et al.* case file, United States District Court, Madison; Melmer, "Menominee Lose," A1, A3; Squires, "Teller Hints at Treaty Ruling Appeal"; "Menominee Treaty Rights Claim"; "Judge Dismisses Indian Treaty Rights Claim"; "Menominees to Appeal Decision"; Janetta, "The Constitutional Status," 302–3; Cohen, *A Handbook of Federal Indian Law*, 37–38; *Menominee Indian Tribe of Wisconsin v. Tommy G. Thompson et al.*, 161 F. 3d 449. On the Ojibwe cases, see Whaley and Bresette, *Walleye Warriors*, and Nesper, *Walleye War*.

27. Docket No. 134–67; "Clinton Signs Bill"; Menominee Indian Tribe of Wisconsin, *Menominee Tribal History Guide*, 103.

28. Mason, *Indian Gaming*, 59–66.

29. Edgar Bowen, personal communication with author.

30. Beck, "Return to *Namä'o Uskíwämît*"; Beck, "The Importance of Wild Rice"; Davis, *Sustaining the Forest.*

BIBLIOGRAPHY

UNPUBLISHED PRIMARY SOURCES

American Friends Service Committee Archives, Philadelphia
AFSC Community Relations Division, Native American Affairs, Regional Offices, Midwest (Chicago).

Beinicke Rare Book and Manuscript Library, Yale University Library
Felix S. Cohen Papers, 1916–92. WA MSS S-1325.

Community Archives of NAES College, Chicago
LaDonna Harris Papers.
Robert Rietz Collection. Fort Berthold Papers.

Federal Bureau of Investigation, Washington DC
Freedom of Information Act Files: Alexian Brothers Novitiate.

General
Edgar Bowen, personal communication with author, 29 January 2003.
Interviews with Menominee people, 1991–2000. The author interviewed Menominees, elders, and others knowledgeable of tribal history, both on the reservation and in Chicago. The author retains notes from all of these interviews but offers anonymity to the interviewees in this written study.

Green Bay Area Research Center, Cofrin Library—Special Collections, University of Wisconsin-Green Bay
Ada Deer Papers. MSS 120.
Menominee Enterprises, Inc. Records, 1954–76. Green Bay MSS 70.
Menominee Tribal News Records, ca. 1974–78. M87-395.

Harry S. Truman Library, Independence, Missouri
Oral History Interview with Oscar R. Ewing. Available at http://www.trumanlibrary.org/oralhist/ewing1.htm. Accessed 18 May 2004.

Illinois State Historical Society Library Manuscript Collections
Illinois Federation of Women's Clubs Papers, Box 17.

Indiana State Library
George W. Ewing Collection. Indiana Division.

L. Tom Perry Special Collections, Harold B. Lee Library, Brigham Young University
Arthur V. Watkins (1866–1973) Papers. MSS 146.
Mitchell Al Dodge Papers. Unprocessed as of summer 2004.

Library of Congress
William O. Douglas Collection.

Marquette University Archives
Sacred Heart Franciscan Provincial Indian Records. Microfilm.

Menominee County/Tribal Library, Keshena
George Kenote Papers.
The Indian Way to Education, an historical, descriptive study of the Menominee County Education Committee and the Menominee Community School. Prepared by the Menominee County Education Committee/Menominee Community School. n.d., 149 pp.
Menominee Tribal News.
Scrapbooks, 1977–78.

Menominee Historic Preservation Department, Keshena
Carl "Chummy" Maskewit. Interview. 30 August 1994. Menominee Tribal Historic Preservation Department, Oral History Program. Excerpt transcribed by David Beck, July 1998.
George W. Kenote. Affidavit Concerning Termination and the Menominee Forest. 2 February 1985.
Gordon Dickie Sr. Interview. 16 March 1993. Menominee Tribal Historic Preservation Department, Oral History Program. Interviewed by David Grignon at Keshena Public Library. Excerpt transcribed by David Beck, May 2001.
Gordon S. Dickie Sr. Papers.
Individual Building Report, Office of Indian Affairs. October 1931.
James Washinawatok. Interview. 4 October 1993. Menominee Tribal Historic Preservation Department, Oral History Program, Phase II Interviews. Interview conducted by Carol Dodge, recorded on videotape. Excerpt transcribed by David Beck, July 1998.
Menominee Tribal Enterprises Records.
"Minutes of Board of Directors Meeting, Menominee Enterprises, Inc. Milwaukee, 1

April 1965. Plaintiff's Supplemental Findings of Fact and Exception for the Basic Case, Part 2, Findings 75–115. *Congressional Reference to the United States Court of Federal Claims.* Congressional Reference No. 93–649x, Judge Bruggink, 20 March 1996.

Mitchel Al Dodge. Interviews. Ninety-third Birthday Interview, 1997. Oral History Interview, 29 September 1993. Menominee Tribal Historic Preservation Department, Oral History Program. Interviewed by Rebecca Alegria and Carol Dodge. Excerpt transcribed by David Beck, December 2001.

"Repatriation Notice." June 2001.

"Report of Dr. Katherine Hall, Plaintiff's Exhibit KH-1, Part 1—Report and Appendix." Vol. 3, Pt. 1. Congressional Reference to the United States Court of Federal Claims, Congressional Reference No. 93–649x, Judge Bruggink, 20 March 1996.

Thomsen, Cristina, Hal Neumann, and John F. Schuttler. *The Forests of the Menominee: Forest Resource Management on the Menominee Indian Reservation, 1854–1992.* Prepared for Menominee Tribal Enterprises, Inc., by Heritage Research Ltd. Missoula MT, 1999.

"Transcript of Proceedings, DOE Hearings on the Draft Recommendation Report for the Crystalline Repository Project." Waupaca WI, 8 April 1986.

United States District Court for the Western District of Wisconsin. Complaint signed by Daniel J. Taaffe and Charles F. Wilkinson, NARF. 25 May 1972, 26 pp.

Menominee Tribal Archives, Keshena

DRUMS Newsletters.

John V. Satterlee. Police diaries. Unpublished photocopy.

Keesing, Felix M., and Marie Keesing. *The Changing American Indian: A Study of the Menomini Tribe of Wisconsin.* 2 vols. Typewritten, n.d.

Kenote, George W. "A Personal Memorandum for Menominee Youth, 1972: A Glance at Catastrophe Judicare Style." Typed manuscript, 50 pp.

Minutes of Menominee General Council and Advisory Council Meetings. 1920–33.

Milwaukee Public Museum Archives

Anthropology Correspondence. Skinner, McKern, 1921–27, original box 65.

National Archives and Record Administration, Great Lakes Region (Chicago)

Hill, Edward E. *Historical Sketches for Jurisdictional and Subject Headings Used for the Letters Received by the Office of Indian Affairs, 1824–1880.* Washington DC: National Archives and Records Service, General Services Administration, 1967. Typed. Record Group 75. Records of the Bureau of Indian Affairs.

Records of the Menominee Indian Mills, 1900–1961.

Records of the Keshena/Menominee Agency, 1892–1961.

National Archives and Records Administration, Washington DC
Record Group 46. Records of the United States Senate.
    Special Committee on Indian Affairs, Committee on Interior and Insular Affairs,
        Sen. 83 A-F9 (70th–82nd).
Record Group 75. Records of the Bureau of Indian Affairs.
    Central Classified Files 1907–9, Green Bay.
    Central Classified Files 1907–39, Keshena.
    Central Classified Files 1940–43, Keshena.
    Letters Received 1881–1907. Entry 91.
    Rosters of Indian Police. 75–982.
    Special Case 143. Special Cases, 1821–1907, Green Bay.
    Special Case 147. Miscellaneous (Menominee).
    Special Case 202. Menominee Logging, Flat Files.

The Newberry Library
Edward E. Ayer Collection.

Smithsonian Institution, National Anthropological Archives
Bridgeman, Alfred F. Menominee vocabulary, Keshena WI, 1874–79. MSS 4990 Menominee.
Scott, Hugh L. Box 5 (La-Roe), Ms 4525.

United States District Court, Madison WI
Menominee Indian Tribe of Wisconsin v. Tommy G. Thompson, et al. Case No. 95 C
    0030 C (W.D. Wis. Jan. 13, 1995).

University of Chicago Special Collections
Sol Tax Papers.

University of Colorado Archives
Omer C. Stewart Collection.

University of Wisconsin, Medical School
Department of Pathology. Autopsy records.

Wisconsin Department of Justice
Division of Criminal Investigation files obtained under the Open Records Act:
    Menominee Warrior Society.

Wisconsin Historical Society Archives

Keesing, Felix. "Leaders of the Menomini Tribe, A Sketch from the Contemporary Records and from the Memories of Old Indians of Today." Typewritten paper with hand-corrected notes n. d., ca. 1930. US/Mss/7E, Folder 1.

Menominee Indian Papers. Wis/Mss/BU.

Wisconsin Historical Society Library

Krautbauer, Bishop. "Missions Among the Menominees in Wisconsin." PAM 52–1474.

Nichols, Phebe Jewell. "Stating the Case for the Menominees." Pamphlet Studies of Wisconsin Indian Problems, No. 1. Copyright Phebe Jewell Nichols, 1931.

GOVERNMENT AND LEGAL DOCUMENTS

1994 Annual Report. Menominee Indian Tribe of Wisconsin.

"An Act to amend the law relating to timber operations on the Menominee Indian Reservation in Wisconsin." *Statutes at Large.* 73d Cong., 2d sess., chap. 539, vol. 48 (1934).

"An Act to authorize the cutting of timber, the manufacture and sale of lumber, and the preservation of the forests on the Menominee Indian Reservation in the State of Wisconsin." *Statutes at Large.* 60th Cong., 1st sess., chap. 111, vol. 35 (1908).

"An act to authorize the cutting, sawing into lumber, and sale of timber on certain lands reserved for the use of the Menominee tribe of Indians, in the State of Wisconsin." *Statutes at Large.* 59th Cong., 1st sess., chap. 3578, vol. 34 (1906).

"An Act to Authorize the Sale of Certain Lands for the Use of the Menomonee Tribe of Indians, in the State of Wisconsin." *Statutes at Large.* 41st Cong., 3d sess., chap. 410, vol. 16 (1871).

"An Act to authorize the sale of timber on certain lands reserved for the use of the Menomonee tribe of Indians, in the State of Wisconsin." *Statutes at Large.* 51st Cong., sess 1., chap. 418, vol. 26 (1890).

"An Act to confer jurisdiction on the States of California, Minnesota, Nebraska, Oregon, and Wisconsin, with respect to criminal offenses and civil causes of action committed or arising on Indian reservations within such States, and for other purposes." Public Law 83–280, *Statutes at Large.* Chap. 505, vol. 67 (1953), 588–90.

"An Act to Provide for the Allotment of Lands in Severalty to Indians on the Various Reservations." *Statutes at Large.* Chap. 119, vol. 24 (1887), 388–91.

"An Act to refer the claim of the Menominee Tribe of Indians to the Court of Claims with the absolute right of appeal to the Supreme Court of the United States." *Statutes at Large.* Chap. 834, vol. 49 (1935).

"An Act to repeal the Act terminating Federal supervision over the property and members of the Menominee Indian Tribe of Wisconsin. . . ." *Statutes at Large.* P.L. 93–197. Vol. 87 (1973).

Annual Reports of the Board of Indian Commissioners.

"Cases Decided in the Court of Claims During the Term of 1918–19. In Which Judgments Were Rendered But No Opinions Delivered." 54 Ct. Cls. 203.

Census 2000 PHC-T-18. American Indian and Alaska Native Tribes in the United States: 2000.

Congressional Record.

Congressional Reference to the United States Court of Federal Claims, Menominee Indian Tribe of Wisconsin v. United States of America. Congressional Reference 93–649x, Judge Bruggink. Charles A. Hobbs, Attorney for Plaintiff. 20 March 1996.

"Constitution and Bylaws of the Menominee Indian Tribe of Wisconsin. Developed by the Menominee Restoration Committee pursuant to §5 of the Menominee Restoration Act (P.L. 93–197, 87 Stat. 770)."

Docket No. 134–67 in the United States Court of Claims. *The Menominee Tribe of Indians, et al. Plaintiffs, v. The United States of America, Defendant.* Vol. I of VII.

Kappler, Charles J. *Indian Affairs: Laws and Treaties.* Vol. 1. Washington DC: Government Printing Office, 1904.

Letters Received by the Office of Indian Affairs, 1824–81. Microcopy 234. Washington DC: National Archives and Records Service, General Services Administration, 1959.

Lone Wolf v. Hitchcock. 187 U.S. 553.

Margold, Nathan. "Solicitor's Opinion." 25 October 1934. In *Opinions of the Solicitor of the Department of the Interior Relating to Indian Affairs, 1917–1974.* Vol. 1. Washington DC: Government Printing Office, n.d., 445–78.

"Menominee Nation Language and Culture Code, Tribal Ordinance No. 96–22, As Amended."

Menominee Indian Tribe of Wisconsin. "Fact Sheet: Menominee Nation Casino and Bingo." 1991.

Menominee Indian Tribe of Wisconsin v. Tommy G. Thompson, et al. 161 F. 3d 449 (7th Cir. 1998), Supreme Court Case 98–1306.

Menominee Tribe of Indians . . . v. the United States, 179 C. Cls. 496 (14 April 1967).

Menominee Tribe of Indians v. The United States, 95 C. Cls. 232 (1 December 1941). Case No. 44294.

Menominee Tribe of Indians v. The United States, 97 C. Cls. 158 (5 October 1942). Case No. 44299.

Menominee Tribe of Indians v. The United States, 101 C. Cls. 10 (7 February 1944). Case No. 44298.

Menominee Tribe of Indians v. The United States, 101 C. Cls. 22 (7 February 1944). Case No. 44303.

Menominee Tribe of Indians v. The United States, 101 C. Cls. 863 Judgment without opinion. Case No. 44294.

Menominee Tribe of Indians v. The United States, 102 C. Cls. 555 (5 March 1945). Case No. 44296.

Menominee Tribe of Indians v. The United States, 107 C. Cls. 23 (7 October 1946). Case No. 44300.

Menominee Tribe of Indians v. United States, 117 C. Cls. 442 (10 July 1950). Case No. 44304.

Menominee Tribe of Indians v. United States, 118 C. Cls. 290 (9 January 1951). Case No. 44303.

Menominee Tribe of Indians v. United States, 119 C. Cls. 832 (13 July 1951). Case Nos. 44304, 44296, 44298, 44300, 44303, 44305, 44306.

Menominee Tribe of Indians v. United States, 391 U.S. 404.

"Poverty Levels, Rates and Ranks, All Counties." 1990 Census Document CPH-L-100.

"Protest of A. Miller, Delegate of the Stockbridge Nation of Indians." Senate Mis. Doc. 119, 48th Cong., 1st sess. (1884).

Public Papers of the Presidents of the United States, Richard Nixon, 1973. Washington DC: United States Government Printing Office, 1975.

Public Papers of the Presidents of the United States, Richard Nixon, 1974. Washington DC: United States Government Printing Office, 1975.

Reports of the Commissioner of Indian Affairs. 1854–1910.

State v. Sanapaw, 21 Wis. 2d 377, 124 N.W. 2d 41.

State v. Sanapaw, 377 U.S. 991.

U.S. Congress. Ex Doc. No. 4. In *The United States and the Indians, 36th Congress, 1860.* 36th Cong., 2d sess. 1860.

U.S. Congress. House. Committee on Indian Affairs. "Menominee Tribe of Indians to Employ General Attorneys." House Report 1527, 71st Cong., 2d sess. (19 May 1930).

U.S. Congress. House. Committee on Interior and Insular Affairs, Subcommittee on Indian Affairs. Hearings on H.R. 7104, 20 March 1952.

U.S. Congress. House. Committee on the Public Lands. "Report to Authorize Investigation as to the Desirability of the Establishment of a National Park on a Portion of Menominee Indian Reservation in Wisconsin." H.R. 1343, 71st Cong., 2d sess. (30 April 1930).

U.S. Congress. House. HR 6869. 68th Cong., 2d sess. *Congressional Record* (21 January 1925). Vol. 66, pt. 3.

U.S. Congress. House. Representative Morse. S. 4046. 60th Cong., 1st sess. *Congressional Record* (16 March 1908). Vol. 42, pt. 4.

U.S. Congress. House. Subcommittee on Indian Affairs of the Committee on Interior and Insular Affairs. *Menominee Restoration Act, Hearings Before the Subcommittee on Indian Affairs of the Committee on Interior and Insular Affairs, House of Representatives.* (1973). 93d Cong., 1st sess. Serial 93–20.

U.S. Congress. Joint. Subcommittees on Interior and Insular Affairs. *Termination of Federal Supervision Over Certain Tribes of Indians: Joint Hearing Before the Subcommittees on Interior and Insular Affairs.* (1954). 83d Cong., 2d sess.

U.S. Congress. Senate. Committee on Indian Affairs. "Menominee Tribe of Indians to Employ General Attorneys." Senate Report 1582, 71st Cong. 3d sess. (26 January 1931).

U.S. Congress. Senate. Ex. Doc. No. 72. Vol. 41 of *The United States and the Indians, a Collection of Congressional Documents Relating to the Indians.* 34th Cong. (1856).

U.S. Congress. Senate. Hearings Before the Subcommittee on Employment and Manpower of the Committee on Labor and Public Welfare. "Menominee County Aid Hearings on S. 1934." 89th Cong., 1st and 2d sess. 10 and 11 November 1965 and 17 February 1966.

U.S. Congress. Senate. Letter from James Rudolph Garfield, Secretary of the Interior, to Senator La Follette. 21 January 1908. 60th Cong., 1st sess. *Congressional Record* (28 January 1908). Vol. 42, pt. 1.

U.S. Congress. Senate. Report No. 1113. 68th Cong., 2d sess. (3 February 1925).

U.S. Congress. Senate. Report of Senator LaFollette. S. 4046. 60th Cong., 1st sess. *Congressional Record* (28 January 1908). Vol. 42, pt. 1.

United States of America v. Frank Long, 324 F. 3d 475 (7th Cir. 2003).

UNPUBLISHED PAPERS, SECONDARY SOURCES, AND
PUBLISHED PRIMARY SOURCES

Alegria, Francisco. "Menominee Language Training Course." *Menominee Nation News* 28, no. 23 (6 December 2004): 8.

Alegria, Rebecca D. "Historic River Drive Sites on the Wolf." Senior Field Project. NAES College, Keshena WI, 1995.

Allen, E. A. "The Indian—Federal and State Responsibility." *Red Man* 8, no. 2 (October 1915): 39–45.

American Indian Resource Institute. *Indian Tribes as Sovereign Governments: A Sourcebook on Federal-Tribal History, Law, and Policy.* Oakland: AIRI Press, 1988.

"Ancestors Repatriated from Oshkosh Public Museum." *Menominee Nation News* 25, no. 12 (23 June 2001): 18.

Aq-Ua-Chamine (Menominee Talking): The Menominee Restoration Committee Newsletter. 1974–76. In author's possession.

"Armed Indians Take Over Estate in Shawano County." *Milwaukee Sentinel*, 2 January 1975.

Aukofer, Frank A. "$32 Million Settlement for Menominee Indians Clears U.S. Senate." *JS Online: Milwaukee Journal Sentinel*, 3 July 1999.

Ayer, Edward E. *Report on Menominee Indian Reservation*. 1914.

Barrett, S. A. "The Dream Dance of the Chippewa and Menominee Indians of Northern Wisconsin." *Bulletin of the Public Museum of the City of Milwaukee* 1 (November 1911): 252–407.

Barry, Dave. *Dave Barry Slept Here: A Sort of History of the United States*. New York: Fawcett Columbine, 1989.

Basso, Keith H. *Wisdom Sits in Places: Landscape and Language among the Western Apache*. Albuquerque: University of New Mexico Press, 1996.

Beaulieu, David L. "Curly Hair and Big Feet: Physical Anthropology and the Implementation of Land Allotment on the White Earth Chippewa Reservation." *American Indian Quarterly* 8, no. 4 (1984): 281–314.

Beck, David R. M. "'Bribed with Our Own Money.'" Paper presented at American Society for Ethnohistory Conference, October 2001.

———. "'Collecting Among the Menominee': The Failure of Ethnologists to Destroy an Indigenous Culture." Paper presented at the Native American Studies Conference at Lake Superior State University in Sault Ste. Marie MI, October 1991.

———. "Historical Overview." In "Designing the Economic Future of the Menominee Peoples," by Benjamin J. Broome with LaDonna Harris, 2–6. Washington DC: Americans for Indian Opportunity, 1991.

———. "The Importance of Wild Rice in Menominee in Menominee History as Viewed through Some Documentary Sources." Chicago: NAES College Tribal Research Center, August 1994.

———. "The Myth of the Vanishing Race." Edward S. Curtis's The North American Indian Web site, Northwestern University Library and Library of Congress, 2001, http://memory.loc.gov/ammem/award98/ienhtml/essay2.html. Accessed 22 December 2004.

———. "Return to *Namä'o Uskíwämît*: The Importance of Sturgeon in Menominee Indian History." *Wisconsin Magazine of History* 79, no. 1 (autumn 1995): 32–48.

———. *Siege and Survival: History of the Menominee Indians, 1634–1856*. Lincoln: University of Nebraska Press, 2002.

———. "An Urban Platform for Advocating Justice: Protecting the Menominee Forest." In *American Indians and the Urban Experience*, ed. Susan Lobo and Kurt Peters, 155–62. Walnut Creek CA: AltaMira Press, 2001.

Bilharz, Joy A. *The Allegheny Senecas and Kinzua Dam*. Lincoln: University of Nebraska Press, 1998.

Binnema, Theodore. *Common and Contested Ground: A Human and Environmental History of the Northwestern Plains*. Norman: University of Oklahoma Press, 2001.

"Biologists Will Sample Legend Lake for Lake Sturgeon." Submitted article, Menominee Conservation Department. *Menominee Nation News* 28, no. 18 (27 September 2004): 6.

Bittle, Rev. Celestine N., O.M. Cap. *A Romance of Lady Poverty: The History of the Province of St. Joseph of the Capuchin Order in the United States*. New York: Bruce Publishing Company, 1933.

The Book of Mormon. Salt Lake City: Church of Jesus Christ of Latter-Day Saints, 2000.

Burnham, Philip. *Indian Country, God's Country: Native Americans and the National Parks*. Washington DC: Island Press, 2000.

Burt, Larry W. *Tribalism in Crisis: Federal Indian Policy, 1953–1961*. Albuquerque: University of New Mexico Press, 1982.

Caldwell, Charlotte. "Wendell Waukau, 1st Menominee as Superintendent of Schools." *Menominee Nation News* 27, no. 14 (21 July 2003): 16.

Castile, George Pierre. *To Show Heart: Native American Self Determination and Federal Indian Policy, 1960–1975*. Tucson: University of Arizona Press, 1998.

Chapman, Michael. "The Menominee Constitution, Model or Muddle." n.d [1980s]. Unpublished paper.

————. "Reflections on the 30th Anniversary of Menominee Restoration." *Menominee Nation News* 28, no. 1 (12 January 2004): 3. Also in *Shawano Evening Leader*, 31 December 2003.

Clark, Blue. *Lone Wolf v. Hitchcock: Treaty Rights and Indian Law at the End of the Nineteenth Century*. Lincoln: University of Nebraska Press, 1999.

Clinton, Robert N., Nell Jessup Newton, and Monroe E. Price. *American Indian Law: Cases and Materials*. 3d ed. Charlottesville VA: Michie Company, 1991.

"Clinton Signs Bill That Compensates Menominee Indians." Associated Press state and local wires, 17 August 1999, a.m. cycle.

Clow, Richmond. "The Indian Yeoman and His Forest." Unpublished manuscript.

Clow, Richmond L., and Imre Sutton, eds. *Trusteeship in Change: Toward Tribal Autonomy in Resource Management*. Boulder: University Press of Colorado, 2001.

"CMN History." College of the Menominee Nation Web site, http://www.menominee.edu. Accessed 20 June 2004.

"CMN Scores a First with UW-Madison." *Tribal College* 14, no. 1 (2002): 56.

Cohen, Felix S. *A Handbook of Federal Indian Law*. Washington DC: Government Printing Office, 1942.

Collier, John. "The Menominee of Wisconsin and the Klamath of Oregon Cases:

How to make rich Indians poor; and why; and how to destroy established conservation practices; and why. And the immediate issue before Congress." April
1957. Unpublished paper.

Cowger, Thomas W. *The National Congress of American Indians: The Founding Years.*
Lincoln: University of Nebraska Press, 1999.

Cronon, William. *Nature's Metropolis: Chicago and the Great West.* New York: W. W.
Norton and Co., 1991.

Current, Richard Nelson. *Pine Logs and Politics: A Life of Philetus Sawyer, 1816–1900.*
Madison: State Historical Society of Wisconsin, 1950.

Davis, Thomas. *Sustaining the Forest, the People, and the Spirit.* Albany: State University of New York Press, 2000.

Deer, Ada E. "The Menominee Restoration Act." *American Indian Culture Center
Journal* 4, no. 2 (fall 1973): 29–30.

[DeLeon, Verna]. "Menominee Health Care—A Vision for Future Generations."
Menominee Nation News, 26 September 1996. Special Insert.

[DeLeon, Verna]. "Waukau: Dedicated Clinic Administrator for the Past 11 Years."
Menominee Nation News, 26 September 1996. Special Insert.

Deloria, Vine, Jr. *Custer Died for Your Sins.* New York: Avon Books, 1970. First
published 1969.

Deloria, Vine, Jr., and Clifford M. Lytle. *American Indians, American Justice.* Austin:
University of Texas, 1983.

———. *The Nations Within: The Past and Future of American Indian Sovereignty.*
Austin: University of Texas Press, 1998. First published 1984.

Dening, Greg. "History 'in' the Pacific." In *Voyaging through the Contemporary
Pacific,* ed. David Hanlon and Geoffrey M. White, 135–40. Lanham MD: Rowman
and Littlefield Publishers, 2000.

Dickenson, Kamay. "Anniversary: Menominee Casino Longest Running in Indian
Country." *Menominee Nation News* 21, no. 17 (26 September 1997).

DRUMS Newsletter. 1972–74. In author's possession.

Farrell, William E. "Guardsman's Leader Predicts Accord on Indians' Take-Over."
New York Times, 29 January 1975.

"Fire Bombs, Shots Shake Reservation." *Milwaukee Journal,* 11 July 1975, 1, 9.

Fixico, Donald L. *Termination and Relocation: Federal Indian Policy, 1945–1960.* Albuquerque: University of New Mexico Press, 1986.

"Freedom Plan Okayed by Menominee Indians." *Milwaukee Journal,* 23 June 1953.

Fries, Robert F. *Empire in Pine: The Story of Lumbering in Wisconsin, 1830–1900.*
Rev. ed. Evanston IL: Wm. Caxton, 1989. First published 1951 by State Historical
Society of Wisconsin, 1951.

Gachet, Father Anthony Maria. "Journal of a Missionary Among the Redskins—
Journal, 1859." Translated from *Cinq Ans in Amérique,* in *Wisconsin Magazine of*

History 18, no. 1 (1934–35): 68–76; 18, no. 2 (1934–35): 191–204; 18, no. 3 (1934–35): 345–59.

Gauthier, JoAnne M. "Economic Development and the Menominee Indian Tribe of Wisconsin." May 1999. Unpublished paper.

Gordon-McCutchan, R. C., and Frank Waters. *The Taos Indians and the Battle for Blue Lake*. Santa Fe: Red Crane Books, 1995.

"Government Gives Reservation Back to the Menominees." *New York Times*, 24 April 1975, 40.

Grignon, David J. (Nahwahquaw). "Menominee Ancestors Repatriated." *Menominee Nation News* 27, no. 23 (8 December 2003): 1, 4.

———. "New Certified Menominee Language and Culture Teacher." *Menominee Nation News* 28, no. 6 (22 March 2004): 1, 13.

Habig, Marion A., O.F.M. *Heralds of the King: The Franciscans of the St. Louis-Chicago Province, 1858–1958*. Chicago: Franciscan Herald Press, 1958.

Harris, LaDonna, in collaboration with Jacqueline Wasilewski. "This Is What We Want to Share: Core Cultural Values." Bernalillo NM: Americans for Indian Opportunity Contemporary Tribal Governance Series, 1992.

Hart, Paxton. "The Making of Menominee County." *Wisconsin Magazine of History* 43, no. 3 (spring 1960): 181–89.

Hau'ofa, Epeli. "Epilogue, Pasts to Remember." In *Remembrance of Pacific Pasts*, ed. Robert Borofsky, 453–71. Honolulu: University of Hawaii Press, 2000.

Haynal, Patrick Mann. "From Termination through Restoration and Beyond: Modern Klamath Cultural Identity." PhD diss., University of Oregon, 1994.

Hensel, Pat. "Alexians Halt Deal to Give Up Novitiate." *Milwaukee Journal*, 10 July 1975, 1, 14.

———. "Arson Suspected in 2 Fires at Firms Near Reservation." *Milwaukee Journal*, 15 July 1975, 14.

———. "Reservation Area Quiet but Tense." *Milwaukee Journal*, 12 July 1975, 1, 6.

Herzberg, Stephen J. "The Menominee Indians: From Treaty to Termination." *Wisconsin Magazine of History* 60, no. 4 (summer 1977): 267–329.

———. "The Menominee Indians: Termination to Restoration." *American Indian Law Review* 6, no. 1 (summer 1978): 143–86.

Hill, Edward E. *Guide to Records in the National Archives of the United States Relating to American Indians*. Washington DC: National Archives and Records Service, General Services Administration, 1981.

Hobbs, Charles A. "Indian Hunting and Fishing Rights II." *George Washington Law Review* 37, no. 5 (July 1969): 1251–73.

Hoffman, Walter James. *The Menomini Indians*. New York: Johnson Reprint Organization, 1970. First published as one of several reports attached to the *14th*

Annual Report of the U.S. Bureau of Ethnology, 1892–93, Washington DC: Government Printing Office, 1896.

Hosmer, Brian. "Creating Indian Entrepreneurs: Menominees, Neopit Mills, and Timber Exploitation, 1890–1915." *American Indian Culture and Research Journal* 15, no. 1 (1991): 1–28.

Hosmer, Brian C. *American Indians in the Marketplace: Persistence and Innovation among the Menominees and the Metlakahtlans, 1870–1920*. Lawrence: University Press of Kansas, 1999.

———. "Reflections on Indian Cultural 'Brokers': Reginald Oshkosh, Mitchell Oshkenaniew, and the Politics of Menominee Lumbering." *Ethnohistory* 44, no. 3 (1997): 493–509.

Hosmer, Brian Cooper. "Experiments in Capitalism: Market Economics, Wage Labor, and Social Change among the Menominees and Metlakahtlans, 1860–1920." PhD diss., University of Texas at Austin, 1993.

House, Charles. "Abandonment or Freedom? 'Great Knife' Cuts Menominee Bonds; Indians Study Cause." *Milwaukee Sentinel*, 15 August 1954, Profile Section, 1, 2.

———. "Freedom or Abandonment? Menominees Fear Another Betrayal." *Milwaukee Sentinel*, 29 August 1954, Profile Section, 1, 4.

Hurst, James Willard. *Law and Economic Growth: The Legal History of the Lumber Industry in Wisconsin, 1836–1915*. Cambridge MA: Belknap Press of Harvard University Press, 1964.

"Indian Road Suit Deferred, Question of Jurisdiction Raised in Logging Case." *Milwaukee Journal*, 21 September 1929.

"Indian Witness Raps Land Sales." *Green Bay Press-Gazette*, 18 September 1973.

"Indians Block U.S. Log Road, Obtain Writ to Halt Construction from Judge Geiger." *Milwaukee Journal*, 6 September 1929.

Janetta, James M. "The Constitutional Status of Native Hunting and Fishing Rights in Canada and the United States: A Comparative Analysis." In *Native American Values: Survival and Renewal*, ed. Thomas E. Schirer and Susan M. Branstner, 297–309. Sault Ste. Marie MI: Lake Superior State University, 1993.

Josephy, Alvin M., Jr. *Now That the Buffalo's Gone: A Study of Today's American Indians*. New York: Alfred A. Knopf, 1982.

"Judge Dismisses Indian Treaty Rights Claim." *Masinaigan* (fall 1996):15.

Kalinoski, Lynda L. "The Termination Crisis: The Menominee Indians Versus the Federal Government, 1943–1961." PhD diss., University of Toledo, 1983.

Kappler, Charles J. *Indian Treaties, 1778–1883*. New York: Interland Publishing Company, 1972. First published 1904.

Keesing, Felix M. "Applied Anthropology in Colonial Administration." In *The Science of Man in the World Crisis*, ed. Ralph Linton, 373–98. New York: Columbia University Press, 1945.

―――. *The Menomini Indians of Wisconsin: A Study of Three Centuries of Contact.* Madison: University of Wisconsin Press, 1987. First published in 1939.

Keller, Robert H. *American Protestantism and United States Indian Policy, 1869–82.* Lincoln: University of Nebraska Press, 1983.

Kinney, J. P. *Indian Forest and Range: A History of the Administration and Conservation of the Redman's Heritage.* Washington DC: Forestry Enterprises, 1950.

Krautbauer, Rt. Rev. F. X. "Short Sketch of the History of the Menominee Indians of Wisconsin, and the Catholic Missions Among Them." *American Catholic Historical Researches* (October 1887):152–58.

Lawson, Michael L. *Dammed Indians: The Pick-Sloan Plan and the Missouri River Sioux.* Norman: University of Oklahoma Press, 1982.

Legro, Ron. "Deputy Guilty in Kin's Death in '60." *Milwaukee Sentinel*, 24 April 1975.

Loew, Patty. *Indian Nations of Wisconsin: Histories of Endurance and Renewal.* Madison: Wisconsin Historical Society Press, 2001.

Lurie, Nancy Oestreich. "Ada Deer, Champion of Tribal Sovereignty." In *Sifters: Native American Women's Lives,* ed. Theda Purdue, 223–41. New York: Oxford University Press, 2001.

―――. "The Menominee Indians, Menominee Termination: Or, Can the White Man Ever Overcome a Cultural Lag to Progress with the Indians?" *Indian Historian* 4, no. 4 (winter 1971): 31–43.

―――. "Menominee Termination: From Reservation to Colony." *Human Organization* 31, no. 3 (fall 1972): 257–70.

―――. *Wisconsin Indians.* Madison: State Historical Society of Wisconsin, 1987.

Martino, Sam. "Novitiate Wiretap Apparently Improper." *Milwaukee Journal*, 15 April 1975, 13.

Martis, Kenneth C. *The Historical Atlas of United States Congressional Districts, 1789–1983.* New York: Free Press, 1982.

Mason, W. Dale. *Indian Gaming: Tribal Sovereignty in American Politics.* Norman: University of Oklahoma Press, 2000.

McCauley, Clay. "The Dreamers among the North American Indians, as Illustrative of the Origin of Forms of Religion, A Lecture Given Before the Tokyo Conference, . . . March 9th, 1893." *Japan Weekly Mail*, 18 March 1893, 338–40.

McDonnell, Janet A. *The Dispossession of the American Indian, 1887–1934.* Bloomington: Indiana University Press, 1991.

Meier, Peg. "A Photographic Treasure Reappears." *Minneapolis Tribune*, 16 April 1978, Picture Section.

Melmer, David. "Menominee Lose Their Treaty Rights." *Indian Country Today*, week of 30 September–7 October 1996, A1, A3.

Menominee Indian Tribe of Wisconsin Historic Preservation Department. *Me-*

nominee *Tribal History Guide, Commemorating Wisconsin Sesquicentennial, 1848–1998.* Keshena, May 1998.

"Menominee Indians to Back Three-Year Freedom Plan." *Minneapolis Star,* 23 June 1953.

Menominee Nation News. See *Menominee Tribal News/Menominee Nation News.*

"Menominee Nation Recognized for Sustainable Forest Management Model." *News from Indian Country* 6, no. 9 (mid-May 1992): 3.

"Menominee Treaty Rights Claim to Be Appealed." *News from Indian Country* 10, no. 17 (mid-October 1996): 1A, 5A.

Menominee Tribal Enterprises. *Relevant Documents Affecting the Menominee Indian Tribe of Wisconsin.* Rev. ed. Neopit WI, 14 November 1986.

Menominee Tribal News/Menominee Nation News. 1991–2004. In author's possession.

"Menominees to Appeal Decision." *Masinaigan* (fall 1996):15.

"Menominees Will Attempt to Settle Their Difficulties With Government." *Shawano County Journal,* 22 February 1940.

"Menominees' Full Freedom Assured at General Council." *Shawano Leader,* 22 June 1953.

Meriam, Lewis, et al. *The Problem of Indian Administration.* New York: Johnson Reprint Company, 1971. First published 1928.

Metcalf, R. Warren. *Termination's Legacy: The Discarded Indians of Utah.* Lincoln: University of Nebraska Press, 2002.

Meyer, Melissa. *White Earth Tragedy: Ethnicity and Dispossession at a Minnesota Anishinaabe Reservation, 1889–1920.* Lincoln: University of Nebraska Press, 1994.

Meyer, Roy W. "Fort Berthold and the Garrison Dam." *North Dakota History* 35 (1968): 217–355.

"MRC Leaders in Scuffle Leaving Keshena Meeting." *Shawano Evening Leader,* 7 April 1975, 1, 4.

NAES College Catalog. 2000–2002.

Nesbit, Robert C. *Wisconsin: A History.* Madison: University of Wisconsin Press, 1973.

Nesper, Larry. *Walleye War: The Struggle for Ojibwe Spearfishing and Treaty Rights.* Lincoln: University of Nebraska Press, 2002.

"New Deal Possible: Alexians." *Milwaukee Journal,* 13 July 1975, 1, 19.

Newman, James Gilbert. "The Menominee Forest of Wisconsin: A Case History in American Forest Management." PhD diss., Michigan State University, 1967.

Nichols, Phebe Jewell. *Sunrise of the Menominees: A Story of Wisconsin Indians.* Boston: Stratford Company, 1930.

"Offers Indians' Land for Park, Chief Oshkosh Maps New Plan to Thwart Power Invasion." *Milwaukee Journal,* 25 September 1929, 4.

"On, Wisconsin, Stumbling Alexians Worsen Trouble at Gresham." *Milwaukee Journal*, 15 July 1975, 16.

Orfield, Gary Allan. "Ideology and the Indians: A Study of the Termination Policy." MA thesis, University of Chicago, 1965.

Ourada, Patricia K. *The Menominee Indians: A History*. Norman: University of Oklahoma Press, 1979.

Peroff, Nicholas. *Menominee Drums: Tribal Termination and Restoration, 1954–1974*. Norman: University of Oklahoma Press, 1982.

Philp, Kenneth R., ed. *Indian Self-Rule: First Hand Accounts of Indian-White Relations from Roosevelt to Reagan*. Logan: Utah State University Press, 1995.

———. *Termination Revisited: American Indians on the Trail of Self-Determination*. Lincoln: University of Nebraska Press, 1999.

Preloznik, Joseph H., and Steven Felsenthal. "The Menominee Struggle to Maintain Their Tribal Assets and Protect Their Treaty Rights Following Termination." *North Dakota Law Review* 51 (1974–75): 53–71.

Price, John A. "Mormon Missionaries to the Indians." In *Handbook of American Indians*, vol. 4, *History of Indian-White Relations*, ed. Wilcomb E. Washburn, 459–63. Washington DC: Smithsonian Institution, 1988.

Priest, Loring B. "Biography, Flora Warren Seymour." In *Handbook of North American Indians*, vol. 4, *History of Indian-White Relations*, ed. Wilcomb E. Washburn, 684. Washington DC: Smithsonian Institution, 1988.

Prucha, Francis Paul. *American Indian Treaties: The History of a Political Anomaly*. Berkeley: University of California Press, 1994.

———. *The Churches and the Indian Schools, 1888–1912*. Lincoln: University of Nebraska Press, 1979.

"Public Health: Suburban County State's Healthiest." *TwinCities.com*, 29 January 2004, http://www.twincities.com/mld/pioneerpress/news/local/states/wisconsin/7819994.htm. Accessed 26 April 2004.

Ray, Verne F. *The Menominee Tribe of Indians, 1940–1970*. United States Court of Claims Docket No. 134–167, . . . Plaintiff's Exhibit R-1. Escanaba MI: Photo Offset Company, 1972.

Reiter, Donald J. "1st Annual Lake Sturgeon Fishery." *Menominee Nation News* 29, no. 1 (10 January 2005): 14.

"Removal of Indian Office to Chicago Is Accomplished." *Indians at Work* 10, no. 1 (1942): 7.

Rick, Patrick, writer and director. *The Novitiate*. Laguna Hills CA: Counterfeit Bill Productions, 2001. Documentary film.

Rosaldo, Renato. *Culture and Truth: The Remaking of Social Analysis*. Boston: Beacon Press, 1989.

Rosenthal, Harvey D. "Indian Claims and the American Conscience: A Brief His-

tory of the Indian Claims Commission." In *Irredeemable America: The Indians'
Estate and Land Claims*, ed. Imre Sutton, 35–70. Albuquerque: University of New
Mexico Press, 1985.

Rosholt, Malcolm, and John Britten Gehl. *Florimond J. Bonduel: Missionary to Wisconsin Territory*. Rosholt WI: Rosholt House, 1976.

Runstrom, A., R. M. Bruch, D. Reiter, and D. Cox. "Lake Sturgeon (*Acipenser fulve-
cens*) on the Menominee Indian Reservation: An Effort toward Co-management
and Population Restoration." *Journal of Applied Ichthyology* 18 (2002): 481–85.

Runte, Alfred. *National Parks: The American Experience*. Lincoln: University of Nebraska Press, 1979.

Sady, Rachel Reese. "The Menominees: Transition from Trusteeship." *Applied Anthropology: Problems in Human Organization* 6, no. 2 (spring 1947): 1–14.

Sandler, Larry, and Rick Barrett. "State Median Income up 14% in 1990s, but Census
Also Says Gap between Richest, Poorest Areas Widens." *JS Online: Milwaukee
Journal Sentinel*, 15 May 2002.

"Scapegoatism." *Milwaukee Sentinel*, 18 July 1975, 12.

Shames, Deborah, ed. *Freedom with Reservation: The Menominee Struggle to Save
Their Land and People*. Madison: Committee to Save the Menominee People and
Forests, 1972.

Shawano County Advocate.

Shillinger, Sarah. "'They Never Told Us They Wanted to Help Us': An Oral History
of Saint Joseph's Indian Industrial School." PhD diss., University of Pennsylva-
nia, 1995.

Skinner, Alanson. *Material Culture of the Menomini*. In *Indian Notes and Mono-
graphs*, ed. F. W. Hodge, vol. 20. New York: Museum of the American Indian,
Heye Foundation, 1921.

Slotkin, J. S. *Menomini Peyotism: A Study of Individual Variation in a Primary Group
with a Homogenous Culture. Transactions of the American Philosophical Society*.
Philadelphia, N.S. 42, no. 4 (1952): 535–700.

Slotkin, James S. *The Menomini Powwow: A Study in Cultural Decay*. Milwaukee
Public Museum Publications in Anthropology, No. 4. Milwaukee, 1957.

Smith, E. B., comp. *Indian Tribal Claims Decided in the Court of Claims of the United
States, Briefed and Compiled to June 30, 1947*. Vol. 2. Washington DC: University
Publications of America, n.d. [ca. 1976; first published in 1947].

Smith, Linda Tuhiwai. *Decolonizing Methodologies: Research and Indigenous Peoples*.
London: Zed Books, 1999.

Spence, Mark David. *Dispossessing the Wilderness: Indian Removal and the Making
of the National Parks*. Oxford: Oxford University Press, 1999.

Spicer, Edward H. "American Indians, Federal Policy Toward." In *Harvard Encyclo-*

pedia of American Ethnic Groups, ed. Stephan Thernstrom, 114–22. Cambridge MA: Belknap Press, 1980.

Spindler, Louise S. "Menominee." In *Handbook of North American Indians*, vol. 15, *Northeast*, ed. Bruce G. Trigger, 708–24. Washington DC: Smithsonian Institution, 1978.

"Squaws Rule Wigwam Now, Redskin Sighs." *Chicago Tribune*, 7 February 1927. Accessed through *Chicago Tribune* online archive, NewsBank InfoWeb, on 11 August 2004.

Squires, Susan. "Teller Hints at Treaty Ruling Appeal." *Shawano Leader*, 29 September 1996.

Stewart, Omer C. *Peyote Religion: A History*. Norman: University of Oklahoma Press, 1987.

Stockes, Brian. "HHS Nominee Familiar Figure to Tribes." *Indian Country Today* 20, no. 32 (24 January 2001): A2.

Szasz, Margaret Connell. *Education and the American Indian: The Road to Self-Determination Since 1928*. 3d ed. Albuquerque: University of New Mexico Press, 1999.

Tabachnick, David Edgemon. "Fence of Ownership: Common Property versus Individual Property Regimes in England, France, Africa, and the United States." PhD diss., University of Wisconsin-Madison, 2001.

Thompson, Benjamin W. "The De Facto Termination of Alaska Native Sovereignty: An Anomaly in an Era of Self-Determination." *American Indian Law Review* 24, no. 2 (1999–2000): 421–54.

Thompson, Gregory C. "John D. C. Atkins, 1885–88." In *The Commissioners of Indian Affairs, 1824–1977*, ed. Robert M. Kvasnicka and Herman J. Viola, 181–84. Lincoln: University of Nebraska Press, 1979.

Trennert, Robert A. *Alternative to Extinction: Federal Indian Policy and the Beginnings of the Reservation System, 1846–51*. Philadelphia: Temple University Press, 1975.

"Tribal Fund Depleted by Incompetent Officials, Indians Contend." *Milwaukee Journal*, 22 September 1929, 2.

Tronnes, Libby R. "'Where Is John Wayne?' The Menominee Warrior Society and Social Unrest during the Alexian Brothers Novitiate Takeover." *American Indian Quarterly* 26, no. 4 (2002): 526–58.

Tyler, S. Lyman. "Indian Affairs: A Work Paper on Termination, with an Attempt to Show Its Antecedents." A Publication of the Institute of American Indian Studies. Provo UT: Brigham Young University, 1964.

Washinawatok, Karen, and Rose Wayka. "Status of the Menominee Language (1998)." *Red Ink* 7, no. 2 (spring 1999): 72–79.

Watkins, Arthur V. "Termination of Federal Supervision: The Removal of Restrictions over Indian Property and Person." *Annals of the American Academy of Political and Social Science* 311 (May 1957): 47–55.

Weil, Richard H. "Destroying a Homeland: White Earth, Minnesota." *American Indian Culture and Research Journal* 13, no. 2 (1989): 69–95.

Whaley, Rick, with Walt Bresette. *Walleye Warriors: The Chippewa Treaty Rights Story.* Warner NH: Writers Publishing Cooperative, 1999.

Wilk, Stuart. "Armed Men Patrol at Novitiate." *Milwaukee Sentinel,* 14 July 1975, 1, 13.

———. "Novitiate Action Tied to 2 Fires." *Milwaukee Sentinel,* 15 July 1975.

———. "State, Indian Leaders Lash Out at Alexians." *Milwaukee Sentinel,* 12 July 1975, 1, 10.

———. "Tribe Agrees on Restoration." *Milwaukee Sentinel,* 21 April 1975, pt. 1, p. 8.

Wilkinson, Charles. "The Passage of Termination Legislation." In *Report on Terminated and Nonfederally Recognized Indians,* Final Report to the American Indian Policy Review Commission, 1625–49. Washington DC: Government Printing Office, October 1976.

"Wolf River's Beauty Seems Prey to Power, Indians Claim Whites Have Made Money on Other Lands, It's Their Right Now." *Milwaukee Journal,* 15 September 1929.

Youngbear-Tibbets, Holly. "Without Due Process: The Alienation of Individual Trust Allotments of the White Earth Anishinaabeg." *American Indian Culture and Research Journal* 15, no. 2 (1991): 93–138.

lumber barons, xxiii, 22, 23, 46, 51, 53, 68, 73. *See also* Sawyer, Philetus
lumberjacks. *See* loggers
lumber market. *See* Great Lakes lumber market; Mississippi River lumber market; Oshkosh lumber market
Lurie, Nancy Oestreich, 93, 140, 141, 149, 163–64, 167
Lutheran Church, Neopit, 194

Mackinac, xxii
Madison WI, xv, 87, 156, 165, 176; 1972 march to, 163
Māēc Awāētok, 81
Mahchackeniew, 1, 30, 38–39, 41, 50, 51, 54, 205n18, 209n32, 212n18
malnutrition, xxv
mami yamamāēw, 11
Manley, John A., 12, 22, 23, 27, 191
Manypenny, George, 9
Manypenny treaties, 9
maple, 5, 20
maple sugar, *xii–xiii*, 8, 12, 18, 20, 25
Marble, H., 89
Margold, Nathan, 133
Marinette WI, xxiv, 1, 60, 195n4, 200n1
marriage, xxii, xxiv, 80–81
Martin, Morgan L., 12, 19–20, 191
Masschelein, Amandus, 34, 35, 193
Matchapatow, Mary Jane, **128–8**
Mau kah teh pe nas, 203n37
Mazeaud, A. M., 16–17, 34, 193
McCall, George, 85, 222n24
McCauley, Clay, 38
McCord, Myron, 51, 59
Means, Russell, 170
membership. *See* tribal membership
men, xx, 76, 106, 127, 134, 169
Menominee Advisory Council. *See* Advisory Council
Menominee agency, 191
Menominee Business Committee, 60, 63–70, 71, 80, 84–85, 104, 146–47; corruption of, 69
Menominee Common Stock and Voting Trust, 147, 160, 167. *See also* Menominee Enterprises, Inc.

Menominee County Education Committee, 158, 167
Menominee County Shareholders and Taxpayers Alliance, 163
Menominee County sheriff, 175
Menominee County WI, 147–49, 152, 154, 158, 160, 165, 167, 183; establishment of, 145, 147–48; governance of, 148, 154, 167, 184; politics in, 167
Menominee Enterprises, Inc., 147–48, 151–52, 154–55, 159–60, 163–65, 167; board of directors of, 147, 152, 155, 164; shareholders of, 147, 155, 159–60; and voting certificates, 160
Menominee General Council. *See* General Council
Menominee Health Board, 175
Menominee Indian School District, 175, 179–80, 244n68
Menominee Indian Study Committee, 143–44, 147
Menominee Indian Tribe of Wisconsin, Inc., 156
Menominee Language and Culture Code, 180
Menominee League of Women Voters, 100–101, 118
Menominee Legislative Council, 176, 181, 183–84, 244n68
Menominee Logging Camp Museum, 182, 216n68
Menominee MI, xxiv, 60, 200n1
Menominee Negotiating Committee, 170
Menominee News, 145
Menominee Restoration Committee, 164, 166–71, 176–77, 244n68, 247n45; Constitution Committee of, 168; Contracted Services Committee of, 168; Enrollment Committee of, 168
Menominee River, xv, 2
Menominee River band, 3, 5
Menominees for Progress, 163
Menominee Tribal Enterprises, *xiii*, **128–12**, **128–13**, 174, 181; management plan for, 174
Menominee Tribe of Indians v. United States (1968), 157

Lightning Source UK Ltd.
Milton Keynes UK
UKOW042132280113

205512UK00010B/278/A